KNOW THY ENEMY II

A Look at the World's Most Threatening Terrorist Networks and Criminal Gangs

Edited by
Michael T. Kindt
Jerrold M. Post
and
Barry R. Schneider

USAF Counterproliferation Center

325 Chennault Circle
Maxwell Air Force Base, Alabama 36112-6427

November 2007

Disclaimer

The views expressed in this report are those of the author and do not necessarily reflect the official policy or position of the U.S. Government, Department of Defense, U.S. Air Force, or the USAF Counterproliferation Center.

ISBN 978-0-9747403-7-9

Contents

Disclaimer ii

Acknowledgments v

Introduction vii

Section One: Broader Non-state Actor Issues

1   Suicide Terrorism:
Are There Important Counterterrorist Lessons to be Learned? 1
James E. Winkates

2   Al Qaeda's Modus Operandi:
Anticipating Their Target Selection 37
Barry R. Schneider

3   The Mind of the Terrorist:
The Spectrum of Terrorism and Terrorist Psychologies 65
Jerrold M. Post

4   Political Islam and Radical Islam:
The Cases of Pakistan and Bangladesh 85
Stephen F. Burgess

5   Why Women Kill:
A Look at the Evolutionary Role of Muslim Female Fighters 113
Farhana Ali

6   "Like Glitter of the Sun": Iran and Terrorism 167
Gregory F. Giles

7   Terrorist use of WMD 197
James J.F. Forest

Section Two: Specific Non-state Actor Groups

8   Hezbollah: A State Within a State 233
Michael T. Kindt

9	Hamas: The Islamic Resistance Movement .... 263 *Jerrold M. Post*	
10	Al Qaeda 2.0 and the Global Salafi Jihad .... 289 *Jerrold M. Post*	
11	Jemaah Islamiyah Remains Active and Deadly .... 307 *James C. "Chris" Whitmire*	
12	The Mexican Drug Cartels: At War for Control of the U.S.–Mexico Border .... 349 *Dario E. Teicher*	
13	Revolutionary Armed Forces of Colombia (FARC) .... 385 *Jerrold M. Post*	
14	Mara Salvatrucha: A Threat to U.S. and Central American Security .... 401 *Tina S. Strickland*	
	Contributors 437	
	Index 445	

Acknowledgments

This volume is the second in the USAF Counterproliferation Center's *Know Thy Enemy* series. The first book by that title dealt primarily with states that posed serious concerns to U.S. national security. This book picks up that theme but focuses on sub-state actors, terrorist organizations, and criminal gangs that are of serious security concern to the United States.

To complete a major conference and book on this subject requires the work of many hands and a widely diverse expertise. We, the editors of this book, thank the sponsors who provided the resources to make this possible and the many dedicated researchers and staff that have contributed to the final production.

The authors are particularly indebted to the Air Force Culture and Language Center, and its Director, Dr. Dan Henk, who provided the funding that allowed this project to move from vision to reality. We hope by highlighting the backgrounds and motivations of international terrorist and criminal groups that this volume contributes to the Culture and Language Center's critical mission of enhancing the cultural awareness of Airmen at all ranks.

We are also grateful to the outstanding subject matter experts who have provided their keen insights into the critical issues addressed in this volume. Their willingness to work with us in improving understanding of the dangerous and shadowy worlds of terrorists and criminals have made this book what it is.

Generous financial support and expert contributions were transformed into this volume by our exceptional team of editors and administrators. The patient acceptance of multiple revisions and continual editing and formatting by Mrs. Abbey Plant was essential to the smooth completion of this effort. Mrs. Jo Ann Eddy's editing and publication efforts and Col. Susan Wassermann's able management of the money were also critical to our efforts.

Finally, the editors thank their spouses, Lindsey Kindt, Carolyn Post, and Judith Keegan for their continued love and support and the many sacrifices that allowed us the time to complete this volume.

Michael T. Kindt
Jerrold M. Post
Barry R. Schneider

Introduction

International terrorist groups and criminal gangs are presently capable of inflicting great harm on the United States and its allies if not adequately countered. The more potent of these sub-state actors, such as Al Qaeda, are in the hunt for weapons of mass destruction and, should they acquire them, are considered to be more likely to use them than state adversaries that have clear return addresses. That being the case, we appear to be entering into an era when sub-state actors armed with unconventional weapons may be able to inflict the level of damage that was previously only within the capability of great power countries.

Each of the sub-state groups discussed in this book offer a substantial threat to neighbors in their regions and to Americans. Each deserves to be fully understood, and kept from inflicting serious harm if possible. Not all of these threatening terrorists and criminals are front and center on our radar screens at present, but they deserve serious attention, and that is the purpose of this book, to provide detailed information on the looming sub-state threat.

As the current conflicts in Iraq and Afghanistan, as well as the potential conflict with Iran, demand much attention from the military, the government, and the citizenry at large, it is important that we not become too focused on today's immediate challenges and fail to consider threats and obstacles that may be lurking off in the future. This book is an effort to expand that perspective beyond these state actor conflicts demanding today's headlines, and to shine a light on other issues and sub-state groups whose potential challenge to our nation may not be adequately appreciated.

In the same way that failure to adequately assess the risk of insurgency in Iraq contributed to the security dilemma the nation faces today, failure to look ahead at other potential dangers may lead us to be ill-prepared when these threats become apparent. In keeping with the motto of the USAF Counterproliferation Center, "We cannot afford to be the unready confronting the unthinkable," this volume is an effort to both shed light on existing terrorist and criminal gang challenges, as well as to prepare the nation to confront the "unthinkable" threats they may present.

We have directed our effort primarily toward those in the military and government community who, while tasked to fight and win our current conflicts, must also be able to think beyond today to the challenges of tomorrow. This book is intended to provide an easily accessible reference point from which to begin to reframe both our present challenges and to prepare for the future. The chapters that follow should be of value to those encountering the concerns these groups pose from the strategic down to the tactical levels.

In 2003, the USAF Counterproliferation Center published a well-received book entitled *Know Thy Enemy*, which, drawing on Sun Tzu's guidance on the importance of knowing your enemy in order to be successful in battle, focused on expanding the knowledge of the reader regarding nation states that may present threats or challenges to the United States. This book expands the scope of possible enemies and explores the challenges presented to national security by non-state actors. Of course, for most readers, the first thoughts of non-state threats to U.S. security are terrorists groups such as Al Qaeda. Certainly, Al Qaeda and other terrorist organizations, Hamas, Hezbollah, and Jemaah Islamiyah are well-represented in this work, but we have worked to cast a wider net on threats to the nation. Toward this we have included chapters on criminal gangs within and near our borders which pose real, yet often unnoticed, challenges both to the security of our country and also to the security of our neighbors.

We begin this work with several chapters that explore key issues that cut across many different terrorist and criminal groups, or that help to clarify the threats these groups represent. Understanding each of these issues will help the reader to better understand the global challenges that the United States faces as we continue to try to resolve the current conflicts in Iraq and Afghanistan. Chapters in this opening section include a focus on the development of the tactic of suicide terrorism, by James Winkates, an examination of the targeting tendencies of Al Qaeda, by Barry Schneider, an exploration of the psychology of the terrorist mind by Jerrold Post, a review of interactions and conflict between political and radical Islam as displayed in Bangladesh by Stephen Burgess, and a detailed review of the history of women's role in jihad and the disturbing trend of increasing numbers of female suicide bombers by Farhana Ali. In our one examination of another nation, Gregory Giles explores the working of Iran's sponsorship of global terrorism, and finally, James Forest explores both the encouraging and inhibiting factors terrorist groups may weigh in determining whether to pursue and use weapons of mass destruction.

Having set the stage with these issues, the second section of the book examines specific non-state groups that present current and future threats to the nation. This section including chapters on well-known Middle Eastern terrorist groups including Hamas, by Jerrold Post, and Hezbollah, by Michael Kindt, and provides a review of the evolving character of Al Qaeda into what is becoming known as Al Qaeda 2.0, also by Jerrold Post. We then leave the Middle East and examine first the primary terrorist threat in the Pacific region, Jemaah Islamiyah, by Chris Whitmire, before turning our attention to threats much closer to home. A review of the western hemisphere's most notorious native terrorist group Colombia's FARC, by Jerrold Post, is followed by a look at the threat posed by Mexican drug cartels on America's border, by Dario Teicher, and finally Tina Strickland provides an examination of the transnational gang Mara Salvatrucha which operates freely in Latin America as well as in many American cities.

Despite the wide-range of topics presented in this volume, it is impossible to cover the full range of challenges the United States faces in the world. As the sole superpower, instability or hostile groups in any corner of the world may present a challenge to America; however, we have attempted to provide a review of the issues and the emerging groups around the world that, we believe, warrant increased attention today.

CHAPTER 1

Suicide Terrorism:
Are There Important Counterterrorist Lessons to be Learned?

James E. Winkates

The examination of suicide terrorism has taken on more urgency in the past several years. What is decidedly different in the modern, global war on terrorism (GWOT) is that noncombatant civilians have become the most frequent and virtually the exclusive target of violence. Increased resort to extremely violent forms of terrorism revived with the September 2000 inauguration of the Second Intifada, resulting in a tragically heightened number of suicide bombings mostly in Jerusalem and the West Bank, and followed twelve months later by the four suicide aircraft hijackings of September 11, 2001. The unprecedented loss of life in these suicide attacks spurred deep concern among governments and societies alike. In May 2002, FBI Director Robert Mueller concluded that future suicide attacks on U.S. soil were "inevitable."[1] Similarly, then Homeland Security Director Tom Ridge also agreed that domestic suicide bombings "may be inevitable."[2] Continued acknowledgement of likely further attacks and multiple U.S. vulnerabilities has punctuated policy appraisals and press reports virtually without pause since the 9/11 attacks.

Since the end of the Cold War, terrorism has become more lethal despite reduction in the total number of incidents worldwide, and has brought heightened risk and vulnerability especially to U.S. citizenry.[3] The stakes have been raised as traditional constraints (viz. great power conflict control, deterrence, and sanctuary) have dissipated. Prospects of a possible WMD (nuclear, biological, chemical, or radiological) suicide attack have also increased as nuclear designs and materials have been shared covertly. In worst case commentary, senior U.S. officials have concluded that a future terrorist attack involving WMD on U.S. territory becomes ever more likely.[4] Relatedly, the likelihood of more post-9/11 *suicide* terrorist attempts, with or without the use of WMD, becomes a haunting prospect.

Introduction

In three and a half years of the worst post-Intifada ("uprising") violence (September 2000 to February 2004), the combined Israeli and Palestinian deaths of more than 3,500 people, including a recorded 103 suicide bombing events, already approached the total death count for the Northern Ireland conflict since 1969.[5] The spread of the suicide tactic to other regions, including Western Europe (Spain), North Africa (Morocco, Tunisia), Sub-Saharan Africa (Kenya, Tanzania), and Oceania (Indonesia), has fortified U.S. governmental intentions to further deter, defend against, prosecute, pursue, suppress, and craft plans to counter the threat. The sheer U.S. geographic vulnerabilities alone pose a daunting challenge. For example, the continental U.S. has 95,000 miles of coastline, 429 commercial airports with 30,000 daily flights, serviced by a fleet of 4,000 U.S. commercial aircraft, 200,000 registered general aviation (private) aircraft, 361 commercial seaports (official ports of entry), and 104 nuclear power plants.

The primary purpose of this chapter is to assess whether there are important counterterrorist lessons to be learned from the post-September 2000 suicide events, especially in the Middle East, and to begin to judge how best to deter, prevent, and defend against likely future suicide terror attacks in the United States. What can be learned from the known pattern of past suicide terror incidents, about the organizational sponsors and the suicide bombers, to apply defensively or offensively against these likely attacks? Major General Doron Almog of the Israeli Defense Forces (IDF), and in 2004 a Senior Fellow at the Washington Institute for Near East Policy, revealed that the Israeli Government had prevented more than 340 suicide bombings and intercepted 142 would-be bombers since September 2000.[6] This data confirm that suicide terrorists can be stopped.

Definition of Suicide Terrorism

Definitions of "suicide terrorism" illustrate much similarity in content, though vary nonetheless among both scholars and official agencies. Perhaps the broadest version is offered by Menahem Milson, Professor of Arab Literature at the Hebrew University of Jerusalem and Academic Advisor at the Middle East Media Research Institute, who avers that "Anyone who is killed in the course of war with non-Muslims is a shahid [martyr], whether engaged in active fighting or not." He goes on to claim that every Muslim (man, woman, or child) whose death comes about – directly or indirectly – through the actions of enemies of Islam is a martyr.[7]

Jane's Intelligence Review concisely defines it as "the readiness to sacrifice one's life in the process of destroying or attempting to destroy a target to advance a political goal."[8] Ariel Merari of the Jaffee Center for Strategic Studies in Tel Aviv defines it as "the readiness to die in the process of committing a terrorist act." He takes great care to comment on the methodological handicaps confronting the definition in recalling earlier studies that pointedly contrasted a person who is "not just *prepared* to get killed," but who "wants to get killed," and secondly to the uncertainty about the subject's intention and the end result of "attempted versus completed suicide."[9] For true suicide terrorist behavior there is no escape plan, no Plan B, no fear of being caught.

The best litmus test for definitive suicide terrorism is the *intentional and successful* sacrifice of a human life to achieve a terrorist objective. As one analyst explains, "the very act of the attack is dependent upon the death of the perpetrator."[10] The perpetrator's death is a *precondition* for the success of the mission. This narrower interpretation of suicide terrorism excludes the inherently high-risk terrorist attacks, which incidentally may or may not claim the life of the attacker.

Perhaps more intriguing is the question of whether suicide for a cause can be a *rational* act. If suicide terrorism is the pursuit of a purposeful goal or objective, then deliberate self-destruction may indeed be interpreted not as "fanaticism," but a rational act in the mind of the doer. According to one school of Islamic scholars, suicide bombings for the right cause can be legitimate claims to martyrdom in conformance with the Koran. Reminiscent of many world religions, martyrs ("shahid") are those who are killed in God's cause. Indeed, the Arabic term reserved for this deed, "istishad," means to give one's life in the name of Allah. On the contrary, the Arabic term "intihar" refers to suicide prompted by great personal distress and is neither condoned nor sanctioned in the Koran or in the Sharia, Islamic law.

Suicide Terrorists: The Benchmark Precedents

To better understand the act of suicide terrorism, it helps to know about both the individuals and the organization or cause they represent. Modern suicide terrorists are recruited, indoctrinated, and sponsored by terrorist organizations whose cause is furthered by the suicide terrorist. While there certainly is a propensity to envision a suicidal self, there is virtually no self selection. Consequently, the differing motivations of sponsoring groups and willing suiciders become an important distinction.

In the post-WWII era, the earliest resort to a pattern of preferential suicide tactics came with Hezbollah in Lebanon in 1983 and with the Liberation Tigers of Tamil Eelam (LTTE) or Tamil Tigers in Sri Lanka in 1987. Hamas followed in Israel in 1994, the PKK in Turkey in 1996, and finally Al Qaeda in East Africa in 1998 (if not earlier).[11]

There are eleven groups which have demonstrated moderate to considerable capability and preference for suicide tactics. They include Hamas, Palestinian Islamic Jihad (PIJ), Al Aqsa Martyrs Brigade, and Popular Front for the Liberation of Palestine (PFLP) in the West Bank and Gaza; Hezbollah in Lebanon; the Tamil Tigers (LTTE) in Sri Lanka; the Kurdistan Worker's Party (PKK) in Turkey; the Chechnyan rebel group in the south Caucasus; Jemaah Islamiyah in Oceania and Southeast Asia; Al Qaeda in Afghanistan and now decentralized elsewhere, and Ansar al-Islam in Iraq, and with splintered elements in several European countries. The Egyptian Islamic Jihad (EIJ) and Gamaya Islamiya (IG) conducted a few suicide attacks within and outside Egypt (Croatia, Pakistan). Other groups have summoned sporadic capabilities for suicide assaults, but have shown no consistent pattern. Interestingly, the Middle East broadly construed (i.e., the Levant, Southwest and Southeast Asia, South Asia, the southern Caucasus (Chechnya), and North Africa, essentially the extended perimeter of the Islamic crescent), dominate the "suicide zone." To be sure, there are other regions in which suicide acts take place (Argentina,

East Africa, United States) but the terrorist organizations which perpetrated the act originated largely from the Islamic part of the world, at least in the past twenty years.

The contemporary surge in suicide bombing can be traced to Hezbollah, the Lebanese Shi'ite Muslim extremist group, led by Secretary General Hassan Nasrallah and purportedly inspired by Iran's use of "human minesweepers" in the war with Iraq.[12] Unknown at the time of the assaults, Hezbollah directed multiple attacks against Western targets in Lebanon, against the American Embassy in Beirut (April 1983), with 80 killed and 142 wounded, U.S. Marine headquarters near Beirut airport (October 1983), 241 dead and 81 wounded, the concurrent attack against the French Multinational Force (October 1983), with 58 dead and 15 wounded, against the Israeli Defense Force headquarters in Tyre (November 1983), with 88 dead and 69 wounded, and subsequently followed by an attack on the American Embassy in Kuwait (December 1983), with 4 dead and 15 wounded.

The series of rapid-fire Hezbollah attacks succeeded quickly in forcing the withdrawal of U.S. and French forces from all of Lebanon, and moreover prompted the Israeli army in 1985 to withdraw from Beirut to a narrow strip in southern Lebanon.[13] Israel withdrew unilaterally and finally from all of Lebanon in May 2000. These unprecedented suicide attacks fit well the narrow definition of suicide terrorism since all bombers perished in the attacks, and were the first of thirty-one cases of suicide terrorism between 1983 and 1986,[14] an especially violent and indeed brutally successful series of assaults.

Prior to these suicide attacks, terrorist groups shied away from killing large numbers of victims. As noted terrorism analyst Brian Jenkins said at the time, terrorists want a lot of people watching, not a lot of people dying.[15] Hezbollah changed that ethic. Prior to 9/11 it was responsible for more U.S. deaths than any other terrorist organization. While the organization bears clear responsibility for the assault of the Israeli Embassy in Argentina (1992) and the bombing of the Jewish community center in Buenos Aires (1994), Hezbollah has largely confined its suicide attacks and other violence to Lebanon. An exception perhaps is reflected in the indictment of a Lebanese member of Hezbollah for conspiracy in designing the truck bomb used in the Saudi Khobar Towers lethal attack.

Long term, Hezbollah remains dedicated to the liberation of Jerusalem and the elimination of the Israeli state. Currently, it seems most intent on establishing Shi'ite Islamic rule in Lebanon, where since 1992 it has been an influential and legitimate political party holding twelve seats in the Lebanese parliament. Much later, Al Qaeda would resurrect the pattern of near-simultaneous, mass murder, suicide tactics claiming the largest terror casualties in a single day with 9/11.

The second most significant and early precedent for suicide terrorism is that of the Liberation Tigers of Tamil Eelam (LTTE), a robust guerrilla force with an extensive network of overseas Tamils who provide funds, procure weapons, and lobby foreign governments with favorable publicity. Founded in 1972 as a Marxist, ethnically Tamil, religiously Hindu separatist group seeking independence from the Sinhalese Buddhist majority. It has been led since inception by charismatic Velupillai Prabhakaran who commands its approximately 8,000 guerrillas that combat government security forces ten times that number. Its Black Tiger division, launched in 1987 as a unit trained for suicide attacks, murdered former Indian Prime Minister, Rajiv Gandhi (1991) and President of Sri Lanka, Ranasinghe Premadasa (1993). To this day, it is the only terrorist group to assassinate two heads of government. Other Sri Lankan senior officials killed included a presidential candidate, a minister of defence, the chief of the navy, and several area military commanders.

In the period of 1980 to 2000, the LTTE conducted the largest number of suicide attacks (168), more than triple the number credited to Hezbollah and other groups based in Lebanon (52).[16] With the suicide terrorist tempo of the Second Intifada since 2000 and the 2002 ceasefire in the Sri Lankan civil war, combined deaths credited to the Palestinian groups have now exceeded the LTTE numbers.

Walter Laqueur makes a telling point emphasizing the pragmatism of groups reliant on suicide tactics by noting, "Enthusiasm for martyrdom persists as long as there is a reasonable chance that it will lead to victory. Sacrifice must have a purpose."[17] The connection of rationality to purpose reinforces the definitional discussion earlier in the chapter. Hezbollah succeeded in driving Western military forces out of Lebanon, and the considerable political and financial support of Iran[18] has not only sustained but helped grow the Shi'ite religious exclusivity in Lebanon. Norwegian mediation of the Sri Lankan civil war, resulting in a tenuous but so far lasting cease fire since February 2002, offers the prospect of at least political autonomy on the island, short of the LTTE long-proclaimed goal of independence and yet far more than Sinhalese leaders so far have been willing to provide.

Terrorist Organization Benefits

The most elemental organizational purpose of course is to survive. No benefits can be accrued without that basic objective. Boaz Ganor, Executive Director of the International Policy Institute for Counter-Terrorism, nicely summarized the benefits of suicide attacks for the sponsoring terrorist organization.[19] First, suicide attacks result in many target group casualties and cause extensive damage. Second, the attacks attract wide media coverage and display for the attentive public great determination and self-sacrifice. Third, unlike technical or indirect means of bomb delivery, the suicide attacker can virtually guarantee that the attack will be carried out at the desired time, circumstance, and location, striving for the maximum number of adversary casualties. Fourth, it is extremely difficult to counter the attempt once the terrorist is en route to the target; he/she can quickly detonate the charge and at least cause some damage even short of the objective so that at least partial success is achieved. Fifth, there is no need to plan nor execute an escape route, allowing terrorist organization personnel time and resources to be devoted elsewhere. Sixth, since the perpetrator dies in the act, there is no fear of capture, interrogation, or leakage of critical information that might endanger other operatives.

One more advantage not mentioned by Ganor is the extent to which the *reputation* of terrorist organizations is enhanced (or degraded, for that matter), serving to further dramatize their cause, gain popular support, or inspire followers. Nothing succeeds like success. Even in failure, the organization loses little except one or two bombers and perhaps the fleeting negative publicity within terrorist ranks and the negligible psychic cost to the organization of a failed attempt.

What of the key terrorist organizations that continue to rely upon suicide tactics to achieve their objectives? Over the past twenty years since 1983 from approximately eleven terrorist organizations relying on suicide tactics, a *hard core of six groups* has sustained the use of suicide tactics: four are operational almost exclusively in the Israeli Palestinian region including Hamas, Palestinian Islamic Jihad (PIJ), Al Aqsa Martyrs Brigade, and the Popular Front for the Liberation of Palestine, plus Al Qaeda and the Chechen rebels from outside the immediate area. Other groups may be added to this pool if some of them return to the tactics employed earlier or if new groups emerge to use suicide as a methodology for inflicting violence.

Intensive examination of the Al Qaeda network and the Chechen rebels is well beyond the scope of this chapter. The latter group has demonstrated interest only in Russian targets since it seeks independence from Moscow, and is of no operational concern to the U.S. beyond American interest in relations with Russia and their role in the Global War on Terrorism. Jemaah Islamiyah (JI) is a militant Islamist group with roots dating to Indonesian independence. Operationally active at least since December 2000, when they executed a wave of Christian church bombings that killed more than 20 people, the group is thought to be affiliated loosely with Al Qaeda. JI seeks the creation of a pan-Islamic state embracing much of Southeast Asia. They have been credited with four significant suicide car bomb attacks – the October 2002 Bali nightclub bombing which killed 202, the August 2003 Marriott hotel attack in Jakarta leaving 12 dead, the September 2004 attack outside the Australian Embassy in Jakarta killing 10, and the October 2005 Bali nightclub bombing which killed 23. Time will reveal whether Jemaah Islamiyah will continue to employ suicide bombers in the region.

The recurring pattern and substance of the four purely Middle Eastern terrorist organizations that resort to suicide attacks are the primary focus of this chapter. At the general level, the chief objectives are "soft targets," namely commuter buses, popular cafes and restaurants, shopping malls, and places of entertainment which put large numbers of vulnerable civilians at risk in the course of their daily lives.

Yahya Ayyash, reputed master bomb maker for Hamas, reportedly urged its leadership in the early 1990s to use "human bombs" to raise the cost of the Israeli occupation and make their loss of life that much more unbearable.[20] Israeli forces killed Ayyash in January 1996. Since the beginning of the Second Intifada, Hamas, a broad-based social, economic, and military organization, conducted the first of the suicide bomb attacks

(January 2001) and carried out by far the largest number of incidents to date. Their targets have included both Israeli civilian and military personnel.

The PIJ is strictly a terrorist organization, not involved in social good works programs, and is more influential in the West Bank than in Gaza. Hamas and PIJ, both Muslim fundamentalist groups, inaugurated suicide bombings in the mid-1990s, primarily to derail the Oslo Accords and related diplomatic efforts aimed at a Middle East peace formula.

The Al-Aqsa Martyrs Brigade, rooted in secular Palestinian nationalism, is a terrorist group loosely affiliated with now deceased Yasser Arafat's Fatah movement. The group claims about a third of all suicide attacks since September 2000. Since 2002 it has executed more suicide missions than the three other Middle Eastern groups combined. Despite periodic Arafat claims to crack down on suicide attacks against Israelis, Al-Aqsa only increased its lethal assaults. The PFLP, primarily secular and nationalist in orientation, has conducted the smallest number of suicide attacks after the onset of the Second Intifada.

While virtually any terrorist group can mount suicide assaults given the simple, inexpensive body suits[21] used to arm the perpetrator, relatively few groups have established the practice or stayed with this tactic. Indeed, a number of groups no longer practice suicide attacks.

The Barbar Khalsa International (BKI) group, fighting for an independent "Khalistan" in the mostly Sikh state of Punjab, has been largely compromised by Indian security forces and staged but one successful suicide incident. The Armed Islamic Group (GIA) of Algeria, similarly, has only a few suicide operations to its credit. They may well have concluded they have made their point dramatically with an estimated 125,000 killed since 1992. The PKK leader, Abdullah Ocalan, is incarcerated in Turkey initially under a death sentence, commuted to life imprisonment, and has publicly admonished his organization from further suicide attacks (July 1999). His continued incarceration provides the Turkish government with a "permanent" hostage and useful bargaining chip.

As mentioned earlier, the most historically successful suicide terrorist groups, Hezbollah and the LTTE, have desisted from further attacks at this time dependent on sustained legislative success in the Lebanese Parliament or a formal political settlement of civil war with the Sri Lankan government, respectively. Beginning in 2006, the LTTE has resumed its attacks against government security forces.

Select Key Elements in Demographic Profiles

Terrorist profiles have gone through considerable change since the peak Cold War years with major theaters of terrorist violence in western, central, and southern Europe, the Philippines, Lebanon, Egypt, and the Andean ridge countries in South America. The axis has shifted away from leftist, ideologically pure, revolutionary movements to more pragmatic and religiously inspired, even millenarian, formulas.

The answer to **who are suicide terrorists** derives a great deal from the suicide events in Israel since September 2000. To return to the description and analysis of Boaz Gaynor, who examined suicide attacks in Israel since 1993, he found the following:[22] Hamas activists were responsible for 72 percent of the attacks, while the Palestinian Islamic Jihad (PIJ) accounted for 28 percent. He found the majority of the assailants came from a low social status, ranging in age from 18 to 27 years, were single, and unemployed. Most were high school graduates, and were "devoted" students in Islamic fundamentalist schools or religious centers.[23] The "shahid," or martyrs, he recounted, were deeply religious (at the extreme), fervent Palestinian nationalists, and often imbued with a desire for revenge for what the Israeli state or its army has done to the Palestinian cause. Saddled with over fifty years of Israeli occupation, often deprived of their land, laden with many travel and occupational restrictions impacting maintenance of family ties, pursuit of schooling, and lacking an ability to work for a decent living combine to make for a daily demeaning struggle for these recruits. Significantly, many shahid were children who grew up in the refugee camps like the famous terrorist, Abu Nidal (Sabri al-Bana) of the Fatah Revolutionary Council.

The first refugee camps established by the UN soon after creation of the Israeli state in 1948 housed large numbers of displaced Palestinians. Presently there are approximately three million stateless Palestinians in Gaza,[24] the West Bank, and in the original territorial boundaries of Israel. The population of Israel is a little more than six million, about 18 percent of whom are Palestinian Israeli citizens.

One explanation for the vast number of persons with suicidal tendencies incubated in refugee camps points to the combined role of camp **poverty**, the concomitant hopelessness, and long-term immersion in a hostile environment. A 2002 random sample survey of 342 Palestinian refugees living in southern Lebanon showed overwhelming endorsement of suicide attacks against Israel (66 percent) and a high willingness for personal involvement in a suicide attack (39 percent). The study found that political Islam plays "a crucial role in fomenting proneness to participation in suicide attacks, especially among refugee camp inhabitants, where dismal poverty coalesces with radical Islam."[25] Palestinian refugee camps have become institutional sanctuaries for extremist religious ideas, with poverty, humiliation, and disgrace contributing to a proneness to suicidal mentality. The early camps are now nearly sixty years in operation.

While appealing as a single source explanation, the consensus view is that abject poverty *alone* does not cause terrorism. Recall Samuel Huntington's thesis, that "The early phases of modernization are often marked by the emergence of fundamentalist religious movements," and that the attempt to *get out* of poverty, *not the condition of* poverty, explains instability. He continued, "people who are really poor are too poor for politics and too poor for protest."[26] That same observation seems to apply to modern day terrorism.

Analyst Jessica Stern interviewed many religious militants across the globe for her recent book, *Terror in the Name of God; Why Religious Militants Kill*, uncovering multiple proclaimed reasons for terrorist violence, only one of which was economic status.[27] James Q. Wilson cites a research study done by Krueger and Maleckova that concluded terrorism spreads as Middle Eastern economies got *better*, not worse.[28] The roots of terrorism seem to lie in many sources of human behavior, no one of which can be isolated as the sole or even primary causation. Single causation explanations rarely apply to complex human behavior.

There is other corroborating evidence of substantial popular support for suicide bombings among Palestinians. In a mid-2001 opinion poll, more than 70 percent expressed support for suicide attacks, an all-time high, and those results were reinforced in a mid-2002 poll with more than two-thirds favoring the option.[29] The first recorded suicide bombing by an Islamist Palestinian group in the West Bank, notes the author, occurred on

April 16, 1993, which began a "virtual cult of the suicide bomber among many Palestinians."[30] The author further relates Israeli Ministry of Foreign Affairs data which show that, while suicide attacks accounted for less than 1 percent of all Palestinian attacks since the beginning of the Second Intifada (September 2000), almost 44 percent of all Israeli casualties since then were a direct result of these suicide attacks.[31] Those stark numbers certainly convey a very high multiplier effect for suicide attacks, and perhaps the major reason for continued reliance on this killing tactic. A very small number of volunteer assailants who succeed in suicide attacks produce a highly disproportionate number of victims.

The demographic variable of **gender** with respect to suicide attacks provides rather interesting insights into organizational, ethnic, and religious cultures. Of all terrorist groups, active and inactive, the LTTE and PKK by far embodied the highest percentages of female suicide bombers.[32] In the LTTE they participated in 30 to 40 percent of the group suicide assaults. By far the most effective and brutal resort to suicide attacks and for an extended period (July 1987 to February 2000), the organization carried out 168 suicide attacks with "thousands of innocent bystanders dead or wounded."

In Turkey, women in the PKK accounted for 66 percent of all attacks, but in a far shorter time frame (June 1996 to July 1999), when their leader Ocalan directed the cessation of the tactic. Unlike the LTTE, the number of PKK targets killed were relatively low. The suicide initiative for PKK appears linked to the time period when it was used to bolster sagging morale caused by repeated Turkish military offensives against the group in southeastern Turkey.

Following repeated military setbacks against Russian forces, the Chechen resorted to suicide bombings in June 2000, initially with a combined male/female team. Subsequent suicide assaults were executed by female perpetrators about one-third of the time. Two women were responsible for the 2004 Chechnyan suicide bombings of two Russian commercial aircraft, killing all the passengers. The subsequent attack and siege of a school in Beslan, Russia, which killed 330, including 170 children, was the work of 30 Chechnyan terrorists, both male and female.[33]

For some time Islamic groups shunned the use of women as suicide bombers, but in the last decade both Hamas and the Al-Aqsa Brigades have begun to use young women as suicide bombers. The first resort to a female suicide bomber in the Middle East, sponsored by Al-Aqsa, occurred in January 2002. While Al Qaeda and its affiliated groups historically have *refrained* from using women as suicide bombers, this has begun to change. In early 2005 Italy's secret service revealed the existence of *Al Khansa*, a monthly Al Qaeda-sponsored online women's magazine which specifically includes "advice for suicide bombers" and how to achieve martyrdom in holy war.[34]

Palestinian nationalism and organizational pragmatism, it could be argued, overrode the Islamic strictures against women in such prominent, forward roles. Muslim social norms normally preclude women's participation in traditionally "masculine" activities that put them into close contact with men who are not part of their family.

Tactically, however, female bombers offer the element of surprise, can better hide explosives under their garments, and have posed as pregnant women garbed in multiple layers of camouflage clothing. Moreover, there is reluctance to do body searches of women in the traditional cultures of the Arab world.

A high percentage of female suicide bomber assailants have experienced the loss of a family member, often an elder brother or a close friend, killed, wounded, or jailed by the Israeli security forces in the street violence of the West Bank, Jerusalem, or Gaza.[35] Furthermore, most Palestinian residents of the refugee camps are women, a reinforcing issue in terms of self-selection for suicide missions. As one Israeli analyst notes, "Palestinian women have become 'Islamikaze' martyrs."[36]

Martyrdom for the cause has become routine and has emerged as the supreme patriotic instrument to beat the Israeli occupier. Islamikaze attacks sanctify their perpetrators and further incite families, who have already lost a child, to pledge the lives of other sons and daughters to Allah. Contributing to the Palestinian cause, taking revenge on the Israeli occupiers, sacrificing and ultimately seeking martyrdom for the cause of Allah, all may explain women's inclination to serve in suicide missions.

The far more difficult issue to judge is **why individuals choose suicide** as a response to their perceived circumstance. Mark Juergensmeyer offers a thought-provoking explanation.[37] He argues that within every terrorist there is the conviction that he or she is the victim in a "cosmic war" leading toward a final battle that has not yet been fought.

Further, that in a heroic and transforming death, religious warfare reflects a blend of sacrifice and martyrdom. These self-chosen martyrs, sponsored by terrorist groups that are both secular and religious, joyfully surrender their lives for the sake of community and religion.

He notes that audio and videotapes, usually made by the suicide bombers the night before their deaths as a record for family and faithful, proclaim their final act as both personal and redemptive. Martyrdom, of course, has a long history in most religious traditions, especially the proselytizing faiths of Islam and Christianity. Both Christ and Husayn, founder of the Shi'ite tradition, were martyrs. The act of martyrdom is to witness to one's faith. So, in this vein, a suicide mission offers profound redemption by sacrificing oneself for your faith in the cosmic war of good and evil.

Much has been said about the considerable incentives (real and imagined) that accrue to suicide terrorists. While the lists of benefits vary slightly, typically they originate in the *hadiths*, the prophetic sayings and anecdotes of Mohammed, and embellished, many claim, by generations of Islamic scholars and commentators.[38] These include:

- The family is showered with honor and praise and their status immediately rises in their community.

- The suicide person gains "eternal life in paradise."

- He or she gains permission to see the face of Allah.

- 72 young, almond-eyed virgins will love and serve him in heaven.

- He (little is said of female beneficence, perhaps because of their unexpected contribution) is granted the privilege of promising a life in heaven to 70 of his chosen relatives.[39]

- The "shahid" is remembered and revered in his community, neighborhood, mosque, and school, exemplified by the production of picture posters, sponsored poems and verse, and religious parades celebrating his "marriage" in heaven.

- The martyr becomes a source of pride. Pictures of the martyr, often with a copy of the Koran clearly prominent, are produced and traded not unlike sports celebrity cards in the U.S. by children inside the refugee camps. A teenage rock group, known as the

"Martyrs," sings the praises of the latest Shahid to celebrate their entrance to heaven.[40]

- The Hamas organization awards monthly stipends of approximately $1,000 for life to the families of bombers, as well as scholarships for siblings, food for the family, and will pay for resettlement of the bomber families who lose their homes due to Israeli retribution.

- Iran and Iraq, other Arab countries, and Muslim foundations have been known to contribute as much as $25,000 to the family of the martyr.

- Saudi Arabia has provided a trip to Mecca for family members of the suicide bomber, and often offers other fringe benefits such as free family housing.[41]

As Jessica Stern and others have put it, martyrdom operations have become part of the Palestinian popular culture, at least in Gaza and the West Bank.[42]

There does appear to be a growing, perhaps even universal, phenomenon of increasing religious extremism across major world cultures.[43] Religion, once considered by many as a private manifestation of faith and solace, has emerged as a key contender to explain (perhaps even absolve) much of human behavior. The growing propensity to "know the mind of God" creates an incontestable and unwavering religious certainty, even to the extreme of a faith-based right, even duty, to kill.[44] This often arrogant self-righteousness, in contrast to civil tolerance, poses challenges across all world regions.

Others argue that religion seems to be minimally or not at all important in explaining terrorist suicide. One view is that terrorism is an inherently violent and sinful act,[45] and the real reason for the terrorist's suicidal act is sacrifice for a nationalist or ethnic community cause. Certainly with regard to LTTE suicide missions, their aim was to achieve an ethno-nationalist cause (political independence) rather than an explanation derived from their Hindu religion.

Moghadam's research leads him to doubt that "a profound religious belief *alone* will generate a person's willingness to die" (emphasis added).[46] Moreover, he argues that a *combination of motivations* (nationalist, economic, religious, and personal) more likely explains most suicide acts.

Islamic extremists have initiated numerous lethal attacks during the decade of the 1990s, as evidenced in the 1993 bombing of the World Trade Center, the 1994 bombing of a Jewish Community Center in Argentina, the 1996 bombing of Khobar Towers in Saudi Arabia, the 1997 attack on foreign tourists in Luxor, Egypt, and the 1998 twin bombings of the U.S. embassies in Kenya and Tanzania. Even before 9/11, these Islamic attacks illustrated an increase in religiously inspired, and more lethal, assaults.

In a 2003 interview the military chief of the Islamic Jihad claimed no trouble in recruiting suicide bombers, indeed that "young men...come to him begging to be trained."[47] As others point out, however, motivation also includes a heavy admixture of anti-Western and anti-modernization explanations as well as group and societal popularization of the idea that attracts volunteers.[48] However, where there is religious zealotry present, there is no conventional brake on committing violence. Consequently, the trend is very much toward more violence, most especially with respect to suicide attacks.

Robert Pape, on the other hand, finds "little connection between suicide terrorism and Islamic fundamentalism, or any religion for that matter." He, too, cites the Tamil Tigers, who by his count committed 75 of the 188 suicide incidents in the database he compiled for the period of 1980 to 2001. The terrorist organizations which sponsor suicide missions, he concludes, *use* religion to recruit and deploy these human bombs to achieve their *organizational* objectives. In his judgment the "strategic logic of suicide terrorism" clearly becomes evident when one examines the political-military gains derived from suicide missions.[49] The fact that these one-way missions are not isolated, "lone wolf" initiatives gives credence to his thesis. Perhaps distinguishing between *causation and intention* or *sanction and legitimation* might bridge the opposing lines of argument. Religion, after all, has been used to inspire, explain, denounce, support, and rationalize numerous sentiments since time immemorial and across all cultures.

In the Middle East generally, the sponsoring organizations of the suicide terrorists are often responding to key political events. Suicide attacks, for example, increased in frequency after the October 1990 confrontation between Israeli security forces and Muslim worshipers on Temple Mount in Jerusalem. Hamas suicide attacks in April 1994 occurred at the same time of negotiations between Israel and the PLO resulting in the Cairo agreement. Attacks also followed the killing of 39 Muslim worshipers and the wounding of 200 more in a Hebron mosque by an Israeli settler in February 1994. Suicide attacks in Jerusalem in the summer of 1995 coincided with negotiations on elections in the occupied territories, preceding the Oslo II agreement.[50] The four Palestinian terrorist organizations do not want peace talks nor any political settlement with Israel, and used the suicide attacks to derail any efforts in this direction. Suicide events have become the trump card for extremists over efforts by moderates of all sides who seek cease fires, negotiations, and conflict settlement amid the sheer exhaustion of civil violence and mounting civilian deaths. There is a built-in escalation dynamic which is persistently fueled by all of the principal Palestinian and Israeli players in their ongoing conflict.

Utility of Individual Templates and Organizational Profiles

Based on the individual demographics of suicide bombers in the Middle East and the objectives of their sponsoring organizations, there appears to be merit in refining both individual suicide bomber templates and terrorist organization profiles. Moreover, this examination suggests there may be a way to expand and exploit individual and organizational differences. If the gap between organizational goals and martyr objectives can be enhanced and deepened, through interventionist means, there is some prospect for unlinking what often appears to be similar objectives. Governments ultimately may sever the ties between perpetrators and their sponsoring groups. The current, parallel, tactical objectives shared between group and suicider could be determined.

For example, most individual suicide bombers are impelled by religious, familial, or future dream scenarios, while organizations are most interested in coercing democratic governments to make territorial concessions, to gain political advantage, or to posture themselves to defeat peace negotiations or peace agreements. The major motive of Iraqi insurgents and suicide terrorist bombers in 2004 and early 2005 was to prevent free nation-wide elections. Both individuals and groups must rationalize their objectives using different vehicles. And if the potential martyr can be made to question or devalue the worth of the organizational goals, perhaps he/she might not be willing to pay the maximum price for it.

A recent examination of Tamil and Palestinian martyrdom operations, for example, concludes that suicide terrorism is an instrumental tactic with obvious organizational ramifications. Indeed, that resort to suicide operations, "has significantly less to do with the presumed anger, desperation, or frustration of those who actually carry out these attacks, than the strategic requirements set by the leaders of the organizations that send the bombers on their way."[51] Gaps between the individual offering to sacrifice their lives and organizations that are simply using them as a tool to achieve a political goal could be pointed out to the potential bomber community to break the trust necessary to recruit volunteers. Counter-terrorism can communicate the great asymmetry between bombers and their leaders in the "suicide contract." This may well offer vulnerabilities to be exploited. One would think that a counter suicide bomber strategy that greatly decreased public support would thereby reduce the pool of potential recruits.

Further Implications of Lessons Learned

The foregoing examination of patterns of suicide violence suggest a number of further guideposts for enhanced preparedness in the United States. First and foremost, to better support the broader Global War on Terrorism (GWOT), much more knowledge and understanding of key elements of the Islamic faith and the specific culture of key Islamic states and groups is imperative.[52] To know one's adversaries is the first step to better respond to their challenges. Broader understanding of Islam the religion, its multiple and seemingly contradictory beliefs and interpretations, the global Muslim culture and its diverse manifestations, and the political, economic, and military aspects of that wider belief system are essential.

It is relatively well-known that Islam is the world's fastest growing religion and constitutes approximately twenty percent of global population. Less well-known is that the Koran has multiple translations and interpreters, not unlike the many translations and interpreters of the Christian Bible. Additionally, while all Koranic public prayer is in the Arabic language, 80 percent of Muslims are not Arabs (Iranians, Indonesians, and Indians the foremost examples). Beyond the Five Pillars of Wisdom, there is no unified, incontestable interpretation of even the most fundamental of revealed dogma. And unlike Catholicism, there is no single, authoritative spokesperson for the faith.

Many may recall the U.S. response to the successful launch and deployment of *Sputnik*, the first satellite, put into orbit by the Soviet Union. Congress quickly passed the National Defense Education Act, which prompted considerable research, faculty grants, and student fellowships, followed by President Kennedy's commitment to travel to the moon by the end of the 1960s. Applied science research and academic courses, Russian language training, and travel to the USSR ensued. This model seems to have application with the challenge of combating extremist Islamic ideology and associated global terrorist networks.

By all accounts the GWOT will require a multi-decade dedication to counter the terrorist threat. This kind of expected and long-term commitment to the challenge begs for a deep and wide understanding of Islam, well beyond the few Arabists in the Department of State. The FBI, CIA, Department of Homeland Security, and virtually all components of the armed services will need knowledge of Islamic culture and issues to better accomplish their assigned tasks. The lengthy Cold War, race for space, and now the GWOT are all examples of *long-term systemic challenges* that require(d) extensive commitment of national assets, time investment, specialized personnel, and very sustained budget resources.

A New Breed of Terrorists: What to Do?

No individual or organization predicted the devastating 9/11 suicide attacks. Only with 20/20 hindsight did we recognize belatedly the hand of Al Qaeda in sequential attacks leading up to September 11, 2001, starting with the first World Trade Center attack in 1993, the attacks or the forces assigned to the 1993 Somalia humanitarian mission, the Khobar Towers assault in 1996, the U.S. embassy bombings in East Africa 1998, and the USS *Cole* assault off Yemen in 2000. The egregious intelligence failure to link these terrorist attacks and uncover Al Qaeda's role in them prompted major inquiries and investigations, most notably the July 2004, *9/11 Commission Report*. A careful later review of the ample evidence available, dating from at least 1995, indicated that there had emerged "a new breed of terrorist." This new threat was only to be recognized much later, and is quite different from the historic portrait of traditional terrorists.

This new breed of terrorist can be characterized as dogmatically committed to killing large numbers of noncombatants, capable of operating autonomously without an overt state sponsor, is loosely organized, favors a militant Islamic agenda, and possesses an extremist penchant for violence.[53] The first substantive indication of a definitive change from previous terrorist actions occurred in 1995, not in the Islamic crescent, but in the Pacific rim. The Philippine National Police uncovered a bomb-making laboratory in Manila and multiple plots organized by Ramzi Yousef to kill the Pope, kill the U.S. President, bomb the U.S. and Israeli embassies in Manila, blow up eleven U.S. commercial airliners over the Pacific, and crash a plane into CIA Headquarters. These plots pointed to planned mass killings of civilians while attacking symbols of national power. Yousef later was discovered to have ties to Osama bin Laden.

So one begins with what is known of the adversary. No longer would the primary focus of counterterrorism be on state sponsors and the protection of U.S. personnel working overseas. Nor would it be the task of simply ferreting out centralized terrorist networks. Al Qaeda and its affiliates now operate in ungoverned areas and relies on a widespread decentralized network to carry on its fight. And with the 1993 and 2001 attacks, foreign terrorism had come to U.S. shores and directly to the American people wherever they live and work.

To avoid further sins of omission, especially detection of prospective suicide assaults on U.S. territory, analysts need to explore how this form of violence might again revisit the United States. In a strongly dissenting view to the widely acclaimed *9/11 Commission Report*, Judge Richard Posner reminds us that in hindsight it is relatively easy to identify "missed opportunities" that might have prevented the attacks, but **"it is almost impossible to take effective action to prevent something that hasn't occurred previously"**(emphasis added).[54] It appears that even though we are but one step removed from the 9/11 attacks, we are in little better position to take more effective action as the following example illustrates.

There may be a good recent example of what not to do. Symptomatic of past U.S. responses to challenges is to reach for the high-tech option, even if it is not yet an entirely reliable and predictable operational capability (the Anti-Ballistic Missile, Space Shuttle, artificial heart as examples). One currently discussed preventive option is to put antimissile defenses on commercial, civilian aircraft. A January 2005 RAND study concluded that Al Qaeda and its affiliates have both motive and capability to shoot down U.S. aircraft with shoulder-fired missiles.[55] In November 2003, an Al Qaeda-linked group fired two missiles at an Israeli passenger jet taking off from Mombasa airport in Kenya. The aircraft fortunately avoided the missiles.

The RAND study concluded, quite correctly many agree, that equipping the entire U.S. commercial air fleet with anti-missile lasers would be cost prohibitive, with start up expenditures of about $11 billion, and annual operating costs of $2.1 billion. Untested and unpracticed, the system would lack both reliability and predictability of performance. Manpower intensive surveillance coverage of most major U.S. airport perimeters would be a more logical and likely far less expensive preventive option. As folk wisdom, striving for the perfect can be the enemy of the good enough. In this post-9/11 era of vast, appropriated sums of money for all sorts of counterterrorist responses, objective risk assessment tends to become quickly politicized. All fifty states and most cities of any size draft proposals and grant requests seeking federal monies for equipment, training, and additional personnel to join the GWOT.

Still undeveloped is a systematic risk management program that seeks to use finances in the most efficient manner. Monies are not unlimited, and poor choices may do enormous harm to the national economy by forcing substantially unnecessary and irrelevant expenditures.[56] One is reminded of the false protection in building backyard bomb shelters in the 1950s and the civil defense stockpiling measures for all public buildings. Money spent on the wrong measures means insufficient funds for more real protection and diverts attention from truly essential deterrence and defense.

A second, very elemental issue, should post-9/11 risk assessment focus most on likely people concentrations or presumed structure vulnerability? In 2003, President Bush directed the new Department of Homeland Security to develop a database and prioritization of potential physical targets across the fifty states. Logically, the Department solicited candidate sites from state and local governments as well as from private industries (which own approximately 70 percent of all energy installations, for example). The initial list had tens of thousands of potential targets. The vulnerable assets included 87,000 food processing plants; 1,800 federal reservoirs; 2,800 power plants; 2 million miles of pipeline; 500 urban transit systems; 66,000 chemical plants; 80,000 dams; and 460 skyscrapers.[57] The conventional wisdom applies, to try to protect all ultimately protects none.

The suicide terror experience in Israel shows clearly mostly randomly selected human targets in crowded locations have been virtually the exclusive risk. Similarly, while the 9/11 attackers destroyed two highly symbolic structures illustrative of U.S. and Western economic power, the targeted buildings were attacked *after* the beginning of the workday to maximize loss of life. Even the most significant, symbolic, physical structures – such as the Statue of Liberty, Sears Tower, Golden Gate Bridge, even the U.S. Capital, White House, or Lincoln Monument – could be replaced or replicated. The key capability post attack, as James Fallows has suggested, is to contain the damage and then concentrate on "rebound,"[58] which is exactly what New York City did so ably and quickly after the 9/11 attack. They responded well, worked as a team, and rebuilt. The extraordinary relief efforts, extraction of human remains, and rubble clearance proved to be an inspiring example and morale builder for the nation.

Also, one must keep in mind the narrowing distinction between "tactical" and "strategic," both in an attack sense and in a response sense. A tactical terrorist attack could become a strategic setback for the under-prepared defender. The notion of effects-based operations (EBO) may cost the attacker little (financially less than $600,000 in the case of the 9/11 attacks), but create a terrible strategic cost (greater than $100 billion in costs and lost revenue to New York City, for example.)

On the other hand, a strategic attack on structures alone (such as office buildings, defense installations, or transit systems) may result mostly in tactical, physical damage. Recovery and reconstitution may not be a strategic loss. The pertinent ratio is what level of acceptable risk should one assume to lessen greatly the prospect of unacceptable consequences? That is not an engineering or science question, but rather an acute political and societal judgment.

One simply cannot replace or quickly recover from thousands or millions of human fatalities. The worst-case scenario is mass casualty attack on populated cities, especially a WMD attack with catastrophic lingering consequences. The multiplier effect on families, co-workers, and institutions of perhaps several million fatalities would be enormous, possibly threatening systemic civil order. Feelings of devastating loss of this magnitude are incomprehensible. The nation would survive, but at what price to nationhood?

What does this suggest for lessons learned? One lesson is that U.S. deterrent, preventive, and defensive measures need to focus on shielding known, dense, concentrations of people. New York City's Grand Central Station and Macy's Christmas Parade, the Super Bowl, the Boston Marathon, Atlanta, O'Hare, or Los Angeles airport terminals and two Talladega race events become the concerns. Like the 9/11 near simultaneous attacks, so, too, high value, soft targets *in real time rapid sequence* are the expected targets of opportunity.

Just as Israel can point to the Second Intifada in September 2000 as the onset of a sustained pattern of suicide terrorism against its civilian citizenry, one can trace the source of Al Qaeda suicide attack planning for the continental U.S. to 1996, when bin Laden officially "declared war" on the United States. His February 1998 fatwa (religious edict) called for the killing of *any American* (civilian and military) anywhere in the world. Al Qaeda's objective is to kill the maximum number of *innocent* Americans.

It is the judgment of several leading national security specialists that Al Qaeda aspires to acquire and detonate a WMD weapon, likely a dirty nuclear bomb, on U.S. soil.[59] As an apt generalization, Pape says "In practice…suicide terrorists often seek simply to kill the largest number of people." Moreover, he also concludes that maximizing the number of enemy killed would alienate large numbers who might be sympathetic to the terrorist's cause. Implicitly, what appears to be the maximum leveraged vehicle of terrorism is also its Achilles heel.[60]

To its credit, the U.S. Government has begun to create a necessary framework to deter, prevent, and defend against terrorist and possible mass casualty attacks. Two significant examples are the *National Strategy for Homeland Security* (2002) and the *National Strategy for Combating Terrorism* (2003). The *Homeland Security* document points to the prevention of terrorist attacks within the United States, how to reduce the nation's vulnerability, and finally outlines preparations to minimize post-attack damage and begin recovery operations. The *Combating Terrorism* document outlines a preliminary vision and necessary refocusing to defeat terrorists, deny support to them, and diminish conditions that terrorists seek to exploit. These initial broad strategies serve as provisional skeletal structures on which will hang operational policies and tactical responses to deter, prevent, and defend against further terrorist attacks. A significant omission in both documents, however, are measures to detect and effectively counter suicide terror attacks.

There is much to commend among a litany of proposed U.S. strategies toward the Muslim world, approaches that could constructively engage overseas religious communities, if not reverse hostility toward the United States.[61] One broad-based blueprint, designed to build upon the 9/11 Commission recommendations, concentrates on defeating the Jihadist extremists through the use of full spectrum political, economic, military, and cultural instruments.[62] Terrorism generally, and suicide terrorism specifically, call for multi-pronged efforts to combat the challenge over long duration.

Some Issues for Further Study

One plausible hypothesis to explain the greatest likely danger in modern terrorism is that **religious cults**, which harbor an apocalyptic vision employing outward-oriented violence and a suicidal impulse, are the most probable culprit to use weapons of mass destruction.[63] As pointed out by the author, however, most suicide cults direct their violence *inward* (e.g., People's Temple, Heaven's Gate).

Suicide terrorists on the other hand direct this violence outward, destroying others and enhancing the appeal of their organization and serving as a means to recruit bomb carriers. These suicide terrorists can be characterized by two differing models. The first model is well characterized by Hamas, which preys upon young, single, men and women who have experienced person loss, guilt and embarrassment, and are searching for a meaningful way to make their lives count amid the desperation that engulfs them.

The second model exemplified by Mohammed Atta, the 9/11 bombers, and the recent car bombers in England, are committed extremists. These individuals are more mature, often with considerable education (including physicians and other professionals), healthy, and well-traveled. Rather than being taken advantage of by an organization, this group is truly committed to the cause and willing to sacrifice their worldly accomplishments (including at times spouse and children) in the service of their religious goal.

It would appear that an interventionist policy might exploit the potential cleavage that exists in group one between the organizational interest and the willing, but despairing suicide terrorist. Model two, on the other hand, would seem to offer less opportunity to exploit such cleavage as their motivation of the bomber and the organization are more closely aligned.

There is always a cultural handicap in the selection of relevant variables to understand human behavior. One common and persistent pitfall is that of **mirror imaging.** This natural tendency to assume your adversary will act as you might in similar circumstances often serves to self-deceive. During the four decades of the Cold War, for example, U.S. policy responses to real and perceived Soviet and PRC actions were often premised on what the American mindset *expected* our adversaries to do politically, economically, and especially militarily. The United States, for example, was astonished that China would enter the Korean War (misreading of the correlation of forces and their real fear of U.S. attack on their homeland), or that the USSR would delay fielding the newest generation of its ICBM missiles (the American ethic is to deploy new technologies quickly even if they are imperfect). The key question often overlooked in designing multi-functional responses to a given challenge is, "what did we miss, or not taken sufficient account of?"

Mirror imaging occurred with the 1995 Oklahoma City bombing of the Murrah Federal Building with 168 killed. For a time, security authorities and especially the U.S. public believed the culprit could *only* be a foreign terrorist, certainly not a young, American, military veteran, no matter how disturbed.

There may be a current example of an arguable case for mirror imaging. Al Qaeda first attacked the World Trade Center (WTC) in 1993, causing 6 deaths and 1,000 wounded, and then they returned far more successfully on September 11, 2001, to take nearly 3,000 lives, most of whom were in the World Trade Center.[64] The U.S. Government sees those WTC events as an Al Qaeda pattern, a "return to the scene of the crime" with a subsequent attack. Both then CIA Director Tenet and FBI Director Mueller during congressional testimony in February 2004 pointed to an Al Qaeda network still capable of catastrophic attacks against the United States. Director Mueller affirmed, "There are strong indications that Al Qaeda will revisit missed targets until they succeed...such as they did the World Trade Center. And the list of missed targets now includes both the White House as well as the Capitol."[65] Recall that during the December 2003 Christmas holidays, U.S. and foreign intelligence surfaced information that air flights originating from London and Paris en route to Washington D.C., among other major U.S. cities, may have been targets for hijacking. Multiple British Air and Air France flights were rescheduled or cancelled. Is this an organizational pattern of recurring operations or simply a coincidence? Short of a similar follow-on attack, the answer is moot.

Another issue, **ethno-religious profiling**, finds ready national debate and contentious postures. There are approximately seven million U.S. members of the Islamic faith, among them many Arab families settled here for generations. About two-thirds of the newer domestic adherents to Islam are African-Americans. Does it not make logical (if not political) sense to monitor and investigate Islamic groups for possible terrorist ties? Common sense and ethnic-racial sensitivity easily collide. Given that virtually all of the suicide bombers in Israel were Muslims, all twenty of the 9/11 hijackers Muslims, and 15 of the 19 hijackers Saudi nationals, religious and country-of-origin profiles are self-evident.

The issue acquires even greater significance with the reported dispatch of Islamic extremists to join "sleeper cells" already thought to exist in the United States.[66] The United Press International reportedly obtained a "terrorist survival information kit" in Quetta, Pakistan, including how to survive a long U.S.-led war against terrorism. Enclosed documents repeatedly emphasized the need for Taliban and Al Qaeda terrorists to "merge with the masses" and "become indistinguishable" from local people.[67] These reports, and many others which point to future risk and threat to the United States, raise many issues for intelligence collection and analysis, law enforcement authorities, and the judicial system.

Long before 9/11, terrorist specialist Paul Wilkinson using a hockey metaphor said, "You can make a hundred brilliant saves, but the only shot that people remember is the one that gets past you." How best to detect suicide plots, to deter, prevent, counter, and, if necessary, reconstitute quickly after an assault have become necessary planning imperatives in defending the national interest.

The 9/11 tragedy charges those in decision-making roles to "think the unthinkable," and to try to do so responsively, objectively, insuring preservation of prized civil liberties, and becoming much more intimately familiar with the wide spectrum of the cultural context of human nature. This new realism is a tall order for the pluralistic, open, American society that has only recently encountered deathly attacks on its citizens at home.

Anticipating suicide assaults will test our investigative and analytic capabilities, and no doubt challenge even more how we proceed to thwart future attacks, ensure constitutional liberties, and conduct the business of the nation.

Notes

1. Council on Foreign Relations, "Suicide Terror: Was 9/11 Something New?" *Terrorism: Questions & Answers*, 11 September 2002, 3, On-line, Internet, available from www.cfrterrorism.org/terrorism/suicide.html.

2. For the context of the statement, see Vincent M. Cannistaro, "Balance Wars Against Terror, Iraq," *USA Today*, 1 April 2003, 13A.

3. The most authoritative accounting of global terrorist incidents has long been the annual U.S. Department of State, *Patterns of Global Terrorism, seriatim*. Serious data collection and calculation errors in the initial 2004 report prompted senior policymaker apologies and immediate revision of the annual document. Apologies from the responsible agencies included then Secretary of State Colin Powell, Ambassador Cofer Black, State Department Coordinator for Counterterrorism, and John Brennan, Director of the Terrorism Threat Integration Center (TTIC), in *Remarks on the Release of the Revised Patterns of Global Terrorism 2003 Annual Report*, Washington D.C., 22 June

2004, On-line, Internet, 18 November 2007, available from http://www.state.gov/s/ct/rls/ rm/2004/33801.htm. The revised report, *Patterns of Global Terrorism 2003,* 22 June 2004, On-line, Internet, 18 November 2007, available from http://www.state.gov/ s/ct/rls/crt/2003/. While terrorism statistics often "spike" up or down year to year, there has been a consistent downward trend in incidents but a distinct rise in lethality, i.e., fewer average incidents but more loss of life.

4. Former CIA Director George Tenet reference in reported congressional testimony, John Diamond, "Intelligence chiefs say al-Qaeda will return to missed targets," *USA Today*, 25 February 2004, 5A; Ambassador Robert L. Hutchins, Chairman, National Intelligence Council, "Terrorism and Economic Security," address to the International Security Management Association, Scottsdale AZ, 14 January 2004, On-line, Internet, available from www.cia.gov/nic/speeches_terror_and_econ_sec.html. In the same vein, Cofer Black, U.S. Ambassador at Large for Antiterrorism, in Steven Gutkin, "Terrorists Pursuing WMDs Capability," *Washington Times*, 9 February 2004, 14. The nation's largest municipal police force in New York City, furthest along among U.S. cities in preparing for a possible WMD attack, conducted chemical and biological training for 10,000 officers present at the Republican National Convention, 30 August through 2 September 2004. William K. Rashbaum and Judith Miller, "New York Police Take Broad Steps in Facing Terror," *The New York Times*, 15 February 2004, On-line, Internet, 18 November 2007, available from www.nytimes.com/2004/02/15/nyregion/ 15THREAT.html. The prospects for a mass-casualty CBRN (Chemical, Biological, Radiological, or Nuclear) attack is examined thoroughly in Adam Dolnik, "Die and Let Die: Exploring Links between Suicide Terrorism and Terrorist Use of Chemical, Biological, Radiological, and Nuclear Weapons," *Studies in Conflict & Terrorism*, vol. 26, 2003, 17-35.

5. Josef Federman, "Israeli minister threatens to kill militant leaders," *The Montgomery Advertiser*, 2 February 2004, 4A. The 103 suicide incident count appeared in *USA Today*, 6 October 2003, 12A. By the end of February 2004, the number of suicide attacks rose to 110. Ravi Nessman, "Suicide blast kills 8 on Jerusalem bus," *USA Today*, 23 February 2004, 13A. *The News Hour with Jim Lehrer,* 10 February 2004 reported that approximately 3000 Palestinians and 900 Israelis had been killed in the previous three years, since the beginning of the Second Initifada in September 2000. Suicide bombings accounted for about half of the 900 Israelis killed. Between February, 2004 and late August, 2004 were seven months of relatively little violence. On 31 August 2004, two suicide bombers blew up two Israeli commuter buses in Beersheba, fifty miles south of Tel Aviv, killing 16 and wounding more than 100, the worst bombing in nearly a year. Hamas claimed responsibility, in retaliation for the Israeli assassinations in Gaza of two Hamas leaders, Sheik Yassin its founder, and his successor, Dr. Rantisi. The account may be found in Steven Erlanger, "Twin Blasts Kill 16 in Israel; Hamas Claims Responsibility," *The New York Times,* 1 September 2004.

6. Doron Almog, "Cumulative Deterrence and the War on Terrorism," *Parameters*, vol. XXXIV, no. 4, Winter 2004-05, 4, On-line, Internet, 18 November 2007, available from http://www.carlisle.army.mil/usawc/Parameters/04winter/almog.htm.

7. Menahem Milson, "Reform vs. Islamism in the Arab World Today," *The Middle East Media Research Institute*, 15 September 2004, On-line, Internet, 18 November 2007, available from www.memri.org/bin/articles.cgi?Page=archives&Area=sr&ID=SR3404.

8. "Suicide terrorism: a global threat," *Jane's Intelligence Review*, 20 October 2000, On-line, Internet, 18 November 2007, available from www.janes.com/security/international_security/news/ usscole/jir001020_1_n.shtml.

9. Ariel Merari, "The readiness to kill and die: Suicidal terrorism in the Middle East," in Walter Reich, Ed., *Origins of terrorism; Psychologies, ideologies, theologies, states of mind* (Washington D.C.: Woodrow Wilson Center Press, 1998), 192-193. His reference to the earlier studies, respectively, were to Lord Chalfont's comment in R. Kidder, "The Terrorist Mentality," *Christian Science Monitor*, 15 May 1986 and secondly to G. Lester and D. Lester, *Suicide* (Englewood Cliffs NJ: Prentice-Hall, 1971).

10. Boaz Ganor, "Suicide Terrorism: an Overview," 15 February 2000. This and other topical papers on suicide terrorism were presented originally at an International Conference on Countering Suicide Terrorism, Herzeliya, Israel, sponsored by The International Policy Institute for Counter-Terrorism (ICT), February 2000.

11. The relative indeterminacy stems from the estimated 30 to 40 terrorist groups believed affiliated with Al Qaeda in perhaps 60 different countries. Raymond Bonner and Don Van Natta, Jr., "Regional Terrorist Groups Pose Growing Threat, Experts Warn," *The New York Times*, 8 February 2004, On-line, Internet, available from www.nytimes.com/2004/02/08international/asia/08TERR.html?pagewanted+2&th.

12. David Van Biema, et al., "Why the Bombers Keep Coming," *Time Europe*, vol. 158, Issue 25, 17 December 2001, 31.

13. "The only time that Arab arms have forced Israel to surrender territory," observes Daniel Byman, "Should Hezbollah Be Next?" *Foreign Affairs*, vol. 82, no. 6, November/December 2003, 55.

14. Merari, 203.

15. Brian Jenkins, *The Likelihood of Nuclear Terrorism*, (Santa Monica CA: RAND Corporation, 1985), 6. The operative principle of "kill one, frighten a thousand" served as a widely accepted premise, especially for anti-colonial terrorist incidents. See Bruce Hoffman, "The Contemporary Terrorist Mindset: Targeting, Tactics and Likely Future Trends," *Intelligence and National Security*, vol. 11, no. 2 (1996), 207ff.

Precedent for mass destruction terrorism was not acknowledged conventional wisdom until the 1995 Aum Shinrikyo nerve gas attack in the Tokyo subway, which killed only 12 people but injured more than 5000.

16. "Suicide terrorism: a global threat," op. cit., 7.

17. Walter Laqueur, *No End to War; Terrorism in the Twenty-First Century*, (New York: Continuum, 2003), 97. Robert Pape's data set of 188 suicide terrorist attacks worldwide between 1980 and 2001 shows that the target of *all* attacks were democracies (full or "partly free" according to Freedom House). He concludes that suicide terrorism grows because "terrorists have learned that it works." "The Strategic Logic of Suicide Terrorism," *American Political Science Review*, vol. 97, no. 3, August 2003, 138.

18. Byman, 61, notes that Hezbollah adheres to Iran's ideology of rule by Islamic clerics, that Teheran provides approximately $100 million annually to the Shi'ite group, and that Hezbollah senior leaders proclaim their loyalty to Iran's Supreme Leader, Ayatollah Ali Khamenei.

19. "Suicide Attacks in Israel," in *Countering Suicide Terrorism; An International Conference February 20-23, 2000*, (Herzilya, Israel: The International Policy Institute for Counter-Terrorism, 2001), 137.

20. *Erased in a Moment; Suicide Bombing Attacks Against Israeli Civilians*, (New York: Human Rights Watch, October 2002), 15-16.

21. Israeli troops reportedly found an invoice from the Al-Aqsa Martyrs Brigade which showed expenses of about $150 to produce a standard suicide bomb outfit, cited in Dolnik, 21.

22. Gaynor, "Suicide Attacks in Israel," 140.

23. It should be noted that suicide terrorist profiles *beyond the Israeli region* appear to show much broader demographics. Sprinzak surfaced ample examples of both college-educated and relatively uneducated, single and married, women and men, socially isolated and integrated, and age ranges from 13 to 47. See "Rational Fanatics," *Foreign Policy*, no. 120, September-October 2000, 66-73. The 9/11 suicide terrorists were all students or professionals. Marc Sageman examined 400 Al Qaeda terrorist biographies, and found their average age was 26, 63 percent had gone to college, 75 percent were professionals or semi-professionals, 73 percent were married the vast majority with children, and surprisingly only 13 percent were trained in madrassas, though their common vision was to help create a fundamentalist (Salafi) Islamic state. See his *Understanding Terror Networks*, (Philadelphia PA: University of Pennsylvania Press, 2004). The March 2004 Madrid train suicide bombing, which killed 191 and wounded more than 1,900, showed much educational and professional diversity. Among the

Moroccan assailants included two on Spanish Government scholarships, one was an architecture student, another held a degree in chemical engineering, and the fourth owned a cellular telephone business. The out-of-region significant common thread points to dedicated and extremist Islamic believers as primary culprits.

24. The summer 2004 internal Israeli debate over Prime Minister Sharon's announced desire to depart Gaza entirely because of its virtual indefensibility short of permanent occupation again exemplified the issue of hostile space. The largest Palestinian refugee camp in Gaza, Jebaliyah, houses approximately 106,000 people confined to one-half square mile – one of the world's most crowded places. *The Montgomery Advertiser*, 3 October 2004, 3AA.

25. Hilal Khashan, "Collective Palestinian frustration and suicide bombings," *Third World Quarterly*, vol. 24, no. 6 (2003), 1061, 1064-1065. That conclusion finds further support in Daphne Burdman, "Education, Indoctrination, and Incitement: Palestinian Children on Their Way to Martyrdom," *Terrorism and Political Violence*, vol. 15, no. 1 (Spring 2003), 96-123. Textbooks created by the Palestinian Authority Ministry of Education in September 2000, and to be introduced over a 5-year period, she concludes, indoctrinate children to an ideology of martyrdom. She discovered in new texts, for example, that children are incited to participate in suicide bombings against Israeli Defense Forces.

26. Samuel P. Huntington, *Political Order in Changing Societies*, (New Haven CT: Yale University Press, 1968), 41, 52.

27. Jessica Stern, *Terror in the Name of God; Why Religious Militants Kill*, (New York: Harper Collins Publishers, 2003), and noted in a CSPAN interview with Brian Lamb, *Booknotes*, 12 October 2003. Author notes. Other notable book contributions to the suicide terrorist literature include the account of international correspondent for the German magazine, *Stern*, Christoph Reuter, *My Life is a Weapon; A Modern History of Suicide Bombing*, (Princeton, N.J.: Princeton University Press, 2004), and Deputy Foreign Editor, Knight Ridder newspapers, Joyce M. Davis, *Martyrs: Innocence, Vengeance, and Despair in the Middle East*, (New York: Palgrave Macmillan, 2003).

28. James Q. Wilson, "What Makes a Terrorist?" *City Journal*, vol. 14, no. 1, Winter 2003-2004, 4.

29. Both polling data results are summarized in Assaf Moghadam, "Palestinian Suicide Terrorism in the Second Intifada: Motivations and Organizational Aspects," *Studies in Conflict & Terrorism*, vol. 26, no. 2 (2003), 76. The original polling and analysis was done by the *Jerusalem Media and Communications Centre*, June 2001, On-line, Internet, 18 November 2007, available from http://www.jmcc.org/publicpoll/results/2001/no41.htm, and May-June 2002, On-line, Internet, 18 November 2007, available from http://www.jmcc.org/publicpoll/results/2002/no45.htm.

30. Moghadam, op. cit., 71-72.

31. Ibid., 65. The Ministry of Foreign Affairs calculations can be found at "Victims of Palestinian Violence and Terrorism Since September 2000," On-line, Internet, 18 November 2007, available from http://www.mfa.gov.il/MFA/Terrorism-+Obstacle+to+Peace/Palestinian+terror+since+2000/Victims+of+Palestinian+Violence+and+Terrorism+sinc.htm.

32. This section draws on data and narrative summary in Yoram Schweitzer, "Suicide Terrorism: Development and main characteristics," in *Countering Suicide Terrorism*, 2001, 75ff, On-line, Internet, 18 November 2007, available from www.ict.org.il/articles/articledet.cfm?articleid=112.

33. See the account of Youssef M. Ibrahim, a Muslim and former senior Middle East correspondent for *The New York Times*, "Silence is a danger to Islam," *USA Today*, 8 September 2004, 15A; C. J. Chivers, "The Chechen's Story: From Unrivaled Guerrilla Leader to the Terror of Russia," *The New York Times*, 15 September 2004, On-line, Internet, 18 November 2007, available from www.nytimes.com/2004/09/15/international/europe/15chechen.html?pagewanted=pr. This byline also provides an excellent biographical sketch of Shamil Basayev, the Chechen rebel leader.

34. *Khansa,* reportedly, is a popular name for Arab women and references a 7th century female poet, who subsequently became the historic symbol of the Islamic woman warrior. Arguably, Osama bin Laden may have made a firm choice in favor of "women's emancipation through martyrdom." See John Phillips, "Women's Magazine Offers Tips to Terrorists," *Washington Times*, 17 January 2005.

35. Hudson, op. cit., 183; Ganor, "Suicide Attacks in Israel," 140; Moghadam, op. cit., 68.

36. Raphael Israeli, "Palestinian Women: The Quest for a Voice in the Public Square Through 'Islamikaze Martyrdom'," *Terrorism and Political Violence*, vol. 16, no. 1 (Spring 2004), 66. The author is affiliated with the Truman Institute for the Advancement of Peace, Hebrew University, Jerusalem, Israel.

37. Mark Juergensmeyer, *Terror in the Mind of God; The Global Rise of Religious Violence*, (Berkeley CA: University of California Press, 2000), 165ff.

38. "Martyrdom and murder," *The Economist*, vol. 370, issue 8357, 10 January 2004.

39. Ganor, op. cit., 138.

40. Hudson, op. cit., 185-186.

41. Laqueur, op. cit., 92.

42. Stern, op. cit., 53.

43. See Bruce Hoffman, "Holy Terror: The Implications of Terrorism Motivated by a Religious Imperative," *Studies in Conflict and Terrorism*, vol. 18 (October to December 1995), 271-284. David Rapoport portrays religiously-motivated, contemporary terrorism as the "fourth wave" in the evolution of terrorist violence. The first three waves were linked to the breakup of empires, the decolonization process, and anti-Westernism. "The Fourth Wave: September 11 and the History of Terrorism," *Current History*, December 2001, 419-424.

44. This line of thought as it may apply to domestic U.S. religious explanations for behavior is persuasively presented by Bill Tammeus, editorial page columnist for the Kansas City Star, in "Absolute religious certainty leads to harm," *The Montgomery Advertiser*, 28 September 2003, 13A. This author applies the argument to suicide terrorism.

45. Merari, op. cit., 206.

46. Moghadam, op. cit., 69.

47. Stephen J. Lyons, "The motivation behind 'Martyrs'; Writer searches for what propels Mideast bombers," *USA Today*, 24 June 2003, 5D, in a review of Joyce M. Davis, *Martyrs*, (2003).

48. Peter Chalk, "The evolving dynamic of terrorism in the 1990s," *Australian Journal of International Affairs*, vol. 53, no. 2, On-line, Internet, July 1999, available from www.newfirstsearch.oclc.org/WebZ/FSQUERY?sessionid=sp04sw01-44654-d2p43ay2-1t, 3-4.

49. Robert A. Pape, "Dying to Kill Us," *The New York Times*, 22 September 2003, On-line, Internet, available from www.nytimes.com/2003/09/22/opinion/22PAPE.html.

50. This sequence of political-military events and close correlation with subsequent suicide attacks is described in Rex A. Hudson and Staff of the Federal Research Division, Library of Congress, *Who Becomes a Terrorist and Why; The 1999 Government Report on Profiling Terrorists*, (Guilford CT: The Lyons Press, n.d.), 51-52.

51. Bruce Hoffman and Gordon H. McCormick, "Terrorism, Signaling, and Suicide Attack," *Studies in Conflict & Terrorism*, vol. 27 (2004), 272.

52. A 2004 RAND study, for example, concluded that "Better *cultural intelligence* is needed...(beyond) the relative lack of Arab specialists in military and intelligence

positions [emphasis added]." Angel M. Rabasa et al., *The Muslim World after 9/11*, (Santa Monica CA: RAND Corporation, 2004), xxvii. An excellent example within the U.S. military education community of applied research on Islam is Youssef H. Aboul-Enein and Sherifa Zuhur, *Islamic Rulings on Warfare*, (Carlisle Barracks PA: U.S. Army War College Strategic Studies Institute, October 2004).

53. *Joint Inquiry Into Intelligence Community Activities Before and After the Terrorist Attacks of September 11, 2001, Report* of the U.S. Senate Select Committee on Intelligence and U.S. House Permanent Select Committee on Intelligence, 107th Congress, 2D Session, December 2002, 191-194.

54. Richard Posner, "The 9/11 Report: A Dissent," *The New York Times*, 29 August 2004, On-line, Internet, available from www.nytimes.com. Posner is a judge on the United States Court of Appeals for the Seventh Circuit, a senior lecturer at the University of Chicago Law School, and author of *Catastrophe: Risk and Response* (2004).

55. Matthew L. Wald, "Study Finds Threat to Jets from Missiles; Cost is Cited," *The New York Times*, 25 January 2005.

56. A number of terrorism analysts have speculated that bin Laden seeks to force the U.S. to spend unsustainable amounts of money on defensive measures, thereby weakening the world's leading economy. Between 9/11 and the close of 2004, U.S. defense spending has grown by more than 25 percent not counting supplemental expenditures of approximately $82 billion for U.S. operations in Afghanistan and Iraq and a nearly $40 billion annual budget for the Department of Homeland Security. See Gal Luft, "Al-Qaeda's Economic War against the United States," *Institute for the Analysis of Global Security*, 24 January 2005, On-line, Internet, 18 November 2007, available from www.iags.org/n0124052.htm. On February 14, 2005, President Bush requested another $81.9 billion in supplemental (above budget) spending, primarily for military operations in Iraq and Afghanistan, on top of $419.3 billion requested for the FY 2006 defense budget. Eric Schmitt, "Bush Seeks $81.9 Billion More, Mostly for Forces in Iraq," *The New York Times*, 15 February 2005. Normally, "supplementals" are reserved for "unanticipated war costs." Dave Moniz, "Bush asks for $82B extra, most of it for Pentagon," *USA Today*, 15 February 2005, 6A.

57. Mimi Hall, "Terror Target List Way Behind," *USA Today*, 8 December 2004, On-line, Internet, 18 November 2007, available from http://www.usatoday.com/news/washington/2004-12-08-terror-database_x.htm.

58. James Fallows, "Success Without Victory," *The Atlantic Monthly*, vol. 295, no. 1, January/February 2005, 84.

59. See Warren Rudman, Gary Hart, Leslie H. Gelb, and Stephen Flynn, "Our Hair is On Fire," *Wall Street Journal*, 16 December 2004. Michael Scheuer, who served as

chief of the bin Laden unit at the CIA's Counterterrorism Center (1996-1999), and the once anonymous author of *Imperial Hubris: Why the West Is Losing the War on Terrorism* (2004), says Al Qaeda will do its utmost to obtain a weapon of mass destruction, not as a deterrent, but that bin Laden is "looking for a first strike weapon," quoted in "Are We Winning the War on Terror? An Interview with Michael Scheuer," *Terrorism Monitor*, vol. 2, no. 13, 14 December 2004, On-line, Internet, available from www.jamestown.org/news_details.php?news_id=82. Attorney General John Ashcroft in his valedictory departure from office cautioned that the "greatest danger facing the United States in the war on terrorism" is the prospect that Al Qaeda or its sympathizers could gain access to a nuclear bomb. Statement of 27 January 2005 in "Ashcroft: Nuclear Terror Greatest Threat," *Associated Press*, 1 February 2005, On-line, Internet, available from www.ap.org. For a concise assessment of the terrorist nuclear option, see Council on Foreign Relations, "What would it take for terrorists to acquire a nuclear weapon?" *Terrorism: Questions & Answers*, 15 November 2004, On-line, Internet, available from www.terrorismanswers.org/home/.

60. Pape, "The Strategic Logic of Suicide Terrorism," 133.

61. A fine example is "U.S. Strategy in the Muslim World After 9/11," *RAND Research Brief*, 2004, which argues for a "shaping strategy" to help ameliorate negative trends in the Muslim world that promote extremism and anti-Americanism.

62. The Century Foundation, *Defeating the Jihadists; A Blueprint for Action*, (New York: The Century Foundation Press, 2004). Chaired by Richard Clarke, former National Coordinator for Security and Counterterrorism and senior advisor to four U.S. presidents, the task force report recommends a mix of "hard" and "soft" power strategies to counter global terrorism.

63. Dolnik, 32. He concludes that suicide terrorism as a tactic cannot be correlated easily with mass-casualty WMD scenarios. For a well-argued contrary view, see Graham Allison, *Nuclear Terrorism: The Ultimate Preventable Catastrophe*, (New York: Times Books, 2004).

64. The final body count for the 9/11 attacks for the three sites (WTC, Pentagon, western Pennsylvania) is 2,976 excluding the 19 hijackers. The New York City coroner did not have an authoritative list of by name killed until October 2003 given the difficulty of identification, false claimants, and corroboration of missing, presumed dead by family and friends not only in the U.S. but from 81 foreign nations.

65. Dana Priest, "Tenet Warns of Al Qaeda Threat," *Washington Post*, 25 February 2004, 1.

66. Jerry Seper, "Islamic Extremists Invade U.S., Join Sleeper Cells," *Washington Times*, 10 February 2004, 1. The report claims the FBI and other federal authorities

believe cells are operating in forty states, awaiting orders for new attacks in the U.S., and using Muslim communities for cover, funds, and recruitment support.

67. Anwar Iqbal, "Terrorists Prepped for a Long Conflict," *United Press International*, 14 February 2004, On-line, Internet, available from www.upi.com. This "how to" manual, authenticated by local sources says UPI, has been printed in several languages, including Arabic, Pashto, and Urdu, and distributed in Afghanistan and Pakistan.

CHAPTER 2

Al Qaeda's Modus Operandi: Anticipating Their Target Selection

Barry R. Schneider

The July 2007 National Intelligence Estimate (NIE) on "The Terrorist threat to the U.S. Homeland" states that:

> We assess that Al Qaeda's homeland plotting is likely to continue to focus on prominent political, economic, and infrastructure targets with the goal of producing mass casualties, visually dramatic destruction, significant economic aftershocks, and/or fear among the U.S. population.[1]

According to this NIE, "Al Qaeda is and will remain the most serious terrorist threat to the homeland, as its central leadership continues to plan high-impact plots, while pushing others in extremist Sunni communities to mimic its efforts and to supplement its capabilities." This leads to a series of questions that require answers if the United States is to maximize its defenses against expected terror attacks:

1. Why does the Al Qaeda leadership choose the targets they select for attack? What is their motivation and purpose?

2. What is the likely pattern of attacks planned, financed, and approved by the central Al Qaeda group around Osama bin Laden (Al Qaeda 1.0), and how might such attacks differ from attacks executed by local jihadists not under the direct control of bin Laden (Al Qaeda 2.0)?

3. Given the intentions of these groups, what kinds of targets and key assets exist in the United States that the government and its citizens must attempt to protect?

4. What is the likelihood of Al Qaeda 1.0 and/or 2.0 acquiring and employing weapons of mass destruction, mass casualty, or mass effect in the U.S. homeland?[2]

5. What are examples of the worse-case or most catastrophic types of potential Al Qaeda attacks to defend against?

6. How should U.S. leaders think about prioritizing homeland defenses and Global War on Terrorism expenditures to achieve the best defense of U.S. critical infrastructures, key assets, and the American population with available resources?

Al Qaeda Target Selection: Motivations and Purposes

Why does the Al Qaeda leadership choose the targets they select for attack? What is their motivation and purpose?

Osama bin Laden and his closest associates have stated that their aim is to establish a caliphate, an extreme and fundamentalist Islamic theocracy, to replace the state governments that now exist in the Muslim world. To this end they have declared a religious war on the United States, the West in general, and on existing Muslim-led governments that do not match their brand of Wahhabbism Muslim theology. They believe each of these countries that they have made their foes pose as barriers to achieving their puritanical form of Islam and these they have dedicated themselves to expelling from power these so-called "apostate" regimes which include key U.S. friends such as Saudi Arabia, Bahrain, Kuwait, Egypt, Jordan, and others.

A recent RAND study has examined four hypotheses about what drives Al Qaeda's central leadership in their choice of targets:

1. <u>The Coercion Hypothesis</u>: Cause enough pain and suffering to drive the United States and other Westerners out of Muslim lands.

2. <u>The Damage Hypothesis</u>: Inflict enough damage to the U.S. economy to reduce the resources available to support American foreign policy.

3. <u>The Rally Hypothesis</u>: Take actions that would stimulate support and encourage recruits to join the movement from the Muslim world.

4. <u>The Franchise Hypothesis</u>: Provide inspiration, well-wishing, support, and a possible clearinghouse for jihad plans and operations of affiliated groups.

The conclusions of the RAND study indicated that they surmised that the coercion and damage hypotheses seemed to best capture the sense of the majority of statements made by Osama bin Laden, Ayman Al-Zawahiri, and others prominent in their leadership core group. It is also likely that the attacks chosen were selected to achieve all or most of these effects. Some of these attacks also might have non-logical but psychological sources, or other rationales might also apply such as attacks launched out of hatred or a desire for revenge for perceived injuries (such as Al Qaeda attacks directed by bin Laden at the Saudi regime that targeted him).

Al Qaeda 1.0's and 2.0's Modus Operandi

How might jihadist attacks differ if done by local groups not directly under the control of central Al Qaeda leadership but inspired by them?

Al Qaeda 1.0

The early pattern of Al Qaeda attacks starting in the 1980s and 1990s up until the September 11, 2001, attacks (Al Qaeda 1.0) were characterized by:

- Central, top-down leadership (bin Laden, Al-Zawahiri);

- Drawing up patient, careful plans – 1 to 2 or more years in preparation including careful casing of targets;

- Undergoing thorough reviews before final approval of plans;

- Operating from permanent installations;

- Organized within a fixed corporate structure;
- Use of standardized operating procedures;
- Following regular procedures and decision-processes;
- Engaging in meticulous training (including exercises and trial runs in their Afghan camps);
- Providing central financing of operations with multiple sources of income;
- Making available necessary equipment and materials;
- Relying on experienced operatives with Afghan war expertise;
- Targets selected tend to be identified with West, Jews, or Shiites;
- Timing, personnel, and final attack was approved by central leadership;
- Frequent reliance on suicide bombers – roughly 50 percent of Al Qaeda attacks outside of Iraq and Afghanistan are suicide bombings;[3]
- Launching multiple attacks, near-simultaneous attacks (to achieve greater fear and attention, while creating greater challenges for responders);
- Putting emphasis on visually pleasing "spectacular" attacks;
- Use of bombs as the favorite weapon of choice as opposed to firearms, missiles, poisons, or other means, whether they be car bombs, suicide bombs, IEDs planted in the path of targets, airliner bombs, or other explosive devices;
- Allowing operatives ample time to get in place;
- Training sleeper cells trained to "blend in" the local area prior to attacking;
- Repeat attacks on targets previously missed; and
- Selecting difficult but important targets, such as:
    - Leaders (e.g., White House, Capitol);

- Symbolic Targets (e.g., Pentagon, World Trade Center, U.S. Embassies, Washington Monument, Statue of Liberty, Wall Street, Capitol, and Pentagon);
- Military Targets (e.g., Pentagon, USS *Cole*, Fort Dix); and
- Economic Targets (e.g., Airlines, Wall Street).

Al Qaeda 2.0

After the U.S.-led coalition in Operation Enduring Freedom and the Northern Alliance expelled Al Qaeda and the Taliban from Afghanistan, bin Laden and his core leadership lost their unrestricted safe haven and were forced to remain hidden in the remote foothills of the Federally Administered tribal areas of Pakistan. The continuing Global War on Terrorism (GWOT) has largely kept Al Qaeda's core group on the run, playing defense rather than offense. This has given rise to a modification of how they and their admirers have had to pursue the global salafi jihad, what we will call Al Qaeda 2.0.

What we term Al Qaeda 2.0, for the purposes of this analysis, is really a collection of three different types of groups. First, there are Al Qaeda affiliates that have created formal ties to Al Qaeda 1.0 and bear the name Al Qaeda in their title. For example, formal agreements were signed extending the Al Qaeda brand name to Al Qaeda in Iraq and the Al Qaeda organization in the Maghreb. In the later case, Al Qaeda 1.0 accepted into the fold the members of the Algerian-based Salafist Group for Call and Combat after they pledged their allegiance to Osama bin Laden, promising to:

> [G]ive him the proceedings from our hands and the fruit from our hearts, to continue our jihad in Algeria as soldiers under his…instructions. He can use us to strike whomever and wherever he wishes, and he will find nothing but obedience from us and shall only receive what pleases him.[4]

Second, there exists a group of like-minded extremist Islamic groups, not formally bound to Al Qaeda, that often act in concert with its goals and sometimes are connected to it via financing or training programs.

These groups, in addition to Al Qaeda, embrace the need to carry on a violent form of Jihad against local governments and Westerners. Some examples are the following:[5]

- Jemaah Islamiyah (JI) in Southeast Asia
- Ansar al-Islam in Iraq
- Dahmat Houmet Daawa Salafici in Algeria
- Mujahideen Suura Council in Iraq
- Moroccan Islamic Combat Group
- Salafiya Jihadia in Morocco
- Egyptian Islamic Jihad
- Islamic Movement of Uzbekistan
- Chechen Jihadists
- Libyan Islamic Fighting Group
- Tunisia Combat Group
- Al Itihaad al-Islam in Somalia
- The New Somalian Jihad: Network
- Harakat-up-Jihad-Islamic in Bangladesh
- Jaish-e-Muhammed in Pakistan and Kashmir
- Laskar-e-Jhangri in Pakistan
- Laskar-e-Taiba in Pakistan and Kashmir
- Harakat-ul-Mujahideen in Pakistan and Kashmir

These formal groups of insurgents or terrorists from time-to-time have received help from Al Qaeda in the form of financing, weapons, training, inspiration, or other assistance.

A third type of group of insurgents or terrorists, jihad fellow travelers, are ad hoc small cells that have formed to carry out violent operations although they may have no formal or direct connections to Al

Qaeda other than the example set or one-way messages through the Internet. In some cases these examples of "spontaneous Muslim combustion" include members who have had a previous terrorist or insurgency experience or training but no direct present connections to bin Laden's organization.

Al Qaeda 2.0 operations are characterized by the following:

- Autonomous groups are involved;
- Al Qaeda 1.0's role is their inspiration and pattern;
- Operations are locally planned;
- Operators are locally trained, if at all;
- Operations are locally funded;
- Attacks are locally executed;
- Decisions are decentralized – not directed by AQ 1.0 leaders;
- Attacks are more spontaneous, less patient;
- Operations are less meticulously planned than by Al Qaeda 1.0 and the initiate riskier attacks with more outcomes left to chance;
- Operators have less of a strategic view – local grievances are emphasized;
- Affiliates launch comparatively unsophisticated attacks;
- Attacks are more designed to provoke fear than to inflict mass casualties or mass destruction; and
- Weapons typically used are conventional explosives and small arms.

In the current situation, "Al Qaeda inspires and guides local groups from afar but establishes no visible operational or logistical links."[6] Al Qaeda 2.0 attacks have been directed and executed by a growing network of Al Qaeda affiliates, "franchises," and jihadist copy cats and ideological fellow travelers. Some of these Al Qaeda 2.0 individuals and groups are members of the Internet virtual community of Islamic extremists who reinforce each other's violent deeds and jihadist impulses.

For example, one 1,600 page volume titled *The Call for a Global Islamic Resistance* has provided a strategy for all those who would take up arms in a decentralized jihad. Written by a Syrian-born engineer, Mustafa Setmariam Nasar, this volume argues for "a strategy for a truly global conflict on as many fronts as possible and in the form of resistance by small cells or individuals, rather than traditional guerrilla warfare. To avoid penetration and defeat by Security services, he says, organizational links should be kept to an absolute minimum."[7]

Thus, one theory about Al Qaeda 1.0 targeting preferences is the so-called, "franchise hypothesis," suggesting that:

> Although Al Qaeda retains its influence and reputation, it (currently) lacks the resources necessary to carry out attacks itself or to directly control the acts of others. Believing in the need to maintain fear and embolden supporters, Al Qaeda (1.0) serves as an inspiration, well-wisher, supporter, and perhaps clearinghouse for the plans and operations of affiliated jihadist groups.[8]

It is clear that Al Qaeda 1.0 exists but that the majority of jihadist attacks since September 11, 2001, have been of the Al Qaeda 2.0 variety. Note that, with one possible exception (the defeated 2005 plot to blow up airliners departing from Heathrow airport in the United Kingdom), every terrorist strike since 2002 has been conducted by a franchised or unaffiliated group.[9] Only the July 2005 plot to blow up airliners that would take off from Heathrow Airport in the United Kingdom was closely coordinated with the central Al Qaeda leadership in Pakistan. Notably, this attack plan was more conceived to inflict a mass effect than the other 2.0 attacks.

This might suggest that the main threat to the U.S. homeland likely would be extremist Muslims living within our borders inspired by Al Qaeda. A small number of violent Islamic extremists have recently been arrested inside the United States and, although, in the words of the July 2007 NIE, the "internal Muslim terror threat is not likely to be as severe as it is in Europe,"[10] the possibility still exists that others will be influenced to take violent action.[11]

The members of the Al Qaeda 1.0 and 2.0 community share some common traits. For example, these recruits mostly come from middle or upper class families, are well educated, particularly in the sciences and professions, and in their mid-twenties when they joined. Most are family men with children who have little or no criminal behavior in their previous backgrounds. There is no evidence that these Al Qaeda 2.0 recruits are emotionally unstable, or were religious zealots prior to recruitment. Most did not attend primarily religious schools. Indeed, most joined when asked by a friend or relative and tended to join when they were abroad in the West outside the borders of their native countries. Only after joining the group did they intensify their religious/political views and become radicalized, bonding firmly with their group and deepening hostility toward outsiders. Once in the group, most never found a way to leave.[12]

The active members making up Al Qaeda 1.0 consist of several types of recruits:[13]

- Central-level operational coordinators;
- Central-level specialists;
- Field-level operational coordinators;
- Field-level specialists;
- Soldiers and guards; and
- Suicide operatives.

The makeup of independent local groups and terror groups affiliated with the Al Qaeda 2.0 variety may be less stratified and members who do the planning may double as the operators to provide the necessary personnel to complete the targeting task.

Both Al Qaeda 1.0 and 2.0 groups tend to be flat, horizontal organizations, rather than vertical, deep hierarchies. Even Al Qaeda 1.0 has always been a somewhat flat and distributed network of participants loosely affiliated with a central command structure.

In the beginning the organization and its affiliates were more centralized under Osama bin Laden and a few associates than appears to be the case today when bin Laden, Al-Zawahiri, and others most closely associated with those at the top appear to be somewhat isolated from many of their jihadist allies worldwide.

Al Qaeda 1.0 still exists and periodically attempts strategic level attacks, but most of the attacks since 9/11 have been directed by Al Qaeda

2.0 groups. More and more, operational planning and execution of attacks is being taken by a diversity of local groups operating largely independent from the central Al Qaeda leadership which is thought to be cut off and isolated in villages in the Himalayan foothills along the Afghan-Pakistan border.

Obviously, it will be more difficult to generalize too much about Al Qaeda 2.0's tendencies since, for example, a Moroccan-based group in Madrid, Spain, might decide on targets, weapons, and tactics independently of Osama bin Laden and his chief lieutenants in Pakistan even when being inspired by them and following some suggestions communicated in general via the Internet. Further, this Madrid modus operandi might differ somewhat from attacks adopted by, for example, Muslim expatriates living in London. Extremists who pay lip service to the leadership of bin Laden may well act on their own and strike out in directions he neither controls nor approves.[14] Indeed, it appears that as you look at the actions of local groups and cells, targeting seems to have been more a function of local access (Fort Dix) and local grievances. Such actions have also been directed at softer targets. Thus, any generalizations made should identify whether we are talking about Al Qaeda 1.0 or 2.0, since the patterns are likely to differ somewhat. Indeed, the variance in the pattern of attacks within the Al Qaeda 2.0 categories could be considerable.

In reviewing these attacks, the first question that occurs is why did the attack take place? What were the motivations of the decision makers? And, do we know who they were?

It is assumed in this report that the most important decision maker in at least approving attack operations is Al Qaeda's leader, Osama bin Laden. Likely the second most important is Al Qaeda's number two leader, Ayman Al-Zawahiri. Then, third in importance, is whoever these central AQ 1.0 leaders approve to plan the specifics of the operation. The leaders of the Al Qaeda 2.0 attacks will vary from group to group and event to event and cannot be predicted with much confidence at present.

In the case of the September 11, 2001, attacks on the World Trade Center towers and the Pentagon building, the appointed operations leader was Khalid Sheik Mohammed,[15] who is now in U.S. custody and whose interrogation has revealed the outlines of Al Qaeda thinking about that event.[16] Financing, support, and approval of the plan was taken at the top levels of Al Qaeda.

At least, this appears to have been the Al Qaeda 1.0 model where the top Al Qaeda leadership provided overall guidance, exercised a veto on proposals, provided seed money for operations, approved operational leaders, and sometimes tapped specific personnel to join the attack teams, complete with special training and rehearsals.

Let us start with bin Laden's reasons for the specific kinds of attacks he has helped plan and has authorized to date. A review of bin Laden's statements indicates that his purpose is to inflict so much damage on the United States and its citizens that the U.S. Government will withdraw its forces from Muslim states, withdraw its financial and other support from Israel, and cease its support for so-called apostate Muslim states that are relatively friendly-to-the-West such as Jordan, Egypt, and Saudi Arabia.

In order to create this level of damage, bin Laden does not differentiate between military targets and civilian targets. In his own words he has stated:

> [S]o the struggle is both financial and physical…It is possible to strike the economic base that is the foundation of the military base, so when their economy is depleted, they will be too busy with each other to enslave poor peoples. So, I say that it is important to focus our attacking the American economy by any means available.[17]

Bin Laden argued that "it is just as important to strike at the U.S. economy by all means available as it is to fight U.S. troops and those allied with them."[18]

The Al Qaeda leader liked the results of the 9/11 attack because it was highly cost-effective in terms of the cost to Al Qaeda versus the cost to America. He has stated that:

> …Al Qaeda spent $500,000 [dollars] on the September 11 attacks, while America lost more than $500 billion [dollars] at the lowest estimate, in the event and its aftermath. That makes a million American dollars for every Al Qaeda dollar by the grace of God Almighty.[19]

> This is, in addition to the fact that it lost an enormous number of jobs – and as for the federal deficit, it made record losses, estimated at over a trillion dollars.[20]

> Still more serious for America was the fact that the mujahidin forced Bush to resort to an emergency budget in order to continue fighting in Afghanistan and Iraq. This shows the success of our plan to bleed America to the point of bankruptcy, with God's will.[21]

During his interrogations, it is reported that Khalid Sheik Mohammed discussed the targeting options under consideration prior to the 9/11 attacks. He had proposed a broader plan whereby hijackers would have taken over airliners on both coasts and run them into high-rise buildings on both coasts. He also said that targets under consideration in the D.C. area included CIA headquarters, the Capitol Building, the White House, the Pentagon, as well as the World Trade Center towers. This combination would hit at a number of types of targets:

1. Symbols of the U.S. economy (e.g., Twin Towers) located next to Wall Street; (as well as an attack on the U.S. airline industry);

2. Symbols of U.S. Government (e.g., White House, Capital, CIA HQ, Pentagon); and

3. U.S. leadership – decapitation strike attempts, putting the top U.S. political leaders in jeopardy.

Bin Laden and Al-Zawahiri trimmed the scale of the 9/11 strikes back to the East Coast attacks that took place. Bin Laden appears to view the United States as a bit of a paper tiger that, while mighty in appearance is fragile and capable of being collapsed if its foundation were struck at vulnerable key nodes.

For example, bin Laden stated that:

> We can conclude that America is a superpower, with enormous power, but that all this is built on foundations of straw. So it is possible to target those foundations and focus on their weakest points which, even if you strike one-tenth of them, then the whole edifice will totter and sway, and relinquish its unjust leadership of the world.[22]

In similar fashion, bin Laden sees the War in Iraq as another chance "to bleed America to the point of bankruptcy."[23]

Al Qaeda and WMD Possibilities

What is the likelihood of Al Qaeda acquiring and employing chemical, biological, radiological, or nuclear weapons – so-called CBRN weapons or weapons of mass destruction? President George W. Bush, three years after 9/11, gave his opinion that "in the hands of terrorists, weapons of mass destruction would be the first resort – the preferred means to further the ideology of suicide and random murder."[24]

The U.S. National Security Strategy has stated that "the gravest danger our nation faces lies at the crossroads of radicalism and technology."[25] Indeed, the world appears to have entered into a new era where a few persons or even a single individual might one day soon unleash the kind of killing or destructive power once reserved only to great power status.[26]

There is evidence that Al Qaeda's leadership is pursuing nuclear weapons, biological arms, and lethal chemical devices, and that if they were to obtain them, they would be likely to use them. Unlike rogue states that possess such weapons, Al Qaeda's leaders have no known and specific return address. Thus, they can be less easily deterred than rogue state leaders who know they might well be signing their own death warrants if they launched a WMD attack on the United States.

The July 2007 U.S. National Intelligence Estimate on "The Terrorist Threat to the U.S. Homeland," states this finding clearly:

> We assess that Al Qaeda will continue to try to acquire and employ chemical, biological, radiological, or nuclear material in attacks and would not hesitate to use them if it develops what it deems is sufficient capability.[27]

In his recent memoir, former CIA Director, George Tenet, writes that:

> ...Of all [Al Qaeda]'s efforts to obtain other forms of WMD, the main threat is the nuclear one. I am convinced that this is where Osama bin Laden and his operatives desperately want to go. They understand that bombings by

cars, trucks, trains, and planes will get them some headlines to be sure. But if they manage to set off a mushroom cloud, they will make history.

Such an event would place [Al Qaeda] on a par with the superpowers and make [b]in Laden's threat to destroy our economy and bring death into every American household. Even in the darkest days of the cold war, we could count on the fact that the Soviets, just like us, wanted to live. Not so with terrorists. [Al Qaeda] boasts that while we fear death, they embrace it.

One mushroom cloud could change history. My deepest fear is that this is exactly what they intend.[28]

It is documented that Al Qaeda has sought all types of chemical, biological, radiological, and nuclear weapons. For example, two nuclear scientists from the A.Q. Khan Laboratories at Kahuta, Pakistan, traveled to Afghanistan in August 2001, just one month prior to the 9/11 attacks in the United States, and spent two weeks talking with Osama bin Laden and his Al Qaeda and Taliban associates about the path to building a nuclear bomb and/or radiological weapons.[29]

One of them, Sultan Bashirrodan Mahmood, was the former Director of Pakistan's Atomic Energy Commission. He was eager to share his expertise with fellow jihadists as he is a religious zealot with an apocalyptic vision.

The other visitor from Pakistan, Chadri Andul Majeed, was a recently retired nuclear engineer specializing in nuclear materials enrichment for the Pakistan Institute of Science and Technology.[30]

Both of these nuclear weapons manufacturing experts belonged to a Pakistani non-governmental organization called the Umma Tameer-e-Nau (UTN) that was designed by its founder and chairman, Mahmood, to aid the Taliban and Al Qaeda. UTN offered help not only to these extremist groups but also approached Libya with an offer to assist Qadhafi's regime with the development of nuclear, biological, and chemical weapons. Along with detailed expert advice, Dr. Mahmood also provided bin Laden with a hand-drawn rough nuclear bomb design.[31]

There were reports from several sources that Al Qaeda operatives had attempted to purchase suitcase bombs from the Former Soviet Union.

Further, they were alleged in 1999, 2000, 2001, and 2002 to have successfully purchased samples of anthrax, plague, ricin, and botulinum toxin. Other reports indicated Al Qaeda representatives may have produced crude radiological materials for radiological dispersal device (RDD) use.

Clearly, the Al Qaeda leadership would entertain the use of nuclear weapons if they had them. In his February 1998 Fatwa, Osama bin Laden stated that "we – with God's help – call on every Muslim who believes in God and wishes to be rewarded to comply with God's order to kill the Americans and plunder their money wherever and whenever they find it."[32]

Two Al Qaeda operatives who were close associates of bin Laden in Sudan, the Syrian physician Muhammed Bayazid and the Iraqi agronomist Mubarak al-Duri, both felt the group had the right to kill masses of infidels. One of them flatly stated that "I think it is legitimate to kill millions of you because of how many of us you have killed."[33]

According to Suleiman Abu Ghaith, a cleric of Kuwaiti origin and spokesman for Al Qaeda, stated in June 2002 that "Al Qaeda has the right to kill four million Americans, including one million children, displace double that figure, and injure and cripple hundreds and thousands."[34]

Although the math is a terrible distortion of historical fact, the fact is that this is a line of thought pursued and spread by Al Qaeda's leadership and might be seen as the justification for a WMD attack on the United States.

Former CIA Director Tenet reports that in the fall of 2001 right after the 9/11 attacks, the Agency was receiving "unsubstantiated rumors from several reliable foreign intelligence services that some sort of small nuclear device had been smuggled into the United States and was destined for New York City."[35]

What would be the effect of a nuclear explosion on a major U.S. port city? A recent RAND report cites the likely effect of a 10 kiloton nuclear explosion on the port at Long Beach, California. Such a detonation would kill 60,000 residents, cause 3 million more to evacuate the city for up to 3 years, would destroy or make uninhabitable 600,000 homes, and would cost an estimated $1 trillion worth of damage.[36]

Ayman Al-Zawahiri, bin Laden's senior associate and number two in the Al Qaeda chain of command has stated that an objective of the global jihad against the United States and its allies is "to inflict maximum casualties against the opponent." He argues that "targets as well as the type and method of weapons used must be chosen to have an impact on the structure of the enemy."[37]

Al-Zawahiri, a medical doctor who has long ignored the Hippocratic Oath (*to do no harm*), has shown a special interest in biological and chemical warfare, and established Al Qaeda's chemical and biological warfare (CBW) research program, codenamed "curdled milk."[38]

His interest in chemical and biological weapons was sparked by Western alarms about possible CBW threats[39] that were fueled primarily by United Nations inspector discoveries about the Iraqi chemical and biological programs after Operation Desert Storm, and by revelations about the enormous size of the CBW programs of the Former Soviet Union.[40]

In their 5,000 page *Encyclopedia of Jihad*, Al Qaeda spells out in detail methods by which chemical and biological weapons can be made.[41] Materials, laboratories, and videos of animal testing were found abandoned in their Afghan camps after Operation Enduring Freedom forced them to flee, and revealed their interest in developing weapons from anthrax, ricin, botulinum toxin, bubonic plague and cyanide.[42] Trace elements of EMPTA, a VX nerve agent ingredient were also found at a Sudanese pharmaceutical plant site that Al Qaeda had invested in prior to their move back to Afghanistan.[43]

It is possible that Al Qaeda has *already* used biological weapons in the United States. The origin of the October – November 2001 anthrax letter attacks that followed on the heels of 9/11 has never been proven. Note that the Al Qaeda anthrax program pre-dates 9/11 and that for some reason, Mohammed Attah, the operational leader of the 9/11 airliner attack, spent some time checking out the availability of crop-duster aircraft prior to the 9/11 airliner attacks. Was one of the options to deliver anthrax spores by air? We do not know yet, but that is a possibility.

Al Qaeda's past operations in Iraq and in the United States give further grounds for fearing future chemical and biological attacks. In Iraq, insurgents allied to Al Qaeda have begun blowing up chlorine tanks with conventional explosives to create the crude chemical weapons effects.[44] This is the so-called "TICs and TIMs" problem that every state in the world has vis-à-vis terrorists or insurgents. Chlorine, for example, is used throughout Iraq to purify water supplies and is carried in trucks in literally thousands of places.

Conventional explosives can distribute these chemicals and, thus, can be used as a weapon to contaminate and harm adjacent people and property. Toxic Industrial Chemicals (TICs) and Toxic Industrial Materials (TIMs) are found in practically every urban center worldwide in the form of fertilizer plants, natural gas storage tanks, and trucks and rail cars carrying hazardous materials like phosgene and propane. This hazardous material travels next to us every day on the highways and rail lines and is stored at multiple sites throughout our cities.

Indeed, two of the 16 critical infrastructures that the Department of Homeland Security has focused its protection efforts upon is the U.S. chemical industry and U.S. nuclear reactors because conventional attacks on such sites could yield Al Qaeda a possible WMD effect on adjacent populations and assets. According to one Homeland Security expert, the United States has 66,000 chemical plants to defend as well as roughly 300,000 oil refineries and chemical or petroleum storage vessels, in addition to 104 nuclear reactors.[45]

In 2006, the then-leader of Al Qaeda in Iraq published an advertisement seeking to recruit and employ Muslim physicists, chemists, and biologists to construct CBRN weapons for the use of his group. Some believe that Al Qaeda in Iraq, being made up increasingly of Sunni Iraqis, may be content to focus their fury on local adversaries among the Shia and Kurdish communities in Iraq when and if the U.S. military withdraws, rather than continue a vendetta against the United States in North America.

On the other hand, early in 2003, the CIA preempted a cyanide attack on the New York City subway that was to be implemented by the use of a Mobtaker, a simple dispersal device. This operation was being planned by an Al Qaeda affiliate cell based in Bahrain. CIA subsequently learned that Ayman Al-Zawahiri had called off the operation before the CIA intervention because, as he told the planners, "We have something better in mind."

When looking into the subway cyanide attack, the Bahrain jihadists sought religious justification, a fatwa, for such chemical attacks. A Bahrain cleric, Shaykh Nasir bin Hamid al-Fahd, obliged them with his fatwa titled, "A Treatise on the Legal Status of Using Weapons of Mass Destruction on Infidels."[46]

In summary, Al Qaeda 1.0 operatives and leaders give every indication of an active program to acquire and, then, to use WMD and they say plainly that their aim is to kill Americans and that inflicting mass U.S. casualties is a far better outcome than attacks causing fewer dead and wounded.[47]

While it seems likely that Al Qaeda operatives would use chemical, biological, radiological, or nuclear weapons if they possessed them, there still exists a minority school of thought on this.

For example, it is possible that Al Qaeda's leaders might conclude that too horrific an attack might repel the Muslim community that they would hope to win over to their side. If bin Laden's goal is to reestablish the Caliphate under his radical Sunni banner, he might not risk being labeled a mass murderer by that community.

Indeed, it might be possible to conclude from Al Qaeda 1.0's failure to successfully attack the continental United States since 2001 that the Al Qaeda leadership does not want to attack targets in the United States and then rouse American public opinion to support an even more dramatic escalation in the War on Terror, or give new support to the U.S. military effort in Iraq, a place Al Qaeda hopes to win as a new base for their operation. A WMD attack on the United States might create a fury that could lead to their demise along the Pakistan-Afghanistan border when the United States retaliated in force.

Another argument against Al Qaeda WMD use, even if they had the capability to use it, is that some kinds of WMD, namely chemical, biological, or radiological weapons are not visually dramatic or pleasing. The media payoff might thus be muted and could dampen the effect they wish to achieve of spectacular events the whole world will remember.

Biological agents infect their victims over time but do not produce visual effects unless there were thousands of casualties produced. BW agents do not make good photo opportunities. Chemical weapons create immediate casualties but are strictly tactical weapons unless used in huge quantities. Radiological weapons are good at inflicting economic damage on areas but their radioactivity is invisible to the naked eye. Only nuclear and high explosives create significant visual and audio effects that can shock the observers or the public through media pictures.

Another reason Al Qaeda operatives may steer clear of WMD weapons use, although it would fit their desire for spectacular attacks, is that the organization is accustomed to and adept at using conventional high explosive bombs. CBRN weapons require niche scientific capabilities, are dangerous to use, and may not be required to destroy a target. Al Qaeda operatives seen wedded to the use of conventional explosives and may decide that if their weapons work, why change?[48] Further, use of CBRN arms is a relatively new, unproven, means of attack that could be both harder and less reliable. Note, for example, the numerous failures with biological weapons that plagued the Aum Shinrikyo cult in its BW attempts. They had no BW successes in nine attempts.[49]

Another argument against the use of WMD is that Al Qaeda may require the assistance of friendly states or friends within states. If the WMD connections were traced back to these allies, they might well be subject to U.S. reprisal attack. Knowing this, Al Qaeda supporters might be deterred from involvement in WMD strikes by that terrorist organization.

Finally, if Al Qaeda were to acquire just one or a small number of WMD, they might save them for a time when they need them to deter attacks on their safe havens by threatening to use them to respond to any attacks on their territory. This argument will gain more weight if Al Qaeda were to succeed in gaining a sanctuary in Afghanistan again or in Pakistan, or in Iraq, for example. If indeed, bin Laden were to succeed in establishing Al Qaeda's presence in a friendly country or in a restored Caliphate, WMD might be used to guarantee its continued viability by posing a retaliatory threat against adversary states.

U.S. Critical Infrastructure and Key Assets at Risk

Within the United States alone there are at least 3.5 million lucrative targets that Al Qaeda and associated jihadists might strike within the sixteen critical infrastructures and key assets in the country. The critical infrastructures and key assets of the United States include:[50]

1. U.S. Government and operations and structures;

2. Banking and finance institutions;

3. Electrical systems;
4. Nuclear power facilities;
5. Gas and oil processing and storage;
6. Dams;
7. Food and water assets;
8. Agricultural farms, herds, and supply chain;
9. Chemical plants;
10. Defense industry and military features;
11. Transportation systems (air, road, rail, ship);
12. Ports and waterways;
13. Postal and shipping services;
14. Emergency services;
15. Health systems; and
16. Telecommunications and Internet assets.

Further, it is also important to protect U.S. cities and their populations as well as large gatherings like New Years' gatherings at Time Square or stadiums full of sports fans at NFL or college football games, and important events like the President's State of the Union address and Presidential inaugurals every four years at the U.S. Capitol Building.

With so many assets to defend, and possessing finite budgets for such defense, how should U.S. leaders prioritize what potential targets to protect first and most completely with limited resources? To get an answer to this question, answers to several others need to be provided first, namely:

- What are the critical nodes of U.S. society that, if damaged or destroyed, would be the most catastrophic losses to our country? What are the key nodes within our critical infrastructures and key assets? What are the urban centers whose destruction would cause the most mass suffering and deaths?

- Given what we know about Al Qaeda and its associated jihadist groups worldwide, what are its tendencies when planning terrorist attacks and selecting targets?[51]

Prioritizing Defenses against Worst Case/ Most Likely Threats

Given the Al Qaeda threat to the United States, where do we put scarce U.S. resources into defenses of United States critical infrastructure and key assets? First, as previously discussed, one way of prioritizing defense investments is to identify Al Qaeda's tendencies in target selection and to defend these assets most heavily. Second, this process of defense prioritization can be further refined if analysis produces the answer to a second question, what kinds of terror attacks could cause the most catastrophic effects on the United States and its citizens?

U.S. defenses should be most heavily reinforced around those assets (targets) that are both in the categories of (1) most likely to be hit and (2) most catastrophic if destroyed. Where these two target sets overlap, special U.S. defensive preparations are required.

Even if the most likely and most catastrophic if destroyed target set is identified, this still might leave too many sites to be able to mount an effective defense of each. Defenses might be stretched too thin. Therefore additional means ought to be employed to narrow the list to receive maximum protection. Three additional criteria should be employed to prioritize defenses of the target set:

- Targets specifically mentioned by Al Qaeda operatives (see interrogation notes of interviews with jihadi prisoners, signals intelligence intercepts, Al Qaeda leader statements, jihadi website statements, and Al Qaeda publications).

- Targets in the locales of jihadist cells and Muslim groups living in the United States and allied states.

- Lucrative targets whose defenses can be most readily protected utilizing available defensive budgets.

All these defensive preparations against Al Qaeda attacks can be made more effective if coupled with an active offensive counterterrorist campaign. In a case where we cannot adequately defend all targets, the best defense is often a good offense. A post 9/11 multi-pronged offensive counter-terror attack has already killed or captured 75 percent of the original core leadership of Al Qaeda. Those running for their lives, hiding in caves, forced to operate in secret, driven into very remote mountain regions will find it more difficult to mount terror strikes against the West.

Also, an offensive against the sources of Al Qaeda's funding may have begun to dry up the resources they need to sustain themselves, finance foreign operations, and recruit and train new operatives. Finally, U.S. and allied diplomatic efforts and pressures on various governments have mobilized an international counterterrorist coalition to work to identify, isolate, and track Al Qaeda operatives.

Should the core leadership of Al Qaeda 1.0 finally be located, targeted, killed, or captured, the common wisdom is that Al Qaeda 2.0 will carry on and that we face a long war, perhaps 40 or 50 years, to finally quell that threat. Perhaps this is true, but this author believes that the decapitation of Al Qaeda's core leadership, especially if deep enough, could quell much of the current threat, especially against the continental United States. It is likely that the WMD threat will be substantially reduced against CONUS. Furthermore, a headless chicken may continue to run around right after the decapitation, but soon runs out of energy and direction. The same might be true of Al Qaeda 2.0 if deprived of its guidance and inspiration.

It is possible that the jihad might end with a whimper rather than a bang if Osama bin Laden, Ayman Al-Zawahiri, and their chief lieutenants were eliminated, so too might be the inspiration for jihad and attacks against the "far enemy." Without unity of command, the Al Qaeda remnants might well continue their local attacks for local reasons, but the unified global jihad may well be reduced to a shadow of its former self. That is the optimistic view, but prudence would argue for preparing for a long and bitter struggle and in leaving little to chance given the possibility of the worst case.

Notes

1. Key Judgments from the July 2007 National Intelligence Estimate, "The Terrorist Threat to the U.S. Homeland," On-line, Internet, available from www.dni.gov. Also quoted in "'Key Judgments' on Terrorist Threat to the U.S.," New York Times, 18 July 2007, A6.

2. WMD for the purposes of this chapter are defined as chemical, biological, radiological, and nuclear weapons. The author does understand that not all such CBRN attacks will result in massive destruction, mass killing, or even mass effect.

3. Bruce Lawrence, Editor, *Messages to the World: The Statements of Osama Bin Laden*, (London, UK: Verso, 2005), 179.

4. Rita Katz and Josh Devan, "Franchising Al Qaeda," *Boston Globe*, 22 June 2007, 1.

5. Angel Rabasa, et. al., *Beyond Al Qaeda: The Global Jihadist Movement*, (Arlington, VA: RAND, Project Air Force, 2006), 80.

6. Karen DeYoung, "Attempts Seen as Model for New Attacks on U.S. Soil," *Washington Post*, 3 July 2007, A1.

7. Craig Whitlock, "Architect of New War on the West, Writings Lay out Post 9/11 Strategy of Isolated Cells Joined in Jihad," *Washington Post*, 23 May 2005, A1. Nasar, now in custody, uses the pen name Abu Musab al-Suri.

8. Martin C. Libicki, Peter Chalk, and Melanie Sisson, *Exploring Terrorist Targeting Preferences*, (Santa Monica, CA: RAND Corporation, 2007), xiv. These RAND analysts observe that, "Al Qaeda has been increasingly forced to reconfigure its operational agenda away from centrally controlled strategic assaults executed by an inner core of militant jihadist activists, and toward tactically oriented strikes undertaken by affiliated cells as and when opportunities arise," 69.

9. Ibid., 70. The lone exception might be the attack on the Taba Hilton in October 2004, unless investigators simply have not found the links back to centralized Al Qaeda leadership.

10. July 2007 National Intelligence Estimate on, "The Terrorist Threat to the U.S. Homeland," See "6 Key Judgments' on Terrorist Threat to U.S.," New York Times, 18 July 2007, A6.

11. See video of "Jihad in America," produced by Steve Emerson to understand the degree of radical Islamic meetings in the U.S. prior to 9/11.

12. Marc Sageman, "Global Salafi Terrorist Networks," presentation in a Johns Hopkins University Applied Physics lab series entitled *Rethinking the Future Nature of Competition & Conflict Seminar Series*, 15 August 2006. Video of this presentation can be found On-line, Internet, 26 November 2007, available from http://www.jhuapl.edu/POW/rethinking06/video.cfm. See also, Lawrence Wright, *The Looming Tower: Al Qaeda and the Road to 9/11*, (New York: Alfred A. Knopf, 2007), 301-305.

13. Lewis Dunn, "Can al Qaeda Be Deterred from Using Nuclear Weapons?" Occasional Paper, Center for the Study of Weapons of Mass Destruction, (Washington, D.C.: NDU, July 2005), 7.

14. See Craig Whitlock, "Architect of New War on the West, Writings Lay Out Post-9/11 Strategy of Isolated Cells Joined in Jihad," *Washington Post*, 23 May 2006, A01. This article discusses the thousands of pages put on the Internet of how Jihadists should conduct a decentralized worldwide attack versus the United States and its allies. The author is a Spanish-Syrian strategist named Mustafa Setmarian Nasar who war captured in 2006 in Pakistan, an important catch since he was the most prolific and systematic theorist preaching how to conduct Jihad 2.0 within the extended Al Qaeda family of terrorist groups.

15. KSM as he is called had a long list of possible targets that he suggested that Al Qaeda hit including the Pentagon, White House, Capitol, World Trade Center, skyscrapers on the West Coast, the Sears Tower in Chicago, CIA Headquarters in Virginia and others. Previously, he and his nephew, Ramzi Yousef, plotted to bomb a dozen U.S. airliners over the Pacific, planned to try to assassinate Pope John Paul and President Bill Clinton in Manilla, and a host of other attacks in Asia.

16. Cited in the report of the 9/11 commission on KSM testimony.

17. Lawrence, *Messages to the World: The Statements of Osama Bin Laden*, 151.

18. Ibid., 145.

19. Ibid., 202.

20. Ibid.

21. Ibid.

22. Ibid., 195.

23. Excludes wars in Iraq or Afghanistan.

24. George W. Bush, "remarks on weapons of mass destruction," National Defense University, Washington, D.C., 11 February 2004.

25. "The National Security Strategy of the United States of America," On-line, Internet, available from http://www.whitehouse.gov/nsc/nss.html.

26. As CIA Director Tenet told President Musharaf of Pakistan, "the current state of play between weapons design and construction and the availability of the needed materials made it possible for a few men hidden in a remote location – if they had enough persistence and money, and black enough hearts – to obtain and use a nuclear device." See George Tenet, *At the Center of the Storm: My Years in the CIA*, (New York: Harper Collins, 2007), 266.

27. "Key Judgments," from the July 2007 National Intelligence Estimate on *The Terrorist Threat to the U.S. Homeland*, On-line, Internet, available from www.dni.gov. Also quoted in "Key Judgments' on Terrorist Threat to U.S.," *New York Times*, 18 July 2007, A6.

28. Tenet, *At the Center of the Storm: My Years in the CIA*, 279-280.

29. Ibid., 262-63.

30. Ibid. Upon learning of the visit of the Pakistani scientists to Afghanistan with Al Qaeda and Taliban leaders, Vice President Cheney's response was, "if there is a one percent chance that Al Qaeda has WMDs, you have to pursue it as if it were true," 264.

31. Ibid., 268.

32. Lawrence, *Messages to the World: The Statements of Osama Bin Laden*; In reply to an Al-Jazeera interviewer who asked if Bin Laden would confirm that he and Al Qaeda were seeking to acquire nuclear weapons, the terrorist leader implied they were, saying "There is a duty on Muslims to acquire them, and America knows today that Muslims are in possession of such a weapon (e.g., Pakistan), by the grace of God Almighty," 72.

33. Tenet, *At the Center of the Storm: My Years in the CIA*, 271.

34. Ibid., 269.

35. Ibid., 268-269. Also, from late 2002 to spring 2003, U.S. intelligence received reports that Al Qaeda operatives in Saudi Arabia were negotiating to buy 3 Russian nuclear bombs, 272.

36. Charles Meade and Roger C. Molander, Considering the Effects of a Catastrophic Terrorist Attack, (Santa Monica, CA: RAND Corporation, August 2006), 7, On-line, Internet, 24 July 2007, available from http://www.trb.org/safety/RAND-Aug-2006.pdf.

37. Marc Sageman, *Understanding Terror Networks*, (PA: Penn Press, 2004), 23. See also, Jaime Gomez, Jr., "Terrorist Motivations, Extreme Violence, and the Pursuit of Weapons of Mass Destruction," *Cultic Studies Review*, Vol. 5, No. 2, 2006, 10.

38. Lawrence Wright, *The Looming Tower: Al Qaeda and the Road to 9/11*, (New York: Alfred A. Knopf, 2007), 303.

39. Ibid.

40. Ken Alibek, *Biohazard*, (New York: Random House, 1999).

41. Gomez, op cit., 10.

42. Wright, *The Looming Tower: Al Qaeda and the Road to 9/11*, 303-04.

43. Ibid., 282. Al Qaeda, for example, had set up a lab near Jalabad to test cyanide gas effects on dogs. They set up a second laboratory at Kandahar to look into the production of weapons grade anthrax.

44. See Damien Cave and Ahmad Fadam, "Iraq Insurgents Employ Chlorine in Bomb Attacks," 21 February 2007, Baghdad, Iraq. Previously the late Abu Musab al-Zarquawi tested cyanide on an associate in his group, killing him. Zarquawi had plans for the use of poisons and chemicals and poisons plots were uncovered in several European states before they could be implemented – France, Spain, Italy, the United Kingdom, and others.

45. Mr. Robert Stephen, Department of Homeland Security, said this in a presentation to the Air War College Homeland Security elective class in December 2005.

46. Tenet, op. cit., 274.

47. Not everyone is convinced that Al Qaeda cannot be deterred from such mass killings using WMD. For example, Major General Robert Smolen, USAF Retired, believes that while Al Qaeda's leaders may be satisfied to send followers on suicide attacks, none of the leaders have so volunteered to be martyrs. A WMD attack on U.S. soil attributed back to Al Qaeda may trigger such a fierce reprisal that the United States might invade the Federally Administered Tribal Areas along the Afghan border and risk the potential backlash in Pakistan to remove Al Qaeda. Bin Laden already has lost one safe haven in Afghanistan when he probably miscalculated the ferocity of the American response to 9/11. He may be gun-shy after that experience, or so the argument goes.

48. As Lewis Dunn has written, "Turning to Al Qaeda's choice of means, what stands out is its preference for bombs of all kinds in executing its attacks: car bombs, boat bombs, concealed bombs, aircraft as bombs, and human bombs. Thus, use of

chemical, biological, and radiological weapons would be inconsistent with this aspect of its operational code." See Lewis Dunn, "Can Al Qaeda Be Deterred from Using Nuclear Weapons?," Occasional Paper of the Center for the Study of Weapons of Mass Destruction, (Washington D.C.: NDU, July 2005), 16.

49. W. Seth Carus, *Bioterror and Biocrimes: The Illicit Use of Biological Agents in the 20th Century*, (Washington, D.C.: NDU, April 2000.)

50. *The National Strategy for the Physical Protection of Critical Infrastructures and Key Assets*, (Washington, D.C.: The White House, February 2003).

51. To estimate what Al Qaeda 1.0's modus operandi looks like, we would have to assess what has been learned from:
- Al Qaeda leader statements in their messages to the world (fatwas, books, press interviews, videotapes, and other public pronouncements)?
- Captured jihadist planning documents, hard drives of computers, and messages left on websites or transmitted via the Internet.
- Information gleaned from interrogations of prisoners who belong to Al Qaeda and associated jihad groups?
- Intercepts of internal terrorist communications gained by various intelligence means?
- Past attacks and the types of target struck? What do we know about or might we infer from these past attacks?

CHAPTER 3

The Mind of the Terrorist: The Spectrum of Terrorism and Terrorist Psychologies

Jerrold M. Post[1]

To counter an adversary optimally requires a nuanced understanding of their psychology, motivations, and decision-making. The secret, clandestine nature of the terrorist adversary makes developing such an understanding particularly difficult. In this overview of terrorist psychology, I shall review current understandings of the spectrum of terrorism and the range of psychologies associated with the different terrorist types. Note the plural—psychologies. When one considers how broad that spectrum is, there would be no reason to assume there is one terrorist mindset, or one terrorist psychology.

Considering the difference in backgrounds, attitudes, and goals of some of the group types represented in Figure 3.1, it would be unreasonable to assume there is one governing terrorist psychology. What, after all, does a nationalist-separatist Tamil Tiger terrorist have in common with a neo-Nazi right-wing terrorist, or a militant Islamist Al Qaeda terrorist with a single-issue terrorist, such as the Earth Liberation Front?

There is a widespread popular misconception that groups and individuals who kill innocent victims to accomplish their political goals must be crazed fanatics; surely no psychologically "normal" individual could perpetrate such horrific acts. But in fact, terrorist scholars who have studied terrorist psychology have concluded that most terrorists are "normal" in the sense of not suffering from psychotic disorders. My own comparative research on the psychology of terrorists does not reveal major psychopathology.[2]

Martha Crenshaw, a prominent international terrorism expert, has observed that "the outstanding common characteristic of terrorists is their normality."[3] McCauley and Segal, in a major review of the social psychology of terrorist groups, found that "the best documented generalization is negative; terrorists do not show any striking psychopathology."[4] In his recent book, *The Psychology of Terrorism*, John Horgan has emphasized that there are no individual psychological traits that distinguish terrorists from the general population.[5]

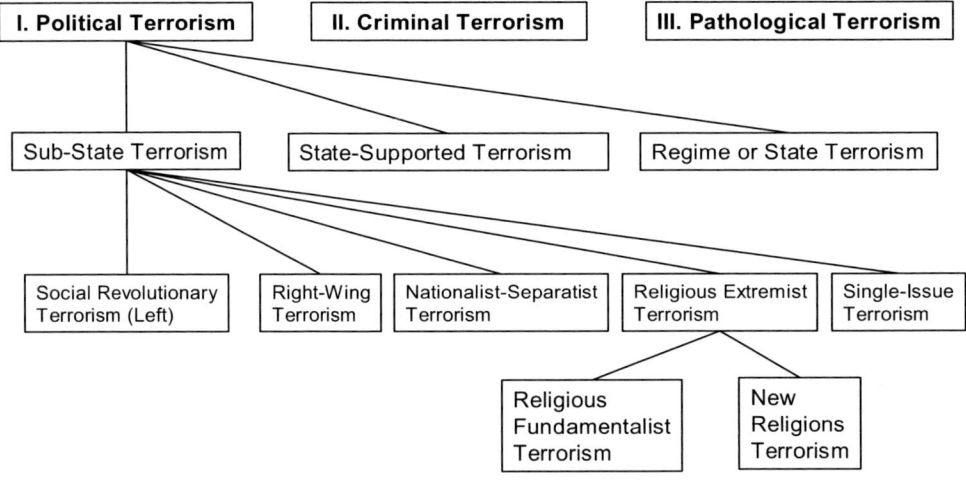

Figure 3.1 New Typology of Terrorism[6]

A consensus conclusion of the Committee on the Psychological Roots of Terrorism for the Madrid Summit on Terrorism, Security, and Democracy, held in Madrid on the first anniversary of the 2004 bombing of the Madrid train station bombing, was that "[e]xplanations at the level of individual psychology are insufficient in trying to understand why people become involved in terrorism. The concepts of abnormality or psychopathology are not useful in understanding terrorism." Rather, we concluded that "[g]roup, organizational and social psychology, with a particular emphasis on 'collective identity,' provides the most constructive framework for understanding terrorist psychology and behavior."[7]

Some psychologically disturbed individuals have carried out acts of violence in the name of a cause individually, but terrorist groups regularly screen out individuals who are emotionally unstable. Just as the Delta Forces would not wish to have an emotionally unstable individual in their ranks because they would pose a security risk, for the same reason neither would a terrorist action cell wish to have an emotionally unstable member in its ranks.

"Criminal terrorism" refers to acts of terrorism by a criminal enterprise in order to further its goals. So, when the narco-terrorists in Colombia assassinate a judge, the goal is not merely eliminating a judge who has threatened their enterprise, it is also to intimidate other judges in order to give the terrorists the freedom to operate that they desire. It is terrorism in support of their criminal enterprise.

For "political terrorism," there are two main subdivisions represented in the graphic – at the middle tier, the level of the state; and in the lower tier, sub-state terrorism. "State terrorism" refers to circumstances when the state uses its own powerful resources – the courts, the police, and the military – against its own citizens. Argentina during the "dirty wars" is a prime example, when citizens opposed to the state were "disappeared." Another example of terror by the state would be Saddam Hussein's al-Anfal campaign of 1986-1989 against his own Kurdish citizens, in which more than 100,000 Kurdish Iraqi citizens were killed with firing squads, aerial bombings, and poison gas, wiping out more than 4,000 Kurdish villages.[8]

"State-supported terrorism" refers to the circumstance when a state covertly provides support to a terrorist group or organization to further its own national goals. This support can be financial, logistical, training, or otherwise, and the degree of influence/control by the state will vary. The annual State Department list of state supporters of terrorism usually includes: Iran, Iraq, Syria, Libya, Sudan, North Korea, and Cuba. Since the conflict in Iraq, Iraq has been removed from this list, and in return for ceasing its program of developing weapons of mass destruction, Libya's name was removed in May 2006.

"Sub-state terrorism" represents terrorism from below. In the beginning of the modern era of terrorism, two types predominated: social revolutionary terrorism and nationalist-separatist terrorism, also known as ethnic-nationalist terrorism. Steeped in Marxist-Leninism, the social revolutionary terrorists, represented by such groups as the Red Army Faction in Germany, the Red Brigades in Italy, and the Weather Underground in the United States, seek to overthrow the capitalist order. These groups have significantly declined since the end of the Cold War and the dissolution of the Soviet empire, although Latin American social revolutionary groups, especially the Revolutionary Armed Forces of Colombia (FARC), remain a significant security threat. The nationalist-separatist terrorists, represented by such groups as the Irish Republican Army (IRA) in Northern Ireland; Fatah, the Palestinian Front for the Liberation of Palestine (PFLP), and other secular Palestinian groups; and Basque Fatherland and Liberty (ETA), seek to establish a separate nation for their minority group.

In the beginnings of the modern era of terrorism, these groups regularly sought to call public attention to their cause. There were often competing claims of responsibility for their terrorist acts. Then in the late 1980s and early 1990s, the situation gradually changed; no responsibility was claimed for upward of 40 percent of terrorist acts. These were the acts of religious fundamentalist terrorists. They were not trying to influence the West but to expel the West, with its secular, modernizing values. And they did not need a *New York Times* headline or a CNN story to claim responsibility, for they were "killing in the name of God," and God already knew. In addition to religious fundamentalist terrorists, the category of religious extremist terrorists also includes millenarian or new religions terrorists, exemplified by the Aum Shinrikyo terrorists responsible for the first major chemical weapons terrorist attack, the sarin gas attack on the Tokyo subways in 1995.

With the decline in social-revolutionary terrorism at the end of the Cold War, there was a concomitant rise in right-wing terrorist groups pursuing racist, anti-Semitic, and "survivalist" ideologies. The same groups that used to warn against the communist menace that had invaded the United States now turned their venom against what they characterized as the illegitimate federal government. Timothy McVeigh and Terry Nichols, responsible for the destruction of the Alfred P. Murrah Federal Building in Oklahoma City, were right-wing terrorists. It is widely believed by security officials that the wave of anthrax letters in the fall of 2001 was perpetrated by an unknown right-wing extremist.

And finally, single-issue terrorism refers to terrorism in pursuit of causes, such as the environment and animal rights. The fact that groups, such as the Animal Liberation Front (ALF), would be motivated to commit criminal acts of violence in order to preserve animal life or, as in the case of the Earth Liberation Front (ELF), to preserve the environment suggests that *the cause is not the cause*. Rather it is the justification, the rationale for frustrated, alienated individuals who have had their frustration channeled against a particular group.

As there is a diversity of terrorist causes, the typology of terrorist groups also reflects a diversity of generational provenance. The X in the upper-left-hand cell of Figure 3.2 indicates that individuals who are at one with families who are at one with the regime do not become terrorists. Generational issues are particularly prominent for the two types of terrorism that dominated the scene at the onset of the modern era of terrorism: social-revolutionary terrorism and nationalist-separatist terrorism.

	Parents' Relationship to the Regime	
Youths' Relationship to Parents	**L**oyal	**D**isloyal Damaged Dissident
Loyal	X	National-Separatist Terrorism
Disloyal	Social Revolutionary Terrorism	

Figure 3.2 Generational Pathways to Terrorism9

As reflected in Figure 3.2, in many ways, the generational dynamics of social revolutionary terrorists and nationalist-separatist terrorists are polar opposites. The social revolutionary terrorists, whose generational dynamics are represented in the lower-middle cell, are striking out against the generation of their parents that is loyal to the regime. Their acts of terrorism are acts of revenge for hurts, real and imagined. A member of the German terrorist group, Red Army Faction, declared, "These are the corrupt old men who gave us Auschwitz and Hiroshima." Jillian Becker addresses this dynamic with the German social-revolutionary terrorists in her aptly titled book, Hitler's Children.10

It should be observed that the generational dynamics described for social revolutionary terrorists are those of Osama bin Laden, the leader of Al Qaeda. After all, when he criticized the "apostate leaders" of Saudi Arabia from Sudan for permitting infidel bases in the land of "the two cities," i.e., Mecca and Medina, he was criticizing the royal family that had enriched his family and himself. For his caustic criticism of the Saudi leadership, bin Laden was deprived of his Saudi citizenship and the bin Laden family turned their back on him. Thus while Osama bin Laden is a leader of the trans-national radical Islamist terrorist organization Al Qaeda, his generational dynamics are those of the social revolutionary.

In contrast, the nationalist-separatist terrorists, represented in the middle-right-hand cell in Figure 3.2, are loyal to parents and grandparents who are disloyal to the regime, were damaged by the regime. They are carrying on the mission of their parents and grandparents. Whether in the pubs of Northern Ireland or the coffeehouses in Gaza and the occupied territories, they have heard of the social injustice visited upon their parents and grandparents. They have heard their parents complaining of the lands stolen from them and have been raised on this bitter gruel of victimhood. It is time to stop talking and start acting.

The variation in the generational dynamics described above emphasizes the importance of understanding the historical, cultural, political, and economic context in which terrorist identities are shaped. This is a major theme of Martha Crenshaw's *Terrorism in Context*.[11]

As observed earlier, social psychology and especially "collective identity" provides the most powerful lens through which to understand terrorist psychology and behavior. Especially for nationalist-separatist terrorist groups, this collective identity is established extremely early, so that from childhood on, "hatred is bred in the bone." The importance of collective identity and the processes of forming and transforming collective identities cannot be overemphasized. This fact, in turn, emphasizes the socio-cultural context, which determines the balance between collective identity and individual identity. Especially for nationalist-separatist terrorists, they have subordinated their individual identity to the collective identity, so that what serves the group, organization, or network is of primary importance.

This subordination to the cause, in turn, gives the leaders of these terrorist groups who frame the cause a major role in creating the dominant terrorist psychology. As my committee at the Madrid summit on terrorism noted:

> It is important to distinguish leaders from followers. The role of the leader is crucial in drawing together alienated, frustrated individuals into a coherent organization. The leader provides a 'sense-making' unifying message that conveys a religious, political, or ideological justification to their disparate followers.

Being a fighter for the cause, consumed by righteous rage, becomes the primary identity for the followers.

The Cauldron of Life Experiences of an Abu Nidal Terrorist[12]

In 1997, I had the opportunity and challenge of assisting the Department of Justice as an expert on terrorist psychology in the trial in Federal Court in Washington, D.C., of Mohammad Rezaq, an Abu Nidal terrorist who played a leading role in the skyjacking of an EgyptAir passenger jet in which more than fifty lost their lives in the skyjacking and the subsequent SWAT team attack on the hijacked plane in Malta. The defendant epitomized the life and psychology of the nationalist-separatist terrorist. The defendant assuredly did not believe that what he was doing was wrong, for from boyhood on Rezaq he had been socialized to be a heroic revolutionary fighting for the Palestinian nation. Demonstrating the generational transmission of hatred, his case can be considered emblematic of many from the ranks of ethnic/nationalist terrorist groups, from Northern Ireland to Palestine, from Armenia to the Basque region of Spain.

In 1948, when Rezaq's mother was eight, as a consequence of the 1948 Arab-Israeli war, her family was forced to flee their home in Jaffa in Israel. They left for the West Bank, where Rezaq was raised. In 1967, when Rezaq was eight, the family fled their pleasant West Bank existence during the

1967 war, ending up in a crowded Palestinian refugee camp in Jordan. She told him bitterly that this was the second time this had happened to her.

There he went to school funded by the UN agency UNESCO and was taught by a member of Fatah whom he came to idolize. At the time, Arafat's stature as a heroic freedom fighter was celebrated in the camps. Rezaq was taught that the only way to become a man was to join the revolution and take back the lands stolen from his parents and grandparents. He first joined Fatah after going AWOL from the Jordanian Army. When he first participated in a terrorist action, he felt at last he was doing what he should do. He left Fatah after becoming disillusioned with Arafat's leadership and ended up in the most violent secular Palestinian terrorist group, the Abu Nidal Organization. When he ultimately was assigned a command role in the skyjacking of an EgyptAir airliner, he felt he was at last fulfilling his destiny. He was taking a bold action to help his people. He was a soldier for the revolution and all of the actions that he directed that led to the major loss of life were seen as required by his role as a soldier for the cause, a cause that ultimately would lead to the restoration of his family's lands.

Secular Palestinian Terrorists in their Own Words[13]

While most Fatah members reported their families had good social standing, their status and experience as refugees was paramount in their development of self-identity.

> I belong to the generation of occupation. My family are refugees from the 1967 war. The war and my refugee status were the seminal events that formed my political consciousness, and provided the incentive for doing all I could to help regain our legitimate rights in our occupied country.

For the secular terrorists, enlistment was a natural step. And it led to enhanced social status.

> Enlistment was for me the natural and done thing ... in a way, it can be compared to a young Israeli from a

nationalist Zionist family who wants to fulfill himself through army service.

My motivation in joining Fatah was both ideological and personal. It was a question of self-fulfillment, of honor and a feeling of independence…the goal of every young Palestinian was to be a fighter.

After recruitment, my social status was greatly enhanced. I got a lot of respect from my acquaintances, and from the young people in the village.

View of Armed Attacks

Armed attacks are viewed as essential to the operation of the organization. There is no question about the necessity of these types of attacks to the success of the cause.

You have to understand that armed attacks are an integral part of the organization's struggle against the Zionist occupier. There is no other way to redeem the land of Palestine and expel the occupier. Our goals can only be achieved through force, but force is the means, not the end. History shows that without force it will be impossible to achieve independence.

In addition to causing as many casualties as possible, armed action provided a sense of control or power for Palestinians in a society that had stripped them of it. Inflicting pain on the enemy was paramount in the early days of the Fatah movement.

I regarded armed actions to be essential, it is the very basis of my organization and I am sure that was the case in the other Palestinian organizations. **An armed action proclaims that I am here, I exist, I am strong, I am in control, I am in the field, I am on the map.** An armed action against soldiers was the most admired. …the armed actions and their results were a major tool for penetrating the public consciousness.

The various armed actions (stabbing, collaborators, martyrdom operations, attacks on Israeli soldiers) all had different ratings. An armed action that caused casualties was rated highly and seen to be of great important. An armed action without casualties was not rated. No distinction was made between armed actions on soldiers or on civilians; the main thing was the amount of blood. The aim was to cause as much carnage as possible.

Socialization of Hatred

The hatred socialized towards the Israelis was remarkable, especially given that few reported any contact with Israelis.

You Israelis are Nazis in your souls and in your conduct. In your occupation you never distinguish between men and women, or between old people and children. You adopted methods of collective punishment; you uprooted people from their homeland and from their homes and chased them into exile. You fired live ammunition at women and children. You smashed the skulls of defenseless civilians. You set up detention camps for thousands of people in sub-human conditions. You destroyed homes and turned children into orphans. You prevented people from making a living, you stole their property, you trampled on their honor. Given that kind of conduct, there is no choice but to strike at you without mercy in every possible way.

Defensive Intensification of Nationalist Identify in Reaction to Attempted "Identicide"

Mustafa Kemal Ataturk, the founder of the modern state of Turkey, in his zeal to create and consolidate a Turkic identity after his defeat of the Ottomans, made the use of the Kurdish language illegal and denied the existence of the Kurdish people, referring to them dismissively as "mountain Turks." This in turn led to a defensive intensification of Kurdish nationalism which Abdullah Ocalan, founder of the Kurdish Workers Party, the PKK, exploited. Ruthless in eliminating rivals, Ocalan achieved godlike stature for his beleaguered people, to the point that his followers would give their lives for the cause he so eloquently championed, committing suicide terrorism for the charismatic Ocalan.

Similarly, the lack of recognition of the rights of the Tamil minority by the Sinhala majority of Sri Lanka led to a defensive intensification of Tamil identity, exploited by the founding father of the Tamil Tigers, the LTTE, Vellupillai Prabhakaran who has charismatic status for his followers, as well, and they too have given their lives for the faith of their founding father, committing suicide terrorism.

Both Ocalan and Prabhakaran saw themselves as idealized models for their followers to emulate. Ocalan, for example, stated:

> Everyone should take note of the way I live, what I do and I don't do. The way I eat, the way I think, my orders and even my inactivity should be carefully studied. There will be lessons to be learned for several generations for Apo (referring to himself by his nickname) is a great teacher.[14]

Equally messianic and narcissistic is Prabhakaran, of whom his biographer Swamy said, "If the peace process were to fail for whatever reason, the destiny of Sri Lanka with its 20 million people would still be in the hands of one man, Vellupillai Prabhakaran."[15] When the leader is both charismatic and authoritarian, and the leader is killed or captured, (Ocalan was captured in 1999) it is a mortal blow to the organization.

For both the Irish Republican Army (IRA) and the Basque insurgent terrorist group Basque Homeland and Liberty (ETA), the cause was passed from generate to generation, with heroic figures in each generation of leaders, but these groups were not so centrally identified with the charismatic stature of their leaders.

Social Revolutionary Terrorism

The social revolutionary terrorists were steeped in Marxist-Leninist rhetoric, and seeking to overthrow the capitalist order and replace it with a communist society. With the implosion of the Soviet Union, the social revolutionary terrorists of Europe, exemplified by the Red Army Faction of West Germany and the Red Brigades of Italy, have largely faded away. But social revolutionary terrorism in Latin American has continued to provide major security threats, especially FARC, the Colombian social revolutionary terrorist group, which controls territory the size of Switzerland, roughly 40 percent of Colombia.

Founded in 1964, its 80-year-old ailing founding father, Manuel Marulanda, who continues to espouse Marxist-Leninist doctrine, still leads the group. Its two primary goals at its founding, to overthrow the state and replace it was a communist-agrarian state, are unchanged. The next generation is much less ideological, although still giving voice to the same revolutionary principles, many of the younger generation have joined the group for economic reasons, and have departed from the revolutionary fervor of the founding father, indeed have become more criminal terrorists, serving as narco-terrorists in relation to the Colombian *narco-trafficantes*. As one FARC official explained, "We tax everything under our control. Everybody else lives on this money. Why shouldn't we? We regulate drug areas, defending the rights of campesinos who have little other opportunities."[16]

A violent insurgency, Sendero Luminoso, the Shining Path, was founded in 1970 in Peru by Abimael Guzman, a professor of philosophy at Ayacucho University. Inspired by Mao Zedong's writings and practice, he provided charismatic authoritarian leadership to the Shining Path, and went by the pseudonym of Gonzalo. Seeing himself as the very embodiment of his organization, he designated Gonzalez thought as "The fourth sword of Communism," the first three being Marx, Lenin, and Mao.

He celebrated violence and self-sacrifice for the cause, calling for the shedding of blood.

> This is nothing but a good start, a fruitful beginning, watered with good blood…this is nothing but a preview…This blood steels us…it makes us…more willing to ford any river, to cross hell, and to assault the heavens…the cost, in the end, is small.[17]

And like the PKK when Guzman, the authoritarian charismatic leader, was captured in 1992, it was a mortal blow to the organization.

Islamist Fundamentalist Terrorism

The beginning of the modern era of terrorism, usually dated to the late 1960s, was dominated by nationalist-separatist terrorists and social revolutionary terrorists. Claiming responsibility for their acts, they were seeking to call attention to their cause through their terrorist violence—it was violence as communication. The intended audience of influence was the West and the establishment, calling attention, for example, to the cause of the Palestinian people. Too much violence would be counter-productive for the cause, leading to a certain degree of constraint. For the radical Islamist terrorists, however, their goals are not to influence the West and the establishment, but rather to expel the West with its corrupt secular modernizing values, to seek revenge against the West, and to overthrow the establishment the apostate establishment and replace the government with one guided by the *sharia*. Thus the constraint against the extent of violence present for groups interested in influencing the West is not present for the absolutist Islamists.

Interview with a Tanzanian Embassy Bomber

In the spring and summer of 2001, I had the opportunity to interview at length one of the defendants in the Al Qaeda bombing of the U.S. embassy in Tanzania. Raised on Zanzibar off the coast of Tanzania, he was eight when his father died and then was educated in a madrassa, where he was taught never to question what you are told by learned authorities. When he was the equivalent of a junior in high school his brother directed him to leave school and help him in his grocery store in Dar es Salaan. There he was miserable – alone, friendless, isolated, except for his attendance at the Friday prayer services at the mosque, where he learned from the Imam that they were all members of the *ummah*, the community of observant Muslims, and had an obligation to help Muslims wherever they were being persecuted.

He was shown videos of Muslim mass graves in Bosnia and the Serbian military, of the bodies of Muslim women and children in Chechnya and the Russian military. He became inspired and vowed to become a soldier for Allah. But he was informed that he could not do this without obtaining training. So, using his own funds, he went to Pakistan and then on to a bin Laden training camp in Afghanistan, where he was taught weapons and explosives handling in the mornings and had four hours of ideological training each afternoon.

After seven months when he could not join the struggle in Bosnia or Chechnya, although offered the opportunity to fight in Kashmir, he returned to Dar es Salaan, where he again pursued his menial existence as a grocery clerk, frustrated at his inability to pursue jihad. Three years later he was called in he middle of the night and asked, "Do you want to do a jihad job," and without further inquiry, he accepted. What had been a positive motivation to help suffering Muslims gradually was bent to his participating in this act of mass casualty terrorism.

Religious Fundamentalist Terrorists in their Own Words

The mosque was consistently cited as the place where most members were initially introduced to the Palestinian/Israeli conflict, including members of the secular groups. Authority figures from the mosque are prominent in all conversations with group members, and most dramatically for members of the Islamist organizations. The introduction to authority and unquestioning obedience to Allah and authority is instilled at a young age and continues to be evident in the individual members' subservience to the larger organization.

This preconditioning of unquestioning acceptance of authority seems to be most evident among the members of the Islamist groups such as Hamas and Islamic Jihad. Note what several such individuals had to say about their actions:

Theme: Unquestioned Acceptance of Authority

> I came from a religious family, which used to observe all the Islamic traditions. My initial political awareness came during the prayers at the mosque. That's where I was also asked to join religious classes. In the context of these studies, the sheik used to inject some historical background

in which he would tell us how we were effectively evicted from Palestine.

The sheik also used to explain to us the significance of the fact that there was an IDF military outpost in the heart of the camp. He compared it to a cancer in the human body, which was threatening its very existence.

At the age of 16 I developed an interest in religion. I was exposed to the Moslem brotherhood and I began to pray in a mosque and to study Islam. The Koran and my religious studies were the tools that shaped my political consciousness. The mosque and the religious clerics in my village provided the focal point of my social life.

Theme: Community support was important to the families of these fighters as well

Families of terrorists who were wounded, killed, or captured enjoyed a great deal of economic aid and attention. And that strengthened popular support for the attacks.
Perpetrators of armed attacks were seen as heroes, their families got a great deal of material assistance, including the construction of new homes to replace those destroyed by the Israeli authorities as punishment for terrorist acts.

Theme: The Emir blesses all actions

Major actions become the subject of sermons in the mosque, glorifying the attack and the attackers.

Theme: Joining Hamas or Fatah increased social standing

Recruits were treated with great respect. A youngster who belonged to Hamas or Fatah was regarded more highly than one who didn't belong to a group, and got better treatment than unaffiliated kids.

Anyone who didn't enlist during that period (intifada) would have been ostracized.

Theme: Inflict mass casualties

The more an attack hurts the enemy, the more important it is. That is the measure. The mass killings, especially the martyrdom operations, were the biggest threat to the Israeli public and so most effort was devoted to these. The extent of the damage and the number of casualties are of primary importance.

Theme: No sense of remorse/absence of moral red lines

When it came to moral considerations, we believed in the justice of our cause and in our leaders...I don't recall every being troubled by moral questions.

In a jihad, there are no red lines.

The Justification of Suicide Bombings

The Islamist terrorists in particular provided the religious basis for what the West has called suicide terrorism as the most valued technique of jihad, distinguishing this from suicide, which is proscribed in the Koran. One suicide bomb commander in fact became quite angry when the term was used in our question, angrily exclaiming, *"This is not suicide. Suicide is selfish, it is weak, it is mentally disturbed. This is istishad,"* (martyrdom or self sacrifice in the service of Allah).

Several of the Islamist terrorist commanders interviewed called the suicide bomber holy warriors who were carrying out the highest level of jihad.

A martyrdom operation is the highest level of jihad, and highlights the depth of our faith. Bombers are holy fighters who carry out one of the more important articles of faith.[18]

It is attacks when their member gives his life that earn the most respect and elevate the bombers to the highest possible level of martyrdom.

I asked Halil what this was all about and he told me that he had been on the wanted list for a long time and did not want to get caught without realizing his dream of being a martyrdom operation bomber. He was completely calm and explained to the other two bombers, Yusuf and Beshar, how to detonate the bombs, exactly the way he had explained things to the bombers in the Mahane Yehuda attack. I remember that besides the tremendous respect I had for Halil, and the fact that I was jealous of him, I also felt slighted that he had not asked me to be the third martyrdom operation bomber. I understood that my role in the movement had not come to an end and the fact that I was not on the wanted list and could operate relatively freely could be very advantageous to the movement in the future.[19]

Mohammed Hafez, in his *Manufacturing Human Bombs*, indicates there are three prohibitions against suicide terrorism in the Koran, the prohibition against suicide, the prohibition against killing Muslims, and the prohibition against killing innocents. The radical extremists quoted above have reframed these acts as martyrdom operations, and endowed them with sacred significance. Hafez has observed that three conditions are necessary for a campaign of suicide bombing: a culture of martyrdom, a strategic decision by the organization to carry out such a campaign, and a willing supply of volunteers.

While as we have observed earlier, there is an absence of psychopathology, a suicide bomber dispatcher interviewed by Anat Berko asked recruiters for "sad guys."[20] The interview revealed that what he meant by "sad guys" was not depressed individuals, but "those who were social nonentities and had no status but who might get recognition by dying, those with low self-esteem…, men and women who have trouble finding themselves, …bitter…at their marginality …who are willing to try anything to feel they have worth and to win the approval of society and their families." The issue of underlying low self-esteem and the redemptive consequences of becoming a suicide terrorist has been emphasized by Raphael Israeli, who concluded that becoming "Islamikazes" gave "them the opportunity to expand their own ego, and the newly acquired comradeship sustains their self-esteem and self-importance."[21] This concept of the "expanded ego" relates of course to the collective psychology of charismatic leader-follower relationships.[22] No longer an isolated failing individual, now he is identified with the collective esteem of the *shaheeds*, the martyrs.

In *The Staircase to Terrorism,* Fathali Moghaddam addresses the progress to terrorism as a series of steps on a narrowing staircase, with each step making it increasingly difficult to turn, further narrowing the range of options ahead until the act of commitment to join the group.[23] By implication, in a still narrowing staircase, there is a series of steps from terrorist to suicide terrorist, another way of conceptualizing Merari's "suicide bomber assembly line."

The foregoing review of terrorist psychologies has differentiated the group psychology in relationship to the terrorist group type. In summary, terrorism is not a function of psychopathology, but rather of social psychology, with a particular emphasis on "collective identity." Thus, it is important to understand each terrorism in its own unique political, cultural, and historical context, and that a nuanced understanding of each terrorist psychology is required for optimal counter-terrorism.

Notes

1. Professor of Psychiatry, Political Psychology and International Affairs, and Director, Political Psychology Program, The George Washington University, Washington, D.C. Dr. Post is also the Chief Behavioral Scientist of the USAF Counterproliferation Center in a consulting role.

2. Jerrold Post, "It's Us Against Them: The Basic Assumptions of Political Terrorists," *Irrationality in Organizational Life*, Kranz, J. (ed.) (Washington, DC: A.K. Rice Institute Press, 1987) and J. Post, "Terrorist Psycho-logic: Terrorist Behavior as a Product of Psychological Forces," *Origins of Terrorism*, Reich, W. (ed.) (New York, NY: Cambridge University Press, 1990).

3. Martha Crenshaw, "The Causes of Terrorism," *Comparative Politics*, vol. 13 (July 1981), 379-399.

4. Clark R. McCauley and M. E. Segal, "Social Psychology of Terrorist Groups," *Group, Organizational and Intergroup Relations, Annual Review of Social and Personality Psychology*, vol. 9, ed. C. Hendrick, (Beverly Hills, CA: Sage, 1987).

5. John Horgan, *The Psychology of Terrorism*, (New York: Routledge, 2005).

6. This graphic is adapted from a typology introduced by Alex P. Schmid, *Political Terrorism: A Research Guided*, (New Brunswick, NJ: Transaction Books, 1983).

7. Jerrold Post, "The Psychological Roots of Terrorism," *Addressing the Causes of Terrorism: The Club de Madrid Series on Democracy and Terrorism*, (Madrid: Club de Madrid, 2005), vol. 1, 7-12.

8. Bruce Hoffman, *Inside Terrorism*, (New York: Columbia University Press, 1998), 25.

9. This generational matrix was first introduced by the author in Jerrold M. Post, "Notes on a Psychodynamic Theory of Terrorism," *Terrorism* 7, no. 3, (1984).

10. Jillian Becker, *Hitler's Children: The Story of the Baader-Meinhof Terrorist Gang*, (New York: J.B. Lippincott Company, 1977).

11. Martha Crenshaw (ed.), *Terrorism in Context*, (University Park: Pennsylvania State University Press, 1995).

12. Jerrold Post, "Murder in a Political Context: Profile of an Abu Nidal Terrorist," *Bulletin of the Academy of Psychiatry and the Law*, (Spring, 2000).

13. This material is drawn from Jerrold Post, E. Sprinzak, and L. Denny, "The Terrorists in their Own Words: Interviews with 35 Incarcerated Middle Eastern Terrorists," *Terrorism and Political Violence*, vol. 15, #1, 171-184, Spring 2003.

14. Beat Witschi, "Who is Abdullah Ocalan?" *cnn.com*, 1999, On-line, Internet, 10 October 2005, available from http://www.cnn.com/SPEIALS/1999/ocalan/stories/ocalan.profile/.

15. M.R. Narayan Swamy, *Inside an Elusive Mind: Prabhakaran, the First Profile of the World's Most Ruthless Leader*, (Colombo: Vijitha Yapa Publications, 2003), 277.

16. Commentary of Malcolm Deas, St. Anthony's College, Oxford, at Colombian Security Forum, 12 November 2003, "What are FARC's Current Political and Military Strategies?"

17. Quoted in Gustava Gorriti, *The Shining Path: A History of the Millenarian War in Peru*, (Chapel Hill: University of North Carolina Press, 1999), 187.

18. Hassan Salame, responsible for the wave of suicide bombings in Israel in 1996, in which 46 were killed. He is now serving 46 consecutive life sentences.

19. Quote from prisoner sentenced to 26 life terms for role in several suicide-bombing campaigns.

20. Anat Berko, *The Path to Paradise: Palestinian Suicide Bombers and their Dispatchers*, (Westport, DT: Praeger, 2007), 7.

21. Raphael Israeli, *Manifestations of Islamic Martryology*, (Portland, OR: Frank Kass Publishers, 2003).

22. Jerrold Post, "Narcissism and the Charismatic Leader-Follower Relationship," *Political Psychology*, vol. 7, no. 4, 1986.

23. Fathali M. Moghaddam, "Psychological Processes and 'The Staircase to Terrorism,'" *American Psychologist*, December 2005, vol. 60, no. 9, 2005.

CHAPTER 4

Political Islam and Radical Islam: The Cases of Pakistan and Bangladesh

Stephen F. Burgess

It is important in "knowing one's enemy" in the post-September 11, 2001, world to comprehend the connections between "political Islam" and "radical Islam" as well as to understand the instances in which there are no links. With the rise of extremist Islam groups and with Al Qaeda's declaration of war against the United States and U.S. interests, the possible links between Islamic political movements and parties and radical Islamic groups are of concern. It is also important to understand how (and if) political Islamic movements and parties can be encouraged to move towards the political mainstream and be disconnected from radical Islam.

Political Islamists strive to roll back secularism and Western influence and completely institute or move closer to the institution of Islamic *sharia* law through largely peaceful, political processes.[1] With the introduction of elections and other forms of peaceful political activity in the Islamic world, Islamist political parties increasingly have been drawn into the process and are contesting elections in seeking political power. There are those who believe that political Islam can be a positive force in helping to build democracy and dry up support for radical Islam.[2] On the other hand, this will be a positive development only if Islamic parties that have gained power in the electoral process are willing to permit a turnover of power to secular parties that win in subsequent elections.

The Muslim Brotherhood, which has been present in several countries, including Egypt for eight decades, is the most prominent manifestation of political Islam.[3] It has been able to reach out to the poor and middle classes through its message of "equality under Allah" and its social programs. In Turkey, the Islamist Justice and Development Party won over a majority of the electorate partly through its proven ability to provide for the social welfare and institute reforms necessary to earn consideration for entry into the European Union.[4] In Afghanistan, many of the members of the recently elected national assembly are political Islamists. In Iraq, the two main Shiite parties and their leaders, and some of the Sunni parties and their leaders, are political Islamists. In northern Nigeria, political Islamist governors helped to bring about the restoration of sharia law in reaction to the loss of power to southern Nigerians in 1999.

Political Islamists have been known to resort to radical measures and back radical Islamists when the peaceful path to change has been blocked. For example, in a case that will be examined, Pakistani political Islamists have supported radical Islamists fighting for change in Afghanistan against the Soviet Union and, later, against certain warlords. They have also supported radicals in Kashmir who take up arms against Indian occupation. In turn, the interrelationship has radicalized many Pakistani political Islamists. For the most part, however, these political Islamists view radical Islamists as extremists who make the task of establishing Islamic rule more difficult.

Radical Islamists tend to view political Islamists as impure Muslims or heretics for engaging in "Western" political processes that are "non-Islamic." Further, radical Islamists are prepared to use violent means, including terrorism, in order to drive Westerners and secularists out of the Islamic world and establish Islamic rule.[5] Radical Shiite Islamists came to power in the Iranian revolution of 1979 and established a theocracy. In the 1990s, that Islamist regime opened, to some extent, the political process to moderate political Islamists but maintained control over the levers of police, military, and electoral power. In Sudan, in the 1990s, radical Islamists were given a role in the military regime and invited into their country the Sunni radical, Osama bin Laden, and his Al Qaeda movement as well as the Shiite Hezbollah movement, allowing both to establish bases. Pressure by the United States helped to force Al Qaeda out of Sudan in 1996.[6] Currently, Saudi Arabia, with its adherence to Wahhabi fundamentalism, must be considered the most "Islamic" state, which produces one of the largest recruiting grounds for Islamic extremists and terrorists.[7]

Radical Islamists have occasionally used the political process to achieve their aims. For example, in Algeria radicals joined with moderate political Islamists in the Islamic Salvation Front (FIS) that engaged in the electoral process in 1991, with the expectation that, once elected to govern, the radicals would establish a theocracy and not hold elections thereafter (the "one man, one vote, one time" problem). In December 1991, the military intervened to preclude a FIS victory, which led the radicals to launch a terrorist campaign against the military and precipitate a bloody civil war.[8] Similarly, the Palestinian Islamist movement, Hamas (a radical Muslim Brotherhood) emerged as an alternative to the secular Fatah and contested elections after the Palestinian Authority was established in 1994. Hamas was elected to govern in 2006, took over the Gaza Strip in 2007 by force, and suppressed Fatah. Thus, as these two examples demonstrate, the line between political Islam and radical Islam can blur. Indeed, in some cases they coincide.

In several Islamic countries, there is no established political process and little political space for groups opposing the government. In such situations, political Islam is not an option. In Saudi Arabia, where there is little opportunity to affect changes in policies, Islamists are either servants of the monarchy or anti-regime radicals or fundamentalist critics. When the Saudi monarchy allowed experimental local elections held in 2006, Islamists won every seat.

In Somalia, where there has been no state since 1991, (only warlord-controlled areas) and little opportunity for political participation since the 1960s, Islamists formed the "Islamic Courts" to administer justice using sharia law.[9] The "Courts" created the Islamic Courts Union (ICU) and used force to temporarily drive the warlords from Mogadishu, Somalia, and established a short-lived Islamist regime.[10] However, some of the leaders of the ICU were radical Islamists who also claimed Ethiopia's Ogaden region for Somalia. This, in turn, sparked a military intervention by Ethiopia backed by the United States that removed the ICU from power.

In this analysis, the links between political Islam and radical Islam are examined using the cases of Pakistan and Bangladesh. Political Islamists in Pakistan and Bangladesh have played significant roles in political processes for decades, and some have established links with radical Islamists. In recent years, both countries have been destabilized, and political Islamists have gained in importance relative to secular parties.[11] Bangladesh has suffered from feuding between the two main secular parties, which has caused instability and provided opportunities for political Islamists to gain in influence and radical Islamists to escalate violent activities. In this analysis, greater attention will be paid to Pakistan, where the links between political Islamists and radical Islamists, particularly Al Qaeda and the Taliban, pose the greatest terrorist threat.

Finally, this analysis will examine ways in which radical Islam can be rolled back and moderate political Islamist parties can be encouraged to reject links with radicals and accept modern governance. Political Islam could be either an "enemy" or "ally" in the war against radical Islam. More needs to be known about that relationship. Greater attention will be paid in this review to Pakistan, where the challenge of rolling back radical Islam is especially daunting.

Political Islam in Pakistan

Political Islam was generally moderate, and Islamist parties in Pakistan were adept at playing the political-electoral game from the 1950s until the 1980s. However, in the 1980s, many political Islamists became radicalized as they established links first with the Afghan mujahideen and later in the 1990s, with the Taliban and Kashmiri Islamic extremist fighters and other Islamic radicals. In addition, the youth leagues of the parties have tended to be more militant if not radical. Thus, Pakistani political Islamists (as well as the radicals) continue to be a concern today in the war on terror in the Islamic world. The central question is, can political Islamists be brought into the political mainstream and be disconnected from radical Islam?

The *Jamaat-e-Islami* (Islamist Party) was founded in India in 1941, as one of the first Islamic revivalist movements in the world, and the party led the campaign in Pakistan after independence in 1947 for the Islamization of politics and society and the grounding of Pakistan's constitution and institutions in Islamic law. The *Jamaat-e-Islami* has had a large contingent of *Mojahirs,* who came to Pakistan from India, migrating especially to the Karachi region of Sind Province in Pakistan after the 1947 partition. They associated with the Islamist party and ideology as a way of competing for their rights against native Sindhis, who supported Zulifkar Bhutto's Pakistan People's Party (PPP). The *Jamaat-e-Islami* mounted the first political Islamist challenge to secular rule in Pakistan, first contesting the 1951 general election and has competed in every subsequent general election, except the one in 1997, which it boycotted.[12]

In 1950, the more puritanical *Jamiat-e-Ulema-i-Islami* (Islamist Scholars and Priests Party) also was founded in Pakistan. Eventually, it drew many of its supporters from among Pashtun tribes in the North-West Frontier Province and the Baluchi tribes in the southwest. The *Jamiat-e-Ulema-i-Islami* became prominent first in the 1980s as a sponsor of the mujahideen in Afghanistan and later in the 1990s as a sponsor of the Taliban. The strictly Sunni *Jamiat-e-Ulema-i-Islami* was especially anti-Shiite in its views and policies. From the 1950s until 2002, the *Jamaat-e-Islami* and *Jamiat-e-Ulema-i-Islami* together won less than 10 percent of the vote in general elections. Their strength remains more in mass mobilization and protests than in contesting elections.

In the 1980s, the military dictator, General Zia ul-Haq brought *Jamaat-e-Islami* into his government. A devout Muslim, Zia attempted to transform Pakistan into his vision of an Islamic state and society, with an Islamist military equipped with nuclear weapons. During his rule, Zia began the practice of using Islamist parties and groups as political instruments. However, he did not grant them any substantial power, instead concentrating power in his own hands. Zia adopted a number of initiatives to strengthen his position, Islamize Pakistan's government and politics, and weaken the established secular political order. His Islamization package included the massive expansion of *madrassas* (Quranic schools). Also, Zia instituted the "hudood laws" that extended Islamic sharia law to a wide-range of Pakistani life, which has led to the increasing subjugation of women, and made Pakistan an Islamic state under military rule (as opposed to the theocratic Islamic state of Iran).[13] In sum, Zia helped political Islam to achieve some of its goals in the 1980s.

In 1988, the political Islamists lost influence when the Pakistan People's Party (PPP) returned to power and Benazir Bhutto became the Prime Minister. In 1990, the opposition Muslim League and the Islami Jamhoori Ittehad front of parties, including the *Jamaat-e-Islami* and *Jamiat-e-Ulema-i-Islami*, came to power for the first time led by Prime Minister Nawaz Sharif. Political Islamist parties worked to oppose Pakistan's alliance with the United States. In 1990 and 1991, the *Jamaat-e-Islami, Jamiat-e-Ulema-i-Islami*, and other anti-U.S. forces in the government opposed U.S. intervention in the Gulf War and the Sharif government's support of the United States. The U.S. presence in Saudi Arabia (in the same country as the holy cities of Mecca and Medina) from 1990 onward inspired anti-Americanism among Pakistani Islamist groups.

In the late 1980s and early 1990s, the *Jamiat-e-Ulema-i-Islami* became increasingly radical as it helped to create the Taliban in the region around Quetta, Baluchistan, and among Pushtun tribes in the North-West Frontier Province. The *Jamiat-e-Ulema-i-Islami* built a support base among a Durrani group of Pushtun refugees who originated from the Kandahar region in southern Afghanistan. The establishment of madrassas was a key element, as militants in the *Jamiat-e-Ulema-i-Islami,* who were part of the strict Sunni "Deobandi" sect,[14] passed their beliefs on to the Taliban students in the madrassas. The Taliban became even more extreme in their beliefs, especially in regard to women and Shiites. The future leaders of the Taliban, including Mohamed Omar, fought against the Najibullah regime after the Soviets left in 1988. In 1992, the Mujahideen overthrew the Najibullah regime, and many future Taliban returned to Pakistan (especially around Quetta) to take advantage of the madrassas of the *Jamiat-e-Ulema-i-Islami* for themselves and their families.[15]

In October 1993, the PPP and Benazir Bhutto returned to power. In striving to build a majority coalition, the secularist Bhutto turned to the Islamist *Jamiat-e-Ulema-i-Islami* and its leader, Maulana Fazlur Rahman, who agreed to join the government in exchange for high-profile positions. Upon joining the PPP-led coalition, Fazlur Rahman became Chairman of the National Assembly's Standing Committee on Foreign Affairs. He made numerous trips to Saudi Arabia and the Gulf States to seek financial and military help for the Taliban. He arranged hunting trips for Arab princes to Kandahar, where they made their first contacts with the Taliban.[16]

The *Jamiat-e-Ulema-i-Islami* inherited camps in Pakistan used to train the Taliban, as well as Al Qaeda fighters. Pakistani Islamist militant groups used the camps to train a new generation of fighters. For example, the radical Islamist group, *Harkat ul-Ansar*,[17] trained recruits in Camp Badr near Khost on the Pakistan-Afghanistan border and sent the fighters to Kashmir, Chechnya, and Yugoslavia.

In February 1997, Prime Minister Benazir Bhutto and the PPP-led government (including the *Jamiat-e-Ulema-i-Islami*) lost power to Nawaz Sharif and the Pakistan Muslim League-led coalition. However, by this time, the *Jamiat-e-Ulema-i-Islami* had already helped launch the Taliban and helped put it in control of most of Afghanistan, and the Taliban returned the favor by offering its support to the *Jamiat-e-Ulema-i-Islami* and related groups in Pakistan.

In 1997, the *Jamaat-e-Islami* refused to return as part of the coalition, having boycotted the elections. The party became more radical and revivalist and rejected the corruption of secular politics. The *Jamaat-e-Islami* created and was supporting the Kashmir-based Hizb-ul Mujahideen (Freedom Fighters Movement), which was one of the largest radical groups fighting in Jammu and Kashmir.

After September 11, 2001, General Musharraf first clamped down on political Islam, as a first step as he later changed course in order to erect a new political order dominated by the military. In the wake of September 11, 2001, Musharraf moved against political Islamist leaders, charging Maulana Fazlur Rahman (the cleric and leader of *Jamiat-Ulema-e-Islami*) with sedition. Rahman was accused of spurring violent protests against the U.S.-led attacks on Afghanistan and placed under house arrest. Maulana Azam Tariq (radical cleric and leader of the anti-Shiite *Sipah-i-Sahaba* militant movement) was also placed under house arrest. The political Islamist leader of *Jamaat-e-Islami*, Ameer Qazi Hussain Ahmed, was arrested and jailed.[18] However, the leaders were soon released and led their parties' campaigns in the October 2002 parliamentary elections.

In the October 2002 parliamentary elections, the Islamist block, the Muttahida Majlis-e-Amal (MMA), took advantage of the forced absence of Pakistan's two civilian leaders, Benazir Bhutto and Nawaz Sharif, to win a larger share of the vote and gain seats, thereby becoming the official opposition in parliament to Musahrraf's party, the Muslim League. From 2002 to the present, the MMA took advantage of its position and its ability to mobilize supporters onto the streets to block Musharraf's efforts to roll back Islamism and move in a more secular direction. Elections have been scheduled for December 2007, and the outcome for the MMA is not predictable because of the uncertain status of Musharraf and Benazir Bhutto. If Bhutto returns, the secularists stand to grow in strength and reverse political Islamist gains.

Pakistani secularists see the political Islamists of the MMA as a continuing obstacle to progress and security, who strive to make Pakistan an even more Islamic state and drive it backwards. In September 2006, the MMA was able to stop the repeal of many of the "hudood laws," especially one which made it exceedingly difficult for a woman to seek justice for rape. As usual, the MMA Islamists were able to mobilize its supporters and get them onto the streets. The Islamists have been elevated to a position where they can block progress by the Pakistan military and political elites, who have traditionally used Islam and Islamic groups to further their political and military strategic ends. Sectarianism has flourished as a result of the influence of radical Islam, and Sunni militants (e.g., from the Deobandi sect) who have continued to attack Shiites and other Islamic sects.[19]

Radical Islam in Pakistan

The seeds of radical Islam in Pakistan were sown during the military dictatorship of General Zia ul-Haq and the war against the Soviet occupation of Afghanistan in the late 1970s and 1980s. Zia encouraged the propagation of Islamist influence over Pakistani society, state, and the military during this period. Also, radical Islamists, including *Salafists* (e.g., Osama bin Laden) from Saudi Arabia,[20] began operations in Pakistan to wage a guerrilla campaign against the Soviets and began proselytizing and building Islamist movements inside Pakistan. Wealthy and radical Saudi *Salafists* helped to fund hundreds of madrassas that taught radical versions of Islam. In the 1980s, radical Sunni movements arose that began to persecute Shiites and other Islamic groups, giving rise to the sectarian violence that persists today.

In the 1980s, three million Afghan refugees settled in Pakistani refugee camps and became the basis for the anti-Soviet *mujahideen* in the 1980s and, in the 1990s, the Taliban. Pakistani and foreign Islamists rose to prominence and came to define jihad as radical Islamist warfare against infidels, and they formed the vanguard of Islamic extremist fighters.[21]

In the 1980s, Pakistan welcomed Islamic extremist fighters from throughout the Islamic world to fight the Soviets in Afghanistan. The Pakistani intelligence agency (ISI) and CIA worked together to aid Afghan, Pakistani, and foreign mujahideen in the campaign against the Soviet Union. Inside Pakistan, the CIA and ISI worked with the Islamist *Jamaat-e-Islami* and Islamic extremist fighters. Arms were shipped primarily to the Ghilzai Pushtun group in central and northeast Pakistan.[22]

Zia also encouraged the rise of Islamist militants in Kashmir, and the ISI and Islamists organized Islamic extremist fighters to launch an anti-Indian campaign there. This interaction with the ISI allowed Islamist parties in Pakistan to extend their influence over armed forces personnel.[23]

In the 1990s, Islamic extremist fighters attacked the Indian presence in Kashmir. The extremist campaign and Indian repression helped confirm to a majority of Pakistanis that Kashmir was part of their national identity. Thus, in their view, Pakistan's identity as a state for Muslims would not be complete for them if it did not include the Muslim majority territory of Kashmir. Throughout the 1990s and afterwards, Pakistan supported the insurgency by training and supplying both Kashmiri and foreign Islamic extremist fighters to fight India's presence.

In 1994, the Taliban used Pakistan as the base to launch its campaign to seize control of Afghanistan. After subjecting most of Afghanistan to their rule, the Taliban subsequently invited Osama bin Laden and Al Qaeda to establish a presence in Afghanistan in 1996. The Taliban (and Al Qaeda) have continued to maintain an active presence in Pakistan after 1996 and have worked in cooperation with Pakistani Islamists.

The costs of radical Islam and extremist campaigns were high for Pakistan. In order to mount the Afghan and Kashmiri insurgencies, the Pakistan Army used Islamic extremist fighters, thus legitimizing their role in Pakistani society. The socio-economic costs were high, as for years, Pakistan's budget went primarily towards military expenditure, debt repayment, and civil administration. There was very little left to invest in the development of the country. In the education sector, madrassas developed to provide much basic education and often took the place of public schools. As a result of the Islamic extremist military operations, Pakistan's domestic situation became even less secure.

Radical Islamists of Kashmiri and Pakistani militant groups continued to maintain a presence and popularity in Pakistan, both among the masses and some elites. Post-September 11, 2001, attacks on U.S. and western interests demonstrated that Islamic extremism was robust in Pakistan's cities. Al Qaeda and Taliban forces moved from Afghanistan into western Pakistan in the Federally Administered Tribal Area (FATA), where the central government had little control, and some moved into Azad (Pakistani controlled) Kashmir on Pakistan's side of the Line of Control where they attempted to incite war between India and Pakistan.

Radical Islam has had a negative impact on South Asian stability with Islamic extremist fighters conducting military and terror campaigns in Afghanistan (especially the Taliban and Al Qaeda) and in Kashmir (especially Lashkar-e-Taiba and Jaish-e-Mohammad, which have been named as terrorist organizations by the United States) and by conducting terrorist actions in Pakistan and India. Radical Islam has been a contributing factor to the war in Afghanistan and a near-war between Pakistan and India in 2002.

After an attack by Islamic extremist fighters on the Indian parliament on December 13, 2001, Indian and U.S. pressure led General Musharraf to offer, in a speech delivered on January 12, 2002, support in combating cross-border terrorism from Pakistan into Indian-controlled Jammu and Kashmir. However, Musharraf found it difficult to follow through on his commitments without risking his own position within Pakistan, especially in the army. This balancing act also applied to efforts to roll back radical Islam.

In 2004, Musharraf finally sent the Pakistan army into the mountainous tribal areas of North and South Waziristan to fight against the Taliban and Al Qaeda. The United States named Pakistan a "non-NATO major ally" in support. After two years of fighting in which hundreds of people were killed, the Pakistan army had made little progress. Finally, in September 2006, Musharraf made a deal with the tribal leaders in North Waziristan, in which the army would leave the area and stay out in return for tribal leaders agreeing to keep the Taliban from crossing the frontier with Afghanistan. The pact was followed by a tripling of Taliban attacks on U.S. and NATO forces across the border in Afghanistan.[24] Thus, the deal fell through in July 2007, and the Pakistan government has been ineffective in stopping Taliban attacks into Afghanistan.

The links between political Islam and radical Islam in Pakistan have existed for more than two decades. The links still exist in the North-West Frontier Province and Baluchistan. Several questions about political and radical Islamist movements in Pakistan remain to be answered. First, do efforts to marginalize or suppress political Islamists push them to cooperate more with radical Islamists? Second, can political Islam be disconnected from radical Islam and be maintained in the political mainstream?

Political Islam in Bangladesh

Political Islam in Bangladesh was present with the birth of the country in 1971. The *Jamaat-e-Islami* party (present in both West and East Pakistan) supported the unity of the country and opposed separatism in the East in 1970 and 1971. These Islamists backed the Pakistan army in 1971 when it brutally suppressed Bengali activists in East Pakistan and then opposed the independence of Bangladesh. The party in Bangladesh has maintained close relations with the one in Pakistan. The leader of the party in Bangladesh, Motiur Rahman Nizam, is still accused of leading a group called Al Badr that allegedly tortured and executed those fighting against Pakistan in the 1971 war. The *Jamaat-e-Islami* was banned from 1971 to 1979 in Bangladesh and did not become the force within the army and society that other political Islamists in Pakistan became. Starting in the 1980s, Saudi groups entered Bangladesh and began funding community associations and madrassas, fueling the radical Islamist movement.

In 1991, given a political vacuum after years of military rule, the Jamaat-e-Islami contested elections and won more than 10 percent of the vote. In the 1996 and 2001 elections, the two main secular parties won an increasing share of the vote, while Jamaat-e-Islami's share was reduced. However, the party succeeded in building grassroots support from its community projects. For example, the Jamaat-e-Islami started an Islamic bank, which has been successful. The party also spawned a militant student wing, Islami Chhatra Shibir, some of whose members have engaged in political violence such as the killing of members of one of the two main secular parties, the Awami League. This is a case where political Islam morphed into radical Islam.

In addition, during the 1990s, other Bangladeshi Islamist movements and organizations emerged. One was the hard line Islami Oikya Jote (IOJ) party, whose leader Maulana Azizul Haq was arrested in February 2001 and charged with a policeman's murder during a general strike called by the Islamist parties. Another was the hard line Islamist group, Jamaat ul-Mujahideen, whose five members were arrested in March 2003, suspected of setting off a number of explosions in Bangladesh.

For more than a decade, the two major secular parties – the Bangladesh Nationalist Party (BNP) and Awami League – competed for

Jamaat-e-Islami support in their attempts to form governments. The bidding put the *Jamaat-e-Islami* in an advantageous position. From 2001 to 2006, the *Jamaat-e-Islami* had two cabinet ministers in the BNP government, and the *Islami Oikya Jote* party has also been part of the government. The result has been that the Bangladesh government has come to support many *Jamaat-e-Islami* positions, including Islamization of institutions and the introduction of *sharia* law at the local level, which has resulted in religious leaders issuing fatwas (decrees) usually against women and minorities. The *Jamaat-e-Islami* in Bangladesh condemned U.S. attacks on Afghanistan and Iraq and persuaded some members of government to do so.

In Bangladeshi society, the influence of political Islam has led to the increasing use of the veil and *hejab* over the past decade. Islamists are becoming the leaders of universities and campus associations. Some estimate that more students are now attending madrassas than public schools. Another disconcerting trend has been acid revenge attacks on women by rejected male suitors. Despite these incidents and trends, the political Islamist *Jamaat-e-Islami* is still not seen by some experts as a major threat in Bangladesh, since the party is supported by less than 10 percent of Bangladeshis. They have limited access to political power, and the cabinet seats that the party held in the BNP government before 2006 were not the most powerful ones.

Some observers in Bangladesh assert that the more that political Islam grows, the greater will be the level of political violence in the country. Evidence of a connection between political Islam and radical Islam is indicated by recent events such as coordinated cinema bombings during a Muslim holiday and several other attacks in Bangladesh against targets of Islamist displeasure. Comparisons are made between such Islamist groups and the mafia, where infiltration, recruitment, and acts of violence start at the community level but, as they grow in strength, they adopt strong-arm tactics and sponsor violence through militant groups. Thus far, there has been considerable circumstantial evidence linking political Islamist parties and radical Islamists groups and terrorists, although an indisputable connection has not been found.

Radical Islam in Bangladesh

Radical Islam in Bangladesh has been manifested in small-scale terrorism and violence. Even this small-scale radical Islamist violence has discouraged positive international engagement of other states and businesses with Bangladesh. The Pakistan-based radical Islamist group, *Lashkar-e-Taiba*, which operates mainly in Jammu and Kashmir, has a presence in Bangladesh, as do a number of Islamist "splinter groups."[25] Political violence and terrorism against Indian, U.S., and other international targets has led some to refer to there being a state of "political chaos" in Bangladesh.

The radical Islamist bombing of an Awami League rally led by the leader of the opposition, Sheikh Hasina, on August 21, 2004, was the most egregious event to date. Also capturing attention was an attack by the radical Islamist "Bangla Bhai" on the British High Commissioner in northeast Bangladesh. Despite this, the Bangladeshi prime minister at the time, Zia Khaleda, when asked about the problem of religious extremism, denied there was a problem. While the Bangladeshi leadership turned a blind eye to the problem, threats have also been made against the American Ambassador and the resident World Bank director.[26] For all these reasons, Bangladesh has been put on the U.S. terrorist watch list, Bangladesh nationals in the United States have been forced to register, and the U.S. Ambassador has condemned the actions of a radical Islamist group in north Bangladesh. India also has accused Bangladesh of harboring Islamist guerrillas who Indian authorities had reported operating in the northeast region of India.[27]

In the last decade, there has been other violence in Bangladesh with a radical Islamist flavor. Radical Islamists have attacked shrines of the Islamic Sufi sect in Sylhet Province and elsewhere, as well as targeting cinemas, cultural events, and secular political parties. Incidents have included the bombing of Sufi saints' tombs, musical programs, and Bengali New Year festivities as well as attacks on member of the Ahmadiya Islamic sect, Christians, and leftists. The Islamist leader, Motiur Rahman Nizam, had incited attacks against the Ahmadiya sect. Radical Islamists launched coordinated bombings of four cinemas in Mymensingh during the *Eid-ul-Fitr* holiday in 2002. These bombings were coordinated, which indicates a sophisticated Islamist terrorist presence. The bombings of cinemas in Mymensingh as well as in Sylhet were the work of Islamists who opposed nudity and sexuality in films being shown. Islamist terrorists also attacked an *Udychi* cultural function in Jessore, the Bangla New Year festival at Ramna, and a Suranjeet Sengupta meeting at Sunamgonj, as well as the mayor of Sylhet.[28]

Other areas of concern in Bangladesh are Islamist guerrillas and criminal gangs that operated in remote Chittagong (southeast), Sylhet (northeast), and Jessore (southwest) provinces. In July 2002, a senior member of Bangladesh's largest terrorist group, the 2,000-strong Al Qaeda-allied *Harkat-ul-Jihad-al-Islami* (HUJI), reported that 150 men who entered Chittagong in southeastern Bangladesh were Taliban and Al Qaeda fighters from Afghanistan. In April 2004, a large arms shipment to this group was seized in Chittagong. Further, it has been reported that Islamist militants were being trained in the southeastern hill country, and that arms shipments were being made through Chittagong. A growing indigenous base of the population is supporting radical Islamist groups in the country. Islamists groups, linked with Al Qaeda, have been operating in the hill regions of Bangladesh's coastal belt. Further, they have been recruiting and hiding among the Muslim Ruhingya refugees from Burma/Myanmar and cross into and out of Bangladesh across its unprotected borders and coastlines.[29]

The presence of Islamist militants and guerrillas in Chittagong and the Northeast region of Bangladesh was partly the result of poverty that spurs rebellions and remote rough terrain that provides safe havens for them. Sylhet and Chittagong have been separatist regions and their populations heretofore have been more conservative in nature. Chittagong is a troublesome region, which is kept in turmoil by a combination of criminals, Islamic extremists, and separatists. It is a seaport, but most of its trade is with the Arabian Peninsula, which makes its population more politically conservative and traditional. Overall, these events and trends placed Bangladesh on the U.S. radar screen in the Global War on Terrorism (GWOT) since it reportedly has become another safe haven for Al Qaeda.[30]

The political Islamist *Jamaat-e-Islami* party, while it was part of the government, has been linked to guerrilla and criminal activity in Chittagong. Bangladeshi "philanthropic" organizations, associated with *Al-Haramain* and *Harkat-ul-Jihad-al-Islami*, were identified as having raised funds for Al Qaeda. Based on the work of investigative agencies, it appears that extremism in Bangladesh has advanced well beyond the incubation stage. Observers point out that the major parties – the Awami League and the Bangladesh Nationalist Party – have "lost the ability to reason," and are politicizing everything, opening the way for extremists. The government is chaotic, manifesting a decline in civil service and administrative leadership and performance, and by a rise in the degree of government corruption. The multi-fiber agreement that provided a guaranteed market for Bangladeshi clothing exports expired, and many textile and clothing workers have lost their jobs, which add to their militancy. The inability of the Bangladeshi government to fully investigate the attacks by extremist organizations also has led to the spread of rumors and fears about Islamic extremism.[31]

Differences between Pakistan and Bangladesh: In spite of the radical Islamist threats to U.S. and other interests there, Bangladesh has not degenerated yet to the level of Pakistan, where radical Islam and terrorism, especially in the form of Al Qaeda and the Taliban, are still more widespread and where protection of U.S. assets is a major concern. Political Islam has more connections to radical Islam in Pakistan than is the case in Bangladesh. The latter has a generally more moderate form of Islam, a stronger civil society and NGO sector, and a public with higher levels of education and literacy than Pakistan. Furthermore, Bangladeshi leaders are not fixated on the status of Jammu and Kashmir or Afghanistan, a focus that has encouraged the formation of armed Islamic extremist groups in Pakistan. The topography of much of Pakistan is mountainous, an easier place for radical Islamists to hide and operate within its territory, whereas Bangladesh is heavily populated, has fewer ungoverned regions, and thus is a more difficult place in which to hide and operate.

Rolling Back Radical Islam and Mainstreaming Political Islam

The cases of Pakistan and Bangladesh raise questions of how to roll back radical Islam and if it might be possible to bring political Islam into the mainstream. A "proactive" strategist would contend that, first, underlying socio-economic problems need to be addressed, especially improving education and providing greater job opportunities, in order to begin the process of rolling back radical Islam. Second, accountable democratic institutions and participation need to be developed so that political Islamist parties can be channeled into the political mainstream. In contrast, a "containment strategist" might recommend that the United States and its allies support authoritarian regimes like Musharraf's that are more inclined to suppress radical Islam and take authoritarian measures to put limits on political Islamist parties.

Both Pakistan and Bangladesh's most troublesome and enduring security challenges, and a source of radical Islam's growth, continue to come from the fact that those countries have some of the fastest growing and youngest populations in the world. They are burdened by the fact that they have poor educational systems, provide mediocre economic prospects for their people, and have high unemployment rates. Madrassas in Pakistan and Bangladesh remain a problem, and they need more qualified teachers, less propagation of extremist viewpoints, and beg for more regulation. At present, they produce young men with few marketable skills who could easily be radicalized. Pakistan and Bangladesh are weak states with low capacity, as evidenced by those governments' inability to collect taxes and their failing economies, which fail to export much beyond textiles. Pakistan and Bangladesh's economic recoveries are dependent on infusions of Western aid and debt forgiveness. The two countries will remain dependent on such assistance at least in the near future in order to avoid even deeper crises. However, if extremist violence continues, they are unlikely to attract the desired levels of foreign direct investment.

Presently, U.S. aid to Pakistan is mostly focused on military hardware with only around 10 percent devoted to socio-economic aid intended to undermine extremism and terrorism. Other aid consists of assisting with the investigation of bombings, gunrunning, and Islamic extremist activity in Pakistan. U.S. aid for Bangladesh is focused on poverty alleviation – a good thing – but not enough is being directed explicitly towards undermining the sources of extremism and terrorism. There is not enough aid being directed towards intelligence and law enforcement in Bangladesh or towards transforming madrassas into less radical and more productive educational institutions.

The Challenges of Rolling Back Radical Islam in Pakistan

In focusing on Pakistan alone, because it is the source of such major threats, the country faces a number of continuing and emerging challenges in its immediate domestic security environment and in rolling back radical Islam. While Musharraf has made commitments to hold democratic elections before the end of 2007 and may eventually return Pakistan to civilian rule, it is questionable if Pakistan will achieve a transition to the kind of liberal and secular state and society that can overcome the country's security dilemma.

Pakistan continues to be dominated by the army, whose corporate identity remains strong. As long as Pakistan continues to fight Islamic extremist fighters along the border with Afghanistan and defend against India, the army will continue to play a dominant role and view itself as Pakistan's indispensable institution. The dominance of the military makes relations with the United States and the West more complex, and it creates formidable challenges for the development of a liberal democratic state and society with a dynamic economy. The military still strives to control political and economic life and finds pretenses to maintain power. While fewer civilians are willing to accept army interference than in the past, the army's central role has to weaken before civilians have a chance to rule. After that, civilians must prove their competence to rule to the army. On a positive note, it appears that the army will not side with radical Islamists, though there will continue to be a significant number of such Islamists in the army. Finally, there appears to be little chance that radical Islamists will seize control of the country and its nuclear weapons.

In Pakistan, the United States has mounted an aid campaign (initially, $1.8 billion) to try to help the country overcome the effect of twenty years of radical Islamist development, especially aimed at regulating radical madrassas. The United States has assisted Pakistan with investigative services since September 11, 2001. Besides adverse democratic and economic trends, Pakistan is threatened by the prospect that the United States will tire of the Global War on Terror and such aid will evaporate in the future.

In Pakistan, there are two different views of General Musharraf and the government's efforts (with U.S. assistance) to roll back radical Islam. The supporters of the Musharraf regime emphasize that it has done much to capture Al Qaeda operatives, fight the Taliban in the tribal areas, and roll back radical Islam. They stress that Pakistan is a predominantly conservative Islamic country and that one must be careful in distinguishing between conservatives and radicals.[32] They point out that the army did its best in the tribal areas of Waziristan but had not been successful and that the best course of action would be to try to work with tribal leaders in countering the Taliban and Al Qaeda.[33] The Bush administration acknowledges these points and claims that the Musharraf regime has done more in the war on terror than any other government.

Secular critics of the Musharraf regime, such as Samina Ahmed of International Crisis Group, Prof. Pervez Hoodbhoy of Quaid-e-Azam University, and Prof. Abdul Hameed Nayyar of the Institute of Sustainable Development Policy, point out that the government is not doing enough to roll back radical Islam. They see the problems of radical Islam as very threatening.[34] They provide evidence that so far madrassa reform has been a failure and that public education reform has been inadequate. In regard to the campaign against the Taliban and Al Qaeda in Waziristan, the critics observe that it has been handled by the Pakistan army strictly as a military campaign, and there has been no effort to win hearts and minds there. They assert that Musharraf and the army have not tried hard enough in North Waziristan and that the Taliban and Al Qaeda will be able to operate there.

The critics assert that the government has been heavy-handed in crushing local opposition in Baluchistan. They believe that opening up and democratizing Pakistan would be the best course of action to roll back radical Islam. The problem is that there is no structure for political governance in Pakistan or control over its territory. It would appear that the best approach would be to open up the democratic process in order to roll back radical Islam in Pakistan.[35]

Indoctrinated youth and radical madrassas are viewed as an important aspect of the growth of radical Islam and are a threat to Pakistan and international security.[36] The government is using a colonial law that applies to a range of educational institutions to try to regulate madrassas. It should update the law in order to enact specific measures relevant to Islamic places of learning to bring the madrassas under control.

Another problem is the lack of capacity and effort to combat terrorist financing. The Ministry of Finance indicates that there are no present

Pakistani laws prohibiting money laundering. With regard to countering terrorist networks, the Musharraf regime makes a distinction between Al Qaeda and Pakistani terrorist networks and Kashmiri Islamic extremist fighters, opposing the former but turning a blind eye to the latter. However, they have a shared ideology and philosophy, and are often the same people. The government continues to make the distinction, which is questionable. Islamic extremist fighters are still operating in Kashmir and pose as a threat to India. However, because of the overlap between the two extremist Islamist groups, and similar goals of both, until the government cracks down on local Islamic extremist fighters, they will not deal with Al Qaeda sufficiently.

Furthermore, the regime has been cooperating with Islamist religious leaders in order to curry public support, which makes it difficult to roll back radical Islam. Until this stops, Pakistan cannot roll back radical Islam and terrorism. The United States needs to act now by stepping up aid and support, because, otherwise, without action to improve education and crack down on all Islamic extremist fighters, radical Islamism will become more entrenched.

Socio-economic factors, such as a poor educational system and a lack of opportunity; religious factors, such as proselytization by radical sects; and demographic factors, such as a fast growing population, have contributed to the development of alienated youth and radical Islam in Pakistan. In addition, reactionary movements, such as the Taliban, benefit from the fact that almost half of the population is illiterate and that, while the national per capita income has increased to US$720, the poor and rural inhabitants of Pakistan are being left behind. For example, access to sanitation in Pakistan in rural areas is 30 percent lower than in other countries with similar income. Forty-one percent of the population lives below the poverty line (i.e., a dollar a day) in rural North-West Frontier Province, the main base of support for the Taliban.[37] Radical teachers in madrassas have played a role in propagating and shaping radical Islam in Pakistan.[38] Improved and less radical education is one answer, but the problem is larger and more complex in Pakistan, involving a number of socio-economic, religious, and political factors.[39]

Education reform is moving slowly. It may take several decades to bring satisfactory results. Most of the change to date has been symbolic. The power of the Pakistani Islamists is increasing and their opposition is slowing education modernization. Some Islamists want to continue to control much of Pakistan's education for indoctrination purposes. In 2004, the Islamist block, the Muttahida Majlis-e-Amal (MMA) was on the defensive, and the reform of education policy and curricula was proceeding. However, the government has now gone into reverse, and the MMA is stronger and is making a heavy strategic investment in creating an Islamic educational system. Currently, Pakistan's government spending on education is only 2.7 percent of its GDP; and it will probably not rise to the target of 4 percent of GDP. All educational sectors (primary, secondary, tertiary) are inadequate, except for some elite private sector education. Although there has been a massive increase in higher education funding, which is presently five times higher than in 2001, Pakistan's educational faculties are poorly staffed and have not been able to make proper use of the funds. Presently, there is not enough manpower to run their universities, and talent is not nurtured. The result is that half of the school age population in Pakistan is not going to school, and half of the school goers drop out before graduation.

All is not yet lost, however, on the Pakistani educational front. The United States has poured tens of millions of dollars into aid for Pakistan that was intended to, among other things, roll back radical Islam. The U.S. Agency for International Development (USAID) established projects in education, as well as investments in better governance, health care, and economic growth. USAID's education grants program included both basic and higher education, and was geographically concentrated in underserved districts of Sindh and Baluchistan provinces, and in the Federally Administered Tribal Areas, such as North and South Waziristan. USAID estimated that the program was benefiting 367,555 children and 18,000 teachers and that USAID education funding was approximately $64 million.[40] From 2002 to 2006, 172 teachers and administrators were trained in the United States. USAID supported teacher training in methods that emphasized the development of critical thinking skills and participatory education for young children, and USAID estimated that over 18,000 Pakistani primary school teachers were trained. USAID also worked to improve the examination system for high school admissions.[41] Critics point out that U.S. aid has been largely spent in the United States, when it should be spent much more efficiently in Pakistan.[42]

Despite these efforts, there are 15,000 to 25,000 madrassas that are providing a large proportion of primary education in Pakistan. The much-vaunted madrassa reform campaign that started in 2002 had been farmed out to the provinces in 2004. However, there had only been a handful of officials with an inadequate budget in each province appointed to register madrassas and begin the reform process.[43] Therefore, because of a lack of political will and state capacity, and resistance from MMA Islamists, the madrassa reform campaign never really got off the ground. Islamic radicalism is also fostered in the public education system. On the positive side, there have been some curriculum and textbook changes that have revised and softened the depiction of India in Pakistan's public education system. It is too early to assess the extent to which these changes will help to improve relations between Pakistan and India.

In sum, the struggle to roll back radical Islam in Pakistan has made progress since September 11, 2001. However, there is still very much to be done, and the present government is losing the will and appears to lack the capacity to continue the struggle. In the meantime, radical Islam remains a resilient force in Pakistan. Given this deteriorating situation, it may well be that an elected and legitimate democratic government (perhaps led by Benazir Bhutto and the Pakistan Peoples Party) might do better than one that rests on the Pakistan army as its main power base.

Conclusion

This analysis has drawn a distinction between political Islam and radical Islam in "knowing one's enemy," focusing on Pakistan and Bangladesh. The problems of rolling back radical Islam and bringing political Islam into the mainstreaming have been addressed within the South Asian context. The analysis has found support for, and problems with, the "proactive" and "containment" strategies that have been recommended by policy analysts. The "proactive" view is that the restoration and development of democracy in Pakistan and Bangladesh will dry up support for political Islam and lessen the role of political Islamists in parliament. Perhaps this will be the case in Bangladesh and with the *Jamaat-e-Islami* in Pakistan. However, the "containment" view is that political Islam in Pakistan (and in Bangladesh to an extent) has been entangled with radical Islam and Islamic extremist fighters for two decades and that it is impossible to disentangle them. Therefore, democratization would not make much of an impact and would undermine the secular authoritarian regime in Pakistan and the semi-authoritarian regime in Bangladesh. Indeed, the fear is that such Islamist political parties might be included to indulge in "one man, one vote, one time" strategies, where, once in power, they would be unwilling to relinquish it in later free elections. The better strategy, according to the containment school, would be to contain political Islam through surveillance and law enforcement.

The proactive view of rolling back radical Islam places great faith in the provision of aid that will develop public education, regulate the madrassas, build a healthy economy, and provide job opportunities for young people. In the long run, such an approach, if achievable, holds promise. However, the containment view focuses on the structural problems of corrupt and ineffective if non-authoritarian governments that will not be able to deliver the necessary education and jobs. Also, in this containment view, it is perceived that the scale of illiteracy and unemployment is so immense in Pakistan and Bangladesh that aid will have little effect in the near term. Thus, it is argued that it is better to continue to focus aid in Pakistan on containing radical Islam in North-West Frontier Province and Baluchistan and in defeating offensive actions by the Taliban and other radical movements.

The cases of Pakistan and Bangladesh are instructive for efforts to "mainstream" political Islam elsewhere (e.g., Egypt). Democratization does compel political Islamists to compete in the public arena where they will either be defeated by secular parties, as in Pakistan and Bangladesh when there have been democratic elections, or will prove themselves as effective governors and make gains, as in Turkey. However, regimes in the Islamic world are, for the most part, weak, and the likelihood exists that radical political Islamists could take over, as Hamas did in Gaza, and impose their will and seek to advance radical Islamism, while progress in modernization and developing civil society take a back seat. It is also difficult to disentangle political Islam from radical Islam in some cases, and the fear is that once in power such parties may turn their regimes into theocratic dictatorships.

Rolling back radical Islam, once it gains a foothold, is even more problematic. The hope that education and job creation will turn young people away from radical Islam is dependent on a number of other variables. Most important in achieving progressive and stable societies are a long time horizon in which to work and good governance over an extended period. Presently, progressive and stable societies and good governance are commodities that are in short supply in the region.

Notes

1. Sami Zubaida, "Trajectories of Political Islam: Egypt, Iran, and Turkey," *The Political Quarterly*, vol. 71, Supplement 1, August 2000, 60-79. Peter Mandaville, *Global Political Islam*, (London: Routledge, 2007). R. Aslan, *No God but God: The Origins, Evolution, and Future of Islam*, (New York: Random House, 2006). G. Fuller, *The Future of Political Islam*, (New York: MacMillan, 2003).

2. Robert S. Leiken and Steven Brooke, "The Moderate Muslim Brotherhood," *Foreign Affairs*, vol. 86, no. 2, March/April 2007, 107-121. Jillian Schwedler, "Democratization, Inclusion and the Moderation of Islamist Parties," *Development*, vol. 50, no.1, March 2007, 56-61. Saad Eddin Ibrahim, "Toward Muslim Democracies," *Journal of Democracy*, vol. 18, no. 2, April 2007, 5-13.

3. Leiken and Brooke, op. cit., 107-121.

4. Ergun Özbudun, "From Political Islam to Conservative Democracy: The Justice and Development Party in Turkey," *South European Society and Politics*, Vo. 11, Nos. 3 & 4, September 2006, 543-557.

5. J. Calvert, "The Mythical Foundations of Radical Islam," *Orbis*, vol. 48, no. 1, Winter 2004, 29-41. Hendrik Hansen and Peter Kainz, "Radical Islamism and Totalitarian Ideology," *Totalitarian Movements and Political Religions*, vol. 8, no. 1, March 2007, 55-76.

6. Alex de Waal and A.H. Abdel Salam, "Islamism, State Power, and Jihad in Sudan," in Alex de Waal, ed., *Islamism and its Enemies in the Horn of Africa*, (Bloomington, Ind.: Indiana University Press, 2004), 71-113.

7. Mohammed Ayoob, "South-West Asia after the Taliban," *Survival*, vol. 44, no. 1, 5-6.

8. William B. Quandt, "Algeria's Uneasy Peace," *Journal of Democracy*, vol. 13, no. 4, October 2002, 15-23. Stathis N. Kalyvas, "Commitment Problems in Emerging Democracies: The Case of Religious Parties," *Comparative Politics*, vol. 32, no. 4, 2000, 382.

9. Roland Marchal, "Islamic Political Dynamics in the Somali Civil War," in Alex de Waal, ed., *Islamism and its Enemies in the Horn of Africa*, (Bloomington, Ind.: Indiana University Press, 2004), 114-145.

10. Michael Shank, "Understanding political Islam in Somalia," *Contemporary Islam*, vol. 1, no. 1, June 2007.

11. Tom A. Peter, "National Intelligence Estimate: Al Qaeda Stronger and a Threat to the US Homeland," *Christian Science Monitor*, 19 July 2007, On-line, Internet, available from http://www.csmonitor.com/2007/0718/p99s01-duts.html. Furthermore, the 2007 U.S. National Intelligence Estimate designated Pakistan as the most important state in the war on terror because of the presence of Al Qaeda, the Taliban, and Pakistani radical Islamists; thus, the role of political Islamists is of interest.

12. S.V.R. Nasr, "Islam in Pakistan," in John L. Esposito, ed. *Political Islam: Revolution, Radicalism, or Reform?* (Boulder, Colo.: Lynne Rienner, 1997), 136-138.

13. Jessica Stern, "Pakistan's Jihad Culture," *Foreign Affairs*, 79, 6, November/December 2000, 117.

14. Dietrich Reetz, "The Deoband Universe: What Makes a Transcultural and Transnational Educational Movement of Islam?," *Comparative Studies of South Asia, Africa and the Middle East*, vol. 27, no. 1, 2007, 139-159. P.W. Singer, "Pakistan's Madrassahs: Ensuring a System of Education not Jihad," Brookings Institution Analysis Paper #14, November 2001, 2, On-line, Internet, available from http://www.brook.edu/views/papers/singer/20020103.pdf.

15. Tim Judah, "The Taliban Papers," *Survival*, vol. 44, no. 1, Spring 2002, 69-80.

16. Itifkhar H. Malik, "Pakistan in 2001: The Afghanistan Crisis and the Rediscovery of the Frontline State," *Asian Survey*, vol. 42, no. 1, 2002, 204-212.

17. C. Christine Fair, "Militant Recruitment in Pakistan: Implications for Al Qaeda and Other Organizations," *Studies in Conflict and Terrorism*, no. 27, 2004, 489-504. For example, the radical Islamist group, Harkat ul-Ansar, trained recruits in Camp Badr near Khost on the Pakistan-Afghanistan border radical Islamist group.

18. "Pakistan Arrests Dozens of Islamic Activists," CNN, 23 October 2001. At the end of February 2002, Ameer Qazi Hussain Ahmed was released from prison and resumed his campaign of denunciation against President Musharraf.

19. Samina Ahmed, The State of Sectarianism in Pakistan, Islamabad, Pakistan, *International Crisis Group*, no. 95, 18 April 2005, On-line, Internet, available from http://www.crisisgroup.org/home/index.cfm?id=3374&l=1.

20. Trevor Stanley, "Understanding the Origins of Wahhabism and Salafism," *Terrorism Monitor*, vol. 3, issue 14, 15 July 2005, On-line, Internet, available from http://jamestown.org/terrorism/news/article.php?articleid=2369746. See also Ahmed Rashid, "The Taliban: Exporting Extremism," *Foreign Affairs*, November/December 1999. Benjamin E. Schwartz, "America's Struggle against the Wahhabi/Neo-Salafi Movement," *Orbis*, vol. 51, no. 1, Winter 2007, 107-128.

21. M. Ehsan Ahrari, "Jihadi Groups, Nuclear Pakistan, and the New Great Game," Carlisle, Penna.: Strategic Studies Institute, U.S. Army War College, 2001.

22. Ahmed Rashid, "Pakistan and the Taliban," in William Maley, ed. *Fundamentalism Reborn? Afghanistan and the Taliban*, (New York: New York University Press, 1998), 74.

23. Ajay Behera, "Is Musharraf Spooked by His Spy Agency?," *Asia Times*, 12 March 2002.

24. Pamela Constable, "In Tribal Pakistan, an Uneasy Quiet: Pact Fails to Deter Backing for Taliban," *Washington Post*, 28 September 2006, A01.

25. Sreeradha Datta, "Islamic Militancy in Bangladesh: The Threat from Within," *South Asia: Journal of South Asian Studies*, vol. 30, issue 1, 145-170.

26. "Wallich," *Bangladesh Observer*, 12 September 2004, 1. Christine I. Wallich, Director of the World Bank officer in Dhaka received a bomb threat, allegedly from Islamist militants and left the country for Delhi. Such bomb threats may lead to a retreat of IGOs, NGOs, aid agencies of foreign governments, and private companies from Bangladesh. In addition, "South Asians for Human Rights," headed by former Indian Prime Minister Inder Gujral criticized the Bangladesh government for doing little to curb the bombings by Islamist militants. Also, Jamaat-e-Islami persecution of the Ahmadiya sect was criticized.

27. F. Alam and S. Rahman, "Perry's Fiction Coming True?," *Bangladesh Observer Magazine*, 3 September 2004, 9.

28. Datta, op. cit., 145-170.

29. Ibid.

30. Alex Perry, "Deadly Cargo," *Time Magazine*, 14 October 2002, On-line, Internet, available from http://www.time.com/time/magazine/article/0,9171,501021021-364423,00.html.

31. Prem Shankar Jha, "That other neighbor," *The Hindustan Times*, 13 August 2004, op-ed page. The article claims that ULFA extremists and other militants have camps in Northeast Bangladesh that are staging post for Islamist extremists attacking India. The growth in Islamist extremists was blamed on the large numbers (3 million) of guest workers who go to Saudi Arabia and elsewhere and return radicalized with Wahhabi-style Islam. The failure of state education system and rise of madrassas is a problem. Islamists are driving Hindus out of Bangladesh. According to the article Jagrata Muslim Janata Bangladesh is a terrorist organization, with "Bangla Bhai as one of its leaders, with 10,000 members and 300,000 supporters.

32. Interview with Moeed Yusuf, Institute for Sustainable Development Policy, who has links with Jamaat-e-Islami, 15 September 2006. He claims that 95 percent of Pakistanis are conservative Muslims and that less than 5 percent are radicals.

33. Interviews with Dr. Pervez Iqbal Cheema, Director, Islamabad Policy Research Institute; Dr. Bashir Ahmad, Senior Researcher, Institute of Regional Studies; Ishtafaq Ul Haque, journalist, Dawn newspaper; and Dr. Shireen Mazaria, Institute of Strategic Studies, September 2004.

34. Interview with Dr. Samina Ahmed, Director, International Crisis Group-Islamabad office, 14 September 2006. Interview with Prof Pervez Hoodbhoy, Department of Physics, Quaid-e-Azam University, Islamabad, 16 September 2006. Interview with Prof. Abdul Hameed Nayyar, Institute for Sustainable Development Policy, 16 September 2006.

35. Interview with Prof Pervez Hoodbhoy, Department of Physics, Quaid-e-Azam University, Islamabad, 16 September 2006.

36 Interview with Dr. Samina Ahmed, Director, International Crisis Group-Islamabad office, 14 September 2006.

37. "Pakistan: Data, Projects and Research," *The World Bank*, On-line, Internet, 17 September 2007, available from http://www.worldbank.org/pk.

38. Charles M. Sennott, "Radical Teachings in Pakistan Schools: Madrassas back Taliban, bin Laden," *Boston Globe*, 29 September 2006, 1.

39. Stephen Philip Cohen, "Demographic, Educational, and Economic Prospects," *The Idea of Pakistan*, (Washington, D.C.: The Brookings Institution, 2004), 231-266.

40. "Partnership for Education, July – September 2007," USAID, On-line, Internet, 17 September 2007, available from http://www.usaid.gov/pk/education/index.htm.

41. Ibid.

42. Interview with Prof. Abdul Hameed Nayyar, Institute for Sustainable Development Policy, 16 September 2006.

43. Interviews with James Rupert, Correspondent, *New York Newsday*, Islamabad, 13 September 2006.

CHAPTER 5

Why Women Kill:

A Look at the Evolutionary Role of Muslim Female Fighters

Farhana Ali

The numbers of Muslim female suicide bomber attacks are on the rise. Since at least 2000, women have participated in no fewer than 50 suicide operations. Most of these attacks have been conducted by Palestinian and Chechen women, but women of other nationalities and countries have either threatened the use of suicide or committed attacks, including events in Pakistan, Kashmir, Jordan, Egypt, Uzbekistan, and more recently, Iraq. In the present conflict in Iraq, as of August 2007, female bombers in Iraq have participated in at least ten suicide operations, but evidence from Arabic websites suggests that more Iraqi women are joining the Sunni insurgency to fight coalition Forces.[1]

Compared to male jihadis, the numbers of Muslim female bombers is low, but the slow and steady increase of *mujahidaat* participating indicates that the phenomenon is growing. Even with the relatively few attacks by Muslim women inspired other women to perpetrate acts of violence, particularly when they perceive that there are no non-violent solutions to the present conflicts in the Islamic world.

In the Arab-Israeli conflict, for example, the first contemporary women's suicide attack, by Palestinian Wafa Idris, motivated four other women to commit attacks within four months of her January 2002 self-destructive bombing attack in a Jerusalem marketplace.[2] Other Muslim women have referenced the successful attacks by Palestinian and Chechen women as cause for women in other countries to follow by example.[3] With no end in sight to various ongoing conflicts and armed struggles, additional women can become vulnerable to recruitment by Al Qaeda and other terrorist groups, such as Sunni and Shia militias in Iraq, to commit acts of violence for the benefit of male-dominated terrorist organizations.

Therefore, the gradual progression of suicide attacks conducted by Muslim women in new theaters of operation like Iraq suggests that women are just as capable of striking the enemy as men, and, in some cases, far more effective in evading an arrest and detection by rival security forces. For example, if covered in a Muslim dress, female bombers have been able to bypass suspicion from authorities, particularly in Islamic countries where Muslim women are traditionally respected for their roles as mothers, sisters, daughters, and wives of Muslim men – a status that by tradition bars men from touching or looking at another woman. These cultural and religious norms enable some women to exploit their gender to bypass security and get close to targets, thereby conducting successful attacks.

Why and how are Muslim women recruited or self-selected for suicide attacks? For terrorism analysts, the answer often lies in the woman's connections, direct or indirect, to the terrorist leader, other group members, organization, or the conflict. The answer may be traced to the ideological, historical, socio-political, or economic factors that impact their decision to choose suicide as a tactic of warfare. Some Western scholarship on this subject has emphasized the role of female emancipation within Islamic patriarchal societies, assuming that all would-be female terrorists are second-class citizens.

Clearly, it is difficult to draw firm conclusions about the motivations of all *mujahidaat* for a number of reasons. There is not much data yet on the record about their motivations. The sample is small, if growing. Only 50 cases have occurred in the past seven years. These 50 women conducted suicide attacks across several conflicts and the situations that motivated a *mujahidit* in Chechnya likely differed somewhat from those in Iraq, Afghanistan, Pakistan, Uzbekistan, or the Gaza strip. It is also likely that different women acted for different reasons, some personal to themselves, some in response to unique regional conflicts and circumstances.

What is clear is that something new appears to be happening. Progressively, more Muslim men and women are engaging in suicide or martyrdom attacks in numerous parts of the Muslim world. The recent use of women as suicide bombers is an even newer phenomenon that may require new responses by rival security forces.

Clearly, more work needs to be done to understand the possible motivation of potential *mujahidaat* in Iraq and elsewhere in order to reverse the present trend and influence them to take less violent and less self-destructive paths to conflict resolution.

As a consequence of more Muslim women ready to detonate by hiding the bomb under the *abaya*, security services will need to craft more innovative tools and strategies to counter a threat that is malleable, unpredictable, and seemingly invisible. Effective counterterrorism methods needs to include solutions that aim to improve the lives of women, particularly those living in war, occupation, and armed conflicts, as well as consider ways to deter women living in Western societies from joining terrorist organizations or encouraging their men to participate in suicide attacks. Thus, a multi-faceted strategy with a wide-range of options will provide security services, law enforcement, and intelligence officers the tools they need to mitigate a threat that has the potential to exponentially increase over time.

Abstract

In the past decade, more and more Muslim women have become suicide bombers, a new phenomena and a new threat to be understood and countered. Profiles of women in the global violent jihad tell us nothing about the female bomber, except that she could be anyone. While numerous studies of Muslim female fighters, or the *mujahidaat,* place emphasis on the profiles of individual female bombers, few researchers have looked at the relationship of the woman and her family, the terrorist organization to which she belongs, and the male clerics that justify her violent acts.

This chapter aims to address the sources of violence, motivational factors, and the space afforded to more Muslim women today to participate as suicide bombers. Secondly, behind most female bombers are Muslim men – from terrorist handlers to clerics – who recruit, reenergize, and are responsible for keeping the violent jihadi movement alive. This chapter contextualizes the arguments made by these men to understand the justifications they use to encourage Muslim female bombers.

Finally, recognizing the problem is not enough. Equally important to an examination of the threat are viable solutions that the United States and its allies could consider to minimize the emergence of more *mujahidaat*. This chapter offers policy recommendations to undermine the appeal of terrorism for women through bolstering Muslim women's empowerment and place in their societies. To this end, this chapter highlights important strategies to help reshape these women's identities and bolster constructive activism in the societies in which they live.

Introduction

Long before Al Qaeda began to see the utility in female bombers, some secular, nationalist terrorist groups have recruited women for suicide attacks. In Sri Lanka, nearly 50 percent of all terror group attacks were perpetrated by women belonging to the secular, nationalist terrorist group, the Tamil Tigers Elam, or the LTTE. In Chechnya, roughly 80 percent of attacks were initiated by women. In the Arab-Israeli conflict, increasing numbers of women are attempting or have succeeded in conducting suicide attacks, though the actual number of women remains unknown.[4] And in Iraq today, as of July 2007, at least ten women have committed terrorist attacks against Iraqi or American forces. Many of these women represent the anonymous or "invisible" face of jihad because their identities remain unknown to the public. Even Islamic websites taking credit for female bombers in Iraq rarely mention them by name, leaving no footprint of their background, citizenship, and marital status.

In my earlier work, I have argued the significance to these women fighters of identifying with other similar women, and conclude that these women are often greatly influenced by the example of others.[5] A *mujahida* who stages a particularly spectacular attack against a target, or whose ability to survive and excel in the male-dominated world of jihad, achieves stardom within her community and is a role model for emulation by other women worldwide. The female martyr serves as a model for future imitation and inspiration. Her fame can inspire other women to emulate the bomber's actions. I have asserted that "previous precedent set by women in a particular conflict or country has been shown to encourage other women to follow by example."[6]

Women suicide bombers are now participating in the insurgency in Iraq predominantly. Within the first six months of 2007, three women had already attempted suicide attacks. On June 6, 2007, a woman dressed in the *abaya* (ankle-length covered gown) was encountered by Iraqi police and refused to respond, prompting police to shoot at her and causing the explosives underneath her dress to explode before she reached her target. Unlike this failed suicide bomber, two other women in 2007 evaded detection by Iraqi and American authorities and were successful in their attacks. On April 10, 2007, an unknown female bomber in northeast Baghdad killed more than a dozen people while another woman in February 2007 entered a university and killed more than forty people.[7]

While it is too early to tell if more women will commit suicide via attacks in Iraq, information on Arabic websites from Iraqi-based Sunni insurgents and Shia militias suggests that their women are ready to sacrifice themselves for the "love of their country and faith."[8] A radical Iraqi Sunni website that is anti-coalition posted a statement from an anonymous insurgent source from al-Ramadi which stated that "there were four Arab female martyrs" who took part in the battles in al-Falluja, al-Mosul, al-Ramadi, Hadeetha, Tal Afar, Al-Qa'im, Ba'quba, and other cities throughout Iraq. Postings on the Internet suggest that women play an important role in the conflict in Iraq, and their inclusion in the war confuses the enemy and makes more difficult the efforts of coalition forces to distinguish between Iraqi civilians and the varied Sunni and Shia militants. These incidents signal an emerging trend of women in Iraq launching suicide attacks, or fighting alongside male insurgents, to weaken U.S. and pro-government Iraqi forces.

Attacks by Muslim women in Iraq are an Al Qaeda innovation. The use of women in Iraq is credited to the late terrorist leader, Abu Musab al-Zarqawi, the first *Salafi-Jihadi* to recognize a woman's operational utility. Known for his anything-goes, no-limit style (e.g., he initiated beheadings of kidnapped foreigners), it is no surprise that Zarqawi would use women – local and foreign – to strike at his perceived enemies. After Zarqawi's death, the tactic of using female bombers has continued. Zarqawi's cohorts and a plethora of Iraqi Sunni insurgent groups are now exploiting women more regularly to conduct attacks. Evidence on Sunni and Shia websites on the Internet are a clear indication that women, both Arab and

Iraqi nationals, are increasingly participating in the conflict as fighters, suicide bombers, and "mothers of the martyrs."[9]

To date, there has been no comprehensive study of the *mujahidaat* in Iraq. With few female bombers, in comparison to men, in Iraq, attention has naturally shifted toward other conflicts where the identities of female bombers are known or the use of female bombers has become an accepted norm. Unlike Palestinians and Chechen women before them who fought in their own nation, many of the female bombers in Iraq are not local Iraqis. Of the publicly known cases in Iraq, only one female bomber is identified as an Iraqi national, and she is the only one to have survived an attack – Sajida Rishawai. She is also the first Al Qaeda woman to have been tried and sentenced to life for a failed suicide attack in Amman, Jordan, in November 2005. While Sajida is a known operative, other female bombers in Iraq are a mystery to security forces. Therein lies the challenge.

If authorities do not know the identities of the women who have committed attacks in Iraq and elsewhere, how can they be expected to mitigate this new, emerging threat? To date, only a few women have openly declared their love for jihad by appearing in martyrdom videos. But the expression of female support for this movement is increasingly seen on the Internet. An insurgent group known as The Islamic Army in Iraq posted an article entitled "This is How Women Should Be" to encourage Muslim women to offer their husbands support in jihad until her death. More women are using the Internet to connect and reach a larger Muslim female population by logging onto female-only chat rooms on Islamic and Arabic websites, thereby enabling would-be *mujahidaat* to engage in an open and lively discussion about their role in jihad, martyrdom, and ways they can join terrorist organizations dominated by militant men. These websites include www.mujahidaat.com, www.ummah.com/forum, www.talk.islamic network.com, and http://forum.ribaat.org. Before its closure in June 2007, the website http://minbar-sos.com also provided a venue for women to seek justification for jihad.[10]

Motivations Vary

Given the clear role women are playing in jihadi operations, it is important to explore why and how Muslim women in different conflicts worldwide are recruited or are self-selected for martyrdom. It is accepted that we may never know the full range of motivations that push female bombers to suicide terrorism. Their reasons may vary from person to person, group to group, and conflict to conflict. As no two conflicts are alike, neither are the motivations of two Muslim female operatives, who likely join in the violence for a variety of reasons, some specific to themselves (i.e., individual retribution), some shared with others. For example, many Chechen women, including Hawa Barayev – the first Chechen female suicide bomber – sought revenge for the loss of male family members. For Barayev, the act was personal; she targeted her husband's assassin. For other women, including Belgium-born Murielle Degauque, who exploded her device on November 9, 2005, near a U.S. military patrol in Iraq, the motivating factor may have been to support the insurgents' fight against the coalition. Others fight to show their own patriotism. For many Palestinian women, the Israeli paper *Haaretz* noted that "suicide bombings have pulled women out of the boxes created by society – the box of a weeping, wailing creature always crying for help... Can anyone say that men are greater patriots than women?"[11] Still others take action to motivate their male counterparts, like Palestinian female suicide bomber, Ayat Akras, who said in her videotaped message before she detonated in a Jerusalem supermarket in March 2002: "I am going to fight instead of the sleeping Arab armies who are watching Palestinian girls fight alone."[12]

Despite varying motivations among women, research indicates certain common themes and patterns among these female bombers:

- Revenge for the loss of family members, and/or loss of community/ nation;

- Respect from the larger Muslim community for her sacrifice;

- Reassurance that she is a capable and equal partner in jihad; and

- Recruit other women to follow her example thereby glorifying martyrdom.

This list is not meant to exclude other factors that could inspire women to participate in terrorism. Professor Andrew Silke maintains that certain factors exist within a given community that enables groups to employ suicide. His argument assumes that groups using suicide have a "cultural precedent for self-sacrifice; the conflict is long-running...and involves casualties on both sides; and the protagonists are desperate."[13] Silke highlights the psychology of vengeance, social identification (i.e., the need to belong to a local or international community of believers), accessible entrée into a terrorist group, status and personal rewards, and the feeling of exclusion from mainstream society which leaves individuals vulnerable to religious indoctrination.[14]

Two factors in particular offer women a heightened sense of awareness of the world in which they live: a breakdown of a woman's societal structures (including, foremost, the loss of her family and community) and increased opportunities for women to volunteer for and join terrorist groups. With new openness to the participation of women, some – even those not living in war, occupation or armed struggle – may now embrace becoming members of a larger community, or what Islam calls the *Ummah* (Global Islamic Community). Scholars and psychiatrists refer to this as embracing a "collective identity."[15] Through the identification process, increasing numbers of women are being mobilized into terrorist organizations.[16]

The quest for identity and solidarity is, thus, seen as a powerful motive for some women to joint terrorists groups. However, this motivation may be only part of the story. Other researchers focus on ideological factors as the main reason why both men and women choose martyrdom operations, but more research still needs to be done to determine the importance of ideology as a motivator for women's inclusion into religious-based organizations. According to Mia Bloom, employing religious language to justify suicide attacks does not detract from the terror organizations' pursuit of power; "their political survival is ultimately more important than any ideology."[17] That a selective interpretation of Islam provides a powerful narrative and umbrella that legitimizes the creation of tactics used by terrorists, such as suicide, is important but may not be the only reason why male jihadis (and the women who join them) choose the tactic.[18] Few researchers insist that some women involved in terrorism may be motivated by the desire to be treated as equals by male members of their society, choosing violence as a means of trying to assert their rights as equals in Islamic patriarchal societies.[19] This view overlooks the historical context from which female terrorists emerge and fails to recognize the important role women have had across the Muslim world in nationalist struggles.

Most scholars agree, however, that jihadi leaders may encourage female participation in martyrdom operations to achieve tactical and operational success for the simple reason that women presently have a greater ability to get closer to their targets.

While it is difficult to discern the multiple reasons women may conduct attacks, there are common themes among them. First, female martyrdom in the Muslim world exists in a political framework that enables male terrorist leaders to mobilize segments of the population for its cause. For years, women have been a part of these secular, nationalist, and leftist movements, but in recent years, more women are perpetrating attacks on behalf of or in the name of Al Qaeda and its myriad of loosely affiliated groups. However, to date only few women have been known to lead resistance or participate violently in terrorist movements.

In the Muslim world, much attention has been given to Palestinian and Chechen female bombers and fighters, where we have the largest data of Muslim women engaged in conflict. The Arab-Israeli conflict is one of the oldest conflicts in which Muslim women have orchestrated attacks. This provides us with access to information about the region's network of male and female terrorists. Data collected by Yoram Sweitzer suggests that there were sixty-seven Palestinian women participating in martyrdom operations from January 2002 to May 2006.[20] This figure now seems too modest a number. Last summer, as many as 100 more Palestinian women belonging to the al-Aqsa Martyrs Brigade had reportedly been recruited to launch suicide attacks against Israel. A woman known as Um al-Abed told reporters in July 2006, "We are expecting more female suicide bombers. The new unit [of female attackers] is now preparing to launch attacks against Israel in response to the Israeli aggression and crimes against our people in the Gaza Strip."[21]

Second, the political goals of militant organizations are cloaked in Islamic terminology to give groups greater appeal, outreach, and the legitimacy they need to mobilize citizens into their social, political, and religious movements. Political aims vary and could include greater mobility and operational freedom for extremists (most groups exist within authoritarian regimes, are constrained by external pressures, or are under occupation); the creation of a recognized nation-state with increased political power to the terrorist organization; and/or the establishment of a *Khalifah* (Caliphate) which extends beyond national boundaries.

Third, women likely adopted suicide attacks as a mode of attack when conventional tactics were unable to have a considerable impact on the enemy or to affect the outcome of local conflicts. According to one female commander:

> The body has become our most potent weapon. When we searched for new ways to resist the security complications facing us, we discovered that our women could be an advantage.[22]

Fourth, some women view themselves as part of a larger Muslim family and simply want to take part in its struggles. According to one woman, "We're all freedom fighters. My brother's son is a martyr. He died fighting the Israelis. My cousin's son was killed by the Israelis... That's my family." In short, social affiliation to male bombers and radicalization born when they die provides women motivation for them to join and fight with terrorist organizations. Evidence from Palestinian female bombers seems to indicate that many of the female bombers to date were related to a male member of a Palestinian militant group. Finally, while the numbers of Muslim female suicide bombers are increasing, they are still extremely low relative to the much larger number of women who serve in an important, auxiliary role.

Existing data on female operatives indicate they are both young and old, single and married, educated and illiterate, as well as a mixture of mothers and women without children. The diversity among women participating in terrorist attacks today discounts any single "profile" of a female suicide bomber. The evidence suggests that the *mujahidaat* could be anyone. Moreover, the relative invisibility of the female bomber and lack of data about her makes her difficult to profile. Rather, an important area of research that "profiles the circumstance" of such attacks may be a more useful approach.[23]

What we do know is that an increasing number of Muslim women are joining the global violent jihad and claim to participate in attacks for the same reasons as militant men. Like men, the *mujahidaat* are impacted by personal, familial, organizational, and societal factors. While these women likely share the same frustrations, despair, and disillusionment with their male counterparts, women may have additional grievances that could stem from *personal* experiences and the roles they play within the larger community. Suicide may become the preferred choice when Muslim women believe their social structure, which is the fabric of an Islamic society, is threatened, has been violated, or is weakened by external and internal pressures.[24] Additional research will need to be conducted to confirm these hypotheses, although terrorists' propaganda, female chat rooms, and communiqués by women suggest that they choose violence when they can no longer nurture or sustain their role as mothers, wives, sisters, or daughters of the Muslim family and by extension, society. Today, with the steady increase in incidents involving Muslim female suicide bombers, there is a growing need to understand the evolution of women's role in Islam and particularly in conflict.

The Status of Women in the Koran

Any study of Muslim female fighters needs to consider the role and status of women in Islam in order to understand their motivations, and how their loss of rights in contemporary Muslim societies might affect them.

Numerous texts by Muslim and non-Muslim authors have highlighted an earlier golden age of Islam for Muslim women. For women, the coming of the Prophet Muhammad elevated their status within Arabian society. The birth of Islam abolished some pagan Arab rites, such as infanticide for newborn girls and the practice of prostitution. The Prophet's teachings also helped women achieve greater justice, protection, and emancipation, as is illustrated in several verses in the Koran, where for the first time in these societies, men and women are considered as equals in the eyes of God.[25]

These verses include:

> *And women shall have rights similar to the rights against them, according to what is equitable (2:228); And their Lord hath accepted of them and answered them: 'Never will I suffer to be lost the work of any of you, be he male or female: ye are members, one of another (3: 195);* and *If any do deeds of righteousness, be they male or female, and have faith, they will enter Heaven (4:124).*

Stressing the importance of women's equal footing with Muslim men, the Koran makes it clear that Muslim women are to be treated equally in matters of faith and accountability. Another illustration of this is highlighted in verse 16:97: *Whoever works righteousness, man or woman, and has faith, verily to him/her We will give a new life that is good and pure and We will bestow on such their reward according to their actions.* Therefore, men and women both are responsible for fulfilling their religious obligations, although Islam allows women exemption from Islamic teachings under certain conditions.[26]

In classical Islamic literature, women's role as mothers of an Islamic society is highly regarded. Among the most notable and popular *hadith* is "paradise lies at the feet of mothers."[27] The respect, honor, and status granted to mothers of Islam is not matched by any other role, not even that of a wife. But like mothers, who sacrifice their time and expend great efforts to raise their children and take care of the household, female martyrs are also honored for sacrificing the pleasures of earthly life for death, or martyrdom, to attain the Afterlife, or Paradise. Thus, women who participated in the early battles against the pagan Arab tribe, the Quraysh, to protect the survival of the new faith, were not only granted a place in Heaven but considered role models for adopting "correct" Islamic behavior.

These acts gained women an aura of respectability that enabled them to inspire other women in a different time and place to follow their stead. In addition, their sacrifices reshaped the context by which women in later conflicts could justify participation in violent action.

However, it is worth stressing that the sacrifice committed by Muslim women in the early Islamic period differs vastly from present-day female bombers. First, the first female warriors of Islam did not engage in suicide missions – a contemporary innovation that would have been considered heresy or *haram* (forbidden) by the classical scholars, including Muhammad, the Prophet of Islam. Second, the early women were considered heroines for having fought bravely against the enemies of Islam. Though few women were actually trained as fighters, most women performed an important auxiliary function as mothers, sisters, daughters, and wives of male fighters. Women who defended their homes while their husbands were at war are no different than women in other conflicts throughout history who have provided for their children and elderly in the absence of men.

But unlike her predecessors, the present day *mujahidaat* are employing terrorist activities that have been legitimized and sanctioned by some extremist Muslim clergymen who have revised the teachings of the prophet to increase the rate of adversary casualties, garner additional media attention, and more importantly, further the goals of the terrorist movement. How these Islamist leaders, who include terrorist leaders and ideologues, have generated arguments to attract, appeal, and accept women into patriarchal organizations can be explained by the need for collective action. Without women, who comprise one half of society, militant men probably understand that increased crackdowns by security services place them at greater risk for capture or being killed. With more militant Muslim men at risk, their women are being encouraged to fill an important gap.

A primary contention of this research is that the rise of Muslim female bombers is dependent on local conditions and are, thus, a consequence of terrorist leaders' ability to mobilize, recruit, and persuade women (and men) to join the global violent jihad in return for *immaterial* or other-worldly gains, such as the rewards of martyrdom for both men and women (*shahida*, feminine for martyr). Even women who are far removed from conflict and war, such as Muslims living in the West, have a shared sense of identity, religious affiliation, and ties to the *Ummah*. To the degree that such Muslim women are persuaded that the United States and the West were at war with Islam, they might sympathize or identify with Al Qaeda's cause, particularly if they were not fully integrated into the societies where they presently live.

A full account of Muslim female activism – and by extension, the role of men who recruit women – requires further attention, and should consider the impact of values and norms within a particular society that could act to persuade some women to choose violence. Thus, the role of culture and ideas, as interpreted by male jihadi leaders and their followers, can alter the choices women make and convince them that there is glory in suicide attacks. Couched in religious symbols and language, some Muslim women might choose to express their real-world grievances through violence.

Who Are the *Mujahidaat*?

The *mujahidaat* are Muslim women engaged in warfare. In the early centuries when Islam thrived under the Prophet's era and during the four proceeding Caliphates, the *mujahidaat* was a term that included women on the battlefield as well as those offering auxiliary support. They included women providing logistics, facilitation, and moral support. The term was applied loosely to include female nurses tending the wounded on the battlefield, women who donated their jewelry and wealth for the warfront, as well as women who encouraged their men – brothers, sons, husbands – to join the jihad to save the Muslim community[28] from falling prey to its earliest enemy, the pagan Quraish Arab tribe that rejected monotheism and prayed to any one of three hundred and sixty gods inside the Ka'aba, a house built in Mecca, Saudi Arabia, by Abraham, whom Muslims consider the Father of all religion. Other women accompanied men on the battlefield, dancing, beating drums, and singing verses of encouragement, to motivate the Arab men to fight: *We are the daughters of the Morning Star, our necks are adorned with pearls, our hair perfumed with musk. Fight fiercely and we will crush you in our arms.*[29]

In this study, the term *mujahidaat* is a specific reference to Muslim female suicide bombers of the past seven years and onward. Unlike the first female warriors, the role of the *mujahidaat* has evolved, to include the increasingly accepted tactic of suicide attacks when all "other strategies have failed to yield the desired results, and when faced with a hurting stalemate."[30] With this amended definition, the rules of engagement have been broadened; terrorist groups argue that fighting an asymmetrical war against more powerful foes forces them to consider new tactics and strategies to defeat their enemies. Like Jihadi men, some Muslim women view suicide as a legitimate act of defense, even though it is apparent that women rejected it in earlier centuries and the Koran bans it.

While suicide is increasingly used in select Muslim conflicts, nowhere in the historical religious literature is suicide or the killing of non-combatants sanctioned. Noted by an Islamic scholar, "Muslims are reminded in many Koranic verses that they should never commit aggression even towards their sworn enemies. Their response must not be disproportionate or go beyond the limits of the permission for armed jihad."[31] According to the Prophet of Islam, suicide prohibited a believer from entering Paradise, and yet the current literature of martyrdom by present-day jihadi groups argues the opposite. The main distinction is that militants reject the Western use of the word 'suicide' and choose to label their attacks 'martyrdom operations' (*'amaliyat istishhadiyaa*), recognizing that Islam strictly forbids suicide.[32]

The First Female Islamic Warriors

Classical Islamic literature and religious sources, including the Koran (Islam's holy book) and *hadith* (oral traditions) are rich with stories and examples of women contributing to the war effort. The tales of these heroic women are recorded not only in Islamic literature but were told to following generations to highlight the significant contribution women made to the faith in the seventh century A.D. Of these stories, the example of Nusayba bint Ka'ab – also known as Umm Umarah – is most widely known. In the Battle of Uhud (625 C.E.), it is reported that she lost one arm and suffered eleven wounds while defending the Prophet Muhammad.[33] She is one of the most celebrated Muslim fighters, having fought in at least six battles during her lifetime, and is mentioned in the Koran.[34]

While she was not the only woman on the battlefield, Umm Umarah's sacrifice for the Prophet and the new faith has been recorded in Islamic textbooks, stories, and historical memory.[35] An account of Umm Umarah's participation in the Battle of Uhud is described by Islamic scholar Nimer Busool:

> I went out early in the day to see what was happening. I carried with me a vessel full of water. I reached the Prophet and his companions while the Muslims were winning…but when they [the men] were defeated, and they started to flee, only ten men, my two sons, my husband and I stayed with the Prophet to defend him.[36]

This account would suggest that Umm Umarah was skilled in military training, unless by chance she knew how to use a sword to defend herself and the Prophet. A Western account of this story indicates that Umarah "pulls the sword from her girdle and cuts [a man coming towards her] on the thigh."[37] Busool concludes that women like Umarah, who fought using the archer and the sword, were trained and skilled in warfare.[38] Like Umm Umarah, Umm Sulaim and her sister Umm Haram bint Milhan from the tribe of *Ansar* in Medina joined the Prophet in the Battle of Uhud. Carrying a dagger, Umm Sulaim is recorded as having said, "O Messenger of Allah! I carry the dagger, so if any disbeliever approaches me, I will split his stomach open!"[39] Umm Sulaim's martyrdom is recorded in a *hadith*, in which the Prophet said, "I entered Paradise, and I heard somebody walking. I said, 'Who is this?' They said, 'This is al-Ghumaisa' bint Milhan (Umm Sulaim)."[40]

Like these women, the Prophet's own female relatives took part in warfare. His wife, Ayesha, led the Battle of the Camel, and his granddaughter Zaynab bint Ali fought in the Battle of Karbala. The Prophet's aunt and sister of his beloved uncle Hamza, Safiya, is "noted for killing a spy with a tent peg while her terrified male guard cringed nearby."[41] In the Battle of the Trench, Safiya killed a warrior and threw away his severed head into the enemy camp. After the Prophet's death, Muslim women continued to take part in warfare.

Most early Muslim women did not participate on the battlefield but provided support to those who fought.[42] Most notable among them is Hazrat Asmaa, who counseled her sons to pursue warfare. When the Syrians took hold of the Ka'aba in Mecca, her son Hazrat Abdullah sought his mother's advice: *My son! Degrading and disgraceful peace for fear of death is not better to being killed because to fight with sword in honor is better than to be beaten with a whip in dishonor.*[43] In another account, she is recorded to have told her son: "if you are fighting for the cause of Allah and are siding with truth, then you must put a bold front. Go and fight as befits a brave man…If you are martyred, it shall be my highest pleasure."[44] While Asmaa is not known for having participated in actual fighting, she "kept a long dagger with her"; she said she would use the weapon in case a thief entered the house.[45] Asmaa died at the age of 100, after the death of her son Abdullah bin Zubair, in the year 73 A.H.[46] Like Asmaa, the mother of Sayed Ahmed Shaheed, encouraged her son to fight in the name of the Islam: *My dear son! Go. But listen don't ever show cowardice. Fight valiantly. And if you run away from the battlefield, I shall never see your face.*[47] Shaheed was eventually martyred, fulfilling his mother's wish.

In later years, Muslim women in leadership positions fought to protect their dynasties. Three Muslim Queens – Sultana Razai Begum of India, Shahajar-ad-Dur of Egypt, and Begum Abish of Iran – led troops to battle and, in some cases, fought together with their warriors against the enemy.[48] Other women directed the affairs of the state in the Turkish and Mongol dynasties and were known by the title of "khatun."[49] In present day conflicts, before the use of suicide tactics, Muslim women continued to prove their military skills by fighting on behalf of the Muslim state.

For example, the late Ayatollah Khomeini extolled the participation of Iran's women in the 1979 war:

> We are proud that our women, young and old, [who fight] side by side with men.... Women who are capable of fighting take military training, which is a major prerequisite for the defense of Islam and the Islamic state.... They have bravely discarded the superstitions created by enemies of Islam and by the inadequate knowledge of friends of Islamic tenets.[50]

Khomeini's support of women on the war front was unique and afforded women an opportunity to address and raise gender consciousness. According to Iranian writer Maryam Poya, the 1979 revolution helped women take a "first step towards improving their status within the family, employment and the wider society."[51]

While Muslim women did not consider participating in suicide attacks until after 2000, one Christian Lebanese woman, Loula Abboud, "may have been the model for the first Palestinian women who became suicide bombers in 2002."[52] Before Palestinian women made headlines by a series of terrorist attacks, beginning in 2002, Abboud, the dark-eyed petite 19-year-old girl conducted a suicide operation in the Bekaa Valley of southern Lebanon in April 1985, "exceeding all expectations" for men and women in war.[53] Described by her brother as a woman "fighting for the liberation of her own homeland," Abboud's struggle for "self-defense" and to "save the children" is echoed by other Muslim women, including women of the first Palestinian *intifada*, who led a campaign to reopen schools, who taught underground classes for children, and who played an important role in "street activism that directly confronted the occupations forces."[54]

In short, Muslim women have recently begun to assume an operational role in warfare. In previous struggles for independence and nationalism, women have been active participants, but their involvement in suicide terrorism and their overall support for the global violent jihad has increased in the past six years.

The Difference between Jihad, Martyrdom, and Suicide

Understanding women in suicide terror requires an examination of how classical sources define jihad, martyrdom, and suicide. Replete with examples, the Koran and *hadith* collection provide historical context and religious rationale for when, how, and by whom jihad could be waged.

The Meaning of Jihad

In its simplest form, jihad is an act of Islamic worship. The Arabic word is derived from the verb, *jahada*, which means "effort and striving."[55] For the larger Muslim world, jihad is simply an everyday living, breathing concept. In recent times, the word "jihad" has been misinterpreted by extremists to suit their individual, organizational, and political objectives. As distinguished professor Mohammed Ayoob notes, "terrorism under a perverted definition of 'jihad' [allows] extremists [to] succeed in making political Islam appear monolithic and supremely dangerous in the eyes of the West."[56]

Contrary to popular Western myth, the word jihad has a broad semantic content, and is different from *qittal* (fighting). Both terms, jihad and *qittal*, have "significantly different meanings and uses in the Koran."[57] The latter word involves killing and bloodshed, whereas jihad, as a concept, is properly understood as defense of life, property, and faith against a clear aggressor. In one word, jihad is best described as *self-defense.* Defense against temptation, defense against Satan, defense against the unjust, and most commonly known in the West, jihad is defense against religious persecution. The Senior Advisor of the Muslim Public Affairs Council (MPAC) in Washington, D.C., Dr. Maher Hathout says:

> Historically, fighting back against aggressors was prohibited during the thirteen years of the Meccan period…[but] after the migration to Medina and the establishment of the Islamic state, Muslims were concerned with how to defend themselves against aggression from their enemies.[58]

After years of persecution and living in exile, the permission to fight came in response to a specific set of circumstances, and was "motivated by the fact that the Muslims suffered injustice and were forced to emigrate...without justification." Among the first Koranic verses for fighting is Verse 22: *Leave is given to those who fought because they were wronged – surely God is able to help them – who were expelled from their habitations without right.*

The rules for jihad are clear in Islam, and the salient points include: (1) jihad is legitimized when it is "recognized and established [by the] Muslim authority, as a policy of the collectivity of the Muslims, to deter aggression;"[59] (2) jihad is to be declared publicly in order to be accepted, vice the *coup de main* that Al Qaeda and other radical groups have been known for, hence, their clandestine lifestyle and operational behavior makes them identifiable with terrorism; (3) jihad is limited to combatants; and (4) finally, the ultimate goal of jihad is to cease hostilities and live in peace, rather than a continuum of conflict.

However, contemporary Islamic literature propagated by terrorists demonstrates a clear shift *away* from the classical sources use of the term jihad. Today, in the view of Al Qaeda and its affiliates, suicide attacks have become commonplace tactics and are rationalized as martyrdom rather than simple self-destruction. This interpretation is in direct opposition to the more popularly cited Koran verse, *And fight in the way of Allah those who fight you, but transgress not the limits. Truly Allah likes not the transgressors.*[60] The Koran permitted jihad within certain perimeters for self-defense. In these verses, the aim of fighting was threefold: "to stop aggression, to protect the Mission of Islam and to defend religious freedom."[61] But these early verses were to be disregarded and new definitions of permissible jihad were created by some Muslims after the fall of the Ottoman Empire in 1924. This might be attributed in part to the absence of a Caliph who could authorize the proclamation of jihad for Sunni Muslims.[62]

How jihad became confused with terrorism is the fault of contemporary jihadis who, in their literature, have ignored fundamental Islamic teachings and reapplied the term to suit their modern-day needs and struggles. To add credibility to the new meanings attached to jihad, some Muslim *ulama* (scholars) have now justified violence against civilian and military targets through numerous *fatwas* (pronouncements) to grant terrorists permission to fight *outside* the original perimeters of Islamic jurisprudence.

These scholars borrow from earlier pronouncements made by Abdallah Azzam, the veteran mujahideen coordinator in Afghanistan, texts by the early Egyptian revolutionaries, and *fatwas* by present-day Saudi-based clerics. Of note is the concept of jihad as *fard ayn*, or religious obligation, that was first introduced in a fatwa written by Azzam in *The Defense of Muslim Lands*: "jihad becomes *fard ayn* on every Muslim male and female."[63] No permission was needed from parents, husband, or creditor to wage jihad against the infidel – a consistent theme played in earlier and later works by such Islamic reformists, theorists, and terrorists.

Drawing selectively on classical Muslim scholars, Azzam quotes Ibn 'Abidin from the Hanafi school of thought in *Join the Caravan*:

> Jihad is fard 'ayn when the enemy has attacked any of the Islamic heartland, at which point it becomes fard 'ayn on those close to the enemy...[64]

In the same piece, Azzam provides sixteen motives for Muslims to fight, which are both for practical and ideological reasons. His sixth reason for waging jihad is to establish a solid foundation as a base of Islam, which, at the time, was to establish an Islamic nation in Afghanistan. Thus, the bulk of his writing focused on winning the 1979-1988 Afghan war.[65]

Defining Suicide

In Islam, suicide is strictly forbidden and considered a grave sin. The Prophet of Islam condemned it and various *hadith* suggest that the "gates of Heaven" would be closed to anyone who committed suicide. Centuries later, some contemporary Islamic scholars are now reaffirming the right of Muslims to defend their faith by participating in martyrdom operations, which they argue is *not* suicide or terrorism. According to Sheikh Faysal Mawlawi, deputy chairman of European Council for Fatwa and Research, martyrdom is justified but suicide is not. This justification is taken directly from the Koran: *"And spend of your substance in the cause of Allah, and make not your own hands contribute to (your) destruction; but do good; for Allah loveth those who do good."* (Verse 2: 195) The Sheikh further states that through the pursuit of martyrdom, a "Muslim sacrifices his own life for the sake of performing a religious duty, which is jihad against the enemy as scholars say."[66]

The Sheikh's statement is a common answer to the question of whether suicide attacks are justified or condemned in Islam. To justify suicide terrorism, terrorists deliberately avoid the term "suicide bombings" (*tafjirat intihariya*) probably to garner support from the broader Muslim community for their actions, and to dispel negative reactions that might occur from the use of the new tactic. Suicide terror also offers the terrorist organization a psychological benefit by way of increased media attention. The media coverage, for example, that female suicide bombers receive, as compared to male bombers, attests to the utility of suicide terrorism as *propaganda by the deed* insofar as it "generates a huge amount of publicity for the cause… [that] enables global awareness."[67]

Describing Martyrdom

Militants today claim that conflicts necessitate new rules of warfare to defeat the perceived enemies of Islam. Rather than use the term "suicide," these actions are described as *martyrdom* operations (*'amaliyat istishhadiyya*). Using this term helps justify the use of suicide or self-destruction as a tactic with religious backing. While available literature on female martyrdom is thin, the classical texts, namely, the Koran and *hadith* provide great detail on a martyr's importance in the religion.

First, the representation of death in Islam is as a part of the continuum of life, itself. Since life in *this* world is temporary, life in *that* world (Afterlife) has great appeal for Muslims, who believe entry into the Other World (i.e., Paradise) will guarantee them an eternal existence. Similar to other cultures and religions, death is understood as the gateway to a higher life, that is arguably more meaningful, long-lasting, and holier than existence on earth. In death, a Muslim is promised a meeting with God. An Indian Islamic scholar, in his seminal work, *What Happens After Death*, compares the believer to a lover, who is waiting to meet his Beloved (God):

> Nothing can please the lover except his meeting with the Beloved. The time of death is the time of meeting. The

lover always remembers the time of union…These are the people who earnestly desire early death.[68]

A similar theme is echoed in classical Islamic texts. In one *hadith*, a believer exclaims, *"O Allah! You know I always…loved death more than life. Give me death early so that I meet Thee!"*

Second, martyrs are held in high esteem in Islam. As evident in the Koran, numerous verses extol the unique position of the martyr. According to one verse, *"And say not of those who are slain in the Way of God: 'They are dead.' Nay, they are living, though you perceive it not."* (Koran 2:154) But now some Islamic theologians and contemporary jihadis distort several *hadith* to suggest that (1) female martyrs receive *fewer* rewards for martyrdom than their male counterparts; and (2) the male martyr is entitled to *more* rewards, though his entitlement to these rewards is mentioned neither in the Koran or popularly cited traditions of Imams Bukhari and Muslim.

Rather, some of the rewards attributed to male martyrs may be intentionally circulated to motivate, inspire, and activate the male bomber.[69] For example, a well-known and widely transmitted *hadith* of Imam Ahmad al-Tirmidhi explicitly notes that male martyrs will enjoy the pleasure of "72 virgins" in Paradise for their willingness to commit suicide. Tirmidhi's opinion on the rewards for the male martyr appears to be all encompassing and arguably enticing for a would-be male fighter:

> The Martyr has seven special favors from Allah: He [or She] is forgiven his sins with the first spurt of blood, He sees his place in Paradise; He is clothed with the garment of faith. He is wed with seventy-two wives from the beautiful maidens of paradise. He is saved from the Punishment of the grave. He is protected from the Great Terror (Judgment Day). On his head is placed a Crown of Dignity, a Jewel better than the world and all it contains, and he is granted intercession for seventy people of his household.[70]

This verse remains controversial. Not all scholars agree that "virgins" is the accurate translation for the Arabic word *houri*. Nowhere does the Koran or authentic *hadith* collections of Imam Muslim and Bukhair mention the rewards of "72 virgins." The promise of 72 virgins is even "reminiscent of the medieval Assassins" doctrine, but this concept is not recognized by the entire Islamic scholarship.[71] The Arabic word in the Koran, *houri*, is characterized in a sexual manner, hence, the translation of the word as "virgin," while others argue this is a reference to "pious companions." Noted in the translation of the Koran by a European convert to Islam, Muhammad Asad, the word *houri* is a reference for "one who is most pure" and "white."

More importantly, scholars opposing Tirmidhi's *hadith* argue that to believe in the verse is to negate all the social rights granted to women by the Prophet. To consider women anything less than equal partners with men would be to offend Islamic scholarship, particularly as it relates to female emancipation. In sum, the "72 virgins" concept has no basis in the Koranic exegesis, but is often cited in jihadi literature and propagated by terrorists.

Are There Rewards and Opportunities for Female Martyrs?

The gradual increase of suicide attacks perpetrated by Muslim female bombers over the last five years has prompted some Western scholars to focus on the question: are women granted 72 *houris* (commonly translated as "virgins") for suicide attacks? Or, more generally, are female warriors entitled to the same rewards of martyrdom as male fighters? Of particular interest to Western scholars is what do Muslim women hope to achieve by participating in suicide terror? Does this act of horror grant her a higher (gender) status? Is this higher status what they are primarily seeking? The issue over whether Muslim women intend to change their status within the society to which they belong remains unanswered but is hotly debated.

First, as noted earlier, most scholars disagree that Islamic men will receive virgins in Heaven, and the same holds true for women. While there is considerable debate on this point, David Cook argues that jihad is reinterpreted for women and, therefore, a female martyr will wait for her husband in Paradise rather than be entitled to numerous companions.[72] While Islam does not require women to join the fight, if she does, she is entitled to the same rewards as her male counterpart. The Prophet's first wife, Khadija, is considered the first female martyr because she supported her husband during the years the Prophet was persecuted by the pagan Arabs. Interestingly, Khadija and other women like her did not die on the battlefield, but is believed to have attained martyrdom by morally defending the faith.[73]

Secondly, assured of the rewards of martyrdom, women, like men, perceive they have nothing to lose. Participation in the conflict to alter the conditions for future generations is a common pattern among women, as noted by Eileen MacDonald when she interviewed Leila Khalid decades ago, as well as other statements made by women in terrorist websites and magazines. Printed in a Hamas monthly publication *al-Muslimah,* Palestinian operative Reem Rayishi said, "I am proud to be the first female Hamas martyr. I have two children and love them very much. But my love to see God was stronger than my love for my children, and I'm sure that God will take care of them if I become a martyr."[74]

One of the deeper questions under-explored in terrorism studies is whether the act of a woman seeking equality in jihad translates into equal rights for her gender from the men within her respective society.[75] While some women have sought a change to the status quo for participating in terrorism, the debate of what women hoped to achieve *as a result* of their involvement in armed conflict and terrorist operations, as opposed to a demand for change irrespective of their joining terrorist organizations, is not entirely clear.

Available literature indicates that Muslim women have participated in terrorist attacks to change the environment under which they live or conditions that could make women vulnerable to suicide terrorism. For mothers, the local context plays a critical role in defining her determination or will to either pursue terrorism herself or to support her children's (i.e., sons) entrée into terror organizations. In an interview with a member of the Palestinian Legislative Council, "Umm Nidal" Farhat, the mother of two male Hamas operatives, she said her role as a mother was to motivate her sons to jihad. In an interview on Saudi television, she said, "Jihad is a [religious] commandment imposed upon us. We must instill this idea in our sons' souls, all the time…this is what encouraged me to sacrifice Muhammad [my son] for the sake of Allah."[76]

Third, while women in much earlier battles of Islam were afforded a higher position in society for contributing to the war front, the same is not true for women in some contemporary battles. For example, Algerian women who formed underground networks and fought against the French colonizers (1958-1964), including in the Battle of Algiers, once again assumed traditional gender roles after Algerian independence.[77] On the other hand, women in the Palestinian *intifada* were determined not to meet the fate of their Algerian sisters. In June 1989, Palestinian women formed a Women's Higher United Council and "had drafted an Equal Rights for Women bill and placed it before the Unified Leadership." According to one woman, "we wanted the men to know that we have teeth too."[78]

By taking part in operations, it appears as though women are contesting the traditional roles assigned to them by patriarchal societies and terrorist groups. While women (including the veteran Palestinian female Leila Khalid involved in a myriad of successful hijackings in the late 1960s and early 1970s) enlisted and played a pivotal role in operations, they have not won greater rights, partly because Muslim women, according to Khalid, "were not on the winning side, at least not yet."[79]

Actions of women martyrs and fighters ensure, in part, that the discourse of women's rights and position in society remains an open issue. Attacks they conduct could stir a needed debate in the Muslim world regarding the role of women that could force a re-examination of existing norms. Reasons why male fighters have welcomed, though previously denied, Muslim women access to operations can be partly explained by organizational and societal needs. The vital contributions of the Muslim woman warrior/martyr are tactical advantages and maximized media shock value that accompanies her participation.

But despite their involvement in war, women in the early Islamic period (7th century A.D.) did not begin to enjoy anything like equal status in the religious law with men until a woman from the Quraysh aristocracy, Umm Salama, one day asked the Prophet, "Why are men mentioned in the Koran and why are we not?"[80] Her reply came in the form of a verse, "*Lo! Men who surrender unto Allah, and women who surrender to Allah, and men who believe and women who believe, and men who obey, and women who obey...Allah hath prepared for them forgiveness and a vast reward.*"[81] This verse, alone, was a "break with pre-Islamic cultural Arab practices, calling into question some of the customs that had defined relations between the sexes."[82]

Moreover, despite the previous prejudices and obstacles, women have an opportunity in present-day conflicts to change the perception that Al Qaeda and local terrorist groups are a male-only confederation. Their participation could prove to other women that she has a right to the "rewards" of martyrdom and her action can change the way local governments respond to the war on terror.

Many women are determined to raise the gender equality issue, even if it is not taken seriously by the male leaders of the organizations under which women serve. According to the Al Qaeda spokeswoman in Saudi Arabia, Umm Usamah, the success of attacks by Palestinian women elevated the status of the Arab woman, particularly after Wafa Idris' suicide bombing. In particular, editorials in Arabic newspapers glorified Idris' attack. For example, Adel Hammudu, editor of the Egyptian opposition weekly, *Saut al-Umma*, referred to Idris as "the bride of heaven, [who] elevated the value of the Arab woman and in one moment, [and] put an end to the unending debate about equality between men and women."

A separate Egyptian paper, *Al-Sha'ab*, hinted that Idris' had shamed Muslim men by committing an attack on behalf of the Palestinian nation: "It is a woman, a woman, a woman who is a source of pride for the women of this nation and a source of honor that shames the submissive men with a shame that cannot be washed away except by blood."[83]

However, it remains to be seen if male and female relations change much in Muslim societies as a result of female participation in violence and self-sacrifice. While her participation in suicide attacks serves the overall group or social movement, her individual contribution is still seldom recognized, except in martyrdom fests within the Palestinian territories where female bombers are deemed necessary for operational and strategic adaptation against a well-armed adversary.

Finally, men are likely able to manipulate some woman's participation in violence by employing religious language to garner her support. In clever propaganda, male jihadis claim that jihad is *fard 'ayn*, or an individual obligation incumbent on every member of society, including men, women, and children. Because no one is exempt, women have a duty to defend the faith, their people, and a larger/virtual Muslim Community. According to the former Palestinian female operative, Leila Khaled,[84] Islam has "only a role in determining the choice in how the [Palestinian] struggle is to be waged."[85] This, ultimately, however does not guarantee women an increased freedom and prestige when the jihad is over.

In short, women's participation in terrorism depended on a number of factors, that include personal motivations, and her desire to enter Paradise through a "martyrdom" (i.e., suicide) operation. While Islam makes it clear that women receive the same rewards as men, the material rewards for women are not equal. It remains to be seen if and when women who sacrifice their lives, property, and in a few cases, children, will stand on equal footing with men in their respective societies for participating in terror groups or acts. Having examined some of the women's motivations and rewards, this chapter now examines women's involvement in modern conflict, to include female support for violent jihad in Europe and the war in Iraq.

Contemporary Female Warriors

Most attacks in the past seven years have been conducted by Palestinian and Chechen women. While they comprise the majority of female bombers, they are not the *only* perpetrators of such violence. Attacks by women in Iraq since March 2003 while few in number (10) have steadily increased, while a larger number of women are attempting or supporting suicide operations in Europe, Kashmir, Israel, and Pakistan and have captured headlines. Thus far, nearly half a dozen Muslim women in Europe have been arrested and tried for terrorist-related activities, raising concerns of a possible growing network of female bombers in the West. In other conflicts, including Iraq, the fractured Palestinian territories, and Pakistan/Kashmir, women appear to be joining terrorist organizations in increasing numbers.

Across Europe, more Muslim women are being charged for their involvement in terrorism. Recent waves of arrests of women in a few European countries this year provide ample evidence that more women are supporting terrorist activities through propaganda, ideological support to male family members, and/or providing cover to male perpetrators.[86] This year, a Dutch Moroccan woman named Bouchara El Hor is currently standing trial for writing a letter to her husband encouraging him to pursue martyrdom. In the letter, she says, "The moment has come that you and I have to separate for the sake of Allah…I am so proud of my husband. I am happy that Allah has granted you the chance to be a martyr."[87] El Hor is an example of the supportive role women have historically provided to men in earlier conflicts and resistance movements, which is ideological and moral support to male family members. Arrests of other women are not yet made public due to ongoing investigations and intelligence collection. They include:

- UK-based sisters Yeshiembet Girma and Muembembet Girma, who are accused of helping the male jihadis involved in the 7/7 bombings escape;

- Samina Malik, a woman from West London is accused of possessing information likely to be useful to a terrorist; and

- Mehreen Haji who is suspected of terrorism fundraising along with her husband.[88]

In Switzerland, a martyr's widow, Malika el-Aroud, was arrested in June 2007 with her second husband for managing a webpage in support of Al Qaeda and the global jihad. In a CNN interview in 2006, Aroud had praised Osama bin Laden and glorified martyrdom. She said, "It's the pinnacle in Islam to be the widow of a martyr. For a woman it's extraordinary."[89] Like Al-Aroud, North African women in the Netherlands belonging to the Hofstad Group were arrested by Dutch police in November 2005, and included 21-year-old Soumaya Sahla for terrorist activities.[90] Sahla was arrested, along with her husband, for their intent to kill Ayaan Hirsi Ali, the former Dutch legislator, before Ali's move to the United States.

As more women across Europe are being tried for terrorism charges, scholars question whether the trend will duplicate itself in the United States. Thus far, only one woman – Pakistani-born Aafia Siddiqui – has been wanted by the Federal Bureau of Investigation for her alleged intent to orchestrate an attack with a band of male terrorists on U.S. soil. She is identified as the only U.S.-based Muslim woman to have had links with Al Qaeda leaders, but little else is known about her since her escape from the United States.[91]

In the Arab world, Palestinian women and local and foreign jihadi women in Iraq continue to present a security threat. Recently published work by Yoram Schweitzer examines the motivations of Palestinian female bombers, including the multitude of women who have failed and are currently serving time in Israeli jails. In his work, he maintains that women have contributed to the Palestinian cause through the intermingling of national and religious rhetoric. For example, the idea of nationalizing motherhood (i.e., the exalted status of the "Mother of the *Shahid*") has a strong appeal among women, who believe that mothers have a special role within Islamic societies. According to other experts, a "favorable social environment and a sympathetic media that disseminates favorable information within the supportive society"[92] helps explain why men are able to mobilize Palestinian women into their organizations. Through her environment, suicide bombers are drawn to the use of "religion, culture, or identity to give meaning to extreme violence"; U.S.-based scholar Mohammed Hafez couches this as "symbolic framings" which enables Palestinian operatives to legitimize "self-immolation as a meaningful act of redemption."[93]

In nearby Iraq, nearly ten known female suicide bomber attacks have been reported, although jihadi websites in Arabic suggest a much larger number, with more – including local and foreign women – fighting alongside Sunni insurgents and supporting Shia militias. Evidence suggests that the female suicide bombers in Iraq have supported Sunni insurgent groups, who have claimed responsibility for the participation of women. For example, the attack at Tal Afar by a "blessed sister" was affiliated with the *Malik Suicidal Brigade* and the *Mujahideen Shura Council* proudly claimed responsibility for a female suicide bombing in al-Muqdadiya in August 2006.

Other Arabic websites highlight the role of women on the battlefield as well as women protecting Iraqi male fighters. In a website known as the Iraqi League, a character called the "mother of the martyrs" or Um Qasim is a 65-year-old woman who is known to have stayed behind in Falluja while it was under siege to bury in her own garden several fighters killed in action.[94] Another website recognizes female suicide bombers in different Iraqi cities and indicates that these women are both local Iraqis and foreign (Arab) fighters, who defended their faith.[95] Other Sunni women in western Iraq are reported to be offering themselves for marriage to Arab fighters committed to fighting Coalition forces. These women are not asking for a dowry – a gift from the groom in exchange for a bride – because they are ready to accept the honor they would receive by becoming a martyr's widow.[96]

Some Iraqi Shia women are also supporting terrorist activities and/or are training for violent attacks. An Internet site indicates the formation of a group of Shia female assassins known as al-Zahra, who reportedly are training to kill Sunni men and women with conventional weapons. If true, it remains unclear who these women are and whether they will employ suicide tactics in the near future.[97] Like militant Sunnis, Shia men are seeking Iraqi wives through a process called *muta'a* or a temporary marriage, which enables them to take a wife during the duration of a war. While the practice is banned by Sunnis, Shia militias use temporary marriages to recruit Mehdi Army fighters – supporters of the al-Sadr organization directed by Muqtada al-Sadr – because it recognizes that most of these young men are unable to afford the expenses of a normal marriage.[98]

While most of the background of the women perpetrating attacks in Iraq is unknown, few suicide bombers have been identified. The only one female bomber to have survived an attack, Sajida al-Rishawi, is an Iraqi national from Ramadi in the Anbar province.[99] Her confession revealed information about her background and ties to Al Qaeda. For example, she revealed that she was the sister of a male terrorist leader killed earlier in Fallujah. She also described her motivations for participating in the attack with her husband who successfully detonated the bomb strapped to himself, killing at least twenty-three other people in Amman. She also identified the logistics of the terror plot.[100]

Another female bomber, who committed an attack on the outskirts of Baghdad on November 2005, was the first European Muslim convert, Belgian-born Murielle Degauque. While her attack failed to hit her designated U.S. target, it generated significant attention from the Western media. One such report stated, "It is the first time we see a Western woman, a Belgian, marrying a radical Muslim, and is converted up to the point of becoming a jihad fighter."[101]

While Al-Rishawi and Degauque are known operatives, many of the female bombers in Iraq represent the "invisible face of jihad."[102] For example, the names of female bombers in February[103] and April 2007[104] remain a mystery. The identities of women who committed earlier attacks in Talafar, northern Iraq, in September 2005 and April 2003 are also unknown. More recently, a failed suicide bomber on June 5, 2007, who was discovered near an Iraqi national police recruitment center near Sadr al-Qanat when she did not respond to orders by police to stop, is an anonymous female jihadi.[105]

Not knowing who the female bombers might be in Iraq poses security problems. A former Marine officer serving in Fallujah told the author, "Searching women is a difficult in a society where there are strict prohibitions against looking at another woman."[106] Intrusive inspections like American travelers go through at airports, including "pat downs" of suspects would be extremely unpopular in such societies. Cultural and religious norms in the Arab Muslim world therefore present unique challenges to United States and Iraqi security forces fighting a myriad of insurgent and militia groups in Iraq. Without the ability to search women closely enough to see if they are wired to explosives, Coalition forces will be vulnerable to female suicide bombers. In addition, the strict Islamic dress codes, where women are covered from head to toe, works to the advantage of females hiding explosive devices.

In several other Muslim countries, women have conducted armed attacks. For example, on April 30, 2005, two veiled Egyptian women in their twenties related to a male operative, Ehab Yousri Yassin, shot at a tourist bus in Cairo. One woman, Negat Yassin, was the bomber's sister and the other, Iman Ibrahim Khamis, his fiancée. They reportedly shot at the bus in revenge for Yassin's death which was caused by Egyptian authorities, and then they shot themselves,[107] probably to avoid capture. It remains unclear if the two women intended to commit suicide or chose the tactic to evade an arrest by Egyptian police.

Another female terrorist detonated a bomb in the ladies room in the Crocodile Coffee Shop in Ankara, Turkey, in May 2003. This may have been accidental for it is not known if the female operative intended to conduct a suicide attack or if the bomb explosion was an accident after she was scared off by the presence of a policeman.[108] That same year, two teenage girls were arrested in Rabat, Morocco, for terrorism offenses and some sources speculate whether the girls intended to conduct an attack against a liquor store.[109]

In Central Asia, outside of the Chechen conflict, only one suicide attack has been committed by a woman. A young Uzbek girl participated in a suicide attack in March 2003. Nineteen-year-old Dilnoza Holmuradova detonated explosives at Tashkent's Chorsu Market, killing at least forty-seven people, including ten policemen.[110] Dilnoza came from a solid middle-class background, was well-educated, spoke five languages, and unlike the vast majority of Uzbek women, she had a driver's license.[111] After dropping out of the police academy she was attending in 2002, Dilnoza began praying regularly, and in January 2004, she and her sister left home without a word to their parents.[112] Her recruitment by the Islamic Jihad Group, a radical offshoot of the Islamic Movement of Uzbekistan (IMU), likely resulted in her decision to carry out the operation. Dilnoza's actions are reflective of a larger problem in Uzbekistan. According to an independent sociologist, the ideological vacuum that resulted in the aftermath of the collapse of the Soviet Union – in which people became "impoverished and demoralized" – partly explains why Uzbek women were susceptible to being influenced by extremist organizations.[113]

In South Asia, radical women sympathetic to Osama bin Laden and Taliban's leader, Mullah Omar, are increasingly being used by Pakistan-based male jihadi groups and extremists, including religious political parties, to serve their interests and promote their cause. This year's protests by women clad in black *burqas* (Urdu for *abaya*) of the Jamia Hafsa seminary in front of the Laal Masjid, known as the Red Mosque, in the capital city of Islamabad is indicative of a trend that not only alarmed the Pakistani government but was an unprecedented move.

Before July 10, 2007, when the Pakistani government demolished the mosque and the madrasa for housing terrorists and threatening the state with suicide attacks, the women of the madrasa had violated the law by illegally encroaching on public land and threatened to initiate suicide bomb attacks should the state refuse to comply with Islamic law. Earlier this year, these women publicly demonstrated and told the press, "We are ready to give our lives for our religion. If any commando action is taken, it will be retaliated [against]. We are ready for *Fedai* (suicidal) attacks."[114] A retired Pakistani Brigadier General told the author that "men of the Laal Mosque are hiding behind these women; the presence of women in these jihadi groups represents the group's weakness. The men are the real cowards."[115]

To date, there have been no attacks by Pakistani women, but reports suggest that Pakistani security services remain on alert of female bombers. Pakistani security agencies were on alert in February 2007 for a possible female suicide bomber wearing "fashionable clothes and sunglasses" who could target the Pakistani Air Force (PAF) installations in Peshawar.[116] On October 1, 2007, it was believed that a suicide attack at a crowded police checkpoint in northwestern Pakistan was conducted by a woman.[117] But Pakistani police have confirmed that the bomber, wearing a *burqa* (head-to-toe-veil) and who killed at least fourteen others, including Pakistani police officers, disguised himself as a woman in the Islamic dress.[118] In the near future, men dressed as Muslim women as well as women in the conservative Islamic dress could both be a threat to Pakistan's internal security.

While female bombers would be a new trend in Pakistan, women's participation in the jihad in Pakistan or Afghanistan exists within the literature of jihadi magazines and has established an ideological role for women to support their men in the violent global jihadi movement – a role that is often overlooked. During the Afghan war, women backed male jihadis with logistics and facilitation support. A number of women also contributed significantly to the Afghan war by publishing articles in jihadi magazines. In one editorial, a woman writes, "We stand shoulder to shoulder with our men, supporting them, helping them…We educate their sons and we prepare ourselves…We march in the path of Jihad for the sake of Allah, and our goal is *Shahada* [martyrdom]." A few women played a more active role, which is unusual given strict customs of the Pushtun (or Pathan) tribe that prohibits women's participation outside the home. Various accounts of female operatives include women "using deception to kill American soldiers by blowing themselves up" or Afghani women taking revenge upon Americans for intruding on their homes and for "tak[ing] liberties with their honor."[119]

The emerging trend of women being motivated by men to chant slogans of jihad can also be traced to female-only *dars* (religious gatherings) across Pakistan and is evident in women's right-wing publications. A private discussion with a female journalist in Karachi indicated that there is an increasing number of Pakistani women, even among the elites, who participate in religious gatherings to protest against U.S. foreign policies and who are calling for jihad.[120] The propagation of jihad in these private, female-only gatherings also encourages women to adopt the ultra-conservative Islamic form of dress and reject Western ideals. According to a female professor of Gender Studies at Peshawar University, female students are now wearing the *burqa* in a city that was once known for its liberal and moderate Islamic practices.[121]

In Pakistani jihadi groups, women are also members of *Lashkar-e-Tayba* (LeT) – which is affiliated with Al Qaeda and is on the U.S. Department of State's list of terrorist organizations. Known as the Lashkar's Women Brigade, it reportedly is running a training camp for female militants in northern Pakistan.[122] In one article, a writer who is a member of Jamaat al-Islami also supported the idea of giving Muslim women basic combat training.

In October 2005, the first female suicide bomber died in an attack in Indian Kashmir, claiming the lives of five soldiers. A spokesman for the militant Pakistan-based group, *Jaish-e-Muhammad*, said the woman was a member of their group.[123] While this is the only suicide attack by a woman in Kashmir, this anonymous female jihadi has now set a dangerous precedent. Established in 1981, the women of *Dukhtaran-e-Millat (Daughters of the Faithful)* support Pakistan-based extremist groups and propagate jihad. According to their female leader, Asiya Andrabi, "Our goal is that this whole universe belongs to Allah…only jihad can protect the Islamic faith."[124]

Clerics Debate Legitimacy of Suicide Tactics and Participation by Female Bombers

In the Muslim world today, there is an important debate about the legitimacy or illegitimacy of suicide as a tactic of warfare. There is a second debate over whether females should be suicide bombers. In the aftermath of the 9/11 attacks and the July 2005 attacks in London, several Islamic scholars denounced the use of suicide as *haram* (forbidden) and *bid'a* (innovation) through *fatwas* (provocations) that were signed in a publicly available documents. Arguing for the rejection of suicide, the former head of Egypt's *Al-Azhar* Fatwa Committee, Shaykh 'Atiyyah Saqr, referred to a *hadith* to argue that the Prophet Muhammad said a believer would be forbidden from entering Paradise if he committed suicide.[125] More recently, a prominent Syrian cleric in London, Abdel Mon'em Mustafa Abu Halima, issued a separate *fatwa* prohibiting suicide operations. Also known as Abu Naseer Al Tartusi, Abu Halima noted, "whoever hurts a Muslim has no Jihad reward," which supports another *hadith* in which the Prophet of Islam is reported to have said: *"whoever murders a non-Muslim enjoying protection under the Islamic state would never smell the scent of Paradise.*"[126]

Despite these references, suicide attacks are justified by other Muslim clerics, including Doha-based Shaykh Yusuf Qaradawi, the late Dr. Abdallah Azzam, and several Saudi sheikhs. They argue that women can participate in jihad and do not describe such self destruction with the word "suicide." According to Qaradawi, the word "suicide is incorrect and misleading," and prefers to use the phrase, "heroic operations of martyrdom." In an interview with an Egyptian newspaper, Qaradawi justified attacks by stating that suicide/martyrdom operations are "the weapon of the weak,"[127] and argued the following point: *"When jihad becomes an individual duty, as when the enemy seizes the Muslim territory, a woman becomes entitled to take part"* in jihad.[128]

Qaradawi first issued a *fatwa* permitting women to partake in violent operations following the first attack by a contemporary Palestinian female bomber, Wafa Idris, in January 2002 at the entrance of a shopping mall in Afula, a city in the northern part of Israel. First published on the Hamas Internet site, www.palestine-info.info, and in the group's journal *Filisteen al-Muslima* in March 2002, Qaradawi said that Muslim women could disregard certain codes of dress and Islamic law to participate in martyrdom operations: "when jihad becomes an individual duty, as when the enemy seizes the Muslim territory, a woman becomes entitled to take part in it alongside men…and she can do what is impossible for men to do," even if it means taking off her *hijab* (headscarf) to carry out an operation.[129]

Before Qaradawi's *fatwa,* Abdullah Azzam in his book, *Defense of Muslim Lands*, argued for empowering women when he wrote they did not need their husband's permission to participate in jihad. In a separate *fatwa* published in 1984,[130] Azzam declared that "jihad was the action required (*fard 'ayn*) of every Muslim, regardless of gender."[131] He appealed to Muslim women to support the male fighters. In Part Two of *Join the Caravan* published in 1988, he wrote, "What is the matter with the mothers, that one of them does not send forward one of her sons in the Path of Allah, that he might be a pride for her in this world, and a treasure for her in the Hereafter through her intercession?"[132] As Azzam notes, mothers were essential to the jihad in Afghanistan against the Former Soviet Union. Through their support for male family members, which included their sons, husbands, and brothers, women were seen as playing a key ideological role.

Today, the debate among the *ulama* on the permissibility of suicide continues to divide the Muslim world; some view suicide as a legitimate tactic while others defy it on the basis that it was never employed by the Prophet of Islam, and therefore, suicide is *haram* (forbidden). Many scholars argue that suicide is one of the major sins in Islam that annuls one's faith,[133] and those knowledgeable of religious text often cite the Koranic verse, *Al Maeda,* which clearly rebukes those who kill: *He who kills anyone not in retaliation for murder or to spread mischief in the land, it would be as if he killed all of mankind, and if anyone saved a life, it would be as if he saved the life of the whole people.*[134]

The issue remains open to interpretation by various Muslim clerics and leaves the question unanswered. Most mainstream Islamic theologians reject the use of suicide as an appropriate response to state sponsored or group initiated violence. Other clerics are far more ambiguous about their position regarding suicide, but one point on which most clerics agree is the role of women in warfare. Several Islamic websites, including www.resalah.net, offer situations in which women could participate in jihad. According to the former website, the different ways Muslim women can support jihad include: raising children to love jihad; to assist male family members in matters in jihad; to engage in *da'wa* (proselytizing); to pray for the male fighters; and provide general support which would include facilitation activities.[135] Nowhere in the preceding statement is a woman encouraged to fight alongside men; the *fatwa* center on www.islamweb.net states "originally war was made a male affair. But women can participate in it if there is a dire need for it, and provided they would not be prisoners."[136]

Increasingly, terrorist leaders, such as Dr. Ayman Al-Zawahiri – Al Qaeda's number two – proudly cite examples of female jihadis, probably to encourage other women to fight for the cause. In an interview with *Al Majallah*, Zawahiri stated, "A British Muslim woman called Umm-Hafsah carried out another operation during which she killed two Americans."[137] Palestinian groups continue to boast about the ready supply of female martyrs to commit attacks against Israeli targets. An Al-Aqsa leader told a London newspaper in 2002, "We have 200 young women from the Bethlehem area alone ready to sacrifice themselves for the homeland."[138] Whether the *fatwas* permitting women to engage in violent action will spark much more use of female suicide terrorism is questionable. What the radical clerics have done, however, is grant would-be bombers, and women sympathetic to extremist causes, a religious justification to participate actively in jihad.

Policy Recommendations

Why women choose to kill or simply to support their men in violent jihad is of growing interest to intelligence agencies worldwide as they develop innovative tools to combat this new and emerging trend. Since 9/11, the focus has been on profiling the female bomber, but as evidence suggests, there is no one profile that matches the diversity of women active in jihad. Without a profile, security agencies and governments have been at a loss on how to counter a growing, and alarming, threat.

Given this diversity, security agencies face an enormous challenge as more women join the fight and commit acts of horror. For the intelligence officer, women are likely to be "invisible" when part of the global jihadi network. They are inaccessible and to the larger (Western) world, faceless. They only become known when they openly call for jihad, as is the case in women-only groups, or after having committed a suicide bombing. In the latter case, these women may never become known to the Intelligence Community.

Thus, the question becomes: how can the West and its allies counter a threat it knows so little about and to which it has little to no access? After all, women *and* men act in unison in the global violent jihad, and thus, any successful counterterrorism strategy must view women as part of Al Qaeda. It bears noting that while only a few women are engaged actively in violent jihad, more women are fighting for democracy and change. Of great encouragement are the vast numbers of Muslim women who oppose violence, which should convince even some skeptics that it is possible to mitigate the growing threat of the *mujahidaat*.

In addition, should the number of Muslim women committing suicide attacks continue to grow, it would still be the exception rather than the rule. Some terrorism experts understand that the jihad movement is not homogenous, and there are places where social mores are perhaps conducive to more "progressive" treatment of women's status. Even in Muslim societies where female fighters *appear* more to be the norm, (i.e., the Palestinian territories) it still remains unclear how long and how frequently Muslim women will conduct suicide attacks.

Despite the unpredictable role of Muslim women in future jihad operations, security agencies have reason to worry, given the number of female bombers over the past six years. While there have been just fewer than fifty incidents, such women have proven to be operationally useful to the terrorist organization and/or the cause for which they are fighting. Countering this new threat forces law enforcement, intelligence agencies, and governing authorities, such as community leaders and religious figures, to reconsider their policies and methods for identifying, targeting, and disrupting female terror networks. That the Federal Bureau of Investigation recognizes that "Al Qaeda is actively recruiting women"[139] is a critical first step that needs to be supplemented with a multi-pronged research and investigative approach that cuts across several disciplines.

First, success against female bombers necessitates that the U.S. Government, in coordination with foreign liaison partners, improve its intelligence gathering capability. In societies where contact with women is permissible, officers may want to evaluate strategies to improve their recruitment of women as intelligence assets to gain a better understanding of women's concerns and the drivers of violence. Recruiting women also can aid in penetrating more difficult and closed male jihadi groups, in which women play an active role. Improving intelligence resources, such as human and technical data collection, must coincide with a deeper understanding of the issues and challenges these women face in their respective societies.

Understanding the various stresses and conditions under which some Muslim women live, particularly in conflicts that further confines them to the home with little opportunities in the public space, (as a result of war or patriarchal norms, such as the Palestinian territories, Iraq and Afghan society), can help female officers gain access to these women. Gaining their trust and developing long-term relationships is one way security officers can help in the design of policies and programs where women are protected and made less vulnerable to terrorist recruitment.

Second, Western commanders, officers, and intelligence officers must think creatively about how to improve their outreach efforts. Western police officers must work more effectively with local imams to gain their cooperation. Female law enforcement officers should initiate contacts with local female activists, community leaders, academicians, and women's NGOs to garner their support in fighting the war against terrorism. Building these relationships is critical to improving the West's overall security against potential *femmes dangereuse*, such as Pakistani-born and American educated Aafia Siddique – the only Muslim woman on the FBI's "Most Wanted List" for her alleged ties with Al Qaeda.

Active recruitment of Muslim female police officers, intelligence analysts and field operators needs to be increased in the Muslim world to perform basic security tasks, such as searching women at airports and, if need be, conducting searches of women in their homes during raids. Using the example of the United Arab Emirates, where Sheika Fatima insisted that women be recruited to join the military to protect the tiny state, other Muslim female leaders worldwide could provide incentives and motivate their female citizens to join the armed forces. With enough evidence from the *hadith* literature and from the Prophet's time, Muslim leaders can show that women *did* fight alongside Muhammad, and therefore, female military officers, police, and intelligence officers are an essential resource for the protection of Islamic nations against terrorists, insurgents, or external threats.[140]

Third, countries need to involve women in peace and security initiatives. Studies have shown that women's inclusion in democratic change and institutions affords them greater opportunities to participate and shape civil society. Governments can advance the peace process by placing women in positions of authority to manage security issues. A forthcoming RAND study indicates that women's earliest inclusion in reconstruction activities is likely to improve the outcomes of post-conflict nation-building.[141] Western support for Muslim activist women, such as Malalai Joya, an elected representative to the December 2003 Loya Jirga[142] in Afghanistan and an advocate against violence, is necessary to ensure that women like her speak against radicalization and involve more women in the political process, despite the risks involved with such participation in such a country. Doing so can help women like Joya and others like her, to be a voice of moderation as well as a role model for other Islamic women.

In sum, providing alternative paths to social and political progress, other than through violence can counter the influence male jihadis will have in recruiting or encouraging Muslim women to join in a violent jihad.

These choices must be centered on fostering improving socio-economic opportunities, funding community-based development projects, centering women's activism on social issues (e.g., improving education for women), and supporting Muslim women's rights and social movements to strengthen their participation in the political and civil spheres of their society. Nurturing the different populations of Muslim women is the key to ensuring that the mothers, sisters, daughters, and wives of Muslim men pursue change in a peaceful manner and are less attracted to extremist ideologies and violent actions.

Conclusion

While it is impossible to accurately predict the future of this trend, the evidence strongly suggests women are active in jihad and will remain so in some capacity. We must begin now to counter women's potential to strengthen terrorist movements. Should suicide attacks increase among Muslim women, it would still be the exception rather than the rule. Some terrorism experts understand that the jihad movement is not homogenous, and there are places where social mores are perhaps conducive to more "progressive" treatment of women's status. Even in Muslim societies where female fighters *are* more the norm, (such as in the Palestinian territories) it still remains unclear whether women will win equal rights once the conflict ends in such male-dominated movements and societies.

In the short term, male fighters could encourage Muslim women to join their organizations, but there is no indication that these men would allow the *mujahidaat* to assume authority positions and replace images of the male folk-hero. There is also no evidence that Muslim female operatives will have contact or much influence with senior male jihadi leaders. Instead, their role is likely to be limited to simply executing attacks. Does this mean that those women are simply considered to be expendable?

Iraq will be a revealing litmus test of whether more women will be recruited for suicide operations. To date, nearly ten women have committed suicide attacks in Iraq. That number appears likely to grow. Chatter on Islamic websites over the past year reflect a new death squad in Iraq, a Shia female assassination unit, and Sunni insurgents also boast of women, whose identities still remain a mystery, that have participated in IED attacks. Should more women join Shia and Sunni militias, this might multiply the challenge to forces on the ground.

The solution to minimizing attacks conducted by women in the future in Iraq and elsewhere has to start with a peaceful settlement to the conflict and the provision of the opportunity for a better life. So long as such conflicts, wars, and occupations by forces outside the country in question continue, more women – and men – will join the global jihad.

Notes

1. On-line, Internet, June 2007, available from http://vb.roro44.com/42952.html.

2. It is worth noting that in modern-day resistance movements, an attack by a Christian Lebanese woman, Loula Abboud, may "have been the model for the first Palestinian women who became suicide bombers in 2002." Abboud, a 19-year old girl, conducted an attack in the Bekaa Valley of southern Lebanon in April 1985. For background, see Joyce Davis, *Martyrs: Innocence, Vengeance and Despair in the Middle East*, (New York, NY: Palgrave MacMillian, 2003), 68-72.

3. See interview in *Al-Sharq al-Awsat* with Umm Usama, leader of Al-Qaeda's Women's Organization in Saudi Arabia, (March 2003).

4. Israeli scholars have profiled Palestinian female suicide bombers in their work. For background, see Yoram Schweitzer (ed.), *Female Suicide Bombers: Dying for Equality?*, (Tel Aviv, Israel: Jaffee Center for Strategic Studies, 2006), and Anat Berko, *The Path to Paradise*, (Praeger, 2007).

5. Farhana Ali, "Ready to Detonate: The Diverse Profiles of Female Bombers," *The National Memorial Institute for The Prevention of Terrorism Annual 2006*, (MIPT, Oklahoma), 2006, 43-52.

6. Ibid.

7. "Suicide bomber strikes Baghdad university," *International Herald Tribune*, 25 February 2007, On-line, Internet, June 2007, available from http://www.iht.com/articles/2007/02/25/news/web.0225-iraq.php.

8. A website called The Iraqi Diaspora in Switzerland Forum posted an article and opened a discussion through its chat room on the subject of "The Girls of the Insurgency

and the Tempting Offer," On-line, Internet, available from http://www.iraqi.ch/forum/index.php?showtopic=648&pic=2512&mode=threaded&start=.

9. Ibid. Also, On-line, Internet, July 2007, available from http://www.iraqiarbita.org/index3.php?do=article&id=8267 and http://vb.roro44.com/42952.html. In the latter webpage, a woman by the name of Noofa Ghargan, 40 years of age, is considered the first Iraqi female woman to fall at al-Qa'im battles, where she fought with men against U.S. marines in al-Anbar province.

10. The webpage was directed by a woman of Belgian nationality and Moroccan descent, Malika al-Aroud, who is a widow of an Al Qaeda operative. For background on al-Aroud, see CNN documentary, "In the Footsteps of bin Laden" and article by Paul Cruickshank, "Suicide bomber's widow soldiers on," CNN world, 24 August 2006, On-line, Internet, available from http://www.cnn.com/2006/WORLD/asiapcf/08/15/elaroud/index.html.

11. Article by Arnon Regular, 26 May 2003.

12. Libby Copeland, "Female Suicide Bombers: The New Factor in Mideast's Deadly Equation," *Washington Post*, 27 April 2002, Ci.

13. Andrew Silke, "The Psychology of Suicide Terrorism," in *Terrorists, Victims, and Society,* Andrew Silke (ed.) (Sussex, England: Wley, 2003), 105-107.

14. For background of these factors, see Andrew Silke (ed.), "Becoming a Terrorist," in *Terrorists, Victims, and Society,* (Sussex, England: Wley, 2003), 37-51.

15. See John Horgan, "The Psychology of Terrorism," (London, Routledge, 2005).

16. Mia Bloom, "Mother, Daughter, Sister, Bomber," in *Bulletin of the Atomic Scientists*, Nov/Dec 2005. Bloom indicates that historically, women have served supporting roles but the "advent of suicide bombers has not so much annulled that identity as it has transformed it. Even as martyrs, they may be portrayed as the chaste wives and mothers of revolution," 56.

17. Mia Bloom, "Motivations for Suicide Terrorism," in Ami Pedhazur (ed.), *Root Causes of Suicide Terrorism*, (New York, NY: Routledge, 2006), 39.

18. Farhana Ali, *The Power of the Message: How to Use Information Warfare to Weaken the Enemy*, (RAND, forthcoming, 2008).

19. German-based researcher Katherina Von Knop of the George C. Marshall European Center for Security Studies in Berlin argues that women in patriarchal societies commit suicide terrorism as an act of liberation from male-dominated norms, customs,

and traditions. Other available literature and interviews conducted by other scholars does not come to this conclusion.

20. Yoram Schweitzer, "Suicide bombings: the ultimate weapon?" On-line, Internet, 19 November 2007, available from www.ict.org.il/articles/articledet.cfm?articleid=373.

21. Khaled Abu Toameh, "Al-Aksa announce female bomber unit," *Jerusalem Post*, 10 July 2006, On-line, Internet, 19 November 2007, available from http://www.jpost.com/servlet/Satellite?pagename=JPost%2FJPArticle%2FShowFull&cid=1150885963162.

22. Hala Jaber, "The Avengers," *The Sunday Times* (London), 7 December 2003, Features, 1.

23. This chapter presents several different likely motivators for different women across different conflicts. Because there is no single profile that captures all female suicide bombers, an alternative predictive approach is needed. Instead, profiling the circumstances or environment from which terrorism breeds (i.e., the roots of terror) can offer a useful framework from which to analyze the causal relationships between terrorists and their societies. It is also useful to look at individual relationships between the female bomber and the male handler, leader, or source of inspiration.

24. Research of female jihadis emphasizes personal motivations above all other motives. This includes a woman's personal link to a male member of a terrorist organization as well as the need to forge a new identity and acceptance from the larger community. A number of scholarly works address the importance of the personal individual (rather than group) decision in choosing suicide terror. For this literature, see Farhana Ali, "Ready to Detonate: The Diverse Profiles of Female Bombers," *The National Memorial Institute for The Prevention of Terrorism Annual 2006*, (Oklahoma, MIPT, 2006), 43-52; Farhad Khosrokhavar, *Suicide Bombers: Allah's New Martyrs* (London: Pluto Press, 2005), 131-137; Randy Borum, *Psychology of Terrorism* (Tampa, FL: University of Florida, 2004), 13; Deborah M. Galvin, "The Female Terrorist: A Socio-Psychological Perspective," *Behavioral Science and the Law*, vol. 1 (1983), 19-32; and Joseph Margolin, "Psychological Perspectives in Terrorism," in Y. Alexander and S. M. Finger (eds.), *Terrorism: Interdisciplinary Perspectives* (New York: John Jay, 1977), 273-274, and Ariel Merari, "The Readiness to Kill and Die: Suicidal Terrorism in the Middle East," in W. Reich (ed.), *Origins of Terrorism: Psychologies, Ideologies, Theologies and States of Mind* (New York: Cambridge University Press, 1990), 206. While individual rationale is important, an equally compelling discussion of jihad as a global phenomenon can not be discounted. Having transcended national boundaries, Faisal Devji instead emphasizes the importance of the global effects of jihad. For his viewpoint, see *Landscapes of the Jihad*, (New York: Cornell University Press, 2005).

25. For details of women's status in Islam and historical examples, see Barlas, Asma, *Believing Women in Islam*, (Austin, Texas: University of Texas Press, 2002);

Badawi, Jamal A. *The Status of Woman in Islam*, (Plainfield, IN: Muslim Students Association of U.S. and Canada, 1980), 12-23; Malik, Fida Hussain, *Wives of the Prophet*, Sh. Muhammad (Lahore, Pakistan: Ashraf Publishers, 1983), 24-62; Khairabadi, Ma'il, *The Great Mothers*, (Delhi, India: Markazi Maktaba Islami, 1996).

26. There are several instances under which they may occur; for example, a woman who is nursing her child may be unable to attend mosque prayers. A woman is exempted from fasting during her pregnancy and during nursing, if there is any threat to her health or her baby's.

27. On-line, Internet, July 2007, available from http://islam.about.com/od/elderly/a/mothers.htm and http://www.irfi.org/questions_answers/paradise_lies_at_the_feet_of_mot.htm. This hadith is quoted from Imam al-Tirmidhi, a famous hadith collector.

28. Busool, Assad Nimber, *Muslim Women Warriors*, (Chicago: Al Huda Islamic Educational Foundation, 1995), 34-35 and 64.

29. Heath, op. cit., 196-199.

30. Bloom, Mia, "Motivations for Suicide Terrorism," *Pedazur book*, 39.

31. Discussion with an Islamic scholar in northern Virginia, June 2007.

32. For a genre of literature on the benefits of martyrdom (*shahadat*), see essays by Shia scholars Ayatullah Mahmud Taleqani, Ayatullah Murtada Mutahhari, and Dr. Ali Shari'ati *Jihad and Shahadat: Struggle and Martyrdom in Islam*, Mehdi Abedi and Gary Legenhausen (eds.), (Houston, TX: Institute for Research and Islamic Studies, 1986); Sunni scholarship offers more diverse writings on the subject, including militant and moderate authors. For example, consider Sayyid Qutb, "Jihad in the Cause of God," in *Milestones*, (Cedar Rapids, IA: Mother Mosque Foundation, 1993), 53-76; Yusuf al-Qaradawi, "The Prophet Muhammad as a Jihad Model," Middle East Media Research Institute, Special dispatch no. 246, 24 July 2001, On-line, Internet, available from http://memri.org/bin/articles.cgi?Page=archives&Areasd&ID=SP24601; Majid Khadduri, *War and Peace in the Law of Islam, Book 2: The Law of War: The Jihad* (Baltimore: Johns Hopkins University Press, 1955), 49-73; Ibn Hazm, *Kitab al-Fasl fi al-Milal wa'l-Ahwa'wa'l-Nihal*, vol. 4, 135; Bassam Tibi, "War and Peace in Islam," in *The Ethics of War and Peace: Religious and Secular Perspectives*, Terry Nardin (ed.), (Princeton, NJ: Princeton University Press, 1996), 128-145; Rudolph Peters, "Jihad: An Introduction," in *Jihad in Classical and Modern Islam*, (Princeton, NJ: Markus Wiener, 1996), 1-8; and Moulavi Cheragh Ali, *A Critical Exposition of the Popular Jihad*, (New Delhi, India: Global Media Publications, 2003).

33. Busool, Assad Nimer, *Nisa Muslimaat Mujahimadaat* (Muslim Women Warriors), (Chicago, Illinois: Al-Huda Islamic Educational Foundation, 1995), 13-37.

34. Koran 3:153; and verse 33:35 was revealed after she asked the Prophet about the rights of women for performing duties of men, such as fighting in war. The verse, Surah Ahzab, is the first revelation that places men and women on equal footing in the eyes of God.

35. An Islamic web page, www.nusaybah.com, is dedicated to Umm Umarah. She fought in numerous other battles and is remembered most for having defended the Prophet at a time when female fighters were rare. She also encouraged her four sons to die for Islam.

36. Ibid.

37. Jennifer Heath, *The Scimitar and the Veil*, (Mahwah, NJ: HiddenSpring, 2004), 209-212.

38. Busool, op. cit., 34.

39. Ibid., 39.

40. Ibn Sa'd, volume 8, 430.

41. Heath, op. cit., 199-200.

42. Busool. op. cit., 34-35.

43. Ansari, Maulana Saeed Ahmed, Nadvi, Maulana Abdussalam, Nadvi Syed Suleman, *Women Companions of the Holy Prophet and their Sacred Lives*, (Bombay, India: Bilal Books, 1997), 148.

44. Khairabadi, op. cit., 10-11.

45. Ibid., 151.

46. Ansari, op. cit., 149.

47. Khairabadi, op. cit., 25.

48. Nur Ahmed, *Forty Great Men and Women in Islam*, (Delhi, India: Adam Publishers, 1994), 170-174.

49. For background, see Fatima Mernissi, *The Forgotten Queens of Islam*, (Minneapolis, MN: University of Minnesota Press, 1993), translated by Mary Jo Lakeland, 21.

50. "The Ashura Uprising," *The Words & Messages of Imam Khomeini*, (Tehran: The Institute for Compilation and Publication of the Works of Imam Khomeini, 1995), 11.

51. Maryam Poya, *Women, Work & Islamism*, (London, UK: Zed Books, 1999), 125. Also see 130-138 for Iranian women's political response to the new Iranian Islamic state. Poya argues that the revolution benefited only the religious women rather than the secular women, who responded to the Islamisation of the state by creating various women's organizations, each with their own literature and campaigns for women's rights. It is important to recognize that the revolution served the cause of only one type of women – the religious supporters of Khomeini. For additional background, see Bahar, S. "A Historical Background to the Women's Movement in Iran," in F. Azari, ed., *Women of Iran: The Conflict with Fundamentalist Islam*, (London, UK: Ithaca Press, 1983); Abrahamian, E., *Iran Between two Revolutions*, (Princeton, NJ: Princeton University Press, 1982); M. Afkhami and E. Friedl, *Women in Post-revolutionary Iran*, (London, UK: I.B. Tauris, 1994).

52. Joyce Davis, *Martyrs: Innocence, Vengeance and Despair in the Middle East*, (New York: Palgrave MacMillian, 2003), 68.

53. Davis, op. cit., 68-72.

54. Jennifer Plyler interview with Hanadi Loubani, a founding member of Women for Palestine, "Palestinian Women's Political Participation," WHRnet, 23 November 2003, On-line, Internet, 19 November 2007, available from www.whrnet.org/docs/interview-loubani-0311.html.

55. Jalal Abualrub, *Holy Wars, Crusades, Jihad*, (Florida: Madinah Publishers, 2002), 78-79.

56. Muhammad Ayoub, "Political Islam: Image and Reality," *World Policy Journal*, Fall 2004.

57. Ibid., 11.

58. Maher Mathout, *Jihad vs. Terrorism*, (Los Angeles: Multimedia Vera International, 2002), 49.

59. Hathout, op. cit., 65-66.

60. Koran, 2:190.

61. Mahmud Shaltut, *The Koran and Fighting*, (translation Rudolph Peters), (Leiden: E.J. Brill, 1997).

62. David Cook, *Understanding Jihad*, Berkeley and Los Angeles, California: University of California Press: 2005), 93.

63. Azzam notes in the article that Bin Baz "declared in the mosque of Ibn Ladna in Jeddah and in the large mosque of Riyadh that Jihad with your person today is *Fard Ayn* (global obligation.)" The fatwa also was signed by other Saudi-based clerics, including Sheikh Mohammed Bin Salah Bin Uthaimin.

64. Azzam, *Join the Caravan*, 23.

65. Azzam's understanding of jihad was neither novel nor revolutionary. Classical Muslim scholars and contemporary jihadis before him had provided a religious justification for jihad against the kuffar [disbelievers] and infidel Muslim rulers. Previous revolutionaries and writers had also stressed the importance of restoring hakkimiya [God's law] on earth to replace jahiliyya [barbarism]. They argued that resistance was the instrument to change. A central figure that Azzam references throughout his early work is the thirteenth century Islamic scholar, Taqi al Din ibn Taymiyyah, in present-day Syria. A chief feature of Tamiyyah's work was to unite Muslims at a time when they were divided into sects and innovations in the religion were paramount. His mission was to restore the religion to the al-Salaf al-Salih (the teachings of the Prophet, his Companions, and the first three generations in Islam).

66. For the Sheikh's full comments, see On-line, Internet, July 2007, available from http://www.islamonline.net/servlet/Satellite?pagename=IslamOnline-English-Ask_Scholar/FatwaE/FatwaE&cid=1119503543974.

67. Mia Bloom, *Dying to Kill*, (New York: Columbia University Press, 2005), 39.

68. Saeed, Maulana Ahmed, *What Happens After Death*, (New Delhi, India: Saeed International: 1995).

69. On multiple Islamic websites, such as www.alminbar.net, different Muslim clerics offer rulings on the merits of sacrifice and rewards for the martyrs. In a *khutbah* (Friday sermon) on "the virtues of martyrdom" by Usaamah Khayyaat, numerous *hadith* are cited to motivate Muslims to support Palestine. Among the collections noted, Khayyaat refers to a *hadith* by two well known Islamic narrators, Imams Bukhaari and Muslim: "*Nobody who enters Paradise would ever wish to return to this life again, even if he was to be given the whole world and everything in it – except for a martyr; for he would wish to return and get killed ten times due to the honour that he received (in*

Paradise)." Other Islamic scholars on the Fatwa Bank at www.islamonline.net discuss the merits of martyrdom and the different types of martyrs.

70. Well-known and widely transmitted *hadith* of Imam Ahmad al-Tirmidhi.

71. For a historical background on the Assassins, see Akbar, M.J., *The Shade of Swords: Jihad and the conflict between Islam and Christianity*, (New York: Routledge, 2002), 195.

72. See David Cook, "Women Fighting Jihad?" *Studies in Conflict and Terrorism*, 28 (2005), 380.

73. While Islam offers a broad definition for martyrdom, men and women in warfare are entitled to the following rewards: All their sins are forgiven with the first drop of blood; He/She enters Paradise and Allah makes him/her intercede for 70 family members; a martyr will not feel the grave trial, which begin directly after a person dies [when the soul is questioned by two angels about his/her worship and a person's deeds]; a martyr will not be horrified by the Great Gathering on the Day of Resurrection [Day of Judgment]; and a martyr will not feel pain of the killing except like that of a pinch. These traditions reflect the ultimate reward: the entry to the highest gardens of Heaven (*Jannat al-Firdaws*), also known as the Seventh Heaven, where the Prophets, his Companions, and pious believers are promised entry. In one tradition, the Prophet described a river in Paradise (*Al-Kawther*) with "banks of gold; its mud is Musk; its water is sweeter than honey and it is whiter than ice." The scent of musk is also used for the martyr, whose body will smell of musk when the martyr enters the Afterlife. A vivid description of Paradise for believers and martyrs is described in *Surat al-Rahman*: "*a place where there will be two garden, abounding in Branches; in them each will be two springs flowing free, with fruits of every kind...they [believers and martyrs] will recline on carpets...the fruits of the gardens will be near.*" Therefore, in Islam, the rewards of martyrdom are guaranteed for both men and women alike, regardless of gender.

74. In 2004, an Al Qaeda magazine published a special section dedicated to the recruitment of women for terrorist attacks highlight the story of Umm Hamza, who was "very happy whenever she heard about a martyrdom operation carried out by a woman, whether it was in Palestine or Chechnya." The article further states that Umm Hamza would cry waiting for a martyrdom operation "against the Christians in the Arabian Peninsula," a reference to Saudi Arabia. (See the ninth issue of *Sawt al-Jihad*, Al Qaeda's propaganda arm in Saudi Arabia).

75. Few researchers have tried to answer this question but do not all agree. Professor Cindy Ness contend that female participation in militancy and terrorism "may not indicate a trend in gender reform [but] does speak of a major transformation in the pattern of participation by females in political violence that needs to be understood." See her introduction in *Studies in Conflict & Terrorism*, 28: 349-351, 2005.

76. Interview by Nabil Hammad with Palestinian Legislative Council Member, "Umm Nidal" Farhat on *Iqra* TV (Saudi Arabia), 1 February 2006, On-line, Internet, May 2007, available from Memritv.org.

77. Eileen MacDonald, *Shoot the Women First*, 74-145.

78. Ibid., 7.

79. Eileen MacDonald, *Shoot the Women First*, 8.

80. Tabari, *Tafsir*, Dar al-Fikr edn, vol. 22, 10.

81. Pickthall, *The Meaning of the Glorious Koran*, sura 33, verse 35.

82. Mernissi, op. cit., 119.

83. Cited in MEMRI Inquiry and Analysis Series, No. 84, 13, February 2002, On-line, Internet, 19 November 2007, available from http://memri.org/bin/opener.cgi?Page=archieves&ID=IA8402.

84. Leila Khaled, a member of the Marxist group, The Palestine Front for the Liberation of Palestine (PFLP), became widely known after her role in a series of airline hijackings in 1969-1970. She is most famously known for leading a daring hijacking of four airlines on 6 September 1970, which resulted in the destruction of three aircraft and her own capture.

85. Toby Westerman, "Cheerleader for female suicide bombers," 31 January 2002, On-line, Internet, 19 November 2007, available from http://www.wnd.com/news/article.asp?ARTICLE_ID=26261.

86. The arrest of 27-year old lab technician Marwa Dana in connection with the Scotland and London terror plot in July 2007 could provide clues into women's supportive roles. At this early stage, it is unclear what role she played although her husband, Mohammed Asha, a Jordanian neurologist, appears to have direct involvement with key suspects, including Iraqi doctor, Bilal Talal Abdullah. For background, see Emily Flynn Vencat, "Probing the British Terror Plot," *Newsweek*, 5 July 2007; Kevin Sullivan and Craig Whitlock, "Foreign Doctors Queried in Bomb Plot," *Washington Post*, 4 July 2007, A10.

87. For contents of El-Hor's letter, see "Wife urged man to die for jihad, court told," *The Guardian*, 31 May 2007, On-line, Internet, 19 November 2007, available from http://www.guardian.co.uk/uk_news/story/0,,2091705,00.html.

88. The identities of these women was provided to the author by a former BBC reporter who is now gathering material for a documentary for the United Kingdom's Channel 4 on female jihadis.

89. Paul Cruickshank, "Suicide bomber's widow soldiers on," *CNN World*, 15 August 2006, On-line, Internet, 19 November 2007, available from http://www.cnn.com/2006/WORLD/asiapcf/08/15/elaroud/index.html?iref=newssearch; also see "Swiss to try 2 Muslims accused of supporting terrorism via Web sites," *International Herald Tribune*, 5 June 2007, On-line, Internet, 19 November 2007, available from http://www.iht.com/articles/ap/2007/06/05/europe/EU-GEN-Switzerland-Internet-Terror.php.

90. Article published in 2007 by Lorenzo Vidino of The Fletcher School at Tufts University explores the members of the Hofstad group. See "The Hofstad Group: The New Face of Terrorist Networks in Europe," *Studies in Conflict & Terrorism*, 30:579-592, 2007. Also see "Dutch Police arrest 21-year old Female Terrorist Suspect," *AFP*, 3 November 2005.

91. For background, see Deborah Scroggins, "The most wanted woman in the world," *Vogue*, March 2005. Scroggins is writing a book tracing Siddiqui's ties to Al Qaeda and apparent disappearance to Pakistan, forthcoming.

92. Kimhi and Even; and Reuven Paz, "Suicide and Jihad in Radical Palestinian Islam: The Conceptual Side," Tel Aviv: Moshe Dayan Center for Middle Eastern and African Studies, August 1998.

93. Mohammed Hafez, "Symbolic Dimension of Suicide Terrorism," in *Root Causes of Suicide Terrorism*, edited by Ami Pedazhur.

94. On-line, Internet, July 2007, available from http://www.iraqirabita.org/index3.php?do=article&id=8267.

95. On-line, Internet, July 2007, available from http://www.bramjnet.com/vb3/showthread.php?t=2234.

96. On-line, Internet, July 2007, available from http://www.iraqi.ch/forum/index.php?showtopic=648&pid=2512&mode=threaded&start=.

97. Bakier.

98. Analysis provided to the author by Iraqi expert Dhafira al-Azzawi of the Lincoln Center, July 2007.

99. For al-Rishawi's background, see articles On-line, Internet, November 2007, available from http://www.pbs.org/newshour/bb/terrorism/july-dec05/bombers_11-

14.html; http://news.bbc.co.uk/2/hi/middle_east/5366438.stm; http://news.bbc.co.uk/2/hi/middle_east/4433712.stm.

100. Ibid. Al-Rishawi's confession, On-line, Internet, 19 November 2007, available from www.msnbc.msn.com/id/10027725/.

101. Castle, Stephen, "Girl next door who became a suicide bomber," published in Brussels, 2 December 2005.

102. Farhana Ali, editorial, "The Bomber Behind the Veil," *The Baltimore Sun*, November 2005.

103. Damien Cave and Wisam A. Habeeb, "Blast Kills 40 as Cleric Faults Baghdad Plan," *New York Times*, 25 February 2007, On-line, Internet, 19 November 2007, available from www.nytimes.com/2007/02/25/world/middleeast/25cnd-iraq.html.

104. Haifa Zangana, "The Iraqi resistance only exists to end the occupation," *The Guardian*, 12 April 2007, On-line, Internet, 19 November 2007, available from www.khilafah.com/kcom/analysis/news-watch/the-iraqi-resistance.

105. "Iraqi Cops Say Shot 'Female Suicide Bomber,'" *Iraq Updates Online*, 5 June, 2007, On-line, Internet, November 2007, available from http://www.iraqupdates.com/p_articles.php/article/18055.

106. Interview conducted in April 2007. The officer is now studying law at Harvard Law School.

107. "Attacks injure nine in Egypt," *Columbia Daily Tribune*, 1 May 2005, On-line, Internet, 19 November 2007, available from http://www.showmenews.com/2005/May/20050501News020.asp.

108. See Farhana Ali, "Muslim Female Fighters: An Emerging Trend," *Terrorism Monitor*, vol. 3, issue 21, 3 November 2005, On-line, Internet, June 2007, available from accessed at http://www.jamestown.org/terrorism/news/article.php?articleid=2369824.

109. "Girls guilty of terror charges," *BBC News*, UK edition, On-line, Internet, June 2007, available from http://news.bbc.co.uk/1/hi/world/africa/3153110.stm.

110. IWPR Staff in Central Asia, "Uzbekistan: Affluent Suicide Bombers," RCA No. 278, 20 April 2004.

111. Ibid.

112. Ibid.

113. Ibid.

114. Pakistani newspaper, *Daily Times*, 2 February 2007. Also see article on this subject by Farhana Ali, "Dressed in Black: A Look at Pakistan's Radical Women," *Terrorism Monitor*, vol. 5, issue 8, 26 April 2007, On-line, Internet, May 2007, available from http://jamestown.org/terrorism/news/article.php?articleid=2373351.

115. Phone interview in March 2007.

116 "Female Bomber may Target Pakistan Air Force: Report," *The Peninsula*, 25 February 2007, On-line, Internet, 19 November 2007, available from http://www.thepeninsulaqatar.com/Display_news.asp?section=World_News&subsection=Pakistan+%26+Sub-Continent&month=February 2007&file=World_News2007022521322.xml.

117 "15 Die in Pakistan Blast," 1 October 2007, On-line, Internet, 19 November 2007, available from http://www.cnn.com/2007/WORLD/asiapcf/10/01/pakistan.bombing.ap/index.html.

118 "Burqa bomber kills 16," *Daily Times*, 7 October 2007, On-line, Internet, 19 November 2007, available from http://www.dailytimes.com.pk/default.asp?page=2007%5C10%5C02%5Cstory_2-10-2007_pg1_6.

119. David Cook, "Recovery of Radical Islam in the Wake of the Defeat of the Taliban," *Terrorism and Political Violence* 15 (2003), 40-43.

120. Interview occurred in Pakistan with the Karachi-based journalist in February 2007.

121. This period is the pre-Afghan jihad era. The female professor is of the Pashtun tribe and has lived in Peshawar her entire life. The trend of young girls now adopting the black burqa raises concerns of an austere "Islamization" process that is undoubtedly led and arguably enforced by men.

122. *Times of India*, 6 April 2007.

123. "Kashmir 'woman suicide attacker,'" *BBC News*, 13 October 2005, On-line, Internet, 19 November 2007, available from http://news.bbc.co.uk/2/hi/south_asia/4337412.stm.

124. Interview of Andrabi by Swati Parashar in spring 2007 offers insight into the DeM's motivations, support networks, and ties to male jihadis. Her articles and dissertation are forthcoming.

125. "Ask the Scholar," *IslamOnline.net*, 21 May 2003, On-line, Internet, 19 November 2007, available from www.islamonline.net.

126. "Salafi Jihadi Trend Theorist Turns against Al Qaeda and Issues a Religious Opinion of the Impermissibility of Suicidal Operations," *Al Sharq Al Awsat*, 2 September 2005, News from Al Mendhar, On-line, Internet, available from www.almendhar.com.

127. "Debating the Religious, Political and Moral Legitimacy of Suicide Bombings," MEMRI – No. 53, 2 May 2001, On-line, Internet, available from http://memri.org.

128. "Ask the Scholar," *IslamOnline.net*.

129. Ibid.

130. The idea that jihad is *fard,* or an obligation on all members of the Muslim society, demand that women, like men, play an active role in militant organizations. Even when jihad is not *fard* and is instead, *fard kifaya* (duty for select male members of society), women were not obliged to fight but did participate in warfare in the early days of Islamic history, as indicated earlier. While the concept of *jihad* as a religious obligation for all Muslims is not new, its reintroduction into contemporary jihadi literature signals a shift towards mandating jihad for all Muslims worldwide, making it incumbent for Muslims living *outside* of conflict to help those in need (i.e., wage jihad). Borrowing from the ideas of classical theologians, Azzam reinvents jihad by attaching to it symbolic drama to propagate a consistent Al Qaeda message: Muslims comprise a single "Nation" and must unite to resist anti-Islamic aggression through the use of obligatory defensive jihad.

131. "The Union of Good", On-line, Internet, July 2007, available from www.intelligence.org.il/eng/sib/2_05/funds_f.htm.

132. Abdullah Azzam, *Join the Caravan*, Part Two, (London, U.K.: Azzam Publications, 2001).

133. Abualrub, op. cit., 209-211.

134. Verse 32.

135. On-line, Internet, August 2004, available from www.resalah.net.

136. On-line, Internet, 13 June 2006, available from www.islamweb.net.

137. "Paper Cites Al-Zawahiri's Al-Majallah Interview, 'Sensational Revelations'," in *Al Arab al Alamiyah*, 17 December 2001.

138. Anne Applebaum, "Girl Suicide Bombers," 2 April 2002, On-line, Internet, available from www.slate.com.

139. Jessica Stern, "When Bombers are Women," *Washington Post*, 18 December 2003, sec. 1A, 35.

140. In her book, journalist Geraldine Brooks in the chapter "Jihad is for Women, Too" provides an excellent study of women across the Muslim world who have participated in guerrilla warfare and joined the military. Countries that have encouraged active women's participation in combat also include the Persian state of Iran. See Brooks, *Nine Parts of Desire*, (New York, NY: Anchor Books, 1995), 107-118. Brooks also indicates the disappointment of female fighters, who after returning to their homes at the end of the war between Ethiopia and Eritrea, women had to assume their traditional roles; she writes, "the traditions of the wider society outweighed the culture that had developed at the front" of the battlefield, (117).

141. Forthcoming report, *Women and Nation Building*, RAND Corporation.

142. Known as the Grand Council. Joya was elected to the Loya Jirga convention in Kabul to create Afghanistan's new constitution. According to a report from Democracy Now, at the convention, Joya spoke against the appointment of fundamentalist leaders, who she deemed as "war criminals who should be on trial." Her outspokenness has resulted in a number of death threats against her. See report, On-line, Internet, July 2007, available from http://www.democracynow.org/article.pl?sid=04/09/13/1428254.

CHAPTER 6

"Like Glitter of the Sun": Iran and Terrorism

Gregory F. Giles[1]

> ...[E]xporting the revolution is like glitter of the sun of which rays...brighten the entire world.
>
> –Ayatollah Ali Khamene'i, April 1988[2]

The Islamic Republic of Iran remains the world's leading state sponsor of terrorism.[3] This terror is directed at a range of targets: regime dissidents at home and abroad, Israel, other Muslim states in the region, the United States, and other Western interests. This commitment to terrorism reflects various interlocking motivations but is rooted in the Islamic Republic's founder, Ayatollah Khomeini, who insisted that the regime's survival lay in "exporting the revolution." As the quote above makes clear, Khomeini's successor as Supreme Leader, Ayatollah Khamene'i, fully subscribes to this view.

Khamene'i sits atop Iran's vast terrorism apparatus that includes major government entities such as the Ministries of Intelligence and Security (MOIS) and Foreign Affairs (MFA), as well as the Islamic Revolutionary Guard Corps (IRGC). A number of top current and former Iranian officials are the subject of international terrorist arrest warrants, effectively proscribing their foreign travel. The involvement of its state-owned banks, "charitable" foundations, and front companies has earned Iran the distinction of "central banker of terror."

Moreover, Tehran is at the center of a *global* network of affiliated terrorist groups who often do its bidding, particularly Lebanon's Hezbollah. Iran supports and has linkages with a number of Sunni extremist groups – including Al Qaeda – that defy the usual Shi'a-Sunni antagonisms. In essence, "the enemy of my enemy" is a terrorist art form in Tehran. Directly and indirectly, Iran has conducted terrorism-related operations within the United States and covert action against U.S. forces abroad, as mounting evidence in Iraq and Afghanistan makes clear. Undoubtedly, terrorism will also figure prominently in any Iranian response to U.S. attacks on its terrorist training camps or nuclear facilities.

This chapter addresses the motives and means of Iranian-backed terrorism. It briefly looks back at Tehran's involvement in terror since the early 1980s, considers current dimensions of the problem, and speculates about the future of Iranian terrorism, particularly in the area of weapons of mass destruction (WMD). Finally, the chapter raises important issues for senior U.S. military commanders. As the analysis demonstrates, Iran has been, and is likely to remain, wedded to terror as a major policy tool, requiring a wide-range of U.S. responses.

Patterns of Iranian Terrorism

To be sure, political violence in Iran predates the current regime. Indeed, Persia and Shi'ism bear witness to a history of bloodshed that stretches back over a millennium. Nonetheless, for the last quarter-century, terrorism has been a principal policy tool of the Islamic Republic. This unbroken pattern underscores the contemporary elite consensus behind Iranian terrorism, as it spans the presidencies of all four major political factions: traditional conservatives (Khamene'i, 1981-1989), pragmatists (Rafsanjani, 1989-1997), reformists (Khatami, 1997-2005), and ultra-conservatives (Ahmadinejad, 2005-present). Moreover, the common denominator since 1989 has been former president and current Supreme Leader Khamene'i, who remains committed to upholding his predecessor's violent stance. Iran has modified its approach to terrorism over the decades, but these have been tactical shifts in application rather than repudiation of principle.

1980s: Unbridled Revolutionary Fervor

With their heady victory over the Shah in 1979, Iran's mullahs sought to solidify and validate their Islamic Revolution by replicating it in neighboring states through incitement and support of Shi'a uprisings.

Such prospecting in Lebanon received a major boost following the Israeli invasion of that country in 1982. Iran responded by dispatching between 2,000-3,000 IRGC troops to help organize, train, equip, and direct a fledgling Shi'a militia there which operated under the name "Islamic Jihad" – what has since become known as Hezbollah (Party of God). At Iran's instigation, and with Syrian support, Hezbollah carried out a spectacular series of suicide car bombings in Lebanon in 1983 that killed 241 U.S Marines deployed in Beirut as part of a multi-national peacekeeping force, as well as killing another 26 Americans at the U.S. embassy. Tehran also used Hezbollah to carry out a wave of kidnappings of Americans and other foreigners in Lebanon.

Also during this time, Iranian-backed Shi'a terror spread to Kuwait, Saudi Arabia, and Bahrain, Sunni Arab monarchies that were bankrolling Saddam Hussein's increasingly bloody war against Iran. In parallel with this effort to coerce the Gulf Arabs to withdraw their support for Saddam, Iran also cultivated ties with the militant group al Dawa (Islamic Call) and was responsible for the formation of the Supreme Council for the Islamic Revolution in Iraq (SCIRI). These anti-Bathist Shi'a groups would provide Iran with major strategic advantages over the United States decades later in the struggle for influence in post-Saddam Iraq.

Tehran also used violence to disrupt the annual pilgrimage or hajj to Mecca in 1987-1989 in order to undermine the Saudis' role as protector of Islam's holy places. The types of attacks during this decade included suicide and non-suicide vehicular bombings, assassinations, hijackings, and kidnappings.

Also throughout this period, Iran conducted a major campaign to liquidate regime dissidents at home and abroad. Under Khomeini's orders, many thousands of political prisoners in Iran were summarily executed. Regime opponents were also hunted down and assassinated in neighboring Turkey and Pakistan, as well as across Western Europe and in the United States. Iran's terrorist wrath also broke new ground by targeting private citizens in foreign countries, specifically the author Salman Rushdie, a British national whose novel, *Satanic Verses*, was deemed blasphemous in Iran, and for which Ayatollah Khomeini personally issued a fatwa (i.e., a religious decree) calling for the author's murder.

The 1990s: Global Reach

Iranian-backed terrorism witnessed a relative lull in 1990, mainly due to the crisis sparked by Iraq's invasion of Kuwait. Once the Gulf War passed, however, several of the patterns established by Iran in the 1980s continued to play out in the decade that followed. For instance, former Iranian Prime Minister Shapour Bakhtiar was assassinated in Paris in August 1991. Nearly 30 more regime oppositionists would be assassinated before the Rafsanjani presidency ended in 1997.[4] Among them were four Iranian opposition figures gunned down at the Mykonos restaurant in Berlin. A German court found that Iranian Intelligence Minister Ali Fallahian had ordered the hit with the blessing of President Rafsanjani and Supreme Leader Khamene'i. Anti-dissident assassinations continued under Rafsanjani's successor, Khatami, in such places as Iraq, Tajikistan, and Pakistan, as well as Iran itself. Again, these assassinations would not have been possible without the sanction of Supreme Leader Khamene'i.

The major development of the 1990s was Iran's demonstrated ability to apply its terror tactics around the globe. In 1992, Iran orchestrated the suicide truck bombing of the Israeli embassy in Buenos Aires, Argentina, killing 29 and injuring another 242. Two years later, an attempt to blow up the Israeli embassy in Thailand was foiled when an explosive-laden truck nearby was involved in a traffic accident. Four months later, Tehran struck again in Buenos Aires, killing nearly 100 and wounding over 300 at a Jewish community center in another suicide truck bombing. An Argentine court later determined that the attack had been ordered by top Iranian officials and carried out by Hezbollah operatives.

Sensing increasing isolation and threats to its interests, Iran responded to the U.S.-led triumph over Saddam Hussein's forces in Kuwait and the Madrid Arab/Palestinian-Israeli peace conference in 1991 by stepping up its support for Palestinian rejectionist groups, regardless of religious affiliation. This included Hamas and Palestinian Islamic Jihad (PIJ), notably Sunni organizations. Also during this time, Iranian operatives in Sudan established an informal agreement with Sunni extremist Al Qaeda to cooperate against their common American and Israeli enemies.[5]

The hostage crisis in Lebanon came to an end in 1992, with some Americans being killed while others were released. Evidently, Tehran had concluded that it was time to move on. By 1996, however, Iran had turned its attention back to U.S. military forces in the region. As later announced by U.S. Attorney-General John Ashcroft, Iran had "inspired, supported, and supervised" the attack by Saudi Islamic militants on the Khobar Towers complex in Saudi Arabia, which killed 19 U.S. servicemen.[6]

Since 2000: From Terrorism to Multi-Front Covert War

Having provided support to Hezbollah and Palestinian rejectionist groups for years, Tehran was in a strong position to exploit Israel's withdrawal from Lebanon in May 2000 and the Palestinian uprising or "second intifada" that broke out in the fall. At the beginning of 2002, Israeli forces intercepted the *Karine-A* cargo ship carrying $15 million worth of Iranian arms for Yasser Arafat's Palestinian Authority. The incident marked an unexpected escalation of the Israeli-Palestinian conflict by Tehran, which had previously denounced Arafat for compromising with "the Zionist entity."[7]

The 9/11 Commission later reported that Tehran had facilitated the movement through Iran of many of the Al Qaeda hijackers that executed the September 11, 2001, attacks, although the full extent of any Iranian foreknowledge of the operation remained an open question. As Al Qaeda leaders fled subsequent U.S. attacks in Afghanistan, a number of them found safe haven in Iran and put it to full use. U.S. officials linked the May 2003 suicide bombings in Saudi Arabia, which killed 26 including 9 Americans, to the Al Qaeda leaders Iran was harboring.[8]

Shortly after the fall of Saddam Hussein, Iran began to infiltrate IRGC operatives, clerics, and social workers into Iraq to solidify ties with Iraqi Shi'a and lay the foundation for actively supporting the insurgency against Coalition forces. This included training insurgents to use and build so-called explosively-formed penetrators (EFP), which have taken such a high-toll on U.S. troops in Iraq. More publicly, Tehran began a drive to recruit suicide bombers in Iran for operations against the West. In one of his first TV appearances as president, Mahmoud Ahmadinejad praised suicide bombing as "beautiful, divine art." To increase pressure on U.S. forces in Afghanistan, Iran also supplied weapons to its hitherto sworn enemy, the Sunni extremist Taliban.[9] In essence, Iran has spent the past few years adapting its terrorism apparatus and cultivating ties with co-religionists as well as foes in order to wage a covert war against the U.S. military presence in the Middle East and Central Asia.

Why Iran Resorts to Terrorism

Terrorism has found acceptance as a policy tool in Iran for a variety of mutually-enforcing reasons. As summarized below, some of these have to do with the regime's perceived strengths and weaknesses, others with facets of Iranian culture and Shi'ism. Ultimately, it is the ability of terrorism to deliver the desired results with minimal costs that makes it so attractive to Tehran.

"Khomeini's Legacy: Offense is the Best Defense"

Like revolutions that have preceded it, the Islamic Revolution looked outward for validation, so sure were its architects that they had achieved the model society for mankind. This notion of spreading revolution struck a particular cord in Shi'ism, which sees itself as a persecuted sect and which claims to offer salvation for all the world's oppressed. The Islamic Republic's founder also anticipated that the regime would find a hostile reception internationally, indeed Khomeini personally instigated it:

> We must strive to export our Revolution throughout the world, and must abandon all ideas of not doing so, for not only does Islam refuse to recognize any difference between Muslim countries, it is the champion of all oppressed people. Moreover, all the powers are intent on destroying us, and if we remain surrounded in a closed circle, we shall certainly be defeated. We must make plain our stance toward the powers and superpowers and demonstrate to them...Our attitude to the world is dictated by our beliefs.[10]

Iran's current Supreme Leader hews closely to this line, as evident in a February 2007 message:

> The modern paradigm [of the Islamic Republic] has presented a new course of action to humanity, a course...

aimed at putting an end to the conflict between worshipping the Almighty and populism in practice. Never has it been expected that the systems founded on wealth and military power...would remain inactive in the face of this phenomenon and abstain from opposing it...

Today, the major duty of officials of the Islamic Republic...is not to hesitate about treading the path to the accomplishment of the Iranian nation's noble objectives...By divine favor and assistance, they should take the course of action that has been delineated by the exalted Islam and manifested in the deeds of the late Imam Khomeini and bolstered through the self-sacrifice of martyrs and war-disabled veterans.[11]

Thus, exporting the revolution was shrewdly linked to the regime's survival by its iconic founder. The destruction of Israel was similarly erected as a pillar of Khomeini's creed. To challenge these central precepts is to question his legacy and the regime's raison d'etre. Even if he was so inclined, Supreme Leader Khamene'i lacks both the religious credentials and charisma to mount such a challenge,[12] and the political ascendancy of the ultra-conservative faction embodied by Ayatollah Taghi Mesbah Yazdi and his follower President Ahmadinejad would staunchly resist such revisionism in any event.

The Sanction of Shi'a Islam

A rich tradition of religious scholarship has developed in Shi'ism, where many mujtahids, or Islamic scholars are simultaneously able to offer independent, authoritative interpretations of the Prophet Muhammad's teachings.[13] In many areas, including terrorism-related subjects, it is possible for competing interpretations to exist. For instance, while narrations from the Prophet Muhammad make clear that terrorism is forbidden, the Eighth Imam (a bloodline descendent of Ali, the Prophet's cousin and son-in-law, considered divine or infallible by Shi'a) notes that the "murdering of the infidels" is permitted if they are "murderers or aggressors."[14] Similarly, while Shi'ite jurisprudence absolutely prohibits suicide, Grand Ayatollah Fazel Lankarani declared that, "If one guesses or knows that by defending himself or his relatives, he will lead himself to death, defense is, not only allowed but also obligatory."[15] Such competing interpretations enable the Islamic Republic to assert that it does not engage in terrorism, but rather "legitimate resistance," as sanctioned, if not obligated, by Islam.

Despite the prevalence of Shi'a suicide bombings since 1983, contemporary Shi'ia scholars have yet to take up the issue in a comprehensive fashion. Instead, a small number of individual ayatollahs have issued their personal opinions via fatwas, with evident polarization. Thus for example, moderate Grand Ayatollah Saanei implicitly criticized the Supreme Leader, stating in 2006 that "terrorism must be hated in any form. And if a powerful and influential figure supports only a small number of these terrorists, he must be condemned as well."[16] In contrast, Supreme Leader Khamene'i has written in support of suicide bombing: "if an obligatee, on the basis of his own judgment, feels that the territory of Islam is in danger, he must rise up for defending Islam, even if he might be subject to death."[17] Khamene'i's maximalist stance apparently recognizes no geographic boundaries, for although Shi'ite jurisprudence limits jihad to defense and then only to Muslim lands,[18] the Islamic Republic has conducted terror attacks as far afield as Western Europe, Argentina, and Thailand. In sum, as long as the regime can call upon extremist Grand Ayatollahs to provide Islamic sanction, it is doubtful that a strictly jurisprudential approach can force Iran out of the terrorism business.

Terrorism "Works"

In the eyes of the ruling mullahs, terrorism has yielded some stunning successes over the years, particularly the rapid withdrawal of the U.S. military from Lebanon in 1983, following the U.S. embassy and Marine barracks bombings. These successes fuel Iranian expectations of imminent victories elsewhere. For example, after suffering years of suicide bombings, President Ahmadinejad notes that Israel is now a "dried tree that will fall in a single storm." Doubtless, Tehran hopes to replicate its Lebanon success in Iraq and Afghanistan, as well.

Iran likely perceives a range of other benefits from supporting terrorism:

- Advocacy of unrelenting Palestinian militancy increases Iran's popular appeal amongst Muslim communities while simultaneously depicting rival Sunni Arab regimes as "lackeys of America and Israel." This has given Tehran access to and influence over events in the Middle East that it would otherwise lack.

- More broadly, Tehran's ability to turn up the level of violence in the region at will has enabled it to claim, accurately, that there can be no peace in the Middle East and increasingly Central Asia, without taking into account Iran's views. This "negative power" helps fulfill Iran's self-image as the region's natural hegemon.

- The holding of American hostages in Lebanon gained Iran access to desperately needed U.S. arms for the war against Iraq. Additionally, subsequent exposure of the "arms for hostage deal" by Iranian extremists produced a major domestic and foreign policy setback for the Reagan Administration.

- Terrorism against Israel keeps the "Zionist entity" off-balance, forcing it to focus on internal security and reducing its "appetite" for external military operations against Iran (i.e., pre-emption of its nuclear facilities).

- The threat of terror provides a key escalatory threat that could contribute to deterring direct U.S. or Israeli attacks against Iran, a growing threat in the eyes of some regime leaders.

- The dissident liquidation campaign has minimized the risk of organized opposition to the regime.

- Terrorism provides "employment" for dangerous extremists who might otherwise pose an internal security problem for the regime.

- Terrorist attacks are a ready means to embarrass and undermine domestic political factions seeking better relations with Iran's enemies.

On occasion, pragmatists among the ruling clerics have warned that certain types of terror were working against larger Iranian goals. In particular, then-President Rafsanjani observed by 1985 that terror against the Gulf Arab regimes was hardening their opposition to Iran and not reducing their support for Saddam's war against it. After a hiatus in 1986 failed to produce any tangible benefits for Tehran, however, Iranian-backed terrorism returned to Kuwait and Saudi Arabia in 1987.[19] Indeed, it would be another decade before Riyadh would fully re-establish diplomatic ties with Tehran – on the condition that Iran stops supporting Saudi opposition groups.[20]

Following the April 1997 Mykonos trial verdict, European Union countries withdrew their ambassadors from Iran and only returned them upon receiving assurances by year's end that Tehran would no longer carry out political assassinations in Europe.[21] The common denominator between these episodes seems to be recognition by Khamene'i that real diplomatic and economic isolation imperils the regime.[22] As evidenced by the continued assassination of regime oppositionists in Iraq, Tajikistan, and Pakistan since 1998, however, these bouts of pragmatism produced tactical shifts in the application of Iranian-backed terror, rather than an outright and lasting repudiation of the practice.

"The Advantages of Asymmetric Means"

Iran's conventional armed forces have yet to recover fully from revolutionary purges and losses during the eight-year war with Iraq. Its air force and air defenses remain particularly weak, leaving Iran highly vulnerable to air attack.[23] These systemic deficiencies help drive Tehran into terrorism and insurgency for three reasons: it helps compensate for the lack of traditional power projection forces, exploits adversaries' conventional force vulnerabilities, and provides a cloak by which the mullahs can deny culpability, thereby reducing the risks of retaliation. Thus, for example, in conjunction with terrorist proxies, the IRGC can strike globally, has used EFPs to devastating effect against U.S. troops in Iraq, and – thanks to the fiasco over Iraqi WMD – U.S. claims of such involvement by the IRGC are greeted with official denials in Iran and public skepticism in the United States.[24]

Iran's Terrorism Apparatus

With sustained political, religious, and economic support from the highest levels of the regime and a devout cadre of operatives, Iran has developed a highly effective terrorism apparatus, one that is both institutionalized and results-driven.

Major Organizations

As with other bureaucratic arrangements in Iran, the mullahs' organizational approach to terrorism is a blend of state and revolutionary bodies that appear to have both overlapping and distinct responsibilities. The role of some of the major entities has evolved over time, as summarized below:

- Office of Islamic Liberation Movements (ILM): This revolutionary body was at the forefront of Iran's initial efforts to export the Islamic Revolution and was led by Khomeini's then-designated heir, Ayatollah Montazeri. As a spill-over in the factional competition for influence between Montazeri and Rafsanjani, the ILM was disbanded in late-1986 and its responsibility for directing external revolutionary activities transferred to the Ministry of Foreign Affairs.[25]

- Ministry of Intelligence and Security (MOIS): MOIS is regarded as one of the largest and most active intelligence agencies in the Middle East, with responsibility for identification and liquidation of regime dissidents at home and abroad. MOIS runs its own terrorism training camps in Iran.[26] It was initially responsible for liaison with Al Qaeda, which was subsequently passed to the IRGC.[27]

- Islamic Revolutionary Guard Corps (IRGC) and Qods Force: As the constitutionally empowered guardian of the Islamic Revolution, the IRGC has a broad mandate which encompasses export of the revolution. It carries out both intelligence and clandestine operations abroad, mainly through its Qods (Jerusalem) Force. The IRGC also maintains an intelligence unit that cooperates with MOIS.[28]

The Qods Force has managed to remain in the shadows, with conflicting public accounts of its size, roles, and chain of command. The outfit has avoided scrutiny via highly disciplined operational security, including the use of couriers to thwart electronic eavesdropping.[29] In essence, the Qods serves as Iran's special operations force. Iran officially does not acknowledge the unit's existence, but a reliable public estimates put its strength between 5,000-15,000 men.[30] It is reportedly headquartered in the former U.S. embassy in Tehran and has various geographical directorates to deal with Western countries, the Levant, and Iraq, among others.

The Qods Force is responsible for training both Shi'ite and Sunni fundamentalists in terror, including Hezbollah and Hamas. The Qods Force conducts its training in Lebanon, Sudan, and at some 20 facilities throughout Iran.[31] The Qods Force currently serves as Iran's main liaison with Al Qaeda. Indeed, Al Qaeda apparently learned how to construct vehicular bombs via the Qods and Hezbollah,[32] and the aforementioned senior Al Qaeda leaders in Iran are reportedly residing at Qods Force guest houses in Tehran and elsewhere.[33] The Qods Force "Department 9000" is said to be the liaison between Iran and Iraqi insurgents.[34] Allegedly, the Qods Force uses the Iranian Red Crescent relief agency, the state-run broadcast corporation, and the Kawthar construction company as fronts for its operations in Iraq.[35] In August 2007, a senior U.S. general specified that a 50-man Qods team was conducting insurgent training inside Iraq.[36]

- <u>Ministry of Foreign Affairs (MFA)</u>: MFA puts various Iranian embassies and missions at the disposal of the Qods Force, providing them diplomatic cover for their terrorist activities abroad. It also maintains a special branch that assists the Qods Force in recruiting foreign terrorists by issuing false passports.[37]

- <u>State-owned Banks and Front Companies</u>: Iran uses a variety of state-owned banks and numerous front companies to transfer money to its terrorist proxies.

- <u>"Charitable" Foundations</u>: After the fall of the Shah, Iran's mullahs created a series of organizations referred to as bonyads or foundations, using properties and industries expropriated from the monarchy and its supporters. The bonyads' leaders are hand-picked by the Supreme Leader and answer only to him. A number of these bonyads, which collectively account for an estimated 10 to 20 percent of Iran's annual GDP, directly or indirectly support Iranian terrorism. For example, the Bonyad-e 15th Khordad established and later raised the bounty on Salman Rushdie's head.

Decision-making Processes and Key Figures

Decision-making for terrorism in Iran reflects the variety of participating government and non-government organizations. Thus, clerical and devout lay officials who oversee pertinent state entities are involved in the process, as are senior extremist clerics, some of whom hold no government office but provide Islamic sanction to undertake terror. Given the sensitive nature of terrorism, coordination at the highest levels of the regime is kept to only a handful of decision makers, foremost of which is the Supreme Leader, Khamenei.

For example, in the Mykonos dissident killings, the German court found that the dissident killings had been authorized by a committee that included Supreme Leader Khamene'i, then-President Rafsanjani, the heads of MOIS and MFA at the time, and other officials. This ruling is consistent with the account given by a high-level Iranian defector, Abdolghassem Mesbahi, of the 1994 bombing of the Jewish community center in Buenos Aires. That attack reportedly was ordered at a meeting that included the same group of top officials as the 1992 Mykonos killings.[38] Moreover, Khamene'i himself was said to have issued the fatwa authorizing the 1994 attack. These officials' common membership in Iran's Supreme National Security Council (SNSC) strongly suggests that an executive committee of that body evaluates and recommends Iranian terrorist acts which then take effect, as with all SNSC decisions, with the Supreme Leader's final approval.

This pattern from the 1990s indicates that when it comes to terrorism, the state president is an integral decision maker, directly implicating reformist President Khatami during his tenure, as well as the current incumbent. Indeed, President Ahmadinejad reportedly is currently responsible for presenting Iran's extra-territorial terrorism plans to the Supreme Leader.[39] Given his reported prior links to the Qods Force, including participation in covert operations behind Iraqi lines during the Iran-Iraq War and allegations of his involvement in the assassination of an opposition figure in Austria in 1989, Ahmadinejad is likely a leading proponent of terrorism and irregular warfare within top regime deliberations.[40] It follows that other key members of this cabal today likely include the current ministers of MOIS and MFA, Pourhommadi and Mottaki, respectively. Moreover, although no longer president, Hashemi Rafsanjani probably retains informal influence in the regime's terrorism decision-making process.

As a designated member of the Supreme National Security Council, the IRGC is also a key player in terrorism deliberations. Operationally, however, the IRGC commander, currently Major General Mohammad Ali Aziz Jafari, reports directly to the Supreme Leader who is the constitutional commander-in-chief. The Qods Force commander, currently Brigadier General Qassem Soleimani, also has direct access to the Supreme Leader. This direct access, supplemented with a network of Supreme Leader's representatives or overseers, has led many Iran observers to conclude that, "in general, arguments that Iran's support for terrorism occurs without official sanction and without the knowledge of the senior leadership have proven incorrect."[41] Selected key figures in Iran's terrorism apparatus are listed in alphabetical order in Figure 6.1.

During 2006-2007, as evidence mounted of Qods Force involvement in the Iraqi insurgency, including the detention by U.S. forces of senior Qods operatives in Iraq, a controversy brewed in the United States as to whether this activity was officially sanctioned by the Iranian government and if so, how high. According to Anthony Cordesman, the SNSC gave the Qods Force control of Iran's operations in Iraq in January 2007.[42] Yet, while senior U.S. officials were able to "connect the dots" regarding the Qods, they refrained from publicly claiming that Supreme Leader Khamene'i had authorized its lethal work in Iraq. As Defense Secretary Robert Gates noted in February 2007:

> We know the Qods Force is involved [in the Iraqi insurgency]. We know the Qods Force is a paramilitary arm of the IRGC. So we assume that the leadership of the IRGC knows about this. Whether or not more senior political leaders in Iran know about it, we don't know.[43]

Figure 6.1 Selected Key Figures in Iran's Terrorism Apparatus

Name	Position	Terror-related Activity	Applicable International Arrest Warrant
Ali Fallahian	Former Minister of Intelligence & Security	Oversight of MOIS terrorist operations. Forced to resign following exposure of MOIS's role in the "serial murders" of dissidents in Iran during 1997.	Argentina, Germany, and Switzerland
Ali Akbar Mohtashemi	Member of Parliament	Inspired the formation of Hezbollah in 1982 and was secretary-general of "The International Conference on the Palestinian Intifida," in Tehran, April 2001.[44]	
Hussein Ali Montazeri	Grand Ayatollah	Initially the regime's terrorism front man in the 1980s, overseeing the ILM,[45] Montazeri later experienced a crisis of conscience and has recently renounced suicide terrorism.	
Manouchehr Mottaki	Minister of Foreign Affairs	Former IRGC. As Iranian ambassador to Ankara, oversaw assassinations of regime dissidents in Turkey.	Ordered by Ankara to leave Turkey in 1989 for his terror involvement.
Mustafa Pour-Mohammadi	Minister of Intelligence & Security	MOIS Representative at Evin prison who approved the mass killings of political prisoners in 1988. MOIS Director of Foreign Intelligence, 1990-1999.	
Hashemi Rafsanjani	Chairman of Expediency Council	Provided presidential approval of terrorist attacks, 1989-1997.	Argentina
Mohsen Reza'i	Secretary of Expediency Council	Former Commander of the IRGC. Oversaw IRGC terrorist operations until 1997.	Argentina
Rahim Safavi	Maj. Gen.	Military Advisor to Supreme Leader. Commander of the IRGC from 1997 to August 2007.	
Qassem Soleimani	Brig. Gen.	Commander of the Qods Force.	
Ahmad Vahidi	IRGC Maj. Gen., Deputy Minister of Defense	Former commander of the Qods Force. Responsible for execution of IRGC terrorist operations during the 1990s.	Argentina
Ali-Akbar Velayati	Advisor to Supreme Leader	Oversight of MFA's role in terror plots during the 1990s.	Argentina

Such public conservatism likely reflects the legacy of the Iraqi WMD fiasco, perhaps some genuine gaps in U.S. intelligence, and a deliberate diplomatic effort to persuade Tehran to back off in Iraq while enabling the Supreme Leader to save face. In the event new intelligence is developed or publicly revealed and Iran maintains or increases its support for insurgents, a greater U.S. willingness to fix blame publicly on Iran's top leaders could be expected. Indeed, by summer, the U.S. military spokesman in Iraq, Brigadier General Kevin Berger, declared, "Our intelligence reveals that the senior leadership in Iran is aware of this activity."[46] Also during this time, a senior State Department official accused the government of Iran of knowingly transferring arms to the Taliban, a move described as a "major miscalculation."[47]

Funding: "The Central Banker of Terror"

Having provided hundreds of millions of dollars each year to incite violent extremism using its state banking system, a host of front companies, and so-called charitable foundations, Iran has been aptly described by senior U.S. officials as the "central banker of terror." A primary Iranian means of transferring money to Hezbollah, Hamas, Popular Front for Liberation of Palestine – General Command (PFLP-GC), and Palestinian Islamic Jihad is via the state-owned Bank Saderat (Export Bank of Iran), which has over 3,000 branches (including an office in Beirut) and 200 affiliated companies.[48] In late-2006, the U.S. Treasury Department announced that it had cut off Bank Saderat from the U.S. financial system for its involvement in terrorism funding. Two Iran-based financial companies, Bayt al-Mal and the Yousser Company, were also sanctioned by the U.S. Treasury Department at the time, having designated them as Hezbollah's "unofficial treasury."[49] Washington has been working closely with other Western financial centers, including those based in London, to further constrain these Iranian entities. By August 2007, the United States was considering adding the Central Bank of Iran to its list of sanctioned entities, an indicator that official Iranian funding of terrorism and proliferation runs deep.

Iran is estimated to provide $200 million annually to Hezbollah. Iranian funding for Hamas (averaging an estimated $35 million annually between 1990 and 2000) and PIJ ($2 million to $3 million annually) is often funneled through Hezbollah. Supreme Leader Khamene'i has promised to split PIJ's funding stream from Hezbollah and to increase it by 70 percent to increase recruitment of Palestinian suicide bombers.[50] In addition to these subsidies from the state treasury, relief agencies and foundations in Iran, such as the Bonyad-e Al Shahid (Martyrs' Foundation), Bonyad-e Al Mustaz'afin (Foundation of the Oppressed), and the Imdad Al-Imam (Khomeini Relief Committee), provide these terrorist groups with substantial funding of their own, often to compensate the families of suicide bombers, which helps incentivize new recruits.[51] Of course, Iran also covers the terrorism-related costs of its own operatives and infrastructure – the budget for the Qods Force training camps in Lebanon alone is estimated at $50 million annually.[52]

Iran has applied Western business concepts and practices to ensure maximum output from its terrorist proxies. Iranian funding to groups like Hamas and PIJ is directly indexed to performance; it increases when they carry out successful attacks and decreases when they fail or delay.[53] Iran has given cash bonuses for successful terrorist attacks, which serve both as a reward and recruitment mechanism. Moreover, to undermine Israeli-Palestinian cease-fires, Iran has employed "incentive pricing," where the payment for a terror operation can go from $20,000 to $100,000. Such performance-based/results-driven funding of terrorism has its vulnerabilities, however, as Iran requires documentary evidence of how its money is being spent. Such records fell into the hands of U.S. forces in Iraq, which apparently cracked the case of Qods Force involvement in the January 2007 Karbala raid in which five U.S. soldiers were killed by insurgents.[54]

Mapping Iran's Global Terrorist Network

By virtue of its international diplomatic presence and cultivation of proxies and other co-conspirators, Iran is able to tap a terrorist network that spans the globe. As noted above, Iran's embassies and economic/cultural missions abroad provide ready access to a host of nations. Under the cover of diplomatic immunity, false passports, and sealed pouches, Iranian terrorists are able to plan, equip, and execute bombings, assassinations, and other terrorist-related operations on foreign soil. This modus operandi even extends to the Iranian mission to the United Nations, in New York City (NYC). In 2002 and again in 2004, the United States expelled Iranian security guards working at Iran's UN mission for videotaping and photographing NYC tunnels, bridges, buses, and subways.[55]

Iran has leveraged its global access and further concealed its tracks by cultivating various extremist groups to carry out terrorist attacks and other forms of irregular warfare on its behalf. As Figure 6.2 makes clear, Iran has little compunction about supporting groups it has previously reviled, such as Communists and the Taliban, so long as they qualify as "the enemy of my enemy."

Figure 6.2 Selected Iranian Relationships with Foreign Terror Groups

Organization	Religion/ Ideology	Locations	Nature of Iran's Relationship
Al Qaeda	Sunni	Afghanistan, Pakistan, Iran, South America	Training, Safe haven
Fatah Tanzim, al-Aqsa Brigade	Sunni	Gaza, West Bank	Recruitment, Funding, Training
Hamas	Sunni	Gaza, West Bank, Lebanon, Iran, South America	Political support, Funding, Training, Safe haven, Weapons supply
Hezbollah (a.k.a. Islamic Jihad)	Shi'a	Lebanon, West Bank, Gaza, Iraq, South America, United States, Canada, Europe, Asia	Political support, Funding, Training, Weapons supply, Direction
Iraqi insurgent groups (various)	Shi'a, Sunni	Iraq	Training, Weapons supply
Islamic Movement of Uzbekistan	Sunni	Uzbekistan	Surveillance of U.S. forces in Kyrgyzstan
Kurdistan Workers Party (PKK)	Marxist-Leninist, Kurdish nationalist	Northern Iraq, Iraq	Safe haven, Training, Logistical support
Palestinian Islamic Jihad (PIJ)	Sunni	Iran, Syria, Lebanon, Sudan, Gaza	Political support, Funding, Safe haven, Training, Weapons Supply, Direction
Popular Front for Liberation of Palestine – General Command (PFLP-GC)	Pan-Arab, Secular, Marxist-Leninist	Gaza, West Bank, Syria, Lebanon	Funding, Safe haven, Training, Weapons supply
Revolutionary Armed Forces of Columbia (FARC)	Communist	Colombia	Training
Taliban (2007)	Sunni	Afghanistan	Weapons supply

Iran and WMD Terrorism

Concern about Iran's potential involvement in WMD terrorism is rising. As noted in the U.S. State Department's 2005 report on global terrorism:

> State sponsors of terrorism pose a grave WMD threat... Iran presents a particular concern, given its active sponsorship of terrorism and its continued development of a nuclear program. Iran is also capable of producing biological and chemical agents or weapons... Iran could support organizations seeking to acquire WMD.

To date, there are no public indications that Iran has engaged in such behavior. This likely reflects a calculation of costs and benefits – *from an Iranian perspective*.[56] Tehran's balance of interest could shift, however, based on internal and external developments. In particular, Iran's acquisition of a nuclear weapons capability might lead regime extremists to believe they could engage in more risky behavior with less fear of outside retaliation.[57] Alternatively, a direct attack by the West on Iran could provide an external stimulant to escalate to WMD terrorism, if the mullahs conclude that conventional terrorism had been an insufficient deterrent. As the foregoing makes clear, Iran would have a range of resources to draw upon, should it embark upon this path.

Among the specific causes of concern about Iranian WMD terrorism, including against the U.S. homeland, are the following:

- Organizationally, the IRGC is responsible for Iran's WMD programs *and* terrorism operations, raising the risks that the two mission areas could become conflated at some point.

- The head of Al Qaeda's WMD development efforts, Abdul Aziz al-Masri, has been sheltered in Iran by the IRGC for five years now, presumably strengthening relationships with IRGC operatives and, potentially, improving his access to WMD-related technology, materials, and expertise.

- The IRGC's top strategist, Dr. Hasan Abassi, has warned that Iran will use Islamists in the United States to attack U.S. nuclear weapons.[58]

- A naturalized U.S. citizen returned to his native Iran in 2007 with a laptop computer containing the technical details his former place of employment, the Palo Verde nuclear power station, located west of Phoenix, Arizona.[59] This information might prove useful to Iranian operatives hoping to stage an indirect WMD attack by sabotaging U.S. nuclear power reactor operations.

- Iran has increasingly put fairly crude but sensitive military systems into the hands of its terrorist proxies, including long-range rockets, cruise missiles, and unmanned aerial vehicles. These systems were soon, thereafter, put to use, often with direct IRGC assistance.

- Some of Iran's terrorist proxies have experimented with the use of poisons to enhance the destructiveness of their bombs. For example, in 2000, Director of Central Intelligence George Tenet testified that Hamas was "pursuing a capability to conduct attacks with toxic chemicals." Indeed, Israeli officials have been quietly dealing with a series of Hamas poison plots and actual attacks since the 1990s.[60] In June 2006, members of the al-Aqsa Marytrs Brigades claimed to have manufactured a variety of chemical and biological weapons and to have fired a chemical-armed rocket into Israel in retaliation for the Israeli military intervention in Gaza. While Israel detected no such attack, the incident underscored growing WMD interest among Palestinian terrorist groups.

- The U.S. National Intelligence Council concluded in July 2007, "...Lebanese Hezbollah, which has conducted anti-U.S. attacks outside the United States in the past, may be more likely to consider attacking the [U.S.] Homeland over the next three years if it perceives the United States as posing a direct threat to the group or Iran."[61]

- Iran's highly-politicized and extremist-dominated security apparatus poses the risk of unsanctioned use of nuclear, biological, chemical or radiological weapons, particularly under the stress of crisis and conflict.[62]

As with its approach to terrorism in general, we could expect an Iranian escalation to WMD terrorism to be governed by a deception and denial campaign to provide the regime with plausible deniability. It would also be enabled by a fatwa from a senior Shi'a ayatollah. Indeed, the official Shi'a doctrine of the Islamic Republic, Ja'fari or Twelver Shi'ism, already deems the use of "poisons" in war permissible. Iran, it should be recalled, developed an offensive chemical warfare capability during the 1980-1988 war with Iraq. Despite official Iranian claims to the contrary, the U.S. Department of Defense contends that Iran used chemical weapons against Iraq during that conflict.[63] Finally, because of its global reach, no nation could hope to be immune from an Iranian-backed WMD terrorist attack.

Implications for Senior U.S. Military Commanders

U.S. military commanders are confronted with an increasingly complex and effective threat of terrorism and irregular warfare emanating from Tehran. As demonstrated above, Iran has been targeting U.S. military forces with deadly effect since it became an Islamic Republic, with lethal attacks in 1983, 1996, and since 2003-2004. These attacks have been focused in the Middle East but are clearly spreading to Central Asia and could go further still. Iran's preference for terror is deeply rooted in its political culture, religious conviction, and strategic analysis. Because the United States has not yet responded to Iranian-backed attacks on U.S. soldiers, citizens, and interests with overt military attack against Iran's homeland, Tehran likely sees no reason to discontinue the practice. Clearly the Islamic Republic and the United States are on a collision course over a number of issues, not least of which is terrorism and insurgency. As these tensions mount, U.S. military commanders have a number of force protection and operational challenges with which to contend.

With regard to force protection, Iranian terror and irregular warfare is a pervasive threat, encompassing not only front-line troops in Iraq and Afghanistan but also U.S. forces in supporting roles and deployments, from Africa to Europe and the homeland. Iran has proven itself the "cradle of car-bombing" and continues to innovate, as witnessed by the devastating effect of EFPs on American armor in Iraq. Iran will continue to search for and exploit the vulnerabilities of U.S. forces in an asymmetric manner. As the January 2007 raid on Karbala makes clear, the Qods Force is highly professional, with access to U.S. military uniforms and detailed intelligence about our defenses. United States force protection measures should be constantly reviewed and enhanced with this kind of adversary in mind. This adaptive vigilance must extend to the threat of WMD terrorism. While no nation-state is known to have provided WMD to a non-state actor, this taboo should not be regarded as permanent. Indeed, if any regime were to flout this informal convention, the Islamic Republic of Iran would be the leading contender – and U.S. interests would likely be the initial target.

The Karbala raid has been linked in the media as an Iranian *quid pro quo* for the U.S. holding of Qods Force operatives in Iraq. This seems to miss the larger point in that while the Qods detainees are alive and likely to remain so, the Iranian operation killed five American soldiers. Whether the killings were intended by Tehran or not, the Karbala raid underscores the escalatory potential of this conflict. There have already been calls in the U.S. Senate for the United States to strike the insurgent training camps in Iran. In time, pressures for direct U.S. military action against Iran could build. Contingency planning therefore requires a sober assessment of the associated operational challenges both in the Persian Gulf and at home.

Any U.S. military action against Iran's terrorism apparatus must be rooted within and contribute to an overall strategy to apply the full range of national power to achieve specific ends. While desirable, the full cessation of all Iranian terrorist activities is likely not an achievable military effect. Rather, U.S. and allied military intelligence, diplomatic and economic operations can inflict major damage to Iran's terrorism apparatus, particularly its infrastructure and revenue generating means, with the goal of significantly impeding Iran's ability to organize, train, equip, and execute terror operations for a number of years.

If U.S. and allied forces were ever to target Iranian WMD facilities, a broad strike could physically reduce the infrastructure and materials potentially available to support WMD terrorism. In any event, military effects should be closely coordinated with intelligence and financial instruments to further expose Iran's terrorist network worldwide and choke it off from easy access to the Western financial system. By applying such measures, Iran's residual terrorism capability should be smaller, weaker, more concerned about its own survival than planning attacks and, at the heart of an accompanying U.S. strategic communications campaign, demonstrated to be a lethal and unworthy liability for the Iranian people.

Naturally, the path to a strategic confrontation comes with corresponding risks, of which there are many. Chief among these are the potential escalation to war and stimulation rather than deterrence of further terrorism and even Iranian introduction of WMD. Also at risk is alienation of the Iranian people, in the event their homeland is attacked, regardless of cause. U.S. contingency planning must also explicitly address these risks and how they might be contained, so that policy makers can decide how best to defend U.S. interests. In weighing these risks, our policymakers ought to understand clearly that further failure to hold Iran accountable for its shedding of American blood will only be perceived in Tehran as weakness, emboldening the mullahs to continue if not expand their terrorist campaign against us.

Notes

1. This chapter reflects the views of the author, not necessarily those of Hicks and Associates, Inc., SAIC, or its clients.

2. Quoted in Ely Karmon, "Iran's Policy on Terrorism in the 1990s," International Institute for Counter-Terrorism (Herzliya, Israel), 8 September 1998, n.1.

3. The U.S. State Department formally listed Iran as a state-sponsor of terror on January 19, 1984. Virtually every year since then, Iran has been called out as "the most active state sponsor of terror" in the Department's annual report on global terrorism. In some cases, Iran has "tied" with other countries, such as Libya and Syria. Only twice, in 1990 and 1998, did the State Department not apply the term, apparently in the hopes of building better relations with the "pragmatic" President Rafsanjani and "reformist" President Khatami, initially elected in 1989 and 1997, respectively.

4. Ely Karmon, op. cit.

5. *The 9/11 Commission Report*, (New York: W.W. Norton and Company, 2004), 61, 240-241.

6. "Bush Aide Attacks Iran Terror Link," *BBC News*, 20 December 2001, On-line, Internet, 5 November 2007, available from http://news.bbc.co.uk/1/hi/world/middle_east/1721743.stm.

7. For a comprehensive treatment of this incident, see Robert Satloff, "The Peace Process at Sea: The *Karine-A* Affair and War on Terrorism," *National Interest*, Spring 2002, On-line, Internet, 5 November 2007, available from http://www.washingtoninstitute.org/templateC06.php?CID=653.

8. "Iran a Safe Haven for al Qaeda," *CBS News*, 16 May 2003, On-line, Internet, 5 November 2007, available from http://www.cbsnews.com/stories/2003/05/18/world/main554415.shtml.

9. Jon Hemming, "U.S. Says Iran Knows Its Weapons Reaching Taliban," *Reuters,* 17 July 2007, On-line, Internet, 5 November 2007, available from http://www.reuters.com/article/worldNews/idUSISL6933820070717.

10. Quoted in Bruce Hoffman, *Recent Trends and Future Prospects of Iranian Sponsored International Terrorism*, (Santa Monica: RAND, 1990), 2.

11. "Leader's Message on the Inauguration of the 4th Experts Assembly," 20 February 2007, On-line, Internet, available from http://www.khamenei.ir/EN/Message/detail.jsp?id=20070220A.

12. For a profile of Supreme Leader Khamene'i, see Gregory F. Giles, "The Crucible of Radical Islam: Iran's Strategic Culture and Leaders," in *Know Thy Enemy,* Barry R. Schneider and Jerrold M. Post, eds., U.S. Air Force Counterproliferation Center, Maxwell AFB, Alabama, July 2003, also On-line, Internet, available from http://www.au.af.mil/au/awc/awcgate/cpc-pubs/know_thy_enemy/giles.pdf.

13. Moojan Momen, *An Introduction to Shi'a Islalm*, (New Haven, CT: Yale University Press, 1985).

14. See Davood Feirahi, "Legitimate Defense, Terror, and Marytrdom-seeking Operations in Shiism," February 2004, On-line, Internet, 5 November 2007, available from http://feirahi.com/en/index.php?option=com_content&task=view&id=13&Itemid=36. Feirahi is an Associate Professor in the Political Science Department at the University of Tehran.

15. Feirahi, op. cit.

16. Jackson Diehl, "In Iran, Apocalypse vs. Reform," *Washington Post*, 11 May 2006, On-line, Internet, 5 November 2007, available from http://www.washingtonpost.com/wp-dyn/content/article/2006/05/10/AR2006051001791.html.

17. Feirahi, op. cit.

18. Feirahi, op. cit.

19. Hoffman, op. cit., 21-31.

20. Ray Takeyh, *Hidden Iran: Paradox and Power in the Islamic Republic*, (NY: Times Books, 2006), 225.

21. "Iran: Reformers Insist Hard-Liners' History of Political Assassination Continues," *Radio Free Europe/Radio Liberty (RFE/RL)*, 11 March 2005, On-line, Internet, 5 November 2007, available from http://www.rferl.org/featuresarticle/2005/03/9883c885-de09-4c37-a5d1-73a12c4dfb60.html.

22. Ibid.

23. Tellingly, Iran has been investing its acquisition funds into long-range ballistic missiles and, more recently, sophisticated Russian air defense missile systems.

24. See, for example, Robert Baer, "Where's the Smoking Gun on Iran?," *Time,* 13 February 2007, On-line, Internet, 5 November 2007, available from http://www.time.com/time/world/article/0,8599,1588810,00.html. Baer is a former CIA Middle East field officer.

25. Hoffman, op. cit., 26-27.

26. "Iranian State Sponsorship of Terror: Threatening U.S. Security, Global Stability, and Regional Peace," Testimony of Matthew A. Levitt, Senior Fellow and Director of Terrorism Studies, The Washington Institute for Near East Policy, February 16, 2005, Joint Hearing of the Committee on International Relations Subcommittee on the Middle East and Central Asia, and the Subcommittee on International Terrorism and Nonproliferation United States House of Representatives, 6, 8. Levitt is a former U.S. Treasury official and FBI counter-terrorism analyst.

27. Rohan Gunaratna, "Al Qaeda Network in Iran and Iraq," 31 January 2006, remarks at Woodrow Wilson International Center for Scholars, On-line, Internet, 5 November 2007, available from http://www.wilsoncenter.org/index.cfm?fuseaction=events.event_summary&event_id=167377#. Dr. Gunaratna is Head of Terrorism Research, Institute for Defense and Strategic Studies, Singapore.

28. A. William Samii, "Factionalism in Iran's Domestic Security Forces," *Middle East Intelligence Bulletin*, Vol. 4, No. 2, February 2002, On-line, Internet, 5 November 2007, available from http://www.meib.org/articles/0202_me2.htm.

29. Robert Baer, op. cit.

30. Robin Wright cites Anthony Cordesman of the *Center for Strategic and International Studies* in "Elite Revolutionary Guard Broadens Its Influence in Iran," *Washington Post*, 1 April 2007, On-line, Internet, 5 November 2007, available from http://www.washingtonpost.com/wp-dyn/content/article/2007/03/31/AR2007033101105.html.

31. See "Exclusive: Terrorist Training Camps in Iran," *Iran Focus*, 27 February 2006, On-line, Internet, 5 November 2007, available from http://www.iranfocus.com/modules/news/article.php?storyid=5956. Iran Focus is affiliated with the Mujaheen el-Khaq (MEK), regime oppositionists that the United States has designated a terrorist organization.

32. *The 9/11 Commission Report*, op. cit.

33. Bill Samii, "Tehran Denies Al-Qaeda Members Have Fled," RFE/RL *Newsline*, Vol. 7, No. 156, 18 August 2003, citing a report from the London-based Arabic-language daily *Al-Sharq Al-Awsat*.

34. "Tehran's Secret 'Department 9000,'" *Newsweek*, 4 June 2007, On-line, Internet, 5 November 2007, available from http://www.newsweek.com/id/34320.

35. "Exclusive: Terrorist Training Camps in Iran," op. cit.

36. Megan Greenwell, "Iran Trains Militiamen Inside Iraq, U.S. Says," *Washington Post*, 20 August 2007, On-line, Internet, 5 November 2007, available from http://www.washingtonpost.com/wp-dyn/content/article/2007/08/19/AR2007081901394.html.

37. "Exclusive: Terrorist Training Camps in Iran," op. cit.

38. Daniel Byman, Shahran Cubin, et al., *Iran's Security Policy in the Post-Revolutionary Era*, (Santa Monica, CA: RAND, 2001), 93-94. See also, Levitt, op. cit., 11. See also, Kenneth Pollack, *The Persian Puzzle*, (New York: Random House, 2004), 355-357. For a contrarian view, see Hooshang Amirahmadi of Rutgers University, quoted in Scott Shane, "Iranian Force, Focus of U.S., Still a Mystery," *New York Times*, 17 February 2007, On-line, Internet, 5 November 2007, available from http://www.nytimes.com/2007/02/17/world/middleeast/17quds.html.

39. Dan Diker, "President Bush and the Qods Force Controversy: Lessons Learned," *Jerusalem Center for Public Affairs*, 1-31 March 2007, On-line, Internet, 5 November 2007, available from http://www.jcpa.org/JCPA/Templates/ShowPage.asp?DBID=1&TMID=111&LNGID=1&FID=376&PID=0&IID=1516.

40. President Ahmadinejad's original official biography, which was posted on his website, noted that he had served in the IRGC during the Iran-Iraq War, was stationed at Ramazan Garrison, and had participated in operations behind Iraqi lines. All of this

strongly suggests that Ahmadinejad played a role in the formation and operations of the Qods Force. Apparent concern about this revelation and whether Ahmadinejad had a hand in the U.S. embassy hostage seizure prompted a clumsy sanitization of the President's official biography. The new and current version, complete with mismatching fonts, omits any reference to the IRGC and instead notes that Ahmadinejad served in a lesser paramilitary group during the war. A photograph taken from Iranian state-TV archives, however, apparently shows the young Ahmadinejad standing beside Ayatollah Fazlollah Mahallati, a co-founder and clerical overseer of the IRGC. See "Iran: Ahmadinejad's Past in Revolutionary Guards Invites Scrutiny," *Iran Focus*, 5 July 2005. Opposition sources allege that Ahmadinejad played a role in the assassination of a dissident in Austria in 1989, a claim that the Austrian government is investigating. Dissidents further claim that Ahmadinejad served as an interrogator and executioner at Iran's notorious Evin prison, where Iranian political prisoners are held.

41. Daniel Byman, Shahram Chubin, et al., 93.

42. Robin Wright, op. cit.

43. Scott Shane, op. cit.

44. Reuven Paz, "Iran: More Fuel on the Israeli-Palestinian Fire," *PeaceWatch*, No. 320, 25 April 2001, Washington Institute for Near East Policy, On-line, Internet, 5 November 2007, available from http://www.washingtoninstitute.org/templateC05.php?CID=2011.

45. Hoffman, op. cit., 5, 20, n. 9.

46. Michael Gordon, "U.S. Ties Iran to Deadly Iraq Attack," *New York Times*, 2 July 2007, On-line, Internet, 5 November 2007, available from http://www.nytimes.com/2007/07/02/world/middleeast/02cnd-iran.html.

47. "U.S.: Iran Sending Weapons to Taliban," *Associated Press*, June 2007, On-line, Internet, 5 November 2007, available from http://www.iranpressnews.com/english/source/025508.html.

48. "Treasury Cuts Iran's Bank Saderat off from U.S. Financial System," U.S. Department of the Treasury Press Release, 8 September 2006, On-line, Internet, 5 November 2007, available from http://www.ustreas.gov/press/releases/hp87.htm.

49. "Prepared Remarks by Stuart Levey, Under Secretary for Terrorism and Financial Intelligence, Before the American Enterprise Institute for Public Policy Research, 8 September 2006, On-line, Internet, 5 November 2007, available from http://www.treasury.gov/press/releases/hp86.htm.

50. Levitt, op. cit., 3-5.

51. "Iran Increases Funding and Training for Suicide Bombers," *Special Dispatch Series, No. 387*, 10 June 2002, Middle East Media Research Institute, citing article by 'Ali Nouri Zadeh in the London-based Arabic-language daily *Al-Sharq Al-Awsat*, On-line, Internet, 5 November 2007, available from http://memri.org/bin/articles.cgi?Page=archives&Area=sd&ID=SP38702.

52. Levitt, op. cit., 6.

53. Information in this paragraph is taken from Levitt, op. cit., 3, 5, 9.

54. *DoD News Briefing with General Petraeus from the Pentagon*, 26 April 2007, On-line, Internet, 6 November 2007, available from http://www.defenselink.mil/transcripts/transcript.aspx?transcriptid=3951.

55. Bill Samii, "Iranian Officials Leaving U.S.," *RFE/RL Iran Report*, 1 July 2002, Vol. 5. No. 24, On-line, Internet, 6 November 2007, available from http://www.rferl.org/reports/iran-report/2002/07/24-010702.asp. See also, "U.S. Expels 2 Iranian Guards at United Nations," *CNN*, 29 June 2004, On-line, Internet, available from http://www.cnn.com/2004/US/Northeast/06/29/un.iran/index.html.

56. Gregory Giles, "A Framework for Assessing the Threat of Iranian WMD Terrorism against the United States," Testimony before the House Committee on Homeland Security, Subcommittee on Prevention of Nuclear and Biological Attack, 109th Cong., 1st session, 8 September 2005.

57. Gregory Giles, "Command and Control Challenges of An Iranian Nuclear Force," in *Deterring the Ayatollahs*, Patrick Clawson and Michael Eisenstadt, eds., (Washington, D.C.: Washington Institute for Near East Policy, 2007), 12-15.

58. "Iranian Revolutionary Guard Official in Tehran University Lecture (Part II): We Plan To Target US Nuclear Warheads on US Soil; Should Take Over England," *TV Monitor Project, Clip No. 252*, 23 May 2004, Middle East Media Research Institute.

59. Upon his return to the United States for the birth of his child, Mohammad Alavi was arrested and as of May 2007, was being held without bail in Arizona. See "Accused Nuke Engineer: I Was Showing Off," *Washington Post*, 18 May 2007.

60. See, for example, Jamie Chosak and Julie Sawyer, "Hamas's Tactics: Lessons from Recent Attacks," *Peacewatch No. 522*, Washington Institute for Near East Policy, 19 October 2005, On-line, Internet, 6 November 2007, available from http://www.washingtoninstitute.org/templateC05.php?CID=2382.

61. *The Terrorist Threat to the U.S. Homeland*, National Intelligence Estimate Unclassified Summary, July 2007.

62. Giles, "Command and Control Challenges," op. cit.

63. See Office of the Secretary of Defense, *Proliferation Threat and Response*, January 2001, 35-36, On-line, Internet, 6 November 2007, available from http://www.fas.org/irp/threat/prolif00.pdf.

CHAPTER 7

Terrorist Use of WMD

James J.F. Forest

The international community is facing a terrorist threat of historic proportions. Within the past few years, terrorist attacks have claimed thousands of lives in London, Madrid, Bali, Jakarta, Bombay, Istanbul, Ankara, Tunis, Casablanca, Amman, Algiers, Riyadh, Sharm-el-Sheikh, and of course, Baghdad, Kabul, and many other cities and villages throughout Iraq and Afghanistan. Meanwhile, additional terror plots of significance have been disrupted in Australia, Denmark, Canada, England, Scotland, Germany, Pakistan, Turkey, and the United States, among others.

This growing cadence of attacks and plots has generated increasing concern that it is only a matter of time before we witness a major terrorist attack involving a weapon of mass destruction (WMD). The possibility that a terrorist group (or even a motivated individual) could acquire and use such weapons to inflict unthinkable levels of death and injuries is more than a theoretical discussion, especially in the aftermath of the September 11, 2001, terrorist attacks.

A number of intelligence sources and news media reports in the United States, Europe, and elsewhere have confirmed that terrorist groups like Al Qaeda have attempted to seek WMD material and capabilities. Thousands of chemical and biological weapons, huge quantities of weapons related materials and expertise are scattered all across the globe, and substandard security at nuclear facilities in Europe, Central Asia, Russia, and Pakistan increases the risk of terrorists seizing highly enriched uranium to make crude, but devastating, nuclear explosives. Overall, the threat of terrorists acquiring and using a weapon of mass destruction is a worry that keeps many senior policy makers in Europe and the United States awake at night.[1]

Much of the current debate about the threat presupposes that the acquisition of a weapon of mass destruction will lead directly to its use. Steven Flynn, for example, has suggested it is a question of "when, not if" terrorists will attack the United States with WMD.[2] However, when forecasting a WMD threat, it is important to clarify the intentions of the group(s) of concern, in order to determine whether such weapons would truly be advantageous to their strategic objectives. Thus, understanding and countering the threat of WMD terrorism requires accurate information on both the intentions and capabilities of groups and individuals to carry out violent acts. This chapter seeks to contribute toward that objective. The discussion begins by offering some examples of terrorism involving weapons of mass destruction, and provides a spectrum of terrorist ideologies, identifying a threshold of catastrophic terrorism which divides those groups willing to cause mass casualties and destruction (including, but not exclusively with WMD) from those groups who are not.

This analysis suggests that most violent non-state actors have little interest in using WMD because doing so would not help them achieve their objectives, and in some cases could even undermine their long-term chances of success. Then, the WMD threat from Al Qaeda is reviewed as a case study exemplifying the ideological nature of this analysis. The discussion concludes that the threat of WMD terrorism is still very real, albeit posed by a minority of terrorist groups, and that global cooperation is necessary for preventing catastrophic attacks from occurring.

Examples of WMD Terrorism

While there are varying opinions about what types of violence constitute terrorism, many scholars agree that there is typically a political dimension to those motivated to conduct the attack, and that the victims of the attack are typically not the overall target. That is, while the attacks of 9/11 killed many innocent victims, Al Qaeda's target was (and remains) U.S. public opinion and policy.

The definition of "weapon of mass destruction" is equally vague, but is usually used to describe a variety of weapons that can kill thousands indiscriminately and/or cause massive physical destruction.[3] Although the acronym CBRN (for chemical, biological, radiological, and nuclear) is a preferred technical term used by many analysts and scholars, WMD is a more common short-hand used across many professions and the media.

A review of the historical record reveals surprisingly few examples of WMD terrorism. In 1984, a cult led by the Bhagwan Shri Rajneesh near the town of The Dalles, Oregon, used a biological agent to contaminate several restaurant salad bars in a plot to influence a local election. Soon, a steady stream of patients were reporting to local physicians and hospitals with symptoms ranging from nausea and diarrhea to headache and fever. In total, 751 fell ill, but there were no fatalities. Two members of the group were prosecuted, and there is no evidence that the cult has since committed a similar act of violence.

In June 1990, the Liberation Tigers of Tamil Eelam (LTTE) became the first insurgent, guerrilla, or terrorist organization to stage a chemical weapons attack when it used chlorine gas in its assault on a Sri Lankan Armed Forces camp at East Kiran. As Bruce Hoffman notes, this attack was relatively crude: several large drums of the chemical were transported from a nearby paper mill and positioned around the camp's perimeter, and when the wind currents were judged right, the attackers released the gas, which wafted into the camp.[4] More than 60 military personnel were injured, and the LTTE captured the facility. However, though this was part of a first round in a renewed military offensive, the LTTE did not use a similar weapon in subsequent attacks, in part due to revulsion among their core supporters and constituencies.[5]

In March 1995, Aum Shinrikyo – a Japanese religious cult – launched an attack on the Tokyo subway using sarin gas, killing nearly a dozen people and injuring approximately 1,000 others, sending 5,000 to hospitals for checkups. Their objective in this attack was to disrupt an anticipated effort by law enforcement authorities to arrest members of the group (they attacked subway lines leading to many government ministries). This attack was similar to their use of sarin the previous year in Matsumoto against judicial officials involved in a judicial proceeding against them.[6]

More recently, when Bob Stevens, a tabloid photo editor in Boca Raton, Florida, died of anthrax poisoning in the months following the 9/11 attacks, he became the first U.S. casualty in a new era of bioterrorism threats. In the days and weeks to follow, four others succumbed to anthrax after handling tainted mail – two postal workers in Washington, D.C., a New York City hospital stockroom employee, and an elderly

Connecticut woman. At least 17 others fell ill but survived the still-unsolved post-9/11 bioterrorism attack.[7]

In January 2003, British police raided an apartment in north London and found recipes or instructions in Arabic for making ricin as well as other toxins, along with a mortar and pestle which appeared to contain chemical residue, 20 castor beans (the raw ingredient needed to produce ricin), cherry and apple seeds (which are used in the production of cyanide), and a CD-ROM containing instructions for the fabrication of homemade explosives. According to police documents and testimony at the trial of Kamel Bourgass – the alleged ringleader of this plot – the plan was to target businessmen and travelers on holiday using the Heathrow Express, the train that travels throughout the day between Heathrow Airport and London's Paddington Station.[8]

Meanwhile, Jordanian authorities made public in April 2004 that they had broken up an Al Qaeda plot to employ large quantities of toxic industrial chemicals (TICs), such as sulfuric acid, cyanide salts and insecticides, against the U.S. Embassy, the Jordanian prime minister's office, and the headquarters of Jordanian intelligence.[9]

And recent attacks in Iraq detonating high explosives to spread chlorine gas have given rise to the concern that more groups will begin using WMD in that conflict or in the home countries of coalition members like the United Kingdom or United States. Investigations and thwarted plots in Iraq have enhanced this concern. For example, in January 2004, U.S. forces discovered seven pounds of cyanide salt during a raid on a Baghdad house that was purportedly connected with Al Qaeda members,[10] and in November of that year they discovered a "chemical laboratory" in Fallujah containing (among other items) potassium cyanide, hydrochloric acid, and sulfuric acid.

While this brief review of recent events suggests ample reason for concern about the future threat of WMD terrorism, it also raises serious questions about why we have not seen more (and more successful) attacks using such weapons. One question is whether the "not if, but when" mentality which permeates the WMD terrorism debate is still applicable in all cases of the threat.[11] Based on predictions of the past decade, the world should be awash in terrorist attacks using improvised chemical, biological, radiological, or nuclear weapons by now. The reality is that despite all the ink dedicated to the topic, there have only been a handful of WMD terrorist incidents, few of which have been effective in killing anyone. An analysis of the relevant literature in this area reveals three themes of possible explanation for this: technical challenges, limited strategic results, and ideological constraints.

Technical Challenges versus Strategic Results

During a roundtable on terrorism and proliferation held shortly after 9/11, Jonathan Tucker explained that few terrorists have been willing or able to overcome the technical hurdles of a WMD attack, particularly with regard to handling and using radioactive material or lethal pathogens.[12] Even chemical weapons – often regarded as the easiest category of WMD to acquire and deploy – pose more challenges than some observers recognize, according to a recent study by René Pita, a professor at the Spanish Military NBC Defense School and a toxicologist with the Joint Assessment Team, NATO Multinational CBRN Defense Battalion.

Pita examined several incidents, alleged plots and indictments which indicate repeated attempts among radical Islamist terrorists to acquire and use these weapons. Thus far it seems that hydrogen cyanide, ricin, and toxic industrial chemicals have been the agents of choice, and although there are several guides and manuals on the Internet for how to acquire or develop these agents, the information on delivery systems is limited and of poor quality. Pita concluded that it does not yet seem likely that terrorist groups linked to Al Qaeda have the skills and technical proficiency needed to make a "classical" chemical warfare agent or to disseminate it in an effective manner.[13]

In his study of Aum Shinrikyo's chemical weapons program, RAND terrorism analyst John Parachini described how the success of the entire operation hinged on two critical individuals – the group's chief chemist, Masami Tsuchiya, who joined Aum after receiving his master's degree in organic chemistry from Tsukuba University, and Tomomasa Nakagawa, who was trained as a medical doctor at Kyoto Prefectural University of Medicine.[14] Without these key members, the group would very likely not have been able to venture into the realm of WMD terrorism. Overall, Parachini notes, Aum's experience with chemical agents illustrates the limitations non-state actors encounter when they attempt to develop an unconventional weapons capability on its own from scratch. Indeed, despite 40,000 members and $1 billion in assets, this Japanese and Russian cult was only able to achieve minimal results with their WMD program.[15]

Overall, most scholars of terrorism and WMD proliferation tend to believe that the threat of a catastrophic attack is too often exaggerated. However, Steve Simon and Daniel Benjamin have argued that the unique and destructive attributes of these weapons "will impel terrorists to overcome technical, organizational, and logistical obstacles to WMD use."[16]

Other scholars have recently voiced their concern that the technical challenges to WMD terrorism are eroding. For example, in a recent *Foreign Policy* article, Matthew Bunn and Anthony Wier of the Managing the Atom Project at Harvard University argued that the nuclear materials required to make a bomb are not impossible for terrorists to obtain, and that the difficulties of constructing or stealing a nuclear bomb could be overcome by a reasonably resourceful terrorist group.[17]

Similarly, Dave Franz, a Senior Fellow at the Combating Terrorism Center at West Point, suggests that although the risk of a biological terrorism attack is still probably quite low, technical barriers to the use of biology as a weapon are falling.[18] Indeed, the global biotechnology revolution offers new and frightening ways for individuals or groups to harm our citizens or our economy, particularly when considering the potential for a devastating attack against the nation's livestock and agricultural industry.[19] And, as the case of Aum Shinrikyo demonstrates, even a small group of people – provided sufficient resources and an ability to maintain tight security – can pose a catastrophic danger.[20]

Despite the possibly decreasing technical challenges, WMD are still significantly harder to produce or obtain than what is commonly depicted in the press, and they probably remain beyond the reach of most terrorist groups. One recent Center for Nonproliferation Studies report suggested that while the data "reflect[s] a trend towards the increased use of CBRN materials by sub-national actors," the current threat from CBRN terrorism will be "characterized primarily by 'low-end' agents, delivery systems, and incidents."[21] Most observers of national security have come to believe that, as the Central Intelligence Agency recently suggested, terrorists will likely choose conventional explosives over WMD.[22]

However, others are quick to point out that weak or supportive states can help non-state actors alleviate the difficulties of acquiring unconventional weapons with catastrophic potential.[23] Indeed, according to Steve Bowman and Helit Barel, a terrorist's ability to produce or obtain WMD may be growing due to looser controls of stockpiles and technology in the Former Soviet Union and the dissemination of technology and information.[24]

Other scholars have echoed these concerns. For example, James Adams has suggested that "terrorist groups are more likely to acquire their WMD from friendly nations than they are to develop them."[25] Jonathan Tucker has suggested that state assistance could allow terrorist groups to overcome the technical hurdles that have been perceived as limiting the threat of CBRN terrorism, and expressed his growing concern about "a clear congruence between a number of states that support terrorism and states that have WMD programs."[26] And Karl Lowe has argued that since terrorist groups are not likely to possess the required mix of technical, scientific, and military skills to carry out an effective attack using biological weapons, the group most likely to do so is one that has state sponsorship and access to that state's biological warfare efforts.[27]

Still, others in this debate over the global WMD threat have cautioned us not to assume that state involvement is a necessary element of a terrorist's attack plan. According to Matthew Bunn and Anthony Wier, policy makers have too often been willing to believe in the myth that the only plausible way that terrorists could acquire a nuclear bomb (or the ability to make one) is from a state, a myth that could limit our intelligence gathering and proliferation monitoring efforts.[28]

Overall, there are clearly technical challenges to successfully conducting a WMD terror attack, and many of these challenges could be overcome with the assistance of a state. But these challenges offer one important area of explanation for why there have not already been more frequent and more successful WMD terror attacks already. A second area involves the notion that the strategic benefits of the most plausible/feasible types of WMD are limited; a high number of casualties can be reasonably expected using conventional explosives, which are far easier to obtain and deploy successfully. Further, conventional explosives offer more control over who is injured/killed, versus a more indiscriminate weapon of mass destruction which could potentially cause harm to a terror group's critical support constituencies. In essence, to some terror group leaders the capabilities that a WMD bring may not be worth the hassles, and may not even yield positive results.

A study by John Parachini has recently called into question the notion that terrorists will inevitably graduate to WMD use. He compared the outcomes of several terrorist attacks, some which employed unconventional weapons, and others which used conventional high explosives.[29] His study focused on the Rajneeshee use of salmonella, the use of chlorine gas by the LTTE, Aum Shinrikyo's sarin gas attack, the World Trade Center bombing, the Oklahoma City bombing, and the U.S. Embassy bombings in Africa. The first three used unconventional weapons, while the latter three used conventional high explosives.[30]

Parachini concluded that in the cases involving the use of unconventional weapons, "the attacks proved much more difficult and much less effective than the perpetrators imagined," while the attacks with conventional high explosives "were spectacularly successful." According to his analysis, the use of conventional high explosives resulted in consistently higher casualties than did the use of unconventional weapons, which raises questions about whether terrorist groups would truly benefit at all from pursuing and using WMD.[31]

In sum, the technical challenges of even the least lethal WMD are daunting, and may not yield results for the terrorists commensurate with these difficulties. But perhaps even more importantly, despite what Hollywood would sometime have us believe, most terrorist groups have no interest at all in WMD because they are more familiar with conventional weapons and the use of WMD simply won't help them achieve their strategic objectives or ideological vision of the future. Understanding the ideologies of terrorism is thus vital to a comprehensive analysis of the global WMD threat.

Ideologies and Intentions of Using WMD: Understanding the Landscape

Terrorism can be considered an ideologically-driven phenomenon, a type of violence that transcends criminal or other motivations.[32] Individuals and groups often resort to the use of terrorism because they have a vision of the future that they long for, and that they do not believe will materialize without the use of violence. This vision of the future is articulated through an ideology, a set of ideas and values meant to inspire individual action and rationalize the use of violence in pursuit of this envisioned future. An ideology can be intellectually and emotionally appealing to many individuals, particularly those who seek meaning in their lives. Religious ideologies add a spiritual dimension to this appeal, and can thus be a more powerful motivator for action by justifying an individual's need to conduct violent acts in order to save oneself, one's family, or the world, while achieving God's will.

Our understanding of the potential threat of a terrorist group is informed by recognizing their vision of the future, as well as the strategy through which they hope to achieve that vision. It is equally necessary to understand the broad spectrum of ideologies in order to develop expectations with regard to a specific group's use of violence in pursuit of their espoused future vision. (See Figure 7.1.)

At one end of this spectrum are groups that desire dramatic changes, but do not see the necessity of violent means to bring about those changes. At the other end of the spectrum are those who seek nothing less than the complete destruction of life as we know it. Between the two extreme ends of the spectrum are a variety of groups willing to use some level of violence in pursuit of their objectives, ranging from a desire for religious governance (e.g., Islamic militants seeking to establish a caliphate, where sharia law reigns supreme) to Maoist communism (e.g., insurgencies in Peru and Nepal).

A vision of the future might include retribution for past injustices, changes in the policy directions of a local regime (or perhaps a superpower), a world with greater socio-economic equality, or even a world without certain types of people in it. Some may pursue a vision of a better world for their children; others may pursue a vision of salvation in the afterlife. A vision can be shared by many individuals and groups, but at different extremes, with some adopting a militant, even violent approach to the pursuit of their vision, while others are more passive sympathizers or financial supporters.

At a certain point along the spectrum of ideologies, reflected in Figure 7.1, there is a threshold of catastrophic terrorism (based on the amount of death and destruction generated by the true believers of the ideology), a threshold which relatively few groups have crossed. Indeed, there are relatively few groups or individuals whose ideologies articulate a desire for the end of the world, or at least the end of all mankind, and who can therefore be placed at the opposite end of the spectrum from the nonviolent protestors.

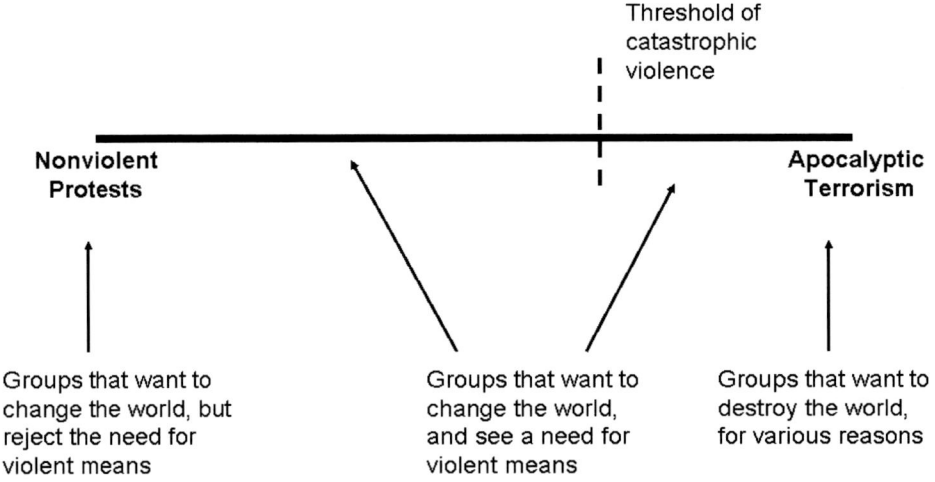

Figure 7.1 Spectrum of Ideologies

Examples include extreme environmentalist cults like the Church of Euthanasia and the Voluntary Human Extinction Movement (both of whom call for the elimination of the human race in order to save the planet), and apocalyptic (doomsday or final judgment) cults. Among the latter category, the most prominent in recent years has been the Aum Shinrikyo, whose leader Shoko Asahara came to believe that a catastrophic world war was imminent, and that only his followers would survive. Shortly thereafter, Anthony Fainberg argued that the United States could expect similar type of attack within a few years, probably from right-wing, neo-fascist groups or religious cults, and Jonathan Tucker's groundbreaking work agreed that groups with extremist ideologies or religious fanaticism are those most likely to turn to CBW weapons.[33] Similarly, in 1999 Steve Bowman and Helit Barel argued that terrorists most likely to attempt attacks with weapons of mass destruction (WMD) are extremist religious millenarian groups and small splinter terrorist cells.[34]

However, it is important to note that beyond small, extremist cults, there is actually a healthy tradition of worrying about the end of history within all of the world's major religions. According to Michael Barkun, doomsday has a fairly exact meaning for religious believers, particularly many Christians, represented in two complementary scenarios. In one, time will cease with God's Last Judgment, and the world will be destroyed and replaced by "a new heaven and a new earth." In the other, this event will be preceded by a sequence of stages, during which escalating conflict between good and evil forces will result in the final, titanic battle of Armageddon.[35] In the Bible, the Book of Revelation (also known as the Apocalypse of John) describes the eventual Battle of Armageddon between the forces of good and evil, leading to judgment day. The Koran does not have a Book of Revelation equivalent to provide a unified narrative about the end of the world, but there are many Muslims (particularly among the Shi'i tradition) who openly yearn and prepare for the return of the Mahdi, the messianic figure who will bring justice to the world and complete the spread of Islam. Apocalyptic strains may also be found in the Buddhist vision of a "Buddha of the future" and in Native American beliefs about the ancestors' return.

Barkun echoes the sentiments of many other scholars that religious terrorists are the most likely source of a WMD attack in the foreseeable future.[36] There are several reasons for this. As British terror expert J.P. Larsson has observed, religious ideologies are often theologically supremacist – meaning that all believers assume superiority over non-believers, who are not privy to the truth of the religion.[37] Second, most are exclusivist – believers are a chosen people, or their territory is a holy land. Third, many are absolutist; in other words, it is not possible to be a half-hearted believer, and you are either totally within the system, or totally without it. Further, only the true believers are guaranteed salvation and victory, whereas the enemies and the unbelievers, as well as those who have taken no stance whatsoever, are condemned to some sort of eternal punishment or damnation, as well as death. Overall, religious ideologies help foster polarizing values in terms of right and wrong, good and evil, light and dark – values which can be co-opted by terrorist organizations to convert a "seeker" into a lethal killer.

In all the examples cited by Barkun, the destruction of the old and corrupt implies the appearance of something new and pure. Regardless of the underlying monotheistic faith, groups that adhere to an apocalyptic ideology see their mission in two general ways: They either want to accelerate the end of time or take action to ensure that they survive the millennium. For example, Aum Shinrikyo wanted to hasten the end of the world (and thus sought nuclear weapons and developed their own chemical and biological weapons programs in pursuit of this objective), while other groups have built compounds (like that of the Branch Davidians near Waco, Texas) in order to survive the apocalypse. Overall, groups which embrace this unique "end of times" form of catastrophic ideology represent a worst-case scenario type of terrorist threat, although to date there have been relatively few groups at this end of the spectrum (and apocalyptic groups have historically had very limited appeal to a broader population).

Thankfully, as indicated in Figure 7.1, a significant majority of terrorist groups have recognized the need to impose constraints on their violence, in order to maintain the popular support necessary for financing their operations and recruiting new members to their ranks. Further, many terrorists throughout history have pursued a vision of the future in which they will someday be in charge of a particular governable space, and this vision may require them to overthrow an existing government but ensure that the space and people they seek to govern are left relatively undamaged. For example, the Marxist ideology of the FARC in Colombia or the Sendero Luminoso in Peru does not lend itself to a WMD attack, nor does the nationalist ideology of the Irish Republican Army ("the Armalite and the Ballot Box").

However, if the envisioned governable space is distinctly different from the larger population of a nation-state (like a separate Basque country, a Tamil homeland, a Chechen or Kurdish state, etc.), there are fewer constraints against a catastrophic terror attack against the governing regime and those who support it (e.g., in Madrid, Moscow, or Istanbul). Perhaps, then, Chechen rebels would deploy a WMD against Moscow or some other densely populated city in Russia, if they felt that doing so would force the government to acquiesce to Chechnya's demands for an independent homeland. But they are likely constrained from pursuing this course of action by the likelihood that a WMD terror attack would produce the opposite effect – heavy handed Russian military reprisals – coupled with inevitable international condemnation for crossing the threshold of catastrophic terrorism. This, in turn, could potentially impact their financial and logistics networks. Thus, as with most other groups, the lack of WMD terrorist attacks by Chechens may be owed more to a lack of strategic benefit and intentions than of capabilities.

As noted earlier, most groups that have already crossed the threshold of catastrophic terrorism (or at least intend to if given the capability and opportunity) appear unconstrained by earthly considerations, and instead see themselves as fulfilling the mandate of a higher power. In essence, the threat they pose is limited solely by the weapons they can acquire. A common thread among these groups is the need for mass destruction and death (indeed, the elimination of all humans, in some cases) in order to bring about a better world envisioned and articulated through some form of catastrophic ideology. Most commonly, this future utopian world is envisioned through the lens of some type of religious interpretation. Some religious extremists are seeking the end of the world, while others just want their religion to dominate the world by any means necessary. Members of Al Qaeda are included in this latter category, and thus provide an important case study for our analysis of the contemporary WMD terror threat.

Terrorist Pursuit of WMD: The Case of Al Qaeda

Today, the threat posed by Al Qaeda is of greatest concern to most security professionals, for reasons of both intention and capabilities. In fact, a Congressional Research Service report in 1999 noted that Al Qaeda warranted "special attention, because they combined the motivation to use WMD with substantial resources,"[38] and the July 2007 National Intelligence Estimate stated:

> We assess that [Al Qaeda] will continue to try to acquire and employ chemical, biological, radiological, or nuclear material in attacks and would not hesitate to use them if it develops what it deems is sufficient capability.[39]

Indeed much has been written about the intentions and capabilities of Al Qaeda, particularly in the years since 9/11. It is equally important to understand the evolving nature of this global threat. According to terrorism expert Bruce Hoffman,[40] Al Qaeda should be viewed not as a normal organization, but as a globally-networked movement with at least four dimensions. Only one of the four dimensions of Al Qaeda provides any semblance of traditional command and control within the movement, the so-called "Al Qaeda central" comprised of leftover leaders of the pre-9/11 organization, ostensibly led by Osama bin Laden, Ayman Al-Zawahiri and a small cadre of others.[41] This dimension of Al Qaeda may be actively engaged in commissioning some attacks, directing surveillance and collating reconnaissance, planning operations, and approving their execution. But the importance of these individuals to the overall objectives of Al Qaeda is actually limited in comparison to the other three dimensions of the movement.

The second dimension of Al Qaeda is comprised of formally established insurgent or terrorist groups like those mentioned above, who have received training, arms, money, "spiritual guidance," and other assistance from Al Qaeda central. These groups are located in dozens of countries across Asia, the Middle East, and North Africa. They include the Islamic Movement of Turkistan, the Jihad Movement (in Bangladesh), Jemaah Islamiyah (in Indonesia), the Abu Sayyaf Group (in Malaysia and the Philippines), the Moro Islamic Liberation Front (in the Philippines), the Islamic Army of Aden (in Yemen), the Libyan Islamic Fighting Group, the Groupe Islamique Combattant Marrocaine (in Morocco), the Groupe Tunisien Islamique (in Tunisia), and an array of militant groups in Kashmir, including *Jaish-e-Muhammad, Lashkar-e-Taiba,* and Harkat *al-Mujahideen*. These so-called "Al Qaeda affiliate groups" – like Jemaah Islamiyah (in Indonesia), the Islamic Army of Aden (in Yemen), Harkat al-Mujahideen (in Kashmir), and the Moroccan Islamic Combatant Group – have been responsible for hundreds of terrorist attacks since before 9/11. Because of these groups' ideological (and sometimes logistical) relationship with Al Qaeda central, we have often attributed these attacks to Osama bin Laden and his close colleagues, regardless of the absence of any direct command or control linkages. This is precisely what bin Laden envisioned for Al Qaeda – armed groups inspired to act on behalf of the global movement.

The third dimension of the movement is comprised of dispersed, ad-hoc groupings of Al Qaeda adherents who may have (or previously had) some direct connection with Al Qaeda, but are not members of any formal group. There are two sub-categories within this dimension: Individuals who have had some prior terrorism experience, and may have been involved in some previous jihadi campaign in Algeria, the Balkans, or Chechnya – or perhaps more recently in Iraq – and may have trained in some Al Qaeda facility, like in Afghanistan, Yemen, or Sudan before 9/11. Examples include Ahmed Ressam, an Algerian who received basic terrorist training in Afghanistan, was given $12,000 in "seed money" along with very non-specific, virtually open-ended targeting instructions before being dispatched to North America, and was arrested in December 1999 at Port Angeles, Washington, shortly after he had entered the United States from Canada.

Similarly, Kamel Bourgass, the 31-year-old Algerian who was apprehended by British authorities in January 2003 after they discovered ingredients, utensils, and instructions for producing ricin in his apartment, had spent several years in Al Qaeda training camps in Afghanistan. The so-called "Ricin Plot" was initially uncovered by Algerians while interrogating Mohamed Meguerba, a member of a North African criminal network who had also spent time training in Afghanistan. And in August 2004, police in London arrested several young British men of Pakistani origin on various terrorist-related charges. Court records indicate they intended to use radioactive "dirty bombs" in a series of attacks against U.S. financial targets, London hotels, and train stations. Among those arrested was Dhiren Barot, a Hindu convert to Islam who had trained at camps in Pakistan, Kashmir, Malaysia, and the Philippines. Individuals like these are conventionally referred to as "Al Qaeda operatives" in the mainstream press, although their connection to Al Qaeda central is minimal.

This dimension of Al Qaeda also includes a second subcategory comprised of persons who have not previously fought in any of the contemporary, iconic Muslim conflicts, but have an identified Al Qaeda connection. Examples here include the suicide bombers who attacked the London underground on July 7, 2005, (two of whom are believed to have received explosives training by an Al Qaeda operational commander in Pakistan) and the five members of a Pakistani community in Lodi,

California, who were arrested by authorities in June 2005 and charged with various offenses related to an FBI anti-terrorism investigation. One of the suspects, 22-year-old Hamid Hayat, admitted in a court affidavit that he had attended an Al Qaeda-supported camp in western Pakistan and received weapons training. These individuals carry no identifiable "name brand" group affiliation, yet are inspired enough by the ideology of Al Qaeda to seek advice, training, and support from its members.

The fourth dimension of Al Qaeda includes radicalized individuals who have absolutely no direct connection with Al Qaeda or any other identifiable terrorist group, but nonetheless are prepared to carry out attacks in solidarity with or support of Al Qaeda's jihadi agenda. Their relationship with Al Qaeda is more inspirational than actual. They are typically motivated by a shared sense of enmity and grievance felt towards the United States and the West, as well as the apostate regimes it supports, and more generally complain about the oppression of Muslims in Palestine, Kashmir, Chechnya, and elsewhere.

An example of individuals in this category is found in last year's so-called "Toronto Plot," in which 12 men and 5 youths were charged with planning a wave of attacks against Parliament Buildings, CBC Broadcasting Centre, and CSIS offices. The members of the group (all of whom were Canadian born or residents of good standing) have no known direct ties to Al Qaeda, but were radicalized (both online and by a local extremist cleric) by the messages of bin Laden to the point of attempting to acquire 3 tons of ammonium nitrate (triple the amount used by Timothy McVeigh in his attack against the Murrah Federal Building in Oklahoma City). Another example is U.S. citizen Daniel Maldonado. Born in Massachusetts and raised in New Hampshire, Maldonado became active on a web forum of highly conservative Salafis, and moved to Cairo in November 2005. A year later, he was motivated by a video by Ayman Al-Zawahiri, released online, calling on Muslims to strike at America's underlings in Somalia, and eliminate the "Zionist-Crusader" presence in the country. Maldonado's journey from young American in New England to jihadi in the Horn of Africa was cut short by malaria, contracted while undergoing weapons and explosive training, and he was arrested by Kenyan authorities after fleeing Somalia.

Overall, a primary objective of Osama bin Laden has always been to encourage and facilitate a worldwide Islamic revolution – to launch a socio-political action movement of global proportion, and to inspire, motivate, and animate radicalized Muslims to join the movement's fight. Join the Jihad. Think globally, act locally. These are the messages of Al Qaeda's massive strategic communications effort. This perspective of Al Qaeda highlights the critical importance of the underlying ideology which motivates members of the Salafi-Jihadi movement.

Understanding the Salafi-Jihadi Ideology

The ideology motivating Al Qaeda and affiliated groups stems from an extremist interpretation of Sunni Islam called Salafism. Within the 1.2 billion-strong Muslim community – people who follow the Koran and the example of Muhammad – there are Sunnis (people who follow the example of the Prophet) and Shi`is (people who follow the example of the Prophet and his descendents through his son-in-law Ali).[42] There are a range of secularists and fundamentalists among both Sunnis and Shi`is, including Islamists – people who want Islamic law to be the primary source of law and cultural identity in a state. Among these Islamists are the Salafis, Sunni Muslims who want to establish and govern Islamic states based solely on the Koran and the example of the Prophet as understood by the first generations of Muslims close to Muhammad. Finally, a distinct minority of Salafis are called Jihadis – the "holy warriors" and today's most prominent terrorists – among whom Al Qaeda and other groups seek to recruit and mobilize toward their particular vision of the future.

This unique Salafi-Jihadi interpretation of Islam draws from a number of sources. First, Ibn Tamiyya, a 13th century theologian, argued that Muslim leaders of his time had strayed from a literal interpretation of the Koran, and called for the eradication of beliefs and customs that were foreign to Islam and a renewed adherence to tawhid (oneness of God). His writings were very influential for Ibn Abd al-Wahhab, an 18th century cleric (and founder of the religious tradition that dominates Saudi Arabia), who argued that if one could not convert an audience to his interpretation of Islam, they could be labeled as infidels and deserved to be killed.

In the early 20th century, an Egyptian named Hassan al-Banna (the founder of the Muslim Brotherhood), carried forward the argument that much of the world had fallen away from true Islam, and encouraged

Muslims to use violence against the corrupting influences of the West (including occupying military forces and apostate regimes).

During this same period, Abu al-Ala Mawdudi, an Indian journalist, gained broad support for his argument that Muslims should not be afraid to use force in their quest to establish a more just society. And finally, another Egyptian named Sayyid Qutb expanded the argument that Islam is the one and only way of ruling mankind that is acceptable to God, and called for the abandonment of all human-created concepts, laws, customs, traditions – even by force, where necessary. He argued that Muslims should resist the influences of Western institutions and traditions that have poisoned mankind and made the world an evil place (*Dar al-Harb* – house of war or chaos).

These and other prominent Muslim figures have contributed significantly to what has become known as the Salafi-Jihadist movement, whose contemporary members are motivated by an ideology that can be summed up as "the world is truly messed up, and only Islam is the answer, therefore we must do all that is necessary to tear down the existing order and replace it with one built on Islam." The Jihadis' vision of the future requires them to overthrow what they consider "apostate" regimes in the Middle East and replace them with governments that rule by Sharia law, but only until the Islamic caliphate can be reestablished to rule over the entire Muslim world.

Attacks against Western targets (to include New York City and the Pentagon, London, and Madrid) are necessary because it is through alliances with powerful, industrialized Western nations that these apostate regimes are sustained. Finally, the magnitude of their long-term objective requires the Salafi-Jihadis to mobilize the entire Muslim community and convince them that catastrophic violence is necessary to remove the obstacles to a better (Islamic) future. There is, of course, much more to the ideology than this simplistic overview, as a quick glance through Internet websites and forums will reveal. But a basic element to keep in mind for the purposes of this analysis is that the Jihadi ideology is derived from Salafi ideology, which in turn is just one of many interpretive traditions of Islam.

A team of researchers at the Combating Terrorism Center at West Point, led by Professor Will McCants, recently produced a comprehensive analysis of the most influential thinkers in the Salafi-Jihadi movement, revealing several important themes about this ideology.⁴³ For example, they discerned that the Jihadi cause is best served when the conflict with local and foreign governments is portrayed as a conflict between Islam and the West; Islam is under siege and only the Jihadis can lift it. Further, Jihadis argue that violence against other Muslims, their governments, and resources is:

1. necessary,
2. religiously sanctioned, and
3. really the fault of the West, Israel, and apostate regimes.

Jihadis are certain of the absolute righteousness of their cause, and want unity of thought. They reject pluralism (the idea that no one has a monopoly on truth) and the political system that fosters it, democracy. And, as Qutb and other early thinkers in the movement have argued, Jihad is the only source of internal empowerment and reform in a state rule by an apostate regime.

Al Qaeda's Interest in WMD

For members of Al Qaeda, the Salafi-Jihadi ideology sanctions the acquisition and use of WMD to annihilate the enemies of Islam. They rationalize the need for these weapons as part of a power/capability/force multiplier calculation within the context of the larger socio-political vision being pursued. Whether the target is foreign or domestic, their interest in a WMD attack is predicated on the notion that if such weapons are made available, then God must intend for them to be used in the service of Jihad.

In October 2006, an audio statement was released by Abu Hamza al-Muhajir, the leader of Al Qaeda in Iraq, calling for nuclear scientists to join his mujahideen group and emphasizing that "the battlefield will accommodate your scientific aspirations." That same month, Dhiren Barot, a British jihadist and convert to Islam (also known as Issa al-Hindi or Issa al-Britani), pled guilty in a London courtroom to a series of attacks on both public gathering places and key economic targets in both Britain and the United States that were, according to prosecutors, meant to cause "injury, fear, terror and chaos."⁴⁴ In one plot, Barot intended to detonate a radiological dispersion device (also known as a "dirty bomb") in London.

These and other recent examples are pointed to as evidence of the global Salafi-Jihadist movement's growing interest in weapons of mass destruction.

Early indications of Al Qaeda's interests in WMD were seen in a May 1998 statement by Osama bin Laden, issued in the name of the "International Islamic Front for Fighting the Jews and Crusaders," titled "The Nuclear Bomb of Islam." In it, the Al Qaeda leader unambiguously declared that "it is the duty of Muslims to prepare as much force as possible to terrorize the enemies of God."[45] When asked several months later by a Pakistani journalist whether Al Qaeda was "in a position to develop chemical weapons and try to purchase nuclear material for weapons" bin Laden replied: "In answer, I would say that acquiring weapons for the defense of Muslims is a religious duty."[46]

Initially, in the late 1990s, Al Qaeda sought to acquire WMD in order to defend their safe haven in Afghanistan. Today, research indicates that Al Qaeda wishes to acquire a WMD to use as a first strike weapon against the United States and its allies. Their calculus for WMD acquisition is rational, not apocalyptic. They believe that WMD will advance their strategic objective of exhausting the United States economically and militarily by forcing the United States to expend massive amounts of money on protecting our critical infrastructure, borders and ports of entry, and on military deployments in Iraq, Afghanistan, and elsewhere. They are convinced that acquiring WMD will allow them to achieve military and strategic parity with the West, bestow credibility on the mujahideen, exaggerate the movement's power and capability, and frighten the enemies of Islam.

They also rationalize the acquisition and use of WMD as necessary to avenge Western "killing of Muslims" by killing large number of Western civilians. In 2003, Al Qaeda received some modicum of religious sanction for the use of WMD against the enemies of Islam by Saudi cleric Nassir bin Hamad al-Fahd, who issued an important and detailed fatwa on the permissibility of WMD in jihad. He stated that since America has destroyed countless lands and killed millions of Muslims, it would obviously be permitted to respond in kind.

Similarly, Al Qaeda spokesman Suleiman Abu Gheith stated in 2002 that "we have the right to kill 4 million Americans, 2 million of them children…and cripple them in the hundreds of thousands. Furthermore, it is our obligation to fight them with chemical and biological weapons, to afflict them with the fatal woes that have afflicted Muslims because of their chemical and biological weapons." And Al Qaeda member Abu Muhammad al-Ablaj noted that a chemical, biological, or nuclear weapon "must be used at a time that makes the crusader enemy beg on his knee that he does not want more strikes."

The apocalyptic "end of the world" doctrine of a cult like Aum Shinrikyo is inconsistent with Salafi-Jihadi ideology. The Koran is filled with predictions about the end of the world, but most Muslims (including many Jihadis) believe that only God decides when this will take place, and thus it is not up to humans to bring about such an event. However, this does not suggest that Jihadis are averse to catastrophic terrorism. Indeed, they do believe that mass killing is permitted in defense of Islam as long as the enemy persists. In his 2003 fatwa, al-Fahd argued that if mass killing is the only way to harm the enemy and bring it to its knees, then so be it. Further, he claims that mass killing of Muslims is also justified if it is necessary to harm the enemy.

In a 9-page open letter to the State Department released in November 2004, senior Al Qaeda strategist Abu Musab Al-Suri described the importance of using WMD against the United States as the only means to fight it from a point of equality. He even criticized Osama bin Laden for not using WMD in the September 11, 2001, attacks: "If I were consulted in the case of that operation I would advise the use of planes in flights from outside the U.S. that would carry WMD."[47] According to Al-Suri, "if those engaged in jihad establish that the evil of the infidels can be repelled only by attacking them with weapons of mass destruction, they may be used even if they annihilate all the infidels."

Like Osama bin Laden and Ayman Al-Zawahiri, Al-Suri has also argued that the United States has declared a crusade against Muslims, and openly seeks to colonize the Middle East. (Of course, an ideology can be compelling to its target audience even if wholly untrue.) Finally, he states that "the defeat of the United States and the end of its ambitions of hegemony over the world is a matter of life and death for Muslims. It is a favor for the entire human race. We cannot imagine that the United States, with its mighty military and economic power, will be defeated and destroyed unless one of the following takes place:

- God Almighty sends a natural disaster and annihilates the United States. He destroys it with meteorites, earthquakes, volcanoes, or floods.

- Muslims will be able to defeat the United States by means of resistance and lengthy guerrilla warfare.

- The last option is to destroy the United States by means of decisive strategic operations with weapons of mass destruction including nuclear, chemical, or biological weapons if mujahideen are able to obtain them in cooperation with those who possess them, purchase them, or manufacture and use primitive atomic bombs or the so-called dirty bombs."[48]

These and other statements of senior Al Qaeda leaders illustrate their rationale for acquiring and using weapons of mass destruction in order to destroy (or at least defeat) the West and save Islam. When their ideology resonates among some parts of the Muslim world, the movement is able to mobilize support which fuels an expanding trajectory of capabilities. From this perspective, it is perhaps only a matter of time before a catastrophic attack with a chemical or radiological (or, slightly less probable, biological or nuclear) weapon is carried out by one or more followers of this ideology. Their use of a WMD against the perceived enemies of Islam would certainly have a dramatic psychological impact on the West as well as the Muslim world, in addition to the potential for catastrophic loss of life and disruption of the global economy. Countering the ideological dimensions of this threat should thus be a priority for the United States and our allies.

Implications for Confronting the WMD Terror Threat

This analysis suggests implications for developing a more sophisticated understanding of terrorist group intentions, capabilities, and opportunities to cause harm and destruction. Unfortunately, a host of pervasive biases tend to get in the way of this.[49] For example, several analysts have suggested that terrorists are unlikely to have the technical skills needed to develop WMD, and are incapable of sustaining a long-term effort to successfully conduct a WMD attack.

Others have argued that because terrorists seek immediate gains and are too impatient to try and develop their own WMD capacity, they are likely to seek state sponsorship and/or try to acquire components and materials from places the United States is most concerned about, and thus if they try to do so our intelligence services will find out. Many terrorism scholars and policy makers have suggested that terrorists cannot be dissuaded or deterred from WMD use, while others have argued that if such an attack occurs, it will be easy to know what group is responsible, making deterrence more possible. Biases such as these contribute to a common set of analytical shortcomings, such as underestimating the capabilities of our enemies, failing to build international nonproliferation partnerships, and focusing on policies that are reactive instead of proactive.

Another bias involves the likelihood assigned to different types of WMD attacks. Security analysts agree that there is a wide-range of potential WMD events, but biological and chemical threats are not often given the same attention as nuclear or radiological threats. The past, the historical record, is not necessarily indicative of what the future will hold, particularly given contemporary advances in biotechnology, where all signs point to an escalating investment in research and development throughout the world. States can be expected to invest more heavily in nuclear and biotechnology research because of the promise these hold for improving the lives of their citizens (particularly in areas of energy and health/medicine), and this in turn will result in a growth of new dual-use technologies in both areas.

These issues have implications for our understanding of a terrorist group's capabilities, and suggest indicators of potential intent that warrant our attention. For example, does the group have a "science and technology division" (as did Aum Shinrikyo), or does it devote significant resources to exploring the development or acquisition of WMD? Is the group actively trying to recruit scientists, chemical storage facility personnel, biotechnology graduate students, hospital radiological lab technicians, and so forth? Does the group have access to laboratories or testing facilities? Do members of the group own front companies, and are they connected to transnational import/export networks?

When forecasting a WMD terror threat, it is also important to clarify the intentions of the group(s) of concern, in order to determine whether such weapons would truly be advantageous to their strategic objectives. Do they maintain an ideology which calls for some sort of cataclysmic event (like Armageddon) in order to realize their vision of a better future? Does their ideology give reason to believe they might be more interested in one type of WMD over another? What does their ideology suggest about potential targets? The statements of a group's leaders, training and indoctrination materials, websites, court records, and a range of other sources should be exploited to identify useful insights on the WMD intentions of any group.

The research literature is fairly rich with additional descriptions of how to forecast a potential WMD terrorism threat. For example, terrorism expert Brian Jenkins has argued that three sets of factors influence the likelihood of CBW terrorism: technical factors, policy factors (actions governments take to limit vulnerabilities), and political factors (terrorist motivations). He also suggests that the technical constraints of obtaining, manufacturing, storing, and effectively disseminating large amounts of lethal chemicals or biological pathogens means that if such terrorism does occur, it will most likely involve chemical rather than biological weapons, will be a small-scale attack, and will more likely involve an agent readily available in an industrialized society (such as cyanide or rat poison) than "more exotic" chemical or biological weapons.[50]

In contrast, Daniel Gressang has offered three different factors that can be used to determine the likelihood of a terrorist group using WMD. The first factor is the core audience with whom the group seeks to communicate. Gressang posits that this can be a human audience (such as a population of constituency that the group operates in support of or on behalf of) or an ethereal audience (such as a religious deity), and that the latter "may be prone to accept greater levels of violence and, perhaps, see considerable utility in the use of mass-casualty weapons."

The second factor is the content of the message directed on the core audience. Gressang argues that most terrorist groups seek social or political change, which is reflected in their message, while some groups preach a message of destruction (of an enemy, a people, a state, etc.). Because the desire to effect change requires that something survive the violence in order to be changed, Gressang argues that only those groups with a message of destruction would likely use CBRN.

The third factor he points to is social interaction, or the level of the relationship of the group to the society in which it exists. This relationship can be reciprocal, with the group receiving some sort of response from the target audience, or it can be the opposite, with the group isolating itself and severing all ties with the society around it. Using these factors, Gressang hypothesizes that groups at the negative extremes of each spectrum would seriously consider the use of CBRN with the intent to cause mass casualties.[51]

In addition, CIA veteran Joshua Sinai has offered three additional areas that should be considered when developing models that can be used by intelligence agencies to forecast the spectrum of warfare that a terrorist group is likely to conduct against a specific adversary.

First, threat assessments need to focus on three types of warfare that characterize this spectrum of terrorist operations: conventional low impact (CLI), conventional high impact (CHI), or chemical, biological, radiological, or nuclear (CBRN) warfare, also known as weapons of mass destruction (WMD).

Second, one needs to focus on the characteristics of terrorist groups that shape and define the type of warfare that they are likely to employ to achieve their objectives, starting with the nature of their leadership, motivation, strategy, supporting constituencies, and other factors such as capabilities, accelerators, triggers, and hurdles that are likely to propel them to pursue CLI, CHI, or CBRN warfare (or a combination of the three).

Third, we must focus our efforts on determining the disincentives and constraints that are likely (or not) to deter terrorist groups away from CBRN warfare, which is the most catastrophic (and difficult) form of potential warfare, particularly when these groups can resort to conventional explosives which have become increasingly more lethal and "catastrophic" in their impact. Analytically, therefore, terrorist groups currently operating on the international scene (or newly emergent ones) need to be viewed as potential CLI, CHI, or CBRN warfare actors (or a combination of the three), based on an understanding of the indicator and warning factors likely to propel them to embark on such types of warfare against their adversaries.[52]

Overall, knowing our terrorist enemies requires thoughtful contemplation of what we need to be thinking about and how to get the kind of information we need to really understand the threat. We must develop the critical thinking skills necessary for identifying at the earliest possible point a terrorist group's interest in acquiring or using weapons of mass destruction. We also need to build a knowledge base of strategies that can be used to dissuade, deter, prevent, eliminate, or mitigate the consequences of terrorists' use of WMD at local levels.

There are also a variety of intelligence gathering activities that are critical to any counterterrorism and counterproliferation effort, including outreach to academic institutions and businesses (especially biotechnology research firms, chemical storage facilities, hazardous transportation companies, hospitals, science and technology think tanks, etc.). Robust interagency working relationships must be established between a variety of federal agencies (including customs and border control agencies) and local law enforcement. International partnerships are critical, as is monitoring the Internet for signs of activity which might suggest target surveillance or attempts to acquire WMD materials, recruit scientists, or mobilize others to carry out (or at least help facilitate) a WMD terror attack in pursuit of the group's ideological objectives.

Our national security strategies have historically focused on constraining an enemy's operational and technical capabilities to cause us harm. This analysis suggests that we must also explore new and creative ways to counter the motivating ideologies of catastrophic terrorism. Combating terrorism that is driven by an extreme religious or apocalyptic vision requires sophisticated skills in public diplomacy and strategic communication, in order to influence the communities which might find these kinds of vision appealing. Furthermore, the communication of compelling ideas and visions to various audiences around the world in the hopes of impacting their behavior – often called strategic influence, "winning hearts and minds," or "winning the war of ideas" – must involve credible voices from within the target audience.

Catastrophic terrorism is inherently indiscriminate, which accounts for the relatively low popular appeal of the most violent ideologies on the spectrum described earlier. Even among the most disenfranchised populations, small-scale violence in pursuit of a better future is seen as more acceptable than indiscriminate death and destruction. As Figure 7.2

illustrates, there is an inverse relationship between the level of violence promoted by an ideology and its potential for popular support.

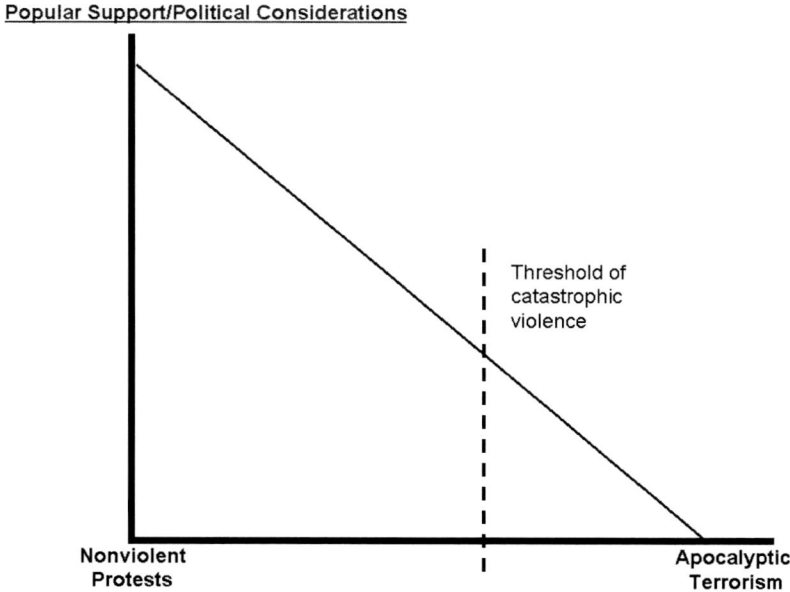

Figure 7.2 Popular Appeal vs. Level of Violence Encouraged by Ideology

In the case of the Salafi-Jihadi ideology, our counterterrorism strategy can capitalize on this inverse relationship by arguing convincingly that while Jihadis claim to be saving Islam, they are hurting their own people and national resources and tarnishing the image of Islam among non-Muslims. There are contradictions inherent in the Salafi-Jihadi arguments, and the movement may very well fall apart someday under the weight of its own ideological contradictions, much like the false utopian promises of Soviet communism. We should seek to accelerate that process.

At the core of Al Qaeda's ideology is the belief in the transformative power of action, jihad-style, at both an individual and global level. In the eyes of the global jihadist, violent action is necessary (and required of all Muslims) in order to prevent the West from destroying Islam.

Ultimately, the goal of the global jihad movement is to establish a worldwide Islamic order, and to achieve this objective jihadis must remove obstacles in their way – like the United States and the regimes it helps sustain – as well as convince Muslims around the world that: (1) Islam is indeed under attack by the West, and (2) the new Islamic order they envision would be a better alternative than the present, and is worth fighting and dying for.

However, Jihadis have lost credibility among mainstream Muslims by attacking women, children, and the elderly. Muslims have been prominent among the casualties of Jihadi catastrophic violence, and thus we should emphasize that when innocent Muslims are killed, they are robbed of their chance to conduct their own personal and spiritual jihad as called for in the Koran.

Jihadis also lose support by creating political and social chaos in the Muslim world (particularly given the Koran's mandate to avoid *fitna*) and by damaging the sources of a nation's wealth (such as tourism and oil). Our counterterrorism strategy must highlight these and other ideologically divisive issues as part of a broader effort to de-legitimize violence against non-combatants.

We must also engage credible Islamic leaders in a global effort to combat attempts to rationalize a WMD attack as God's will. As several recent reports published by the Combating Terrorism Center at West Point indicate, denouncements of prominent Jihadis by other prominent Jihadis are particularly damaging and demoralizing.[53] We must encourage a broad, comprehensive effort involving Salafi scholars – particularly Saudi clerics, who are best positioned to discredit the movement – to reduce the potential appeal of this ideology in the Muslim world by emphasizing the fact that theirs is an extremely radical interpretation of an otherwise peaceful religion, and followers of this interpretation are more cultish than part of a religious movement.

It is particularly important here to highlight how Muslim opponents of the Jihadis use the term "Qutbism" (in recognition that the Jihadis cite Sayyid Qutb more than any other modern author) to describe them, a designation Jihadis hate since it implies that they follow a human and are members of a deviant sect. Adherents of the Al Qaeda-inspired movement consider "Qutbi" to be a negative label and would much rather be called Jihadi or Salafi.

We must emphasize that they are pursuing a totalitarian system of government in which no one is allowed to think for themselves, and anyone who does not share their understanding of Islam will be declared an apostate and executed. In fact, the appeal of this vision of the future is so weak that its adherents must use violence in order to compel individuals to accept it.

Finally, we must convince Jihadis and their potential supporters that their methods are an ineffective and counterproductive means for social change. An important component of this argument involves convincing our enemies of the strength of our own national resilience. We must convince them beyond a shadow of a doubt that they are guaranteed not to achieve their objectives, regardless of the frequency or magnitude of their catastrophic terror attacks. Even the types of weapons they use, including WMD, will never result in a world (or even a Middle East) that is ruled only by Islamic law.

As long as our political and economic systems and our citizens are shown to be adequately resilient to withstand any type of WMD attack, this alone can be a powerful form of deterrence. Denial of the enemy's potential for achieving their objective is a type of strategic constraint that is common in much of the counterinsurgency and counterterrorism research, and should play a more prominent role in combating the threat posed by followers of the Salafi-Jihadi ideology.

Conclusion

Nearly ten years ago, three widely respected scholars (Ashton Carter, John Deutch, and Phillip Zelikow) proposed that while the United States has become reasonably adept at dealing with normal terrorist incidents, it is not at all prepared for what they called "catastrophic terrorism," better known as WMD terrorism. They acknowledged that the task appears insurmountable, yet emphasized that the United States has overcome similar periods of challenge in the past. In order to meet the threat, they recommended reorganization along four lines: intelligence and warning, prevention and deterrence, crisis and consequence management, and coordinated acquisition of equipment and technology. The authors proposed new institutions that should be developed within each of these four areas that they believe would meet the stated needs. (Written in late

1998, some of their suggestions have come to pass after September 11, 2001.)[54]

That same year, Nobel Laureate Joshua Lederberg offered a prophetic observation that continues to ring true nearly 10-years later: "There is no technical solution to the problem of biological weapons. It needs an ethical, human and moral solution if it's going to happen at all."[55] Countering the threat of catastrophic terrorism, especially involving WMD, certainly requires us to counter our enemy's technical and operational capabilities, but as Lederberg suggests, we must also do all we can to address the *behavioral* aspects of the threat. In addition to traditional means of deterrence (e.g., affecting the political will of a state or non-state actor to use WMD in pursuit of their objectives), we must also triumph in the battlespace of the mind, the place where ideologies of catastrophic terrorism can take root and motivate the most destructive behavior known to mankind.

The Salafi-Jihadi ideology which motivates members of Al Qaeda and other like-minded groups is built upon the precepts of an existing tradition within the broader Islamic faith. It is an ideology which resonates in the Muslim world because of several pre-existing perceptions and environmental factors, including a sense of crisis, humiliation, impotence, and resentment directed at their local rulers and powerful Western allies.

Understanding the enablers of an ideology's resonance is important, as it sensitizes us to conditions or events which might *increase* (or, alternately, *constrain*) the appeal of a movement like the Salafi-Jihadis among a broader population. Further, as other terrorism scholars have noted, the primary danger of a WMD attack stems from religious terrorists who are "unconstrained" either by fear of government action or moral considerations, but rather – like the Salafi-Jihadis – are pursuing what they perceive to be God's will (a world that is ruled by Islam), and believe that the acquisition and use of WMD is necessary to achieve this objective. Countering this and other ideologies of catastrophic terrorism must therefore be a critical component of our national security strategy, and requires a collaborative interagency and multinational effort.

Notes

1. For example, see the Congressional Testimony of FBI Director Robert Mueller on 11 January 2007, (Hearing of the Senate Select Committee on Intelligence Annual Threat Assessment).

2. This is a catch phrase used—some may say abused—by several government officials, security experts, academics, and comedians to discuss the likelihood of the use of WMD against the United States. Stephen Flynn, in his book *America the Vulnerable*, (HarperCollins: 2004) spoke of containers as "the poor man's missile" and implied that the question is "when, not if" such containers will be used to deliver WMD into the United States.

3. See Russell Howard, "Preface" in *Weapons of Mass Destruction and Terrorism*, edited by Russell Howard and James Forest, (New York: McGraw-Hill, 2007). See also, Richard Pells, "Not with a Whimper: Visions of Mass Destruction in Fiction and Film," *E-Journal USA-Foreign Policy Agenda*, March 2005, On-line, Internet, available from http://usinfo.state.gov/journals/itps/0305/ijpe/pells.htm.

4. Bruce Hoffman, "CBRN Terrorism Post-9/11," *Weapons of Mass Destruction and Terrorism*, edited by Russell Howard and James J.F. Forest, (New York: McGraw-Hill, 2007).

5. John V. Parachini, "Comparing Motives and Outcomes of Mass Casualty Terrorism Involving Conventional and Unconventional Weapons," *Studies in Conflict and Terrorism*, vol. 24, no. 5, (September 2001), 389-406.

6. This Matsumoto attack did not kill the 3 judges, but did inflict deaths and casualties on neighbors and succeeded in delaying the trial that the Aum thought it might lose. For a list of Aum attacks with biological agents, see David E. Kaplan, "Aum Shinrikyo (1995)," in *Toxic Terror: Assessing Terrorist Use of Chemical and Biological Weapons*, ed. Jonathan B. Tucker, (Cambridge, Mass.: MIT Press, 2000), 221.

7. Peter Franceschina, "Anthrax Attacks Remain Unsolved," *Baltimore Sun*, 15 October 2006, 1. See Russell Howard, "Preface" in *Weapons of Mass Destruction and Terrorism*, edited by Russell Howard and James Forest, (New York: McGraw-Hill, 2007).

8. Hoffman, "CBRN Terrorism Post-9/11," 2007.

9. "Jordan says major al Qaida plot disrupted," *CNN*, 26 April 2004.

10. U.S. Forces in Iraq find some cyanide," *ABC News*, 7 February 2004.

11. Sammy Salama and Lydia Hansell, "Does Intent Equal Capability? Al Qaeda and Weapons of Mass Destruction," *Nonproliferation Review* 12, no. 3, (November 2003), 615-653.

12. "Roundtable on the Implications of the September 11, 2001, Terrorist Attacks for Nonproliferation and Arms Control," *Nonproliferation Review*, vol. 8, no. 3, (Fall-Winter 2001, 11-26.

13. Rene Pita, "Al Qaida and the Chemical Threat," *ASA Newsletter*, Issue No. 108, 9 June 2005, On-line, Internet, available from http://www.asanltr.com/newsletter/05-3/articles/053a.htm.

14. John Parachini, "The Making of Aum Shinrikyo's Chemical Weapons Program," in *The Making of a Terrorist, Vol. 2: Training*, edited by James J.F. Forest, (Westport, CT: Praeger Security International, 2005).

15. Ibid.

16. Steven Simon and Daniel Benjamin, "America and the New Terrorism," *Survival*, vol. 42, no. 1, (Spring 2000), 59-75.

17. Matthew Bunn and Anthony Wier, "The Seven Myths of Nuclear Terrorism," *Weapons of Mass Destruction and Terrorism*, edited by Russell Howard and James J.F. Forest, (New York: McGraw-Hill, 2007).

18. Dave Franz, "Bioterrorism Defense: Controlling the Unknown," *Weapons of Mass Destruction and Terrorism*, edited by Russell Howard and James J.F. Forest, (New York: McGraw-Hill, 2007).

19. For more on this, see Lee M. Myers, "Agriculture and Food Defense," in *Homeland Security: Protecting America's Targets, Volume 3: Critical Infrastructure*, edited by James J.F. Forest, (Westport, CT: Praeger, 2006); Hanley, Brian and Birthe Borup, "Bioterrorism and Biodefense for America's Public Spaces and Cities," in *Homeland Security: Protecting America's Targets, Volume 2: Public Spaces and Social Institutions*, edited by James J.F. Forest, (Westport, CT: Praeger Security International, 2006); and Terrence K. Kelly, Peter Chalk, James Bonomo, John Parachini, Brian A. Jackson, and Gary Cecchine, "The Office of Science and Technology Policy Blue Ribbon Panel on the Threat of Biological Terrorism Directed Against Livestock," Conference Report Prepared for the Office of Science and Technology Policy, April 2004, Santa Monica, CA: RAND Corporation, On-line, Internet, available from http://www.rand.org/scitech/stpi/Bioagpanel.

20. John Parachini, "The Making of Aum Shinrikyo's Chemical Weapons Program," 2005.

21. Jason Pate, Gary Ackerman, and Kimberly McCloud, "2000 WMD Terrorism Chronology: Incidents Involving Sub-National Actors and Chemical, Biological, Radiological, or Nuclear Materials," *Center for Nonproliferation Studies*, 13 August 2001, On-line, Internet, available from http://cns.miis.edu/research/terror.htm.

22. Cited in Steve Bowman and Helit Barel, *Weapons of Mass Destruction—The Terrorist Threat*, (CRS Report for Congress, RS20412), Washington, D.C.: Congressional Research Service, 8 December 1999, On-line, Internet, available from http://www.fas.org/irp/crs/RS20412.pdf; also see Gavin Cameron, "WMD Terrorism in the United States: The Threat and Possible Countermeasures," *Nonproliferation Review*, vol. 7, no. 1, (Spring 2000), 162-179.

23. For example, see John Parachini, "Putting WMD Into Perspective," *Homeland Security and Terrorism*, edited by Russell D. Howard, James J.F. Forest and Joanne Moore, (New York: McGraw-Hill, 2005).

24. Bowman and Barel, *Weapons of Mass Destruction—The Terrorist Threat*, 1999.

25. See Brad Roberts (ed.), *Terrorism with Chemical and Biological Weapons: Calibrating Risks and Responses*, (Washington, D.C.: Chemical and Biological Arms Control Institute, 1997).

26. "Roundtable on the Implications of the September 11, 2001, Terrorist Attacks for Nonproliferation and Arms Control," 2001, 11-26.

27. Roberts, *Terrorism with Chemical and Biological Weapons*, 1997.

28. Bunn and Wier, "The Seven Myths of Nuclear Terrorism," 2007.

29. Parachini, "Comparing Motives and Outcomes of Mass Casualty Terrorism Involving Conventional and Unconventional Weapons," 2005.

30. Ibid.

31. Ibid.

32. An earlier version of this section, "The Final Act: Ideologies of Catastrophic Terror," was presented at the *Threat Convergence Summit*, November 2006 in Arlie, Virginia.

33. Roberts, *Terrorism with Chemical and Biological Weapons*, 1997.

34. Bowman and Barel, *Weapons of Mass Destruction—The Terrorist Threat*, 1999.; Also, for a discussion on what types of groups or individuals might attempt to use bioterror weapons, please see Brian Hanley and Birthe Borup, "Bioterrorism and

Biodefense for America's Public Spaces and Cities," in *Homeland Security: Protecting America's Targets, Vol. 2: Public Spaces and Social Institutions*, edited by James J.F. Forest, (Westport, CT: Praeger Security International, 2006).

35. Michael Barkun, "Terrorism and Doomsday," *The Making of a Terrorist, Volume 3: Root Causes*, edited by James J.F. Forest, (Westport, CT: Praeger Security International, 2005).

36. Ibid.

37. J.P. Larsson, "The Role of Religious Ideology in Terrorist Recruitment," *The Making of a Terrorist (Volume 1: Recruitment)*, edited by James J.F. Forest, (Westport, CT: Praeger Security International, 2005). Also, see James J.F. Forest, "Introduction" in *Teaching Terror: Strategic and Tactical Learning in the Terrorist World*, (Lanham, MD: Rowman & Littlefield, 2006).

38. Bowman and Barel, *Weapons of Mass Destruction—The Terrorist Threat*, 1999.

39. National Intelligence Council, "The Terrorist Threat to the US Homeland," National Intelligence Estimate, July 2007, On-line, Internet, available from http://www.dni.gov/press_releases/20070717_release.pdf.

40. Testimony before Congress, *Combating Terrorism Center's website*, 14 February 2007, On-line, Internet, available from http://ctc.usma.edu/Hoffman_Testimony021407.pdf.

41. A previous version of this section was previously published as "Knowing Al Qaida," by James Forest, in *Family Security Matters*, 22 June 2007, On-line, Internet, available from http://www.familysecuritymatters.org/terrorism.php?id=1087256.

42. This description of Islam and Al Qaeda's ideology is courtesy of William McCants, a Fellow at the Combating Terrorism Center at West Point.

43. William McCants and Jarret Brachman, *The Militant Ideology Atlas*, West Point, NY: Combating Terrorism Center, 2006, On-line, Internet, available from http://ctc.usma.edu.

44. BBC News, "Man admits UK-US terror bomb plot," 12 October 2006, On-line, Internet, available from http:newsvote.bbc.co.uk/mpapps/pagetools/print/news.bbc.co.uk/2/hi/uk_news/6044. See also Alan Cowell, "British Muslim Sentenced in Terror Attacks," *New York Times*, 8 November 2006.

45. Quoted in Ben Venzke and Aimee Ibrahim, *The al Qaida Threat: An Analytical Guide to al Qaida's Tactics and Targets*, (Alexandria, VA: Tempest Publishing, 2003), 52.

46. "Osama bin Laden—Interview, 23 December 1998, Rahimullah Yusufzai Interview" in Ibid., 53.

47. Reuven Paz, "Global Jihad and WMD: Between Martyrdom and Mass Destruction," in Hillel Fradkin, Husain Haqqani and Eric Brown, eds., *Current Trends in Islamist Ideology*, (Washington, D.C.: Hudson Institute, 2005). See also, Peter Bergen, "Reading al-Qaeda," *Washington Post*, 11 September 2005.

48. Ibid.

49. Portions of this discussion paraphrase (by permission) a presentation by Belinda Canton at the Armed Groups Workshop, hosted by the National Consortium for the Study of Intelligence, in Annapolis, Maryland on 19 July 2007.

50. Brad Roberts, *Terrorism with Chemical and Biological Weapons*, 1997.

51. Daniel S. Gressang, "Audience and Message: Assessing Terrorist WMD Potential," *Terrorism and Political Violence*, vol. 13, no. 3, (Autumn 2001), 83-106.

52. Joshua Sinai, "Forecasting Terrorist Groups' Warfare: 'Conventional' to CBRN," *Countering Terrorism in the 21st Century, Vol. 1: Strategic and Tactical Considerations*, edited by James J.F. Forest, (Westport, CT: Praeger, 2007).

53. These reports are all available on the CTC's public website, On-line, Internet, available from http://ctc.usma.edu.

54. Ashton Carter, John Deutch, and Phillip Zelikow, "Catastrophic Terrorism: Tackling the New Danger," *Foreign Affairs*, vol. 77, no. 6, (Nov-Dec 1998), 80-94.

55. Quoted in Richard Preston, "Annals of Warfare," *The New Yorker*, (9 March, 1998).

CHAPTER 8

Hezbollah: A State Within a State

Michael T. Kindt

The oft heard but unattributed quote "One man's terrorist is another man's freedom fighter" is a nearly perfect description of the world's view of the Lebanese group Hezbollah. Some, such as the United States, clearly view this organization as a terrorist group, highlighted by Richard Armitage's statement that "Hezbollah may be the A-Team of Terrorists' and maybe [Al] Qaeda is actually the B-Team."[1] Although this view of Hezbollah as a terrorist group is shared by some key U.S. allies, those holding this view are currently in a definite minority: (U.S., UK, Canada, Australia, Netherlands, and Israel). Most European countries, (and the EU) do not classify Hezbollah as a terrorist group, seeing them instead as a liberation movement on the verge of becoming a political party.[2]

For many in the Arab world, far from being considered terrorists, Hezbollah is seen as a shining example of courage and skill, being the only Muslim group to stand up to Israel and the United States and achieve victory. Their ability to force Israeli withdrawal from its occupation of southern Lebanon in 2000, and its perceived victory over Israel in the summer war of 2006, are accomplishments that no Arab states have been able to match, earning the group hero status in the eyes of many Muslims in the region.[3]

This vast range of perspectives, each holding portions of truth, is a reflection of the complexity and sophistication of the group known as Hezbollah. This chapter will explore the development of Hezbollah, from its roots in the Lebanese civil war, through its entry to politics and continuing conflict with Israel, in an effort to better understand the group's motivations, goals, and likely courses of action.

The Roots of Hezbollah

The area now known as Lebanon has been at the crossroads of many of the world's greatest empires, and this interaction of disparate cultures and faiths has produced an extremely culturally diverse nation that straddles the edge of the Arab world. In fact, many Lebanese, particularly Christians, see themselves not as Arab but as Phoenician.[4] Lebanon today is defined more by religious background than by ethnic culture, with no one religious group claiming an outright majority in the nation. Although it is estimated that 60 percent of the population is Muslim, this group is divided between Shi'a, Sunni, Druze and Alawite sects. The 40 percent Christian is similarly divided between Maronite, Greek Orthodox, Melkite Catholic, and several other Christian sects. Overall, Lebanon recognizes 17 significant religious denominations.[5]

This range of beliefs and backgrounds has played itself out continuously in the history of Lebanon and is at the heart of the turmoil in the country today. It is through skillful manipulation of this conflict that Hezbollah has grown to be a power player both within the country and a source of concern on the world stage. In the independent Lebanon that was created after the 1943 National Pact, political representation and key elected offices were determined by the representation of religious sects in the nation.

The decision to create a Lebanon apart from Syrian control was favored by the Christian groups but not by many in the Muslim communities. This initial split between Christians and Muslims, those desiring a Lebanon leaning toward Europe and those wanting to stay grounded in the Arab world, was to form a basis for a second conflict that continues to play out today. Based on data from a 1932 census, the Maronites were the largest single sect and were constitutionally to hold the office of the President. As the next largest single sect, Sunni Muslims were to hold the office of Prime Minister and the Shi'a, as the third largest group, were to hold the position of the Speaker of Parliament.[6]

This "confessional system" which rigidly assigned representation and power based on what would certainly become outdated census information, perpetuated the power of the Maronites and Sunnis at the expense of the Shi'a and set the stage for increasing resentment and conflict. With a government and civil power structure that favored

Christians and Sunnis, with economic growth and government resources focused on the urban areas populated by these groups, the more rural Shi'a suffered through political and economic blight. The conditions in the rural southern part of the country led to large migrations of Shi'a to the outskirts of Beirut in the late 1950s and 1960s. This created large groups of displaced, disconnected Shi'a often living in slum-like conditions who were ripe for political manipulation.

As dissatisfaction with the dominance of Christian groups grew throughout the Muslim communities during the 1960s and early 1970s, it became increasingly difficult for the political system to resolve differences between the groups. Various religious and political groups began to form militias to protect the interests of their groups and the nation fell into a complex civil war in which alliances between groups rapidly changed, and foreign parties were drawn into the fray. In 1976, Syria entered Lebanon at the request of the Maronite president who feared his side was losing the battle, and by 1978 Israel invaded southern Lebanon in an effort to stop attacks from Palestinian groups who had settled in the region. It is within the context of this instability that a variety of Shi'a coalitions began to form, both to fight for Shi'a interests and to resist the occupation of southern Lebanon by the Israelis.

Amhad Nizar Hamzeh, in his book, *In The Path of Hizbullah*, describes four crises leading up to the civil war which prompted the development of Hezbollah. The first was an identity crisis based on the historic persecution of Shi'a not only in Lebanon but throughout the region at the hands of the British and French and dominant Sunni governments, which left Shi'a feeling a profound sense of alienation. The second crisis, more unique to Lebanon, was the political and economic system which excluded the Shi'a, who, by 1980 may have become the largest single religious group, from both the political and financial mainstream. The confessional system limited their access to power in the government. The third crisis leading to the formation of Hezbollah was the military occupation at the hands of Israel. Although some Shi'a initially welcomed the Israeli invasion in 1978 with hopes that it would remove Palestinians from the area, the campaign did not achieve this and the Shi'a suffered many casualties in the process. By the time of the second Israeli invasion in 1982, opinion had turned against Israel and their presence provided both justification and motivation for a strong resistance movement, brought to life by Hezbollah. The final catalyst for the formation of Hezbollah was the success of the Islamic revolution in Iran, led by the respected Shi'a cleric Ayatollah Khomeini.

While this triumph of an Islamic movement, over a pro-Western government inspired many Islamic communities in their quest for power, the personal, religious, and intellectual connections between the Shi'a religious leaders of the revolution in Iran and the senior Shi'a clerics in Lebanon ensured that this call to revolution was most clearly heard in Lebanon.[7] These conditions combined to create a population that was both desperate from years of political and economic neglect, but newly hopeful that a religious call to arms could bring them to greater freedom and power. Hezbollah, encouraged by both Iran and Syria, began to emerge from this environment to challenge the existing system and eventually lead the Shi'a community both militarily and politically.

But Hezbollah was not the first group to tap into the growing Shi'a discontent with the Lebanese political system. One of the first movements, in the early 1970s, to harness this energy was that of Imam Musa Al-Sadr, a respected cleric whose efforts to strengthen the Shi'a underclass and challenge the existing political system won him high regard with the poor, and enemies among the elites of the nation. A predominately Shi'a group, the Movement of the Deprived attempted to broaden its appeal to all disenfranchised Lebanese with a vision of political change for all. With the descent of Lebanon into civil war in 1975, Al-Sadr's civil movement developed its own militia group AMAL (Battalions of the Lebanese Resistance) to protect the interests of the Shi'a from other growing sectarian militias. The leader of this militia group was Nabih Berri, a young lawyer who grew to prominence and remains a key figure in Lebanese politics to this day. AMAL received its military support initially not from Syria, which was connected with the existing political system, but from Libya.[8]

This relationship with Libya was not without its difficulties and in 1978, the movement's founder and Islamic leader, Al-Sadr, disappeared on a trip to Libya (and is believed to have been killed there), leaving Berri in charge of the overall movement.[9] This mysterious disappearance of the Al-Sadr, which evoked images of the Shi'a belief of the hidden Imam, seriously impacted both the group and the community. Without Imam Al-Sadr, Berri moved AMAL in the direction of cooperation with the government, turning away from its Islamic inspiration, and as a result those looking for religious justification for their political and militant activity began to fall away from AMAL.[10] One of those who left the group was Hussein Musawi, a religious leader who broke away from AMAL to reestablish and emphasize the Shi'a roots of the movement.

Musawi's return to theological underpinnings of social and political change inspired a number of Shi'a religious leaders, many of whom had studied at the Shi'a seminary in Najaf, Iraq. This connection to Najaf is significant as two religious figures critical to the formation of Hezbollah had studied here: Grand Ayatollah Ruhallah Khomeini who would take over Iran and sponsor the Hezbollah movement, and Sayyed Mohammed Hussein Fadlallah who following the death of Imam Al-Sadr became the most influential Shi'a religious leader in Lebanon and would become the spiritual voice for Hezbollah.[11] It was from this group of clerics and individuals disenchanted with AMAL, drawn to a more openly religious movement, with theological connections to Ayatollah Khomeini and his Islamic Revolution in Iran, that Hezbollah would begin to coalesce.[12]

The final catalyst for the development of focused, armed Shi'a revolution in Lebanon was the 1982 invasion and subsequent occupation of southern Lebanon by Israel. Although the Shi'a of southern Lebanon accepted the Israeli invasion and crackdown on the PLO, with whom the Shi'a were also in conflict, the extended occupation and consequences for the Shi'a community quickly led to resentment that gave purpose and support to the founders of Hezbollah. This dynamic is best illuminated by Ehud Barack, a former Israeli Prime Minister, who stated: "When we entered Lebanon there was no Hezbollah. We were accepted with perfumed rice and flowers by the Shi'a in the south. It was our presence there that created Hezbollah."[13]

Hezbollah Announces Its Presence

The date of the actual birth of Hezbollah is a matter of debate. Some within Hezbollah place its founding in the late 1970s when those leaving the AMAL movement began to associate and look toward a more Islamic revolutionary ideal.[14] Others suggest that it was not until the mid 1980s that Hezbollah developed into a true organization, rather than a loose group of like-minded revolutionaries.[15] This also corresponds to Hezbollah's very public announcement of its existence and goals in its "Open Letter to the Oppressed" which was published in February 1985.[16]

From a practical standpoint, however, 1982 appears to have been the year in which the group began to assume a distinct identify and began to garner significant outside support for its Islamic revolution. A number of significant events in 1982 contributed to the consolidation of the group. First in that year, Israel invaded Lebanon for the second time and began their occupation of southern Lebanon. Later that year, the founding members of the organization met and composed their writing of the *Treatise of the Nine*, which outlined their identity and goals.[17] Also in 1982, critical military and ideological support for the group began to flow from Iran. In 1982, Iran is believed to have sent around 1,500 Islamic Revolutionary Guard Corps (IRGC) personnel to Lebanon to begin training the new forces for revolution in Lebanon.[18] This marked the beginning of an ongoing relationship in which Hezbollah both professed and demonstrated loyalty to the religious leadership of Iran in return for military, financial, and ideological support for their actions in Lebanon and Israel.

A further indication that Hezbollah was born in that year was the launching of the group's first claimed suicide bomber attack. In November 1982, a 15-year-old boy, Ahmed Qasir, drove a car loaded with explosives into a building being used by Israeli forces in Tyre.[19] This attack killed 88 people, including 74 Israeli soldiers, and marked the beginning of the use of suicide bombers as means of delivering deadly blows to Israeli and other Western forces in the country.

This attack in Tyre had ramifications far beyond the death and destruction caused on that day as it appears to have sparked the modern use of the suicide bombing tactic in the Middle East.[20] Although this attack was not claimed by the group until several years later, after the death of the attack planner, Raghib Harb, it marked the first in a string of deadly suicide attacks attributed to Hezbollah. This initial attack, and the death of Ahmed Qasir, as well as others the groups considers to have died in the resistance, are recognized by Hezbollah on "martyrdom day" observed annually on the anniversary of this attack.

The suicide attack perpetrated by Ahmed Qasir at the urging of Hezbollah marked the beginning of a terrible wave of violence either directly attributable to, or linked to Hezbollah, throughout the 1980s. Suicide bombings and kidnappings became the weapons of choice in Hezbollah's battle against Israeli occupation and the involvement of Western powers in Lebanon. Their wrath was not reserved for foreigners or infidels as the group also launched attacks against fellow Lebanese competitors (including fellow Shi'a) for control of the Shi'a regions of the country. Attacks on other Lebanese targets, including Shi'a groups, continued through the civil war as each group jockeyed for control of territory and influence over the population. However, Hezbollah's most prominent and deadly attacks came against Western and Israeli targets.

Less than one year after the initial suicide attack, the group launched the attacks that would bring them to the attention of the United States and provide them with their first claimed victory over the West. The first direct attack by Hezbollah against U.S. interests came on April 18, 1983. On this date a truck bomb was detonated in front of the U.S. Embassy building in Beirut, killing a total of 63 people, including 17 Americans. This attack was the first serious attack against U.S. forces in the region and highlighted the dangers of involvement in Lebanese affairs. Although Hezbollah has consistently denied responsibility for the attack, they have expressed understanding for the motivation of such attacks on Western agents in Lebanon, representing them as responses by "the weak to aggression of the powerful."[21] This attack was claimed by a group calling itself "Islamic Jihad," which may have been a transitional name used by those who had split from AMAL and would announce themselves as Hezbollah in 1985. The United States has maintained that Hezbollah, or associated elements, conducted the attack with the support of Iran.

The casualties inflicted on the United States in the attack on the embassy in Beirut were soon dwarfed by the destruction and loss of life in a second attack against the United States. On October 23, 1983, a truck bomb exploded at the barracks of the Marine peacekeepers stationed in Beirut, killing 241 U.S. service members, in what was until 9/11 the most deadly terrorist attack against the United States. Nearly simultaneously, another truck bomb exploded at the barracks of the French contingent to the UN mission killing 80 French soldiers.[22] Hezbollah denied involvement but the attack has been attributed to them. The group made statements praising the attacks and their impacts on the Western powers using them to bolster their cause of resistance against the Israelis and the

West and win the support of the Lebanese Shi'a community. Such comments are epitomized by the statements of Sheik Mohammed Yazbeck, now on Hezbollah's Shura Council, who praised the attacks as "shaking America's throne and France's might. Let America and Israel know that we have a lust for martyrdom and that our motto is being turned into reality."[23] These attacks also highlighted the sophisticated planning and organizational capability of the group. To be able to conduct surveillance, identify vulnerabilities, construct deadly weapons, and attack two Western military powers simultaneously is the mark of a well-prepared and disciplined adversary. While these capabilities are likely to be strongly related to the support and training provided by the Iranian IRGC operatives sent to Lebanon, it is clear that Hezbollah and associated Shi'a militants learned quickly and well from their advisors.

These attacks highlighted the extremely dangerous nature of Lebanon during the 1980s and the barracks bombings, along with apparent threats of further attacks, prompted the withdrawal of U.S. forces from Lebanon in early 1984.[24] This withdrawal provided Hezbollah their first perceived victory in their struggle against the West and empowered them to continue the fight. After the redeployment of American forces out of Lebanon, Hezbollah and other militant groups continued the conflict and pursued different targets and tactics.[25] The group's efforts moved from military targets to targeting individuals associated with the United States and the West as a wave of kidnappings swept the country.

Throughout the mid- to late 1980s, Lebanon was the scene of a rash of kidnappings as various factions in the raging civil war jockeyed for influence and control throughout the country. Some of the kidnappings targeted government officials including CIA officer William Buckley and Army Lieutenant Colonel William Higgins. William Buckley, the CIA station chief in Lebanon, had been captured in 1984 and apparently killed the following year.[26] Lieutenant Colonel Higgins, the commander of a UN observer team in Southern Lebanon, was kidnapped in 1987, tortured and killed with a video of his hanging released in 1989.[27] The bodies of Buckley and Higgins were not recovered until they were found, abandoned during a wave of hostage releases and body recoveries following the end of the Lebanese civil war in 1991.

Many civilians were also among the 30 Westerners kidnapped during the 1980s. These included cases such as Terry Waite, an emissary of the

Church of England, sent to negotiate the release of hostages, who was kidnapped himself and held for nearly 5 years.[28] Perhaps the most prominent of the kidnappings was that of an American journalist, Associated Press reporter Terry Anderson, who was held for nearly 7 years at the hands of Hezbollah, until his release in 1991. In an act of remarkable courage, Anderson returned to Lebanon 5 years after his release and met with Hezbollah Secretary General Hassan Nasrallah, and asked him about the kidnappings of the 1980s. Nasrallah declined to condemn such actions stating, "I'm not saying whether their methods were good or not, right or wrong, these actions were short-term, with short-term objectives, and I hope that they will not happen again." Efforts to negotiate the release of these hostages ultimately involved talks with and weapons transfers to Iran the so-called "arms for hostages" secret negotiations. These covert activities, which were uncovered during the Iran/Contra investigations, became famous in their own right and were known as "Irangate."[29]

Kidnappings were not the only tactics utilized by Hezbollah during the civil war, and in one of the defining scenarios of the era, Hezbollah operator and Ayatollah Fadlallah bodyguard, Imad Mugniyeh, masterminded the skyjacking of TWA 847. On June 14, 1985, TWA flight 847 from Athens to Rome was hijacked with 153 passengers, including many Americans. The flight was diverted to Beirut, and over the course of 3 days the plane moved from Beirut to Algiers and back twice, occasionally releasing some hostages in return for fuel and food. During the plane's second stop in Beirut, the hijackers identified Robert Stethem as a U.S. Navy sailor and subsequently beat him and shot him in the head, throwing his body on the tarmac. The hijackers demanded the release of 766 Lebanese and Palestinian prisoners being held by the Israelis as the condition for the release of the hostages. During negotiations passengers were gradually released until the final 39 were set free 17 days after the initial hijacking.

Mugniyeh was later indicted by the United States for his role in this act of terrorism along with three others believed to be associates of Hezbollah. Only one of the alleged hijackers, Mohammed Ali Hamadi, has been brought to justice. Hamadi was captured in Germany and convicted of the murder of Robert Stethem in 1989; however, he was released on parole by German authorities in 2005 and is today at large along with the other perpetrators. This act of terror again appears to have earned a victory for Hezbollah as in the weeks after the release of the Flight 847 hostages nearly 700 Lebanese and Palestinian prisoners were released by Israel.

Car bombings, kidnappings, murders, and hijackings became a staple of life in Lebanon in the 1980s with rival groups targeting outsiders and each other in a struggle for control of the country. During this time Hezbollah fought not only Israeli and Western forces but also other Lebanese and even other Shi'a groups for power and influence. This period included a war within a war in which the more religiously driven Hezbollah battled the more secular Shi'a group AMAL for control of southern Lebanon and the Dahiya area of Beirut. This conflict, known as "the war of the bombs" persisted from 1988 through 1990, was ended through pressure exerted by both Iran and Syria on the two factions as the Lebanese civil war came to an end with the approval of the Ta'if Accord in of 1990.[30]

Building a State within a State

The end of the Lebanese civil war presented several challenges for Hezbollah. The accord, negotiated in Ta'if, Saudi Arabia, called on all militias within Lebanon to disarm and return to the political process under a slightly reformed constitution and with the acceptance of Syria as a temporary stabilizing force. This challenged Hezbollah as it had denounced involvement in the political process. In fact, AMAL's willingness to participate in a secular government had been one of the factors that had contributed to the formation of Hezbollah as an independent group. To accept any participation in a secular government could then be seen as delegitimizing the group and its call for an Islamic government. Further, after 15 years of civil war, the country was eager for peace and the continuation of violence against other sects would risk alienating the group's supporters.

Just as Hezbollah's founding and initial goal for an Islamic state in Lebanon was inspired by the success of the Islamic revolution in Iran, so too was Hezbollah's ability to balance these dilemmas supported by new political changes within Iran. The succession of Ayatollah Khamenei as Supreme Leader of Iran and Rafsanjani as new President paved the way for a somewhat more moderate approach to foreign policy within Iran and likely support for a more accommodating Hezbollah within Lebanon.[31] Along with this more moderate external influence, within Lebanon, Ayatollah Fadlallah, always the pragmatist, emphasized the multi-denominational nature of the country as being unsuited to Islamic rule and that efforts should be focused on making the nation more accommodating to Shi'a beliefs rather than controlled by them.[32] Additionally Syria, which had been granted *de facto* control over Lebanon was motivated to bring all groups into the new political system in order to consolidate its gains. Finally, the continuing presence of Israeli forces in southern Lebanon provided a justification for Hezbollah to maintain its weapons and focus its resistance against Israel, rather than on the new government of Lebanon.

Despite some members within the group advocating a continued militant stance with Lebanon, the more pragmatic voices of Sayyid Abbas Al-Musawi and Hassan Nasrallah carried the day and the group announced that they would participate in the 1992 Parliamentary elections. In order for this to transpire, Judith Palmer Harik concludes that an agreement was reached in which Hezbollah agreed to only oppose the government within the political system and in return the government would legitimize Hezbollah's continued armed resistance to Israel.[33]

Hezbollah, throughout the 1990s and into the present, has largely maintained this agreement and has played its dual role of political party and resistance movement against the Israeli occupation with surprising success. On the political front, Hezbollah began to establish a more open organizational structure, focused beyond resistance and toward the many roles it must fill as both a national political party and the agent responsible for regional and local governance. Ahmad Nizar Hamzeh provides a detailed analysis of Hezbollah's organization in his book, *In the Path of Hizbollah*. Hamzeh describes Hezbollah as having constructed a fairly elaborate structure in which a Central Council of nearly two hundred senior group members elects seven individuals to serve on the Shura Council, the primary leadership body, for three-year terms. The Shura council then selects from the seven who will serve as Secretary General and Deputy Secretary. The Shura Council directs the rest of the organization. Their decisions are not subject to appeal and are considered to have a level of religious authority over all members of Hezbollah.

While the Shura Council provides strategic direction and policy for the group, day-to-day operations of the far-flung organization are managed by an Administrative Apparatus consisting of five separate councils, in some ways similar to the United States Cabinet. Each council is headed by a member of the Shura and manages the functions within that area. Among the most important of these is the Executive Council which oversees the delegation of key functions of Hezbollah from the central down to the local level. This includes direction of the vast range of social services provided by the group. Key to Hezbollah's success in recruiting fighters and martyrs is its ability to care for its wounded warriors and the families of its martyrs. Providing housing and jobs for the wives of those captured and killed and education for their children, Hezbollah ensures that fighters can be confident their families will be cared for.[34]

While services to fighters may be necessary for recruitment and retention, Hezbollah goes well beyond simply caring for its fighters and has become one of the largest providers of medical, education, and other social services in Lebanon. These efforts, critical to the community's support of Hezbollah, are financed by an estimated $100 million a year from Iran, and serve to knit together the Shi'a community in Lebanon and particularly in the poor suburbs of Beirut, winning Hezbollah the respect and appreciation of the Shi'a community and others whom these services benefit.[35] In fact, the competence and capability of Hezbollah's services have become an embarrassment to the central Lebanese government who cannot provide services throughout the region with the efficiency of Hezbollah. The group has even assumed control of medical facilities in the south and is estimated to treat over 400,000 patients per year.[36]

The Executive Council also oversees Hezbollah's communication and information efforts. Their media wing has capabilities beyond that of any other political party in Lebanon and they use their capability to spread their message to its fullest extent. While other recognized terrorist groups communicate anonymously or covertly through the Internet, Hezbollah as a political party and social organization can communicate openly through licensed media outlets. In addition to at least five newspapers, Hezbollah operates four radio stations and its flagship satellite broadcast television network al-Manar (the beacon). This network, which broadcasts throughout the Middle East, can produce a steady diet of pro-Hezbollah, anti-Israel news and entertainment programming that reaches an estimated 10 million viewers per day.[37]

Not content with merely passive media influence, the Syndicate Unit of the Executive Council works to establish Hezbollah members within the full range of the organizations of civil society. Working to recruit members within labor unions, trade groups, and professional organizations such as medical and legal associations, Hezbollah seeks to have Shi'a interests represented in all facets of Lebanese civil interaction. The Executive Council also maintains branches that perform the role of a state department, negotiating agreements with other parties, as well as with foreign governmental and nongovernmental organizations to meet needs of the organization and expand its influence.

Within Lebanese politics, the Parliamentary Council is made up of those members who have been elected to national office as representatives of Hezbollah. This council works to organize their efforts within the political realm and is the Shura Council's mechanism to ensure that all elected representatives remain true to the decisions and policies of the group. Thus, these parliamentarians are elected by the people they are put forward by and must remain loyal to the party's interests over those who elected them.

Another Council subordinate to the Shura and tasked with managing the activities of the group is the Judicial Council, staffed by religious authorities this represents Hezbollah's reliance on Shari'a in the areas in which it governs. These judges rule on violations of religious law as well as on civil disputes between members and between those in Hezbollah governed communities.[38]

The last primary executive body is the Jihad Council. This body, which is reportedly headed by Secretary General Nasrallah and includes representation of the Islamic Revolutionary Guard Corps, appears to function in the same manner as a National Security Council. This group assesses threats to the organization and its people and develops strategies for countering these threats. The Jihad Council is not an operational body which could take action against threats, rather it would make recommendations to the Shura council which could then task the Military and Security Apparatus to carry out any necessary operations. The Military and Security Apparatus is then responsible for defense against both external and internal threats. These functions include both identifying and training recruits and assessing the reliability and security of those already in the organization, thereby ensuring that Hezbollah is difficult for outside agencies to covertly penetrate.[39]

This brief review demonstrates that Hezbollah has grown to be much more than just a terrorist group. Its capabilities extend far beyond the ability to create fear in an enemy; it has grown to encompass most of the capabilities of a small government. In fact, when compared with the legitimate government of Lebanon, Hezbollah appears more capable of meeting the basic needs of its constituents. This ability to grow its capabilities while moderating its rhetoric has enabled it to win the hearts and minds of many Lebanese and has become a force to be reckoned with in the politics of the country.

Key Leaders

To establish the structures and capabilities of Hezbollah requires consistent leadership, thus it is important to look at the group's most influential leaders. In the development of the ideology and strategy of Hezbollah, two key leaders stand out: the spiritual guide, Ayatollah Sayyid Mohammad Husayn Fadlallah, and the commander, Sheikh Hassan Nasrallah.

Taken at face value, Ayatollah Fadlallah should not be included as leader of Hezbollah as he has repeatedly stated that he is not and has never been a member of the organization. Despite the denial of a formal association between Fadlallah and Hezbollah, it is clear the two are linked, and that religious opinions rendered by Fadlallah are frequently used to inspire the group and provide justification for its actions. Members of the group have acknowledged that it "benefits greatly" from his "opinions, positions and comments."[40] Born to a Lebanese father in the holy city of Najaf, Iraq in 1935, home of some the most respected schools of Shi'a theology where religious hopefuls came from around the world to hone their knowledge and credentials. Growing up in Najaf, it was natural for him to want to study in its famous schools, and he started a step ahead of his peers. As a Sayyid, his family was able was to trace its heritage to the prophet Mohammed and Fadlallah was entitled to wear the black turban which signifies this heritage.[41] In school he showed a desire to make the teachings of the Koran more relevant to changing circumstances in the Islamic world, a desire he would carry out on his return to Lebanon after finishing his training as a top student. He began his teaching in Beirut, which was filling with disenfranchised Shi'a and he worked to make his teachings of the Koran more relevant to their situation.[42] It was this same population who had been drawn to Imam Al-Sadr's AMAL movement, and when he disappeared in Libya in 1978 some of his authority and followers transferred to Fadlallah, who used this influence to move the community in the direct of Islamic sacrifice and martyrdom in an effort to achieve an Islamic state in Lebanon.[43]

His desire to make Islamic teachings more relevant to the disenfranchised in Lebanon was critical to the controversial tactics of the new Hezbollah militia. Fadlallah's teachings blurred the lines between martyrdom and suicide, arguing that there was no difference between entering battle against a superior foe knowing that you would be killed and taking ones own life in a suicide attack against an enemy. He also provided justifications for the kidnappings carried out by Hezbollah and other Shi'a groups noting that such actions as being necessary to battle the Israeli occupation of Lebanon.[44] This religious justification for acts typically deemed to be against the teaching of the Koran, legitimized Hezbollah's actions and facilitated the recruitment of soldiers for these missions.

Fadlallah's value to Hezbollah did not end with his legitimization of violence. He was also instrumental in easing Hezbollah's way into accommodation with the Lebanese political system in the early 1990s, working to convince hardliners that participation in the political process was an acceptable way to advance the goal of an Islamic state within Lebanon.[45] Thus while denying membership in the organization, there is no denying the impact his teachings have had in advancing and legitimizing the strategy and tactics of Hezbollah as they gained power in Lebanon. He continues to be a voice of Hezbollah to other religious communities in Lebanon and to directly or indirectly provide support for the group through his religious teaching.

While Ayatollah Fadlallah has been important throughout the development of Hezbollah, the individual who has been most critical to its survival over the last 15 years has been its Secretary General Sayyid Hassan Nasrallah. Nasrallah was born in Lebanon in 1960 and turned to political activism early in life. In his middle teens he was inspired by Imam al-Sadr's call for the Shi'a to unite and resist the oppression that they were experiencing in Lebanon. When the civil war began in 1975, Nasrallah quickly joined al-Sadr's militia, AMAL. He became devout in his religious practices and was encouraged to undertake more formal training in Najaf, where Fadlallah had previously studied.

In 1979, he was forced to give up his studies and return to Lebanon when Saddam Hussein began persecuting Shi'as who may have been cooperating with the new Islamic government in Iran. In Lebanon he began teaching and rapidly acquired a following as a charismatic leader and speaker. Critical of AMAL's direction after the death of Imam al-Sadr, Nasrallah left the group in 1982 and began associating with those who would become the core of Hezbollah.[46] After fighting with Hezbollah against Israeli and even other Shi'a militia during the civil war, Nasrallah went to Iran to finish his religious training and position himself for greater leadership positions. He returned to Lebanon in 1989 and by the age of 29 had become a leader within Hezbollah.

He served as the group's liaison with Iran, building not only organizational ties with the group's sponsor but also personal ties. These personal ties serve to demonstrate the power Iran maintains over Hezbollah, as following the death of the Secretary General Abbas al-Musawi, Iran's leader Ayatollah Khamenei selected Nasrallah, only 31, over the more senior deputy, Sheikh Naim Qasim, to assume leadership of Hezbollah. Nasrallah built a reputation as a leader with exceptional integrity, who is completely committed to the group and its goals, earning the respect of much of the nation with his dignified speech after his son was killed in an Israeli attack in 1997.[47] Hassan Nasrallah has become a hero to the Shi'a in Lebanon and an icon in much of the Arab world. As the leader who is seen as having defeated Israel twice, driving them from Lebanon in 2000, and forcing a withdrawal again in the 2006 war, he is seen as succeeding where other leaders have failed.

In addition to a successful military leader he has also proven to be very adept politically, ensuring the smooth entry of Hezbollah into Lebanese politics and development of their political influence. He has also managed the other challenges in ways beneficial to the group. He managed to maintain Hezbollah's arms after the Israeli withdrawal in 2000, and maintained influence despite Syria's withdrawal in 2005.

Finally, he has been able to maintain the support of many Lebanese despite precipitating the 2006 war that devastated Lebanese infrastructure and killed over 1,000 civilians.

Politics and Violence

The leadership of Hezbollah has worked to tailor the group's use of violence to meet its political and military goals. The end of the civil war in 1990 left Israel occupying a large section of southern Lebanon which Hezbollah was committed to freeing. Thus while the end of the civil war forced Hezbollah to abandon its fight against other Lebanese parties and join the political process, it freed the group to focus its military attention on evicting the Israelis. Hezbollah subsequently embarked on a ten-year mission to force Israeli withdrawal from the region, with Israel battling to secure southern Lebanon and protect its own northern border. This conflict reportedly developed an informal set of rules. Neither Hezbollah nor the Israelis would benefit from their own civilians being targeted as this could potentially erode their bases of support. Thus, Israel refrained from attacking civilian targets in southern Lebanon, attempting to focus their attacks on Hezbollah units and positions. Hezbollah, in return, limited their attacks to Israeli and Southern Lebanese Army forces in the occupied territory.[48]

There were significant exceptions to this pattern. In 1992, following the death of Hezbollah's then Secretary General Sheikh Abbas Musawi and his family in an Israeli attack, Hezbollah apparently retaliated not by targeting Israel but by bombing its embassy in Argentina, killing 38. A second bombing of a Jewish center in Buenos Aires followed in 1994, killing 95 and wounding 200. It was during this time that Hezbollah began to demonstrate its ability to operate on a global scale well beyond its home territory of Lebanon. The United States, Argentina, and Israel have all concluded the attacks to be the work of Hezbollah with Iranian backing, but the group has consistently denied responsibility. These attacks do not appear to be completely isolated as it is believed the group maintains camps in the South America tri-border region of Argentina, Brazil, and Paraguay.[49]

This balance between the Israeli Defense Forces (IDF) and Hezbollah held, with some exceptions on each side, for nearly ten years until Israel announced its intention to withdraw from Lebanon in 2000. This, of course, was seen as a great victory for Hezbollah as they took credit for forcing the invader from their lands. On the surface, this victory should have voided the justification for Hezbollah to maintain its weapons as they were no longer subject to occupation and had no other force to resist. Of course, this was not the case as both the Lebanese government and Hezbollah claimed that an area known as Shebaa farms belonged to Lebanon and that Israel must withdraw from this region as well. This approximately 10 square mile region had been viewed as part of the Syrian Golan Heights, but Lebanon claimed that Syria had given this land to Lebanon in 1951. Thus, the Shebaa farms region became the new justification for Hezbollah to maintain its weaponry and to continue its battle against Israeli occupation.[50]

Despite occasional clashes in the Shebaa farm region, 2000 to 2006 was a period of relative calm in Lebanon and between Hezbollah and Israel. It was during this time that Hezbollah became more active in its support for another one of Israel's enemies who they saw as remaining under occupation, the Palestinians. Hezbollah's apparent triumph over the Israelis may have had an inspiring effect on the Palestinians and Hezbollah's television station, al-Manar, broadcast pro-Palestinian programming into Palestinian territories. Hezbollah is believed to have played a role in both training and supplying Palestinian militants during the Intifada that began in late 2000 and have continued this support.[51]

Despite ongoing violence between Hezbollah and Israel, the group was able to gain an increasingly prominent role within the Lebanese political establishment. As early as 1992, it began reaching out to other parties and religious groups in the country in order to mend fences and build liaisons for future cooperation. The group established political platforms that emphasized their commitment to social and economic reform, and reiterated their desire to establish Islamic law only with the consent of the nation. These efforts to moderate their position and establish themselves as a nationalist, rather than a purely Shi'a, movement coupled with the reputation for honesty and competence developed through their social programs has led to increasing success at the polls. In each election since 1992, Hezbollah has won more seats in the Lebanese

Parliament and won control of local government in more municipalities. Additionally, they have increasingly worked with other parties to develop a legislative block that controls over one fourth of Parliament.[52]

This political success, however, has not resulted in a turn away from their militant capabilities. Hezbollah remains an extremely well-armed and well-trained adversary that has persisted in anti-Israeli rhetoric and actions. These capabilities were put on full display for the world in July of 2006 when Hezbollah and Israel returned to war.

Military Capability and the 2006 War

Although classified by the United States as a terrorist group, Hezbollah is much more than a group of radical militants attempting to disrupt Lebanon and Israel. Hezbollah maintains an extensive and disciplined military capability that perceives itself, and is seen by many in the Arab world, as accomplishing what no group of Arab states has been able to accomplish, namely defeating Israel in battle. Hezbollah's first claimed victory occurred in 2000, when Israeli forces withdrew from southern Lebanon after a grinding 18-year struggle, in which nearly 1,000 Israeli troops and up to 17,000 Lebanese were killed.[53] In this conflict, Hezbollah relied on guerilla tactics of bombings and ambushes designed to both wear down the Israeli defense force and to provoke disproportionate Israeli attacks which Hezbollah could then use as recruiting and public affairs tools. Israeli withdrawal was a huge military and public relations victory for Hezbollah, garnering the group praise from inside a wide-range of Lebanese, from the groups supporters in Syria and Iran, and from across the Arab world. For the first time, an Arab group had stood up to the Israelis and forced them to withdraw.

This perceived victory, which appeared to meet Hezbollah's previously stated requirement of Israeli withdrawal to allow it to disarm, did nothing of the sort. Rather, Hezbollah began to reinforce Southern Lebanon for future conflict with the Israelis and justified their continued militancy on Israel's continued occupation of the Shebaa farms region. Hezbollah's study of Israeli tactics and capabilities, along with a relatively free hand in the region, allowed it to prepare to aggressively defend against any future Israeli incursions.

Following the withdrawal of Israeli forces, Hezbollah displayed its remarkable strategic planning capability and rapidly began preparing for the next conflict. Despite the expansion of the United Nations Interim Force in Lebanon (UNIFIL) to fill the security gap in the south of the country, Hezbollah was able to create an extensive system of bunkers, fortifications, and missile launch sites throughout the area, designed to prevent heavy Israeli forces from progressing rapidly into the region. Capitalizing on the ability of their fighters to blend into the local population, the group also fortified and stockpiled villages throughout the region that could also become traps for potential advancing Israeli forces.[54]

Preparing not just to be able to defend against an attack from the south, Hezbollah also planned for and acquired the capability to take offensive action against Israel in the form of improved rocket and missile capability. Their ability to stockpile and conceal both short and medium range rockets throughout the region provided them the capability to rain rockets and fear into Israel despite the IDF's efforts to destroy these assets.

Hezbollah portrays conflict with Israel in terms which it says provides their fighters with a distinct advantage. Sheik Naim Kassem highlights their view of the combat motivation of each side. He stated that while the Israelis view the conflict in terms of preserving their lives, Hezbollah's "point of departure is preservation of principle and sacrifice. What is the value of a life of humiliation?"[55] Hezbollah then sees itself as fighting for more than land or rights; it views itself as fighting for dignity and is willing to sacrifice lives for this.

The military capabilities and strategy favored by Hezbollah were clearly and effectively displayed during the 2006 summer war during which Israeli attacks targets in Lebanon by air and ground followed Hezbollah's kidnapping of two Israeli soldiers on the border. Hezbollah displayed not only the possession of, but also the ability to effectively use complex weapon systems to achieve overall strategic goals. Hezbollah's most publicized weapons system during the conflict was the Katyusha rocket. An unguided 122mm rocket, the Katyusha posed little military threat to the Israeli defense forces, but with its 12 to 25 mile range, allowed Hezbollah to bring the conflict home to Israeli civilians by launching approximately 3,000 of the rockets over the course of the 30-

day war.[56] The ability to maintain the near constant barrage of these weapons resulted in the disruption of many social and economic functions in northern Israel and an estimated 300,000 Israelis seeking shelter from the attacks.[57]

While Katyushas created social disruption in Israel, higher technology weapons made Israel's incursion into Lebanon deadly. SA-14 and SA-16 anti-aircraft missiles made aerial operations challenging for the Israeli Air Force. Hezbollah forces also successfully deployed a wide-range of anti-tank weapons, from older AT-4 and AT-5 wire guided missiles to Russian designed AT-13 and AT-14 missiles (believed to have come from Syria) which can damage the most advanced tanks with reactive armor. Use of such advanced weapons along with well-executed ambush tactics allowed Hezbollah to damage 60 armored vehicles (only 5 to 6 of these were completely destroyed).[58]

Terror-causing rockets and ambushes of Israeli forces are consistent with Hezbollah's past guerilla warfare style approach to battling Israel, but they were also able to challenge Israel with an expanding arsenal of higher technology weapons. This capability was demonstrated vividly early in the conflict when an Iranian CS-802 anti-ship missile successfully engaged an Israeli ship, killing 4 sailors. The move into higher tech weapons was also seen in the use of armed UAVs, night vision equipment, and more sophisticated command and control communications equipment.[59] This move toward more complex weapons systems may have served to make Hezbollah's forces more vulnerable to the much superior conventional capability of the IDF. However, Hezbollah was able to integrate this technology with more classic guerrilla capability of blending into the population and using the civilian population both as cover and as a defense.

Anthony Cordesman details how Hezbollah was able to take advantage of their support in southern Lebanon, by building many of their military facilities in communities to make them more difficult to hit without causing significant civilian casualties. This plan of fighting within communities allowed supply lines to military bunkers to flow in the same manner as daily civilian economic activity. Rocket teams were able to be stationed within homes and businesses, moving outside to fire and quickly returning to the shelter of a "civilian" building before being targeted by Israeli forces.[60] This sheltering among civilians appears to have been planned by Hezbollah not only for its value in protecting military assets but also to deliberately draw fire upon civilian communities. Hezbollah was able to rapidly turn Israeli efforts to target these facilities in civilian areas into a significant strategic communications offensive, using their own media resources as well as sympathetic media outlets throughout the world to showcase the devastation caused by Israeli attacks on "civilian" targets.

Papers such as the UK's *The Independent* showed front page pictures of rescuers with dead or injured children and the headline "How can we stand by and allow this to go on?"[61] Such media success helped motivate international efforts which ultimately ended the conflict. Interestingly, the international media highlighted outrage at the civilian casualties caused by Israel's attacks but paid little attention to Hezbollah's tactics of hiding within communities and making these areas viable military targets. The image of Lebanese as "victims" of Israeli attacks quickly led to the evaporation of the initial support for Israeli operations in Lebanon as critical early supporters of attacks on Hezbollah such as Saudi Arabia, Jordan, and Egypt, distanced themselves from Israel and international opinion turned to support Lebanon, and indirectly, Hezbollah.[62] However, the rocket attacks and kidnappings that precipitated the crisis had not been authorized by the Lebanese government, of which Hezbollah was a part. There was by no means unanimous support for Hezbollah's actions which not only devastated the Lebanese infrastructure, but also threatened the already fragile political stability of the nation. In fact, there was considerable criticism of these actions, prompting Nasrallah to claim that they would not have kidnapped the Israeli soldiers had they known how powerfully Israel would respond.[63]

The image of Israel's withdrawal from Lebanon without achieving its goals, including recovery of the kidnapped soldiers, destruction of missile capabilities, and degradation of Hezbollah's military capability, cast Hezbollah in the light of the victor, again protecting Lebanon's sovereignty.[64] Hezbollah was also able to turn the aftermath of the war into a public relations success. Presenting themselves as victors who had now twice driven the Israeli forces from Lebanon, Hezbollah was again able to boast of something no Arab state had been able to accomplish. The costs of this "victory," of course, were very high since the Lebanese infrastructure was devastated, and thousands of people were left homeless.

Hezbollah's ability to energize its welfare system, reportedly financed by an infusion of support equal to over $100 million worth of funding from Iran, allowed them to rapidly put cash in the hands of the victims to help them rebuild or resettle elsewhere. Reports suggested that Hezbollah initially paid displaced victims the equivalent of $12,000 for rent and have paid an additional $4,000 to those whose homes have not been rebuilt.[65] This effort in funneling aid and reconstruction through the government of Lebanon, coupled with the relative inefficiency of the international community, has also bolstered Hezbollah in the opinions of many in southern Lebanon.

This war and its aftermath serves to highlight the incredibly adaptive nature of this organization that combines guerrilla and conventional military capabilities with political and social service arms, all reinforced by mass media communication skills that allows it to seemingly turn every development to its advantage. In confronting Hezbollah, we are not confronting simply an adaptive terrorist group, but an organization with nearly all the capabilities of a nation-state. But unlike a state, it can instantly hide within the innocent civilian population of Lebanon, rendering ineffective the traditional retaliatory means of deterrence that could typically be used against an adversary nation's military forces.

Conclusions

Given what we know about this Islamic group, several conclusions can safely be drawn. First, with large-scale financial, material, and training support from Iran, Hezbollah has become a well-organized, well-financed group of fighters who, by virtue of their training, discipline, and ability to blend into their operating environment, can resist well the efforts of even the most advanced military forces who seek to destroy them. Second, their weaponry allows them to present a clear threat to the safety and security of Israel, but, at this time, not the existence of that nation. Third, Hezbollah possesses connections outside the region that allow them to strike targets with terrorist attacks around the world if such actions are elected by the group. Fourth, although possessing significant terrorist and guerilla warfare capability, fueled by a hatred for Israel and the West, Hezbollah is much more than a fighting group; they are also a recognized and popular political party, a respected provider of social services, and a religious organization. This means that, unlike groups such as Al Qaeda, they have constituencies that they represent and communities that they are responsible for, and they must weigh these factors when making their strategic decisions.

One likely future path for Hezbollah is that it will retain and refine the capabilities and intentions it has demonstrated since the end of the Lebanese civil war in 1990. This would entail further development of its social and political strength not as ends in themselves, but as tools with which deflect criticism over its continued militancy and attacks on Israel. When much of Lebanon depends on Hezbollah for their survival, and possessing the political and military strength to resist actions by the central government, Hezbollah may feel empowered to engage its enemies, the United States and Israel, in other arenas.

The most likely areas for the spread of Hezbollah's militancy are in the occupied territories in support of the Palestinians (where they are clearly already present) and in Iraq where they are recently reported to be aiding Shi'a militia.[66] Both of these areas provide the group the ability to fight Israel and the United States by assisting what they see as resistance movements. Supporting these movements in their fights against "occupation" allows Hezbollah to continue their fight without engaging in what might be seen by the rest of the world as terrorist attacks. By following this course they can gain the allegiance of new fighters, expand their influence and capabilities, and hurt their enemies without significantly risking the credibility they have developed in the world.

The U.S. must be particularly concerned about the development of an Iraqi Hezbollah. If Hezbollah were able to maintain a fight against Israel for more than 20 years, while building popular support in a nation that does not even have a Shi'a majority, how much more effective might they be in Shi'a dominated Iraq, with their sponsor, Iran, immediately next door? Hezbollah is likely to support Shi'a militia in an effort to help bring about a Shi'a government there. This support would likely become much more aggressive and open if the Iraqi government were to ask the United States to leave the country, as this would enable them to more easily frame continued United States presence as an occupation.

Another future path for Hezbollah may be even more dangerous. In response to perceived threats to its existence, either through rejection within Lebanon or possibly large-scale attacks on Iran, the group could return to open acts of terrorism. Hezbollah has demonstrated the ability to carry out deadly attacks across the world and there is no reason to believe that this capability has diminished. Iran is known to have armed Hezbollah with a variety of missiles and other weapons and is believed to possess chemical and biological weapons. If Iran were to have transferred such capability to Hezbollah, the group might be able to complete truly devastating attacks and could present a threat not only to the safety of Israel is but also to Israel's existence.

The one path that does not appear to be open to either the United States or Israel is the easy destruction of Hezbollah or its safe haven. The 2006 war demonstrated their ability to resist the might of a superior military force and to recover quickly. Any more intense military effort to destroy the group would likely cause such collateral damage that the public outcry would render the attack counterproductive. Targeted attacks against key leaders such as Hassan Nasrallah may weaken the group for a time, but other leaders have surely been groomed within the organizational structure.

The only clear path to weakening the group may be a wide reaching effort on the political and diplomatic front. Efforts to strengthen the ability of the government of Lebanon to meet the needs of all it citizens and secure its own borders may weaken both Hezbollah's political support as well as its justification for keeping its weapons. The recent triumph of the Lebanese Army (with some Western military aid) over Fatah al-Islam has boosted the esteem of Lebanon's military and appears to have been a unifying force in the country.[67] Continued aid to strengthen the Lebanese government may weaken the appeal of radical groups and ultimately empower it to openly oppose Hezbollah in future conflicts. Hezbollah has fought this prospect by withdrawing its cabinet members from the current Western-leaning government, creating a political stalemate and demanding veto power over government decisions. Within Lebanon, current struggles between anti-Syrian political groups, several of whose members have been recently assassinated, and pro-Syrian groups led by Hezbollah and AMAL highlight the critical nature of the balance of power in Lebanon and the need for further support of the government. While too much open support from the United States might fuel criticism from Shi'a groups, aid from Sunni Arab nations such as Saudi Arabia and Kuwait, who have no interest in Iran's influence growing in the region, would be less open to such criticism.

Given the group's history and inclinations, it appears that Hezbollah will continue to be a rival of United States interests for some time to come. Efforts to contain, combat, and ultimately defeat such a rival can only be successful if there was also a willingness to see the reality of Hezbollah as the adaptive multi-dimensional group they have become, a state within state, rather than simply viewing them as a terrorist organization.

Notes

1. Hezbollah: "A-Team of Terrorists," On-line, Internet, 21 May 2007, available from http://www.cbsnews.com/stories/2003/04/18/60minutes/main550000.shtml.

2. Official Journal of the European Union, COUNCIL DECISION 2005/221/CFSP, 14 March 2005, On-line, Internet, 21 May 2007, available from http://www.statewatch.org/news/2005/mar/terr-list2.pdf.

3. Hezbollah 'Heroes to Arabs', 4 August 2006, *The Australian*, On-line, Internet, 21 May 2007, available from http://www.theaustralian.news.com.au/printpage/0,5942,20014617,00.html.

4. CIA World Factbook, On-line, Internet, 21 May 2007, available from https://www.cia.gov/library/publications/the-world-factbook/geos/le.html.

5. Ibid.

6. Ahmad Nizar Hamez, *In the Path of Hizbollah*, Syracuse University Press, Syracuse, NY, (2004).

7. Ibid.

8. Judith Palmer Harik, *Hezbollah the Changing Face of Terrorism*, (London: I.B. Tauris, 2004), 22.

9. Sami Moubayed, "Who is Hassan Nasrallah?" *World Politics Review*, 17 July 2006, 2, On-line, Internet, available from http://worldpoliticsreview.com/article.aspx?id=55.

10. Harik, op. cit., 22.

11. Augustus Richard Norton, *Hezbollah*, (New Jersey: Princeton University Press, 2007), 32.

12. Harik, op. cit., 23.

13. Norton, op. cit., 33.

14. Joseph Alagha, *The Shifts in Hizbullah's Ideology: Religious Ideology, Political Ideology, and Politcal Program*, (Amsterdam: Amsterdam University Press, 2006), 34.

15. Norton, op. cit., 34.

16. Alagha, op. cit., 34.

17. Ibid., 35.

18. Hamez, op. cit., 24.

19. Martin Kramer, "Sacrifice and 'Self-Martyrdom' in Shi'ite Lebanon," *Terrorism and Political Violence*, vol. 3, no. 3 (Autumn 1991), 30-47.

20. Jim Winkates, "Suicide Terrorism: Martyrdom for Organizational Purposes," *Journal of Third World Studies*, 2006, vol. 23, no 1.

21. Harik, op. cit., 37.

22. Hamez, op. cit., 82.

23. Robin Wright, *Sacred Rage: The Wrath of Militant Islam*, (New York: Touchstone, 2001), 99.

24. Ibid., 100.

25. Hamez, op. cit., 85.

26. "Body Believed to Be C.I.A. Agent and Hostage Is Found in Lebanon," *New York Times*, 27 December 1991, On-line, Internet, 12 November 2007, available from http://query.nytimes.com/gst/fullpage.html?res=9D0CE1D81039F934A15751C1A967958260&n=Top/Reference/Times%20Topics/Organizations/C/Central%20Intelligence%20Agency.

27. "Body Found in Beirut May Be Colonel's," *New York Times*, 23 December 1991, On-line, Internet, 12 November 2007, available from http://query.nytimes.com/gst/fullpage.html?res=9D0CE5D7143EF930A15751C1A967958260&n=Top%2fReference%2fTimes%20Topics%2fSubjects%2fH%2fHostages.

28. "1991: Church envoy Waite freed in Beirut," *British Broadcasting Company*, On-line, Internet, 12 November 2007, available from http://news.bbc.co.uk/onthisday/hi/dates/stories/november/18/newsid_2520000/2520055.stm.

29. Norton, op. cit., 74.

30. Alagha, op. cit., 40.

31. Hamez, op. cit., 109.

32. Harik, op. cit., 56.

33. Ibid., 47.

34. Hamez, op. cit., 47.

35. Norton, op. cit., 110.

36. Hamez, op. cit., 55.

37. Avi Jorisch, "Al-Manar: Hizbullah TV, 24/7," *Middle East Quarterly*, Winter 2004, vol. 11, no. 1.

38. Ibid., 64.

39. Ibid., 71.

40. Amal Saad Ghorayeb, *Hizbollah: Politics and Religion*, Pluto Press, London, (2002), 6.

41. Martin Kramer, "The Oracle of Hezbollah," in *Spokesmen for the Despised: Fundamentalist Leaders of the Middle East*, R. Scott Appleby ed., University of Chicago Press, Chicago, (1997), 85.

42. Ibid., 91.

43. Hamez, op. cit., 24.

44. Jerrold M. Post, *The Mind of the Terrorist: The Psychology of Terrorism from the IRA to al-Qaeda*, (New York: Palgrave Macmillan, 2007).

45. Harik, op. cit., 70.

46. Sami Moubayed, op. cit.

47. Annia Ciezadlo, "Sheikh Up," *New Republic Online*, 28 July 2006, On-line, Internet, 12 November 2007, available from http://anniaciezadlo.com/pages.php?content=galleryBig.php&navGallID=1&navGallIDquer=1&imageID=9&view=big&activeType=.

48. Norton, op. cit., 85.

49. "The Battle for Lebanon Explodes in Argentina," *PBS Frontline World*, On-line, Internet, 12 November 2007, available from http://www.pbs.org/frontlineworld/stories/lebanon/tl04.html.

50. Gary C. Gambill, "Syria and the Shebaa farms Dispute," *Middle East Intelligence Bulletin*, 200, vol. 3, no. 5, On-line, Internet, 12 November 2007, available from http://www.meib.org/articles/0105_11.htm.

51. Norton, op. cit., 93.

52. Ibid., 102.

53. Nicholas Blanford, *The Information Brief*, no. 8, 29 September 1999.

54. Andrew Exum, "Hizballah at War; A Military Assessment," *Policy Focus*, #63, December 2006, *The Washington Institute for Near East Policy*.

55. Andrew McGregor, "Hezbollah's Tactics and Capabilities in Southern Lebanon," *Terrorism Focus*, vol. 3, issue 30, On-line, Internet, 12 November 2007, available from http://jamestown.org/terrorism/news/article.php?articleid=2370089.

56. Anthony Cordesman, "Preliminary 'Lessons' of the Israeli-Hezbollah War," *Center for Strategic and International Studies*, 17 August 2006, On-line, Internet, 20 November 2007, available from http://www.csis.org/media/csis/pubs/060817_isr_hez_lessons.pdf.

57. Andrew McGregor, "Hezbullah's Rocket Strategy," *Terrorism Focus*, vol. 4, issue 16, On-line, Internet, 12 November 2007, available from http://jamestown.org/terrorism/news/article.php?articleid=2370098.

58. Cordesman, op. cit., 2006.

59. Ibid.

60. Ibid.

61. Robert Fisk, "How can we stand by and allow this to go on?" *The Independent*, 31 July 2006, On-line, Internet, 12 November 2007, available from http://news.independent.co.uk/fisk/article1205977.ece.

62. Cordesman, op. cit., 2006.

63. "Nasrallah: Soldiers' abductions a mistake," *CNN.com*, 27 August 2006, On-line, Internet, 12 November 2007, available from http://cnn.com/2006/WORLD/meast/08/27/mideast.nasrallah/index.html.

64. Cordesman, op. cit., 2006.

65. Alastair Lyon, "Lebanon's reconstruction far from complete," Reuters, 9 July 2007, On-line, Internet, 12 November 2007, available from http://www.topix.net/content/reuters/2007/07/lebanons-postwar-reconstruction-far-from-complete.

66. General David H. Petraeus, "Report to Congress on the Situation in Iraq," 10 September 2007, On-line, Internet, 12 November 2007, available from http://www.mnf-iraq.com/index.php?option=com_content&task=view&id=13904&Itemid=131.

67. Nicholas Blanford, "In Lebanon Soldiers Win New Respect," *Christian Science Monitor*, 28 August 2007.

CHAPTER 9

Hamas: The Islamic Resistance Movement[1]

Jerrold M. Post

Established during the first *intifada* – the Palestinian civil revolt against Israeli occupation, which began in December 1987 – Hamas, the Islamic Resistance Movement, traces its origins to the Muslim Brotherhood, founded in Egypt in 1928 by Hassan al-Banna. The Brotherhood sought to revitalize Islam and to establish an Islamic state, with no distinction between religion and the state. Its members considered Palestine, permanently and exclusively, a Muslim land so designated by Allah.

In their view, it is the duty of Muslims to liberate the entirety of the Holy Land from non-Muslim authority. "Israel will be established and will stay established until Islam nullifies it as it nullifies what was before it," stated the martyred Imam Hassan al-Banna, founder and Supreme Guide of the Muslim Brotherhood. He went on to state, "It is the nature of Islam to dominate, not to be dominated, to impose its law on all nations and to extend its power to the entire planet."

Despite these totalistic goals, which would clearly require jihad at some time in the future, Hamas initially took root as a social and religious movement, building hundreds of mosques in impoverished Gaza, and only declaring jihad after years of developing social support. This stands in contrast to Hezbollah, which began as a violent militia, later combining fighting forces with a network of social services and subsequent electoral success.

Sheikh Ahmad Yassin and his colleagues, who were members of the Muslim Brotherhood, began developing extensive social services in Palestine from 1973 to 1987 through a network of mosques and religious and educational institutions. And only after 14 years of patiently establishing their base did they move into political violence. Growth and evolution have been trademarks of Hamas – a process that is gradual and incremental, but ever moving forward. Renowned terrorism expert Bruce Hoffman, the author of *Inside Terrorism*, noted, "The terrorist campaign is like a shark: it must keep moving forward – no matter how slowly or incrementally – or die."[2]

When the first intifada erupted in 1987, Sheikh Ahmad Yassin convened a group of Muslim Brotherhood leaders. They decided to establish a nominally separate organization to participate in the intifada. This would shield them from blame should the revolt fail, but would allow them to claim credit if it succeeded. They called the new organization Hamas, which means "zeal," "force," and "bravery" in Arabic, but is also the acronym for *Harakat al-Muqawama al-Islamiyya*, the Islamic Resistance Movement. Formed during 1987 and 1988, Hamas prioritized both short-term goals – removing Israeli forces from the occupied territories – and its long-term agenda, the creation of an Islamic state in all of historic Palestine. When Hamas talks about historic Palestine and liberating occupied territories, they are referring to all of contemporary Israel; there is no "two-state" solution in this absolutist ideology.

Hamas issued the group's charter in 1988, entitled *The Charter of Allah: The Platform of the Islamic Resistance Movement*. The Charter unambiguously identifies Palestine as Islamic in nature, indicating Hamas's goal to create an Islamic State: "Palestine is an Islamic Land which has the first of the two Qiblas [the direction to which Muslims turn in prayer], the third of the holy Islamic sanctuaries, and the point of departure for Mohammed's midnight journey to the seven heavens [i.e., Jerusalem]."[3]

Hamas's Charter is fundamental in understanding the group's mentality, particularly in relation to Islam, historic Palestine, and resistance to the Israeli presence in Palestine.[4] Article 13 draws this direct comparison between the land and Islam: "Giving up any part of the homeland is like giving up part of the religious faith itself." In a systematic paranoid exposition, the Charter develops a clear sense of the Jews and the Zionist entity as the enemy, blaming them for virtually every evil that has befallen Muslims and indeed the world as a whole:

> The enemy planned long ago and perfected their plan so that they can achieve what they want to achieve… They worked on gathering huge and effective amounts of wealth to achieve their goal. With wealth they controlled the

> international mass media-news services, newspapers, printing presses, broadcast stations and more... With money they ignited revolutions in all parts of the world to realize their benefits and reap the fruits of them. They are behind the French Revolution, the Communist Revolution... With wealth they formed secret organizations throughout the world to destroy societies and promote the Zionist cause... With wealth they controlled imperialistic nations and pushed them to occupy many nations and exhaust their natural resources and spread mischief in them...
>
> They are behind the First World War in which they destroyed the Islamic Caliph and gained material profit, monopolized raw wealth, and got the Balfour Declaration [which laid the groundwork for the creation of Israel]. They created the League of Nations so they could control the world through that organization. They are behind the Second World War...and set down the foundations to establish their nation by forming the United Nations and Security Council instead of the League of Nations in order to rule the world through that organization... There is not a war that goes on here or there in which their finger are not playing behind it.

Article 32 cites as the authoritative source for this international Jewish conspiracy the anti-Semitic counterfeit text, *Protocols of the Learned Elders of Zion*, proclaiming:

> Today it's Palestine and tomorrow it will be another country, and then another. The Zionist plan has no bounds and after Palestine they wish to expand from the Nile River to the Euphrates. When they totally occupy it they will look towards another, and such is their plan in the 'Protocols of the Learned Elders of Zion.'[5]

A pivotal moment in the intifada occurred in October 1990 following the killing of seventeen Palestinians by Israeli security forces, within the Haram al-Sharif, or Temple Mount. Seizing on this opportunity, Hamas called for jihad "against the Zionist enemy everywhere, on all fronts and with every means."[6] This led to a dramatic increase in Hamas attacks. As Sheikh Yassin noted, "[t]he Israeli occupation demonstrated that words were not enough to bring it to an end. Only armed resistance can achieve liberation."[7] Hamas's move from social services to violence was probably also a reflection of the success of the Fatah political movement, and the recognition by Hamas leadership that without aggressive action, their existing system was insufficient to compete politically with Arafat and Fatah.

A second key turning point occurred in 1992 when Israel deported over 400 members of Hamas, including Sheikh Yassin and other key leaders. These deportations proved an essential catalyst for Hamas' strategic and political growth since, now isolated, the Hamas leadership was allowed time to carefully develop and plan their long-range strategy. The deportation also created interaction between Hezbollah and Hamas, and some members of Hamas even received Hezbollah training in Southern Lebanon.

Hamas became increasingly radical as Palestinians became frustrated with Fatah, angry with Israel, and willing to accept more hostile tactics. During the Oslo negotiations (1993-1994), Hamas initiated its campaign of suicide bombing and kidnapping to undermine the Oslo process and ensure that the Palestinian Authority would not be able to deliver peace. Those Palestinians unwilling to accept negotiations or compromise with Israel and those disappointed by Arafat and the PLO, increasingly turned to Hamas.

Contributing to the rise in Hamas's popularity was the bitter resentment among Palestinian youth in the territories toward the takeover of the leadership and administrative positions by Arafat's men, who came out of exile. The Palestinian youngsters, who conducted the intifada and paid so dearly for their struggle, felt that they, rather than Arafat's cronies, should have been given the power positions in the newly established Palestinian Authority. In an attempt to gain political capital among Palestinians angered with the PLO's movement toward governance and the mainstream, Hamas stepped up terrorist acts in 1995 and 1996.[8]

As with Oslo, Hamas made strong statements against the Camp David II peace efforts:

> The Palestinian people accuses all who seek this [solution] of weaving a plot against its rights and its sacred national cause. Liberation will not be completed without sacrifice, blood and jihad that continues until victory.[9]

There was a growing perception among the Palestinians that Arafat and his government were corrupt. Particularly during the intifada, splintering, fragmentation, and paralysis of the PLO led to increase public and political support for Hamas. Hamas intentionally moved to distance itself from Fatah and Arafat. During the Gulf War, in a calculated attempt to distance itself from Fatah's rhetoric supporting Saddam Hussein, Hamas made public statements criticizing Saddam Hussein and the invasion of Kuwait. By creating a distinction between itself and Fatah, Hamas was able to gain funding and infrastructure development from several Arab Gulf states as a result.[10] With growing militarization, the military wing of Hamas, the Izz al-din al-Qassam Brigades, continued to grow. These military forces armed themselves with weaponry that included light automatic weapons, grenades, rockets, bombs, and explosives.

Leadership from prison has played a vital role in Hamas's strategic decision-making process. Incarcerated Hamas members enjoyed heroic status and legitimacy, based on their imprisonment for their acts for the Palestinian cause, and as the most radical and committed group within the leadership, were able to forward their radical agenda, pushing issues on the boundaries of policy. Their influence has been so extensive that some experts argue that none of Hamas's political actions would prove successful without the support of prison leadership. Sheikh Ahmad Yassin has been the most prominent example, as he directed Hamas activities during years of incarceration.

Sheikh Ahmad Yassin

Sheikh Ahmad Yassin was the principal leader of the militant faction within the Muslim Brotherhood (MB) in Gaza who founded Hamas as the military wing of the MB in 1987. A charismatic force, he remained as its spiritual leader until his death by assassination in March of 2004. Born near Askalon in 1936, Yassin and his family fled to the Gaza strip due to the 1948 Arab-Israeli War. As the result of a childhood injury, Yassin was severely disabled; he was nearly blind, paraplegic, and confined to a wheelchair. In 1957 he became a teacher in Gaza and then went on to study at the Ayn Shamas University in Egypt in 1964-65, where he became involved with the Muslim Brotherhood. Yassin's activities led Egyptian authorities to expel him from the country and return him to Gaza. By the 1980s, Yassin had become the leading Islamic militant in the occupied territories.[11]

Yassin and his Muslim Brotherhood colleagues spent thirteen years, from 1973 to 1987, developing social services in Gaza. Yassin also led the Gaza Strip Steering Committee, a key leadership element within the Hamas organization. Because of resistance activities, he was imprisoned by Israeli authorities in 1984, but released as part of a prisoner exchange a year later. The leader of Hamas when the first intifada broke out in 1987, he was imprisoned again by the Israelis two years later. Ailing and aging, Shaykh Yassin was released in 1997 and flown to Jordan for medical treatment as part of a deal whereby Jordan released two captured Israeli intelligence officers who had been detained for a botched attempt to assassinate a Hamas leader several days earlier. After his release from medical treatment, Yassin returned to Gaza where he received a tumultuous hero's welcome. Until his assassination by the Israelis on March 22, 2004, the wheelchair-bound Yassin provided powerful charismatic leadership to Hamas.

Demonstrating the power of his charismatic leadership and his ability to inspire his young recruits, Yassin conveyed the goals of martyrdom to Nasra Hassan, a Muslim expert with the United Nations:

> Love of martyrdom is something deep inside the heart. But these rewards are not in themselves the goal of the martyr. The only aim is to win Allah's satisfaction. That can be done…in the speediest manner by dying in the cause of Allah. And it is Allah who selects martyrs.[12]

While Yassin's radical anti-Israeli statements reflect the extremity of language in the Hamas Charter, his more "moderate" rhetoric reveals strategic thinking. Particularly in his later years, Yassin made occasional use of less inflammatory statements. He carefully drafted his statements to allow culpability to be placed upon Israel for the continued violence while ensuring that Israel would be unwilling to accept Hamas's terms. His language also carefully avoided end-game solutions, claiming that issues such as 1967 borders and the return of Palestinian refugees were interim agreements, thereby leaving the creation of an Islamic Palestine as a topic for future discussion.

Just prior to his assassination, Yassin made a statement that on the surface seemed to reflect a move away from a strict rhetoric of violence, "Yassin asserted that the movement would agree to a temporary peace with Israel in exchange for the establishment of a Palestinian state 'on the basis of the 1967 borders' and the return of Palestinian refugees to Israel; 'the rest of the land, within Israel, we will leave to history,'"[13] preconditions that Yassin knew full well were unacceptable to Israel. Yassin had made similar comments in the past, both in 1987 and 1989:

> I do not want to destroy Israel... We want to negotiate with Israel so the Palestinian people inside and outside Palestine can live in Palestine. Then the problem will cease to exist.[14]

Negotiation Does Not Mean Renouncing Absolutist Goals

Hamas's mention of negotiating with Israel apparently runs counter to the Hamas Charter, but such statements are not unique or unheard of. Abu Marzuq, the leader of the Political Bureau of Hamas, issued a similar political statement in 1994. Likewise, Abd-al Aziz Rantisi, a radical member of Hamas noted: "The intifada is about forcing Israel's withdrawal to the 1967 boundaries... [this] doesn't mean the Arab-Israeli conflict will be over, but rather that its armed character would end."[15]

This point was emphasized in a remarkably candid statement by Mahmiud al-Zahar, a pediatrician from Gaza and prominent Hamas leader:

> We must calculate the benefit and cost of continued armed operations. If we can fulfill our goals without violence, we will do so. Violence is a means, not a goal. Hamas's decision to adopt self-restraint does not contradict our aims, including the establishment of an Islamic state instead of

Israel... We will never recognize Israel, but it is possible that a truce [muhadana] could prevail between us for days, months, or years.[16]

But in fact, according to Farhat Asa'd, a prominent member of the Hamas political leadership on the West Bank, to enter into negotiations with Israel is to recognize Israel's right to exist and is to recognize the legitimacy of the occupation. This they will not do.

As noted by Shaul Mishal and Avraham Sela in their important study of Hamas, *The Palestinian Hamas*, the principle of "not ceding one inch" is quite consistent in its leaflets.[17] In leaflet no. 28, "Islamic Palestine from the [Mediterranean] Sea to the [Jordan] River," they assert:

> The Muslims have had a full – not a partial – right to Palestine for generations, in the past, present, and future... No Palestinian generation has the right to concede the land, steeped in martyrs' blood... You must continue the uprising and stand up against the usurpers whoever they may be, and until the complete liberation of every grain of the soil of...Palestine, all Palestine, with God's help.

In a March 13, 1988, leaflet they assert: "Let any hand be cut off that signs [away] a grain of sand in Palestine in favor of the enemies of God...who have seized...the blessed land." They are also adamant that there can be no negotiations with Israel, for "[e]very negotiation with the enemy is a regression from the [Palestinian] cause, concession of a principle, and recognition of the usurping murderers' false claim to a land in which they were not born" (August 18, 1988).

Ismail Haniya

Hamas leader and current Palestinian Prime Minister Ismail Haniya was elected in the 2006 legislative elections that brought Hamas to power, a result that shocked the West but confirmed the predictions of the Arab street. Haniya has a long history of close affiliation with the late spiritual leader Sheikh Ahmad Yassin. Haniya was born in the Shati refugee camp, west of Gaza City, in 1962 after his family fled from their original home during the 1948 Arab-Israeli war. Haniya was imprisoned several times, and with Yassin, formed part of the Hamas prison leadership that was fundamental in guiding the group. Haniya was one of over 400 Palestinian fighters and leaders expelled to southern Lebanon in 1992. He spent over a year at Marj al-Zahour refugee camp, where he became part of the exiled movement leadership, developing ideology and strategy for Hamas, and gaining worldwide media exposure.

Stressing the oppression of Palestinians by the Israelis, even after his election, Haniya stated, "Our government will spare no effort to reach a just peace in the region, putting an end to the occupation and restoring our rights."[18]

Statements and Ideology

Hamas has proven a prolific public affairs machine, demonstrated during the intifada when the organization produced and distributed leaflets to the masses directing and coordinating demonstrations, boycotts, protests, and other political activities. Excerpts from these leaflets provide insight into Hamas, and particularly focus on Islam and the anti-Israeli jihad.[19]

> We have no way to defend ourselves. We can only put pressure on Israel, and make clear that 'if you do not withdraw, then we will be able to cause death and destruction on your side.' The Palestinians turned from a cat into a tiger, because they put us in a cage with no chance to move.
>
> —2000 statement by Hamas leader Abu Shanab, assassinated in 2003

> The Jews – brothers of the apes, assassins of the prophets, bloodsuckers, warmongers – are murdering you, depriving you of life after having plundered your homeland and your homes. Only Islam can break the Jews and destroy their dream. Therefore, proclaim to them: Allah is great, Allah is greater than their army, Allah is greater than their airplanes and their weapons.[20]

> The blood of our martyrs shall not be forgotten. Every drop of blood shall become a Molotov cocktail, a time bomb, and a roadside charge that will rip out the intestines of the Jews.[21]

Suicide Bombing[22]

On January 14, 2004, a young mother of two carried out a suicide bombing at a Gaza security checkpoint.[23] To a Western audience, it seems inconceivable that a mother would willingly commit such an act. Yet Hamas has carried out numerous such acts of violence, justifying them through public statements, and systematically instilling the "acceptability" of such martyrdom operations: "If [revenge] alone motivates the candidates, his martyrdom will not be acceptable to Allah. It is a military response, not an individual's bitterness, that drives an operation. Honor and dignity are very important in our culture. And when we are humiliated we respond with wrath."[24]

The wave of suicide bombings has been characterized as a required response to the provocation by Israeli settler Baruch Goldstein, who killed (or wounded) 130 Palestinian Muslims who were praying in the Tomb of the Patriarchs in the West bank town of Hebron. In fact, plans for the campaign had been well laid, and Hamas leadership was awaiting a propitious moment. Indeed, the first suicide operation by Hamas occurred on April 16, 1993; the massacre at the Tomb of the Patriarchs took place on February 25, 1994. But by that time, Hamas and the Palestinian Islamic Jihad had already carried out seven suicide attacks, although to be sure, the suicide bombing campaign was accelerated after the Hebron massacre.

The decision to adopt the tactic of suicide bombings was made at the highest level of Hamas' leadership, as they had determined that anger within the Palestinian community had reached the tipping point. As a result of the massacre at the mosque, Hamas would escalate the conflict and initiate a campaign of suicide attacks against Israeli civilians. A strategic decision by Hamas leadership, it required only a supply of willing recruits socialized to the glory of martyrdom.

Ariel Merari, a noted Israeli terrorism expert, has been a pioneer in emphasizing the key role of social psychology, not individual psychopathology, in producing suicide terrorists. He has pithily described the "suicide terrorist assembly line," which has three key junctures.[25]

First the volunteer or recruit is identified, usually by friends or relatives in the organization, and commits himself to becoming a *shahid*. Then he is publicly identified as a "living martyr," a member of "the walking dead." This brings great prestige both to the prospective martyr and to his or her family.

Finally, just before the mission, he is videotaped reading his last will and testament, in which he explains his motivations and his goals. This cements his commitment, and makes it nearly impossible for him to back out, for it would bring unbearable shame and humiliation. These videos then are disseminated on Hamas websites, where they glorify the martyrs and contribute to further recruitment.

During the period between 1999 and 2004, Hamas faced new pressures. Salah Shehade (commander of the military wing Izza-Din al-Qassam Brigades), published a communiqué supporting and justifying the group's use of martyrdom operations. This communiqué attempted to counter the accusation that Hamas manipulated young recruits to become suicide bombers. Instead, Shehade argued that Hamas applies strict requirements in considering potential suicide bombers: recruits had to be Muslims, with a level of education, and could not be the only provider for their family.[26] Hamas has made a conscious effort to publicize and celebrate its martyrs. In many Palestinian neighborhoods, "[t]he suicide bombers' green birds appear on posters, and in graffiti – the language of the street. Calendars are illustrated with the 'martyr of the month.' Paintings glorify the dead bombers in Paradise, triumphant beneath a flock of green birds. This symbol is based on a saying of the Prophet Mohammed that the soul of a martyr is carried to Allah in the bosom of the green birds of Paradise."[27]

The campaign of martyrdom attacks provided important political benefits for Hamas. In September 2000, with the eruption of the new intifada, Hamas gained significant popularity among the Palestinian population, particularly due to the group's military wing, al-Qassam Brigades, which conducted the suicide bombing campaign.

Despite the glorification of martyrdom, there have been certain periods during which Hamas concealed its involvement in suicide bombing, placing the blame on a mysterious group known as "Islamic

Jihad." For example, Hamas's reluctance to claim responsibility for suicide attacks – and its unsuccessful attempts to hide the identity of the bombers – in 1997 was not the result of criticism of the religious legitimacy of suicide. Rather, it was an attempt to avoid conflict with the Palestinian Authority which, at that time, was under extreme Israeli and American pressure to take measures against Hamas.

Hamas leaders, and many Islamic authorities, have always maintained that "martyrdom" attacks are different from ordinary suicide and are not only religiously legitimate but are praiseworthy.

> The Koran does not permit suicide in principle; on the other hand, it is a religious duty to fight and die for Allah and Islam. In theory, the martyr is supposed to submit to the will of Allah, and it is to be his own personal decision to do so. In practice, the candidates for martyrdom are heavily indoctrinated, chosen by the leadership, and assured that after their death their families will be taken care of.[28]

Clearly, economic difficulties in Palestinian territories have boosted the popularity of Hamas, made martyrdom more acceptable, and legitimized acts of violence in the minds of many Hamas supporters. The Palestinian economy is collapsing, and business activities are handicapped by Israeli checkpoints and barriers, preventing travel and commerce in the occupied territories. Hamas leaders incorporate these visible "symbols of oppression" into their inspiring externalizing rhetoric as they appeal to Palestinian youth to resist the occupation and enter the path of martyrdom. The impoverished occupied territories provide a psychologically bleak environment in which the majority of the population shares a sense of loss or injury, therefore creating a sizable pool of ready recruits, particularly among the young.

Twenty-three-year-old Mona Yousef is one such example. An unemployed translator, Yousef expressed support for Hamas's principles based largely on her own personal loss:

> Hamas must not give up the principles on which it was elected. They must still argue and fight for the prisoners, for the borders and for the Palestinian state. Hamas should not recognize Israel. I strongly believe this… My grandfather died in the 1948 war. My brother was killed in

the first intifada. He was 12, and the IDF shot him on his way to school. People have been sacrificing their lives to fight for their rights. Every house in Gaza has a story like this, a prisoner or someone killed by Israel.[29]

Yousef's story is emblematic of sentiments in the West Bank, and particularly Gaza. Unemployed youth without future prospects, having already lost friends and/or family in violence they view as "Israeli hostilities," are easy targets for manipulation by terrorist recruiters.

Terrorists, both leaders and rank-and-file members, frequently display a number of similarities in their backgrounds and histories. Consider the leaders of Hamas as mentioned previously, Ahmad Yassin, Ismail Haniya, and Mahmoud Zahhar. All were influenced by the Muslim Brotherhood, lived in refugee camps or regions, were educated and involved in Islamic institutions of higher education, were part of the exiled group of Hamas leaders sent to Lebanon in the early nineties, and finally all gained legitimacy through imprisonment and the loss of family members.

The transition between ideological support for terrorist or resistance groups and the significant step of actually engaging in an act of violence or terrorism is incremental. Barber's surveys of 900 Palestinian male adolescent Muslims revealed that in the time period of the first intifada, 1987–1993,

> [P]articipation in violence was high, with stone throwing in particular high for males (81 percent), while over two-thirds experienced both physical assault and were shot at. Over 80 percent of those interviewed by Barber admitted to supplying deliveries to activists, while a similar amount went to visit the families of dead martyrs. Yet from all of these youths, very few are likely to become operational activists for one of the main terrorist groups.[30]

The soil has been tilled, but it may require the loss of a relative or friend, as with Mona Yousef, to move the bitter youth seeking vengeance into the path of terrorism. On the basis of extensive interviews with incarcerated members of Islamist Palestinian groups, we noted commonalities in the terrorist's personal histories.

> The boyhood heroes for the Islamist terrorists were religious figures, such as the Prophet, or the radical Wahabi Islamist, Abdullah Azzam, [who was Osama bin Laden's professor]. Most had some high school, and some had education beyond high school. The majority of the subjects reported that their families were respected in the community. The families were experienced as being uniformly supportive of their commitment to the cause.[31]

This identification with religious and revolutionary figures provides justification or legitimacy for acts of violence by the powerless against the powerful oppressor – in this case, Israel. A member of the military wing of Hamas, who was arrested at age 19 and is now serving three life sentences, related his gradual path to violent action and indicated that Sheik Dr. Abdel Aziz Rantisi was his childhood hero, a source of inspiration.[32]

> I owe my start in the organization to the Moslem Center [established by Rantisi] which was active in the camp and helped residents in every sphere. I attended religious lessons and symposia in the mosque conducted by Muslim Center people and I was active on a voluntary basis in helping needy residents. During the intifada I joined Hamas and my political views grew stronger… The intifada caused many of our young people to join the organization. In fact, Hamas was established with the eruption of the intifada and it spread throughout the territories, growing stronger all the time. The intifada, despite the oppression and difficulties it caused, created a positive dynamic for the organization. After carrying out an action, I felt enormous satisfaction and pride and knew that our success would eventually lead to the realization of our dream of independence and the establishment of a Palestinian state on the soil of Moslem Palestine…I have not the slightest twinge of regret over my chosen path.

Islamic terrorist organizations appear to single out likely candidates for terrorist and particularly martyrdom operations, as noted by John Horgan in *The Psychology of Terrorism*:

Hamas and Islamic Jihad do not apparently favor married young men as potential martyrs, but rather appear more open to selecting and 'preparing' unmarried men, with no families to support – it is likely that the group is aware of the emotional responsiveness of people at a younger age and the increased susceptibility towards greater involvement this might bring.[33]

Clearly, Hamas selected individuals whose lack of personal or social connections made martyrdom a more acceptable option. Recruits became easy targets because they already felt excluded from the group, and yearned for social acceptance. Membership in Hamas carries significant social prestige, as the following interview quote reveals, "Recruits were treated with great respect. A youngster who belonged to Hamas or Fatah was regarded more highly than one who didn't belong to a group, and got better treatment than unaffiliated kids."[34]

Hassan Salame: Suicide Bomb Commander

Hassan Salame, now serving forty-six consecutive life sentences, is considered the most prolific suicide bomb commander in the history of Palestinian terrorism in Israel, and was responsible for the wave of suicide bombings throughout Israel in the run-up to the 1996 election. Salame was born in 1971 in the Khan Yunis refuge camp, considered one of the more radical pockets of resistance to the occupation. The dominant organization there is the Islamic Center, led by Abdel Aziz Rantisi, Hamas founder Sheik Ahmad Yassin's right-hand man. The Center has played a major role in recruiting new members and systematically converting them into suicide bombers. Salame can be considered an exemplar of Hamas terrorism and his compelling interview, previously unpublished, is quoted extensively.

> *We were a normal, well-established and respected refugee camp family. All the children went to school, and were considered quiet and well behaved. No-one in the family was involved in criminal activities; most used to pray in the*

mosque. Within the family we never discussed politics and our social standing was good.

My childhood hero, like many of the kids in the camp, was Che Guevara, whom we saw as a leading revolutionary figure... When I grew up, my hero became Dr Abdullah Azam.

From my childhood I leaned towards Islam. Most of my social activity was focused around the mosque. I attended lessons in religion organized by the Islamic center and that formed the basis for my ideology... As far as people in the camp were concerned, they believed every young Palestinian should enlist. Recruitment was the order of the day and seen as a necessity. Every young person was obliged first and foremost to do what he could for the liberation of the people and the land...

At the start of the intifada, I joined Hamas. I was recruited by Jamil, a friend from the camp... The intifada mobilized the entire Palestinian nation for the struggle, and took the Islamic movement another stage towards achieving its goal... My joining up was the normal thing to do, as all the young people were enlisting.

I felt great satisfaction at having been recruited to Hamas and was proud of my record... I felt very good about what I had chosen to do, and I felt I was fulfilling my duty towards Allah, the Arab and Palestinian peoples, and to myself.

Within the group, there is a feeling of solidarity and common cause. We share a common aim and destiny. There is an atmosphere of brotherhood...

Of course, my family supports me and my organization... Most of the general population supports the recruits.

In general, any organization that fights for the liberation of Palestine is a good thing. But we need to distinguish between religious and secular organizations. Religious organizations understand that we also have to fight for Islam and not only for the nation and the land.

Fatah is a good positive organization, but mistaken in its ideology and deeds. Fatah, in its concessions to Israel, its recognition of the state of Israel, and its joining the peace process, is totally unacceptable to me.

Every young Moslem understood the importance of our armed actions and we never needed ideology to justify them... A martyrdom operation bombing is the highest level of Jihad and highlights the depth of our faith. The bombers are holy fighters who carry out one of the more important articles of Islam.

The armed attacks are an inseparable part of the organization's activities. They are the goal of the military wing, and the reason it was set up. Jihad is conducted in different ways, and the military aspect is the most important. Without the military element, without the armed attacks, the organization will not be able to achieve its goals.

As for the peace process, I personally am against it. It runs counter to our views. It entails recognition of the State of Israel and that runs counter to Islam and the Hamas... Even if there ultimately is agreement between Israel and the Palestinian Authority, it will only be a stage in the long history of Islam. The [Hezbollah] too doesn't say what will happen after you leave Lebanon...Of one thing, I am convinced: in the end Islam will triumph.

In response to Israeli counterterrorist actions, designed to inhibit the carrying out of terrorist activities by destroying the homes of the perpetrators' families, Hamas extolled the acts of the martyrs and supported their families: 'Perpetrators of armed attacks were seen as heroes, their families got a great deal of material assistance including the construction of new homes to replace those destroyed by the Israeli authorities as punishment for terrorist acts.'[35]

Jessica Stern, author of *Terror in the Name of God,* observed that "hopelessness, deprivation, envy, and humiliation make death, and paradise, seem more appealing."[36] The manner in which hopelessness can be exploited is eloquently conveyed by an elderly resident of Jenin she interviewed: "Look how we live here, then maybe you'll understand why there are always volunteers for martyrdom. Every good Muslim understands that it's better to die fighting than to live without hope."[37]

Internet and Public Relations

Hamas has proven particularly effective at mobilizing the new media to support recruitment, information sharing, and coordination of logistics. The Internet site for the al-Qassam Brigades maintains websites that allow communication between Hamas members and other sympathizers who may wish to engage in acts of violence as well as to move non-members sympathetic to the cause along the path of violence. A recent posting discussed the following Internet exchange between two non-Hamas members, Palestinians who used the Hamas Internet site to exchange terrorism information:

> My dear brothers in Jihad…I have a kilo of acetone peroxide. I want to know how to make a bomb from it in order to blow up an army jeep; I await your quick response.

A response came approximately one hour later:

> My dear brother… I understand that you have 1,000 grams of Om El Abad. Well done! There are several ways to change it into a bomb." [He proceeded to explain the specific details for making an explosive for a roadside bomb].[38]

Hamas has created an Internet site providing instructions for building and producing a number of terrorist weapons, including rockets and explosives. Furthermore, the military wing of Hamas created a "Military Academy," which runs online courses for bomb-making, featuring a fourteen-lesson course as part of a program to expand the pool of terrorist bomb-makers. Additional topics include how to manufacture plastic explosives and the selection of terrorist targets. In 1996, the Hamas website posted *The Mujahideen Poisons Handbook,* a detailed, twenty-three page handbook on preparing poisons and deadly gasses intended for terrorist attacks.[39]

2006 Elections

Hamas agreed to an informal truce with Israel in February 2005 in return for Hamas being able to participate in the Palestinian elections. In 2006 Hamas won the elections based on its "promises to provide effective, honest governance." Hamas had long-voiced its acceptance of elections, provided that Palestinian elections were legitimate. Many of Hamas's supporters and members have stressed the point that Hamas will recognize the will of the Palestinian people.

In the Palestinian town of Nablus, a Hamas student leader stated:

> In elections, Hamas will always accept the will of the people. There will be an Islamic state at the end, but only if the majority of the people opts for it. Hamas will never enforce its agenda on anyone.[40]

And Yassin stated prior to his assassination:

> In elections, it is always the people who decide. We will accept their decision as we have accepted their decision in all elections we have participated in.[41]

The issue of corruption played a major role in the 2006 elections. Hamas attacked Fatah on the grounds of practicing corruption and cronyism while neglecting the plight of the Palestinians. Notably, Hamas was able to distribute around 95 percent of its funds to the needy Palestinian poor.[42] This helped to create a legitimate, fair, and just Hamas in the eyes of the public – compared with the corruption of the Palestinian Authority.

In the ensuing elections, Hamas won 76 out of 132 seats on the Palestinian Legislative Council. Despite this majority, only 45 percent of Palestinians voted for Hamas in the January elections. Widespread perceptions of Fatah as corrupt enhanced Hamas's electoral numbers, as some Palestinians voted for Hamas as a vote against Fatah. Overall, the voting results reflected a strong, but not universal support for Hamas's anti-Israeli platform.[43]

Continuing to oppose a two-state solution, consistent with the absolute principles in their founding charter, Hamas still refuses to recognize Israel's right to exist. The United States, the European Union, and Israel have withheld financial support from the Hamas-led Palestinian government, making it clear that the resumption of economic support is contingent upon Hamas foreswearing terrorism, recognizing Israel's right to exist, and reentering the so-called "road map" negotiations that will lead to a two-state solution.

These sanctions have destroyed the already-weakened Palestinian economy – funds to the PA have been cut, and civil servants have gone as long as six months with essentially no pay. Many middle-class Palestinians, particularly those working for the Palestinian Authority, have been plunged into poverty, leading to public protests and rioting. The UN estimates the poverty rate in Gaza at 80 percent.[44] This poverty has contributed to harsh anti-Israeli opinion in the West Bank and particularly in Gaza, leading to a public largely sympathetic to Hamas. The following statements reveal the sentiments of various Gaza residents, and explain why Hamas's anti-Israeli program resonates widely with Gaza's poor.

Majeda al-Saqqa, 37-year-old NGO worker from Khan Younis:

> The situation now is just so bad: socially, educationally, economically. Israel has been destroying Palestinian society... The issue is not should Hamas recognize Israel. The issue is that we are under occupation. We don't have a state yet, Israel does. They have embassies, offices, passports. We are the people who are neglected by Israel and the West. The basis for any solution is for Israel to recognize us.[45]

Fathi Tobail, aged 50, an employee of the Palestinian Authority:

> We are the ones who are oppressed, who need recognition, not Israel. It's for the occupier to recognize the oppressed, not for the oppressed to recognize the occupier. They have their own country, but we are still suffering to get our own state.[46]

Despite the profound economic hardship wrought by the economic boycotts by the European Union, the United States, and Israel, there is no indication of Hamas moving away from its founding principles. They persist in blaming Israel and the United States for the difficulties within Gaza without ever indicating that the economic policies are in response to Hamas's continued support of terrorist violence to obtain their totalistic goals.

As early as 2005, there have been indications of Hamas's increasing radicalization. Following Israel's August 2005 withdrawal from Gaza, Hamas, particularly its military branch, attempted to show the benefits of violence (as opposed to Fatah's diplomacy). Statements emphasized the benefits of "four years of resistance, against ten years of negotiations."[47] Likewise, the political branch produced tens of thousands of flyers titled *The Dawn of Victory*, which displayed masked photos of Hamas commanders, emphasizing their military success.

Since the victory of Hamas in the spring 2006 elections, the Palestinian territories have been disrupted by international sanctions and escalating cycles of Palestinian and Israeli violence. Hamas initiated talks with Fatah, proposing a national government designed to unify the Palestinian factions, but there are no indications that Hamas has changed its ultimate goals. Rather, it probably represented another "strategic" move consistent with Hamas's long-time goal of destroying the Israeli state.

The gap between Hamas and the Western-supported Palestinian Authority is increasing, and what has been characterized as a burgeoning civil war between Hamas and the Palestinian Authority militias is escalating. While it seems that the very future of the peace process, the Palestinian people, and Hamas (as both a terrorist group and as a political party), as well as Israeli security, currently hang in the balance, these crises have regularly plagued the region since the establishment of Israel in 1948.

Notes

1. The goal of this chapter is to convey understandings of the psychology of Hamas leaders and followers. To do this, an overview of the political and cultural context is

necessary. There is no intent to develop a definitive political history of Hamas, and so there will not be an attempt to portray in detail the intricacies of Hamas's role since the 2006 election nor of its relationship to other militant Islamist groups such as the Palestinian Islamic Jihad or secular groups such as the Al-Aqsa Martyrs Brigade, which have also actively participated in the wave of suicide bombings.

2. Bruce Hoffman, *Inside Terrorism*, (New York: Columbia University Press, 1998), 162.

3. Amal Saad-Ghorayeb, *Hizbu'llah: Politics and Religion*, (London: Pluto Press, 2002), 73.

4. Quotations from the charter are taken from Taheri 1987.

5. "The Covenant of the Islamic Resistance Movement (Hamas)" August, 1988. The complete transcript provided by The Avalon Project at Yale Law School, On-line, Internet, available from http://www.yale.edu/lawweb/avalon/mideast/hamas.htm.

6. "Dealing with Hamas," *International Crisis Group Middle East Report, Number 21*, Amman/Brussels, January, 26, 2004, 7.

7. Ibid., 16.

8. Walter Laqueur, *The New Terrorism: Fanaticism and the Arms of Mass Destruction*, (Oxford: Oxford University Press, 1999), 138-139.

9. Leaflet of the Islamic Resistance Movement (Hamas), January 1988, Reproduced in Charles D. Smith, *Palestine and the Arab-Israeli Conflict: a History with Documents, 5th ed.*, (Boston, MA: Bedford/St. Martin's, 2004), 433-4.

10. James Forest, ed., *Teaching Terror: Strategic and Tactical Learning in the Terrorist World*, (Lanham, MD: Rowman and Littlefield, 2006), 194-5.

11. "Biography of Ahmad Yassin," *Encyclopedia of Palestinians*, 12 November 2000, On-line, Internet, available from http://www.palestineremembered.com/Gaza/al-Jura/Story185.html.

12. Nasra Hassan, "An Arsenal of Believers: Talking to the 'Human Bombs,'" *New Yorker*, 19 November 2001.

13. "Dealing with Hamas," op. cit., 3.

14. Interview, *Al-Nahar* (Jerusalem), 30 April 1989, quoted in Abu Amr, *Islamic Fundamentalism,* cited in "Dealing with Hamas," 13.

15. International Crisis Group Interview with Rantisi, October 2002, cited in "Dealing with Hamas," 13.

16. *Al-Quds* (East Jerusalem), 12 October 1995, cited by Mishal and Sela, 71.

17. Shaul Mishal and Avraham Sela, *The Palestinian Hamas: Vision, Violence, and Coexistence*, (New York: Columbia University Press, 2000), 51-52.

18. "Profile: Hamas PM Ismail Haniya," *BBC News Online*.

19. International Crisis Group Interview, Abu Shanab, 5 August 2003, cited in "Dealing with Hamas," 17.

20. Leaflet of the Islamic Resistance Movement (Hamas), January 1988, Reproduced in: Smith, 433-4.

21. Ibid.

22. Hamas is not the only militant Palestinian group engaging in suicide terrorism. The Palestinian Islamic Jihad is a militant Islamist group that also has a campaign of suicide bombing, but, unlike Hamas, does not sustain a web of social services. The success of the suicide bombing campaigns of Hamas and the Palestinian Islamic Jihad can be seen as requiring the secular militant group Fatah to develop a unit that would also engage in suicide bomb attacks, the Al-Aqsa Martyrs Brigade, in order for Fatah to compete organizationally with Hamas for new recruits. In addition to this discussion of Hamas suicide terrorism, an extended consideration of suicide terrorism will be found in Chapter 9, Section 2: *Tactics Old and New: Suicide Terrorism and Weapons of Mass Destruction Terrorism*.

23. "Dealing with Hamas," op. cit., 1.

24. John Horgan, *The Psychology of Terrorism*, (New York: Routledge, 2005), 131.

25. For extended discussions of this social psychological observation, see Ariel Merari, "Social, Organizational, and Psychological Factors in Suicide Terrorism," in *Root Causes of Terrorism,* Tore Bjorgo, ed., (London: Routledge, 2005), 70-86; A. Merari, "Psychological Aspects of Suicide Terrorism," in *Psychology of Terrorism*, B. Bongar, L. Brown, L. Beutler, J. Breckenridge and P. Zimbardo, eds. (Oxford: Oxford University Press, 2007); and A. Merari, "Suicidal Terrorism," in *Assessment, Treatment, and Prevention of Suicidal Behavior*, R. I. Yufit and D. Lester, eds., (Indianapolis: Wiley, 2004), 431-453.

26. Forest, *Teaching Terror*, 198.

27. Horgan, *The Psychology of Terrorism*, 91.

28. Laqueur, *The New Terrorism*, 141.

29. "BBC Panel Interview with Mona Yousef," *BBC News Online*, 13 September 2006, news.bbc.co.uk/go/pr/fr/-/2/hi/talking_point/5339478.stm.

30. Horgan, *The Psychology of Terrorism*, 101. Based on survey by B. Barber, *Heart and Stones: Palestinian Youth from the Intifada*, (New York: Palgrave, 2003).

31. J. M. Post, E. Sprinzak, and L. M. Denny, "The Terrorists in their Own Words: Interviews with 35 Incarcerated Middle Eastern Terrorists," *Terrorism and Political Violence*, vol. 15, no. 1 (2003), 171-184.

32. Previously unpublished interview summarized in Post, Sprinzak, and Denny, "The Terrorists in their Own Words," 171-184.

33. Horgan, *The Psychology of Terrorism*, 102.

34. Post, Sprinzak, and Denny, "The Terrorists in their Own Words."

35. Previously unpublished interview developed in association with terrorist interview project summarized in Post, Sprinzak, and Denny, "The Terrorists in their Own Words."

36. Jessica Stern, *Terror in the Name of God: Why Religious Militants Kill*, (New York: HarperCollins Publishers, 2003), 38.

37. Philip Jacobson, "Home-Grown Martyrs of the West Bank Reap Deadly Harvest," *Sunday Telegraph*, 19 August 2001, 20 as cited in Stern, *Terror in the Name of God*, 38.

38. Reported by Amit Cohen, "Hamas Dot Com," in *Maariv Online*, 2 July 2003, On-line, Internet, available from www.maarivenglish.com/tour/Hamas%20Dot%20Com.htm. Reprinted in Forest, *Teaching Terror*, 119.

39. Forest, *Teaching Terror*, 119-121.

40. "Dealing with Hamas," op. cit., 14.

41. Ibid.

42. Forest, *Teaching Terror*, 199.

43. Shlomo Brom, "A Hamas Government: Isolate or Engage?" *U.S. Institute of Peace Briefing*, March 2006, 2.

44. Alan Johnston, "Palestinian Despair as Donors Meet," *BBC News*, 1 September 2006.

45. BBC Panel Interview with Majeda Al-Saqqa, *BBC News Online*, 13 September 2006, On-line, Internet, available from news.bbc.co.uk/go/pr/fr/-/2/hi/talking_point/5338842.stm.

46. BBC Panel Interview with Fathi Tobail, *BBC News Online*, 13 September 2006, On-line, Internet, available from news.bbc.co.uk/go/pr/fr/-/2/hi/talking_point/5339478.stm.

47. "Enter Hamas: The Challenges of Political Integration," *International Crisis Group, Middle East Report, Number 49*, (January 18, 2006), 7.

CHAPTER 10

Al Qaeda 2.0 and the Global Salafi Jihad[1]

Jerrold M. Post[2]

When Abdullah Ocalan, the authoritarian charismatic leader of the Kurdish separatist group, the PKK, was captured in 1999, it was devastating to the organization. Similarly, when Abimael Guzman, the authoritarian charismatic leader of Peru's Sendero Luminoso, the Shining Path, was captured in 1992, it was a mortal blow to the organization. But, when, as result of the massive air-ground campaign in Afghanistan in the aftermath of 9/11, although Al Qaeda suffered severe losses, it was not their end. This includes the death and/or capture of several senior leaders and the destruction of the centralized headquarters and training sites of Al Qaeda in Taliban-controlled Afghanistan. From there, bin Laden and his chief leaders had administered the group's personnel, finance, recruitment, training, and operational planning. But after being denied their safe haven and while on the run, acting defensively, bin Laden and Al Qaeda adapted to a new reality.

Despite these losses and the dispersal of members throughout the world, it is a testament to its organizational structure and flexibility under the leadership of the charismatic, but *not* authoritarian, Osama bin Laden, and his deputy and designated successor, Ayman Al-Zawahiri, that Al Qaeda remains operationally intact – severely wounded, but certainly not yet destroyed.

Al Qaeda 2.0

Rather, under their guidance, Al Qaeda Version 1.0 with its centralized authority structure adapted smoothly to this grave crisis, morphing into Al Qaeda Version 2.0, a semi-autonomous network under the overall umbrella of Al Qaeda, which provides a consistent ideological framework. Much of the day-to-day control, operational planning, and financing of Al Qaeda was dispersed regionally, providing a much more widespread and difficult counter-terrorist challenge, demonstrating to the victors in Afghanistan the accuracy of the adage, "No good deed goes unpunished."

This adaptive crisis response in many ways reflects the non-authoritarian leadership style of Osama bin Laden, who studied organizational management at the University at Jeddah, and created Al Qaeda according to modern management theory. It is a flat decentralized organization, and the leadership provided by bin Laden is distinctly not authoritarian. Rather he is more akin to the chairman of the board of Radical Islam, Inc., who has "grown" his corporation through mergers and acquisitions.

Unlike the PKK and Sendero Luminoso, bin Laden did identify his own successor, Ayman Al-Zawahiri, who serves as CEO, managing day-to-day leadership. Together they created a redundant leadership structure so that when a key leader is killed or captured, another leader is ready to move into his niche. Thus, when the number three man and chief of operations Muhammed Atef was killed in the early days of the 2001 attack on Afghanistan, he was swiftly replaced by the former director of personnel, Abu Zubaydah; when Zubaydah was captured in 2002, he was replaced by Khalid Sheikh Mohammed, the architect of 9/11; when Khalid Sheik Muhammad was captured a year later, he too was replaced. Scarcely a beat was dropped in these organizational transitions.

For many Al Qaeda followers, the fall 2001 attacks in Afghanistan only served to reinforce their sense of righteous belief in their cause and their perception of the West as anti-Islamic aggressors. Although we have not seen a second large-scale Al Qaeda attack, there is nothing to suggest that Al Qaeda is no longer operational. Despite Al Qaeda's Afghan base having been destroyed and its leadership dispersed, its cellular structure remains intact with both active and sleeper cells throughout the world. It is possible that in setting the bar so high with 9/11, Al Qaeda did not wish to lower their sights.

Moreover, the shift from a more centralized command and control to a more dispersed semi-autonomous network, at least initially, probably delayed plans in track. It is most likely, however, due to the highly-focused international attention, that the next wave of Al Qaeda attacks will be on a smaller scale and undertaken by cells operating semi-independently.

Yet, as witnessed in the 2006 foiled British – U.S.-bound airliner plot, in their new semi-autonomous form, Al Qaeda and the jihadi network retains the capability of mounting a major coordinated attack, the hallmark of Al Qaeda operations, as witnessed by the coordinated twin city attacks on the U.S. embassies in Nairobi, Kenya, and Dar es Salaan, Tanzania, in 1998 and the coordinated twin city attacks of September 11, 2001, on New York City and Washington, D.C.

Death or Capture of bin Laden will not end the Threat from Al Qaeda

With the U.S. tendency to personalize our enmities, there is a wistful hope that the death or capture of bin Laden will end the threat from Al Qaeda. Indeed, the bounty/reward has just been raised to $50 million. But in the event of bin Laden's death or capture, Al Qaeda's flat, dispersed organizational structure, the presence of a designated successor, the nature of bin Laden's and Zawahiri's leadership and charisma, and their global Islamist mission, all indicate that the terrorist network would survive. Bin Laden's loss would assuredly be a setback, but since Zawahiri is already running Al Qaeda's operations on a day-to-day basis, his transition to the top job would be virtually seamless. Indeed, increasingly in recent years major statements from Al Qaeda have been made by Zawahiri, not bin Laden, indicating the leadership succession is already underway. The organization's luster for alienated Muslims would dim to some degree, but within the organization, Zawahiri's considerable stature and charismatic attractiveness should permit him to carry on the network's mission.

While U.S. President George W. Bush and former British Prime Minister Tony Blair took pains to clarify that the War on Terrorism is not a war against Muslims, but a war against terrorism, bin Laden, in seeking to frame this as a religious war, has now laid claim to the title of commander-in-chief of the radical Islamic world, opposing the commander-in-chief of the Western world, President George W. Bush. Many alienated Muslim youth find resonance in bin Laden's statements, and see him as a hero. Al Qaeda has become a catalyst for an international jihadist movement that will likely continue to grow, influenced and operationally facilitated by the original parent organization.

Contributing to the resilience of Al Qaeda is that it is an adaptive learning organization, regularly reviewing and pursuing lessons learned from both successful and failed operations, such as the inclusion of the lessons learned from successful Mossad counter-terrorism operations as applied in the Al Qaeda Training Manual.[3] A less adaptive organization would have been destroyed by the focused attack in Afghanistan. Bin Laden sent out a communiqué in the fall of 2002 which dispersed the organization and established a regional command structure, and said, in effect, "we have shown you the way. From now on it is largely up to you to plan and fund your own operations."

Osama bin Laden's active leadership in formulating specific attacks post-9/11, while not wholly abandoned, was applied to encouraging others to take action in the growing global recruit's movements, other associated or inspired groups and individual fellow travelers in the Jihadist ranks were thereby granted the responsibility to carry on operations against the Western infidel.[4] Since the September 11, 2001, attacks, only one follows the Al Qaeda 1.0 pattern of centralized planning, training, financing, and sanctioning – the aborted attack on airliners originating from UK airports. All others have been of the new Al Qaeda variety. Through the latter, bin Laden continued to maintain symbolic leadership control over the organization through his full praise and hailing of attacks by Al Qaeda-linked groups. In 2002, he embraced attacks in Bali, Yemen, and Moscow as a:

> response to what happened to all Muslim brothers around the world.... The incidents that have taken place since the raids on New York and Washington up until now – the recent operation in Moscow and some sporadic operations here and there – are only reactions and reciprocal actions. These actions were carried out by the zealous sons of Islam in defense of their religion and in response to the order of their God and prophet, may God's peace and blessings be upon him.

In the audiotape, bin Laden speaks on behalf of all the *mujahedin* fighters, but more broadly, the nation of Islam:

> The Islamic nation, thanks to God, has started to attack you at the hands of its beloved sons, who pledged to God to continue jihad, as long as they are able, through words and weapons, to establish right and expose falsehood.[5]

The string of attacks in the last few years by Al Qaeda-linked groups were, with one exception, probably mounted independently. Nevertheless, these groups indicated that the attacks were in response to bin Laden's guidance and were affirmed by him and they added to the luster of Al Qaeda. These operations have largely been perceived as indicators of continued Al Qaeda potency rather than being portrayed as a reflection of bin Laden's and Al Qaeda's eroding influence and a lack of organizational coherence, although the latter interpretation is also plausible.

The new direction taken by Al Qaeda and its allies is seen in the March 2004 attack on the Madrid train station. A December 2003 posting on Al Qaeda websites called for terrorist attacks against Spain on the eve of the election, indicating it would either force the regime to withdraw from Iraq, or would lead to a socialist victory at the polls and the new party would then pull out.[6] In this way Al Qaeda could legitimately lay claim to inspiring the major March 2004 attack, just before the election, that led to the fall of the government and the decision of the successor socialist government to remove troops from Iraq.

In another case the Abu Hafs al-Masri Brigade, a European jihad group linked to Al Qaeda, claimed responsibility for the Istanbul, Turkey, bombings in August 2004, stating that the attack in "Istanbul was only the beginning…[A] group of mujahedeen…did the first attack after all of them [European nations] have refused the truce that was offered by our sheikh,"[7] referring to bin Laden's advice to European states to reject the U.S. War on Terror. (This is an interesting example of the transfer of blame so characteristic of terrorist groups.) This sustained influence of bin Laden over his allies in the extremist Islamic movement has influenced an emerging generation of new blood to carry on the attacks and replace the killed and captured.

Abu Musab Zarqawi, then leader of Al Qaeda in Mesopotamia, in an October 2004 audiotape, communicated the importance of the new generation to continue on the fight to resist the Infidel: "Oh, young men of Islam, here is our message to you. If we are killed or captured, you should carry on the fight. Don't betray God and His Prophet."[8]

Co-opting Potential Rivals: al-Zarqawi and Al Qaeda of Mesopotamia

Part of Al Qaeda's leadership genius under bin Laden and Zawahiri is not to focus on differences, but to co-opt and embrace potential rivals. A striking example was that of Abu Musab al-Zarqawi, whose aggressive campaign of terror in Iraq and Jordan and barbaric ways such as the beheading of hostages displayed on the Internet captivated audiences and proved to rival bin Laden's influence on many levels within the ranks of its affected Muslim youths.

The decision by bin Laden and Zawahari to forge relations with Zarqawi exemplifies the essence of the new global threat of terror – shifting alliances, local leadership, focusing on a variety of new targets, and drawing on new resources. While sheer differences in vision and leadership were apparent, arguably combining resources benefited the overarching jihad mission of Al Qaeda. It also indicated that Al Qaeda was still a force despite its loss of a safe haven in Afghanistan and losses due to the counter-terror operations led by the United States. Captivating media audiences around the world, Zarqawi's violent unbounded approach to waging war against the infidels on the battlefield of Iraq, including Shia brethren, provided a stark contrast to the deeply ideological principles of Islamic Jihad as espoused by bin Laden. In October 2004, Zarqawi swore allegiance "to the sheikh of the mujaheddin, Osama bin Laden," and thereby recognized bin Laden as the "emir" in Iraq.[9] But this was in words only, and by no means did Zarqawi hand over control. "[This is] a cause [in which] we are cooperating for the good and supporting jihad."[10]

Bin Laden recognized the need to provide Zarqawi relative autonomy to carry out operations in Iraq while attempting to retain influence over the jihad, which was diverging from the path of bin Laden's Al Qaeda, as it emphasized sectarian violence and threatened competition as more fighters flocked to Zarqawi's charismatic banner.

A letter intercepted by U.S. forces, dated July 2005, from Zawahiri to Zarqawi attempts to reassert Al Qaeda's priorities in Iraq by calling into question Zarqawi's lack of foresight and planning. This was in part due to the extent of the sectarian violence that Zarqawi was leading, with Sunni Muslims killing Shi'ite Muslims, raising questions about the religious justification for the escalating violence.

> We are extremely concerned, as are the mujahedeen and all sincere Muslims, about your Jihad and your heroic acts until you reach its intended goal. Therefore, I stress again to you and to all your brothers the need to direct the political action equally with the military action, by the alliance, cooperation and gathering of all leaders of opinion and influence in the Iraqi arena.[11]

Zawahiri attempted in this letter to inject an element of reality into Zarqawi's jihadist thinking, which fostered sectarian violence and killing of supporters of the infidel, and he demonstrated an acute awareness of the power of the media:

> Among the things which the feelings of the Muslim populace who love and support you will never find palatable – also – are the scenes of slaughtering the hostages… And your response, while true, might be: Why shouldn't we sow terror in the hearts of the Crusaders and their helpers… However, despite all of this, I say to you: that we are in a battle, and that more than half of this battle is taking place in the battlefield of the media. And that we are in a media battle in a race for the hearts and minds of our Umma.

The Zawahiri letter captured the prevailing frustration at the highest levels of leadership to contain Zarqawi's deviations, which they felt were threatening the reputation of Al Qaeda, and in particular were counterproductive for Al Qaeda's reputation in the Muslim world.[12]

But Zarqawi did not change his indiscriminate tactics. Shortly after the letter surfaced, Zarqawi's Al Qaeda in Iraq claimed responsibility for three suicide attacks in Amman, Jordan, in November 2005 that left many

Muslims dead, demonstrating that Zarqawi was by no means influenced and certainly was not deterred by the firm tone of Zawahiri's letter.

Despite Zarqawi's defiance, in a June 2006 audio speech eulogizing Zarqawi after his death, bin Laden offers up great respect for "one of our best knights, an Emir who was one of the best Emirs." While the eulogy appears to be an effort to defend Zarqawi's role in sectarian violence in Iraq, in fact it is also an opportunity to reassert Al Qaeda's priorities in Iraq and set the record straight.

> To those who accuse Abu Musab al-Zarqawi of killing some segments of the Iraqi people, I say…Abu Musab, may God have mercy upon his soul, had clear instructions [implicitly, from bin Laden] to focus his fighting on the occupying invaders, led by the Americans, and not to target whoever wanted to be neutral, but whoever insisted on fighting along with the Crusaders against Muslims should be killed, regardless of their sect or tribe. Supporting the infidels against Muslims is one of the 10 things that nullify Islam, as stipulated by scholars.[13]

One of the difficulties in moving from centralized command and control to a more dispersed, decentralized organization is maintaining overall control and not having actions by assertive, competitive leaders threaten the organization's overall direction and reputation. This was the dilemma for bin Laden in containing the ambitious Zarqawi, whose sectarian excesses were leading to Muslim criticism of the jihad and were undermining bin Laden's authority. This problem for Al Qaeda's core leaders is exacerbated as the organizational shape of Al Qaeda has progressively evolved into the global jihad movement – how to maintain influence, if not control, and yet claim credit for actions to demonstrate the movement has not left the leader behind.

Some would go so far as to say that Al Qaeda now provides an overarching ideology for groups and organizations largely operating independently. The organizational form of Hamas and Hezbollah is much tighter and more authoritarian, with followers in action cells having little say in the conduct of operations. In contrast to these other radical Islamist terrorist organizations, which are quite hierarchical in organizational style,

Al Qaeda has a much looser organizational form, with distributed decision-making, reflecting the leadership style of bin Laden.

Al Qaeda Reconstituted[14]

In fact, early estimates that the 2001 conflict in Afghanistan had dealt a crippling blow to Al Qaeda and marked the beginning of the end of the end for the organization have proven to be overly optimistic and to have insufficiently considered the adaptive, resilient nature of the organization. The rumors of Al Qaeda's imminent death were premature. There is substantial reason to believe Al Qaeda central has largely been reconstituted. Because of its redundant leadership structure, the significant numbers of senior leaders that have been killed or captured have been replaced by long time Al Qaeda members with demonstrated loyalty to bin Laden and Zawahiri. There is a new generation of Al Qaeda senior leaders, and when one is killed or captured, the organization swiftly replaces him.

Many of the senior leaders have as a central responsibility serving in liaison roles to associated organizations. The resurgence of the Taliban did not occur spontaneously but represents major Al Qaeda influence with several of its senior leaders, such as Mustafa Abu Al-Yazid, who serves as liaison to the Taliban and Khalid Habib, who is an Afghan field commander, playing major roles. Abu Obaidah al-Masri is the current chief of external operations.

Moreover, as exemplified by the London transit bombings of July 2005 and the foiled U.S.-bound airline attack of August 2006 demonstrated, Al Qaeda's role was more than inspirational. In fact, further investigation by British authorities of these plots carried out by British citizens with Pakistani roots have clarified these plots were ordered by Al Qaeda deputies, training was provided in Pakistan by Al Qaeda to the operational leaders, and al-Masri, the chief of external operations reportedly was extremely active in assisting with the August 2006 plot to place explosives aboard U.S.-bound airliners out of Heathrow. This was not mere inspiration, and showed a much firmer guiding hand than earlier believed.

The reconstituted leadership is playing active roles in recruitment, training, and finance. Particularly impressive is their enhanced communication ability; their media arm al-Sahab, has proven to be extremely effective in getting the Al Qaeda message out. Having produced 16 videos in 2005, through September 2007 they had disseminated more than four times this output. And, always adaptive, they have facilitated communications impervious to Western electronic surveillance. Until 2005 they had transmitted their videos to outlets such as Al Jazeera but in the past two years have been posting their videos directly on the Internet.

Al Qaeda Embraces and Supports Southeast Asian Islamic Terrorist Groups

Based in Indonesia, Jemaah Islamiyah (JI) is a Southeast Asian militant Islamist group whose goal is to establish a sharia-based Islamic state in Southeast Asia, including Indonesia, Malaysia, southeastern Philippines, and Singapore. They have been active since their founding in 1993, and trace their origins to a radical Islamic group Darul Islam operating in Indonesia in the 1940s. JI was founded by two Indonesian clerics, Abdullah Sungkar and Abu Bakar Ba'asyir.

After the downfall of the Suharto regime in 1998, JI leader Sungkar made contact with Osama bin Laden. With this liaison, JI shifted gears from a more local focus to becoming part of the global struggle. The Bali nightclub bombing of October 2002, in which 202 people were killed, including many Australians, was the first attack after JI developed this mutually beneficial relationship with Al Qaeda. After the Bali bombing, bin Laden praised this action, and in his embrace, implicitly claimed credit.

JI has a relationship with Abu Sayyaf, meaning "bearer of the sword." Operating in the Philippines, the Abu Sayaff Group (ASG) was founded in 1991 by Abdurajak Abubakar Talibani to create an Islamic state in the predominantly Muslim islands of southeastern Philippines. Talibani had studied Islamic jurisprudence in Mecca, Saudi Arabia, and on his return to the Philippines in 1984 preached militant Wahabi sermons. He joined the Muslim fighters in Afghanistan in their war to expel the godless Soviets from his Muslim state under Osama bin Laden's leadership. The provenance of Abu Sayyaf in relationship to Al Qaeda has its beginnings with this personal relationship of their leaders. After the war, when Talibani returned to the Philippines, bin Laden directed his brother-in-law Jamal Khalifa to travel to the Philippines in 1991 and establish connections with the newly forming group.

Ramzi Yousef, an electrical engineer, now in prison for his role in the 1993 first World Trade Center bombing, was sent to the Philippines by Al Qaeda to train ASG members in explosives. His cell helped organize the so-called Bojinka plot to blow up 11 U.S.-bound airliners in flight, the plot to be executed by ASG. The plot was foiled when he was arrested and his encrypted computer with details of the plot was seized. (This planned coordinated attack of 11 U.S.-bound Asian airlines is notably similar to the foiled August 2006 planned bombing of 10-12 U.S.-bound airliners out of Heathrow by British jihadists of Pakistani origin.)

Thus from its earliest days, the ASG was more tightly connected to Al Qaeda, differing from the looser affiliative relationship with JI, a further reflection of the flexible leadership of bin Laden as he was "growing" his organization.

The Global Salafi Jihad

One of the more alarming developments, which poses profound counterterrorism challenges, is the increase in recruitment to the global Salafi jihad of second generation émigrés to Europe, as exemplified by the March 11, 2004, Madrid train station and the July 7, 2005, London transit bombings as well as the foiled August 2006 coordinated attack on U.S.-bound planes from Heathrow airport in London. Throughout Europe, there is an increased radicalization and recruitment of terrorists from second- and third-generation émigrés to the global Salafi jihad. Although most Muslim immigrants and refugees are not stateless, many suffer from an existential sense of loss, deprivation, and alienation from the countries where they live. Their families had emigrated to Western Europe to seek a better life, but they and their offspring had not been integrated within the recipient society. They are then exposed to extreme ideologies that increasingly radicalize them and can foster entering the path of terrorism.[15]

An estimated 80 percent of new recruits to the global Salafi jihad in Europe are from Muslim diasporas; some estimates reach as high as 87 percent of the new recruits coming from the diaspora.[16]

For example, Mohammad Atta, the ring leader of the 9/11 attacks, and two of his co-conspirators were graduate students in the Technological Institute in Hamburg, Germany. While in this host country, they joined a mosque within the local Muslim community, and were soon attracted to an extremist faction. The Madrid train station bombing of March 11, 2004, was conducted by Muslim émigrés and members of the Muslim diaspora originally from countries in North Africa. The London transport bombings of July 7, 2005, were carried out by Muslim youth with Pakistani family roots, living in a Muslim diasporic community in Leeds, England.

These events raise alarms about so-called "homegrown terrorists," young, second and even third generation residents acting out of their alienation, possibly inspired by the global Salafi jihad, but carrying out these attacks independently of it. Recent events, however, show that "homegrown" may be too simple a characterization. In August 2006, the major terrorist plot to hijack and blow up ten U.S.-bound airliners out of London's Heathrow Airport, was led by British individuals of Pakistani descent who had traveled back to Pakistan, where apparently they had had contact with Al Qaeda members, for training in explosives. Note this attack resembles the pre-9/11 Al Qaeda operations that featured a major role for the central leadership.

The influence and involvement of Al Qaeda (which in a sense is also a transnational diasporic group), suggests that it inspired and facilitated such acts of the disaffected among Muslim British citizens. According to a recent *New York Times* article, Dame Eliza Manningham-Buller, Director-General of MI5, the British security service, stated that the service was "watching 1,600 people who are actively engaged in plotting, or facilitating, terrorist acts here and overseas." She said they had identified nearly 30 plots that "often have links back to [A]l Qaeda in Pakistan and through those links [A]l Qaeda gives guidance and training to its largely British foot soldiers here." She also said that other countries – Spain, France, Canada, and Germany – faced similar threats.[17]

The following item demonstrates Al Qaeda's influence. It was found in the organization's manual published online on its website, four months before the Madrid train station bombing:

> In order to force the Spanish government to withdraw from Iraq, the resistance should deal painful blows to its forces... It is necessary to make the utmost use of the upcoming general election in March next year. We think that the Spanish government could not tolerate more than two, maximum three blows, after which it will have to withdraw as a result of popular pressure. If its troops remain in Iraq after these blows, the victory of the Socialist Party is almost secured, and the withdrawal of the Spanish forces will be on its electoral program.

While the October and November 2006 riots in Marseilles and Paris were not acts of terrorism, they certainly expressed the frustration and alienation of the Muslim émigrés and members of the Muslim diaspora who had not found acceptance in French society, who instead seemed to be confronting a choice between being French and being Muslim. The murder of filmmaker Theo von Gogh in Amsterdam by a Muslim extremist Dutch Moroccan, angered by his film story of the plight of four Muslim women, is another example of this wrath.[18]

In the consensus document of the Committee on the Psychological Roots of Terrorism of the Madrid Summit on Terrorism, Security and Democracy (March 2005) that I chaired, several of the summary statements reflected the role of diasporas and the need to adopt policies to deal with this growing problem:

> Although most Muslim immigrants and refugees are not 'stateless,' many suffer from an existential sense of loss, deprivation and alienation from the countries where they live. They are often exposed to extreme ideologies that increasingly radicalize them and can foster entering the path of terrorism. The diaspora has been identified as particularly important for the global Salafi Jihad, with a large percentage (80 percent) of recruits joining and becoming radicalized in the diaspora.[19]

And the following recommendation was offered:

> Western governments should directly support the development and implementation of community based

interventions aimed at promoting community and individual level changes that would support greater incorporation and integration of refugees and diaspora youth into the political culture of Western liberal democracies. The growing population of alienated Muslim youth in European societies represents a growing internal threat.

The consensus was that while it is important to integrate and incorporate members of the Muslim diaspora into the host society, at the same it was imperative that their cultural and social integrity be accepted. They should not be forced to choose between their new and original cultures, as were the French Muslim girls prohibited by a new law from wearing their traditional headscarves, or Hijabs, while in school. France, which experts on the European Muslim diaspora regard as having the largest and least integrated Muslim community in Europe,[20] experienced the fall 2006 rioting by poor, mostly well-educated but unemployed young men, alienated Islamic youth who were protesting their estrangement from the mainstream French society. To be sure, they were avowedly secular, protesting the economic inequities, but it is just such frustrated youth that were vulnerable secondarily to radicalization and, ultimately, recruitment in the radical mosques in Great Britain and Germany. That their vandalism has also been expressed as hate crimes against Jewish synagogues and Jewish centers in the suburbs of Paris suggests this group frustration could easily become a politically radical force.

Grounded in the everyday experience of secular Muslim émigrés to Western Europe, European social conditions promoted feelings of alienation among young Muslims who felt excluded from the relatively closed European social structure. Not particularly religious, they drifted back to the mosque to find companionship, acceptance, and a sense of meaning and significance. This in turn made them vulnerable to extremist religious leaders and their radicalization within Muslim institutions. Based on his study of jihadi networks, Marc Sageman sees one possible path in the movement as moving toward a global leaderless jihad.[21]

The challenge for bin Laden, Zawahiri, and the founding generation of Al Qaeda will be to continue to provide both inspiration and direction to the jihad under their overall influence. And, given the semi-autonomous functioning of the radical cells within the diasporic communities, this poses a profound challenge to international counterterrorism.

This challenge is further magnified by the increasing role of the Internet in the socialization of youth. There are now some 4,800 radical Islamist websites, according to Gabi Weimann's comprehensive *Terror on the Internet*.[22] And both within and between these diasporic communities this imparts a feeling of belonging that transcends the often isolated individuals. It is interesting to observe, and not without irony, that the Salafi groups so vigorously opposed to modern values rely on the most modern of technologies to spread their extremist messages. The following depicts Al Qaeda's Internet strategy.

> Due to the advances of modern technology, it is easy to spread news, information, articles and other information over the Internet. We strongly urge Muslim Internet professionals to spread and disseminate news and information about the Jihad through e-mail lists, discussion groups, and their own websites. If you fail to do this, and our site closes down before you have done this, you may hold you to account before Allah on the Day of Judgment... This way, even if our sites are closed down, the material will live on with the Grace of Allah.
>
> –from one of Al Qaeda's websites

Thus we have radical Islamist virtual communities of hatred and extremism being formed through messages propagated on the Internet. This is a challenge of Olympian stature that the West has barely begun to grapple with.

Notes

1. This chapter draws particularly on Jerrold Post, *The Mind of the Terrorist: The Psychology of Terrorism from the IRA to al-Qaeda*, (New York: Palgrave Macmillan, 2007) Chapter 15, concerned with Al Qaeda in the post 9/11 era and J. Post, and G. Sheffer, "The Risk of Radicalization and Terrorism in American Muslim Communities," *Brown Journal of World Affairs*, (2007, in press).

2. Professor of Psychiatry, Political Psychology and International Affairs, and Director, Political Psychology Program, The George Washington University, Washington, D.C. Dr. Post is also the Chief Behavioral Scientist of the USAF Counterproliferation Center in a consulting role.

3. Jerrold Post, (editor) *Military Studies in the Jihad Against the Tyrants: The Al-Qaeda Training Manual*, (Montgomery, AL: U.S. Air Force Counter Proliferation Center, 2005).

4. David Johnston and David Sanger, "New Generation of Leaders Is Emerging for Al-Qaeda," *New York Times*, 10 August 2004.

5. "Bin Laden Tape Praises Bali Attack," *The Guardian*, 13 November 2002, On-line, Internet, available from http://www.guardian.co.uk/alqaida/story/0,,838943,00.html.

6. "Jihadi Iraq: Hopes and Dangers," Al Qaeda On-line manual, December 2003.

7. "Rival Groups Claim Turkey Blast," *cnn.com*, 10 August 2004, On-line, Internet, available from http://www.cnn.com/2004/WORLD/europe/08/10/turkey.blasts.twoclaims/index.html.

8. Michele Catalano, "October Turkey," *The Command Post*, 3 October 2004, On-line, Internet, available from http://www.commandpost.org/oped/2_archives/015711.html.

9. "Zarqawi's Pledge of Allegiance to al-Qaeda: From Mu'asker al-Battar, Issue 21," *The Jamestown Foundation*, 16 December 2004.

10. "Letter from Zarqawi to bin Laden," January 2004, On-line, Internet, available from www.cpa-iraq.org/transcripts/20040212_zarqawi_full.html.

11. "Letter from al-Zawahiri to al-Zarqawi," *GlobalSecurity.org*, 9 July 2005, On-line, Internet, available from http://www.globalsecurity.org/security/library/report/2005/zawahiri-zarqawi-letter_9jul2005.htm.

12. "Al-Qaeda in Iraq: Letter to al-Zarqawi Fake," *cnn.com*, 13 October 2005, On-line, Internet, available from http://edition.cnn.com/2005/WORLD/meast/10/13/alqaeda.letter/index.html.

13. "Bin Laden Seizes Opportunities in his June and July Speeches," *The Jamestown Foundation*, 5 July 2006, On-line, Internet, available from http://www.jamestown.org/news_details.php?news_id=186.

14. This section draws extensively from a summary review of the reconstituted Al Qaeda leadership by Craig Whitlock, "The New al-Qaeda Central," *The Washington Post*, 9 September 2007, A1, A21.

15. Muslim Population Worldwide. Retrieved 16 January 2006 from: On-line, Internet, available from http://www.islamicpopulation.com/index.html; J. Cesari and S. McLoughlin, *European Muslims and the secular state*, (Burlington, VT: Ashgate Publishing, 2005); J. Klausen, *The Islamic challenge: Politics and Religion in Western Europe*, (New York: Oxford University Press, Inc., 2005); L. Vidivo, The Muslim Brotherhood Conquest of Europe, (electronic version), *The Middle East Quarterly, 12(1)*, 1-11, 2005; The PEW Forum on Religion and Public Life, *An Uncertain Road: Muslims and the future of Europe*, (Washington, D.C., October 2005); T. Ramadan, *Western Muslims and the Future of Islam*, (New York: Oxford University Press, Inc., 2001); R. Yadlin, The Moslem Diaspora in the west, In M. Ma'oz & G. Sheffer (Eds.), *Middle Eastern Minorities and Diasporas*, (Brighton: Sussex Academic Press, 2002); P. Werbner, *Imagined Diaspora Among Manchester Muslims: the Public Performance of Pakistani Transnational Identity Politics*, (Oxford: James Cueery, 2002); B. Lewis, *The Muslim Discover of Europe*, (New York: Norton and Company, 2001).

16. J. Post, "The psychological and behavioral bases of terrorism: individual, group and collective contributions," *Addressing the Causes of Terrorism, The Club de Madrid Series on Democracy and Terrorism*, Club de Madrid, 2005, (1) 7-12.

17. Elaine Scioline and Stephen Grey, "British Terror Trial Traces a Path to Militant Islam," *NY Times: Europe*, 25 November 2006, On-line, Internet, 12 January 2007 available from http://www.nytimes.com/2006/11/26/world/europe/26crevice.html?ex=1322197200&en=7340a3579b048d42&ei=5088&partner=rssnyt&emc=rss.

18. Norwegian Defense Research Establishment (FFI), *FFI explains al-Qaeda document*, 19 March 2004, On-line, Internet, 16 January 2007, available from http://www.mil.no/felles/ffi/start/article.jhtml?articleID=71589.

19. Jerrold Post, "The Psychological and Behavioral Bases of Terrorism," 2005.

20. Roughly 10 percent of the persons now living in France are Muslims.

21. Marc Sageman, *Understanding Terror Networks*, (Philadelphia: University of Pennsylvania Press, 2004).

22. Gabi Weimann, *Terror on the Internet*, (Washington, D.C.: United States Institute of Peace Press, 2005).

CHAPTER 11

Jemaah Islamiyah Remains Active and Deadly

James C. "Chris" Whitmire

Introduction

Southeast Asia's largest and most deadly militant Islamic terrorist network, Jemaah Islamiyah (JI), is at a crossroads in its existence amid ongoing counterterrorism pressure, but continues to pose a serious threat to Western and regional interests.[1] On-going counterterrorism measures in the past five years have certainly forced JI to adapt, but it remains active and deadly. JI operates primarily out of Indonesia, a country of critical economic and strategic importance and the world's most populated Muslim country with over 194 million followers of Islam.[2] JI is the vanguard of radical Islam in Southeast Asia and preys upon the region's many impoverished and underemployed young people who already have a 66 percent unfavorable opinion of the United States government and are easy targets for jihadist recruiters.[3,4] Additionally, JI exploits the region's vast geography that stretches over 3,200 miles and includes more than 13,000 islands, many of which are ungoverned and ideal as terrorist safe havens.[5]

Jemaah Islamiyah, translated to mean "Islamic Community," disdains Western influence and secular rule.[6] Its members advocate violence and have the capability, sophistication, and will to inflict lethal attacks to further their cause.[7] Ideologically, JI is founded on Wahhabi and Salafi teachings and is a staunch supporter of Islamic rule and universal jihad.[8] Its philosophy holds that "non-Muslims, Muslim apostates, and other anti-Islamic forces that seek to destroy Islam" must be countered with physical force.[9] Its anti-Western rhetoric closely parallels that of other radical Islamic terrorist groups including Al Qaeda.[10] Its ultimate objective is to create an Islamic theocratic state, a caliphate, across Indonesia, Malaysia,

Singapore, Brunei, Cambodia, the southern Philippines, and southern Thailand.[11]

The United States recognizes Southeast Asia as "an attractive theater of support and logistics" for terrorist activity.[12] Extremists continually exploit religious sympathies and discontent as they seek to win support from the impressionable citizens of the area. JI celebrity orators stoke the fires of discontent among frustrated and minimally educated locals by declaring elections and democracy useless, and condemning the West as imperialistic and conspiring against the Muslim world.[13] With the vast number of Muslims to prey upon, JI is definitely a terrorist group that requires close watching.[14]

Admiral Thomas B. Fargo, former Commander U.S. Pacific Command, identified Southeast Asia as a "crucial front in the war on terror."[15] He went on to say, "Destabilization of the governments of that region, moderate, secular, legitimately elected, with large Muslim populations, would sentence the region to decades of danger and chaos."[16] He emphatically proclaimed, "We have to stop the violence."[17] This is especially true given the Western diplomatic and economic interests in the region vulnerable to JI operations.[18]

JI has a dedicated following and furthers its cause by cooperating with other like-minded Islamist groups. It has forged alliances regionally with multiple Islamist separatist forces and this facilitates training, attacks, and safe-harboring of members fleeing capture.[19] Globally, JI cooperates with Al Qaeda in multiple capacities including funding, training, and attack planning.[20] In effect, JI is a "diffuse web of like-minded individuals from different militant, terrorist, or radical groups" focused regionally, but an avid supporter of the international jihadist movement.[21]

The organization is dynamic, adaptable, and its leaders appear to learn from their mistakes. JI has operatives throughout Southeast Asia with cells extending as far as Cambodia, Vietnam, and Australia.[22] Its members are responsible for numerous bombings of soft targets throughout the region over the last decade. Many of these attacks have targeted innocent civilians including tourists and those associated with "Western interests."[23] The most devastating was the triple-suicide Bali attack of October 12, 2002, where 202 people perished and another 330 were wounded including many Westerners in a crowded tourist hotspot.[24] Other significant JI events follow in Figure 11.1.

Figure 11.1 Jemaah Islamiyah's Track Record of Violence[25]

Date	Event	Casualties	Comments
Jun. 2007	Abu Dujana, JI's Syurah (military wing) leader, and Zarkasih, JI's acting amir, captured by Indonesian counterterrorism police unit, Densus-88.	None known	Lost two of a dwindling pool of first-generation JI leaders with Al Qaeda training and Afghanistan fighting experience. These two bridged the factional divides within JI. Abu Dujana participated in the planning of Bali 2002 and Zarkasih master-minded violence in Poso. JI will certainly struggle to replace the skills of these two key leaders.[26]
Mar. 20, 2007	Plots by Abu Dujana-led cells to bomb Satya Wacana Christian University and assassinate the head of the province's attorney-general's office showed JI's continuing resolve to inflict terror and further its cause.[27]	Thwarted	Indonesian counterterrorism units working with Australia's Federal Police arrested seven JI members and killed another during a raid. 1,600 pounds of explosives, 100 pounds of TNT, approximately 200 detonators, and a large cache of weapons and ammunition were seized.[28]
Apr. 28, 2006	Noordin Mohamed Top's bomber faction lost two key operatives.	Two killed and two other operatives arrested	This operation was the result of an Indonesian police stakeout in Wonosobo, Central Java.[29]
Oct. 29, 2005	Several acts of domestic and ethnic violence in Poso.	3 Christian schoolgirls beheaded	These were attempts by JI to undermine governmental authority including assassination attempts.[30]
Oct. 1, 2005	Bali suicide bombings	23 killed including the bombers[31]	This attack was led by Noordin Mohamed Top, the faction leader of JI's bomber group which is considered by many to be a JI splinter group. Top claimed responsibility in the name of Al Qaeda and not JI. It demonstrated continued capability and resilience by the bomber faction to launch coordinated attacks on soft targets despite on-going counter terrorism efforts in the region. While lethal and in-step with previous attacks, logistics and funding for this event were lacking as compared to past operations.[32]

Sep. 9, 2004	Suicide car bombing outside the Australian Embassy in Jakarta.	10 killed and more than 100 wounded[33]	Al Qaeda provided the suicide bomber.
Aug. 5, 2003	J.W. Marriott hotel car bombing in Jakarta.	12 killed and 150 injured	Hambali was arrested August 2003.[34]
Oct. 12, 2002	Bali nightclub triple-suicide bombing targeting Western tourists.	202 killed including 88 Australians; 330 injured	Hambali is believed to have served as an Al Qaeda financial link;[35] Amrozi bin Nurhasyim was convicted; first of 33 convicted for the bombing.
Late 2001 – 2002[36]	Plot to attack U.S. and Israeli Embassies and British and Australian diplomatic buildings in Singapore.	Thwarted	Al Qaeda – JI key link, Omar al-Farouq was involved and captured during the planning phase.[37]
Dec. 31, 2000	Five near-simultaneous bombings in Manila.	22 killed and over 100 injured	Hambali was the planner; Fathur Rahman al-Ghozi had a key role. He was later convicted and killed in a police shootout.
Dec. 25, 2000	Wave of 11 anti-Christian church bombings in Indonesia. Several additional attempts failed to detonate.	20+ killed[38]	Hambali was involved and Bashir was questioned by authorities, but not convicted.
1995	Plot to explode 12 U.S. commercial airliners over the Pacific—code name BOJINKA.	Thwarted	Hambali was a key planner for Ramzi Yousef (1993 World Trade Center operational leader) and Khalid Sheik Mohammed (Al Qaeda 9/11 master-mind).[39]

These previous attacks reflect JI's regional focus as it pursues its objective to establish an Islamic Caliphate in the Southeast Asian region. All of these attacks were aimed at undermining its "near enemy," the governments in the region, which are often viewed as oppressive.[40] Such endeavors also lash out at the jihadist "far-enemy," the West, by hitting globalization and cultural phenomena that are perceived as corrupt to Islamic ideals.[41] Economic and tourism assaults serve this purpose well by destabilizing delicate trade and political balances. Also, exploiting ethnic rifts between Muslims and Christians further compromises governmental authority.[42] This is currently happening in the Indonesian Poso region with Christians being antagonized with attacks.[43]

In such a large group with grand, expansive goals, there is considerable diversity in preferred strategies, tactics, and methodologies.

Within JI three factions exist which often disagree on target selection and means.[44] These factions include: the political, the radical (also known as the proselytizers), and the terrorist (known as the bombers).[45] The most notable of these is the bomber faction and its methods are often criticized or disavowed by the other two. Experts refer to this as "the schism" with many now citing the bomber faction as a splinter group. Whether or not the bomber group is independent of JI or simply operates with little regard for oversight is still subject to debate. Regardless, given JI's intense indoctrination process and member loyalty, the bomber faction is certainly part of the JI network and poses the most significant near term terrorist threat to Western interests.[46]

The bomber faction is comprised of a few dozen hard-line JI members who prefer clandestine operations.[47] From 2002 to 2005 key bomber faction leaders of JI conducted a flurry of hostile activities and the deadly impact of several of these attacks on fellow Muslims came into question.[48] The bomber faction included key JI members, most notably Nurjaman Riduan bin Isomuddin (a.k.a. Hambali), who attended the Ngruki (al-Mukmin) Pesantren for their JI indoctrination and boasted Afghan training where they developed strong Al Qaeda tics.[49] This faction sought to inflict maximum damage to Western and governmental targets.[50]

During this time Indonesia finally acknowledged the significance of the JI threat and began amplified counterterrorism efforts.[51] The Indonesians, in conjunction with crackdowns already in progress in Malaysia, Singapore, and the Philippines, and all aided by the United States and Australia, inflicted numerous setbacks on JI. Several leaders were killed and over 200 members arrested.[52] These losses prompted opposition within JI and key leaders reasoned that JI attacks and government counter-attacks were killing Muslim bystanders as well as those targeted, and, hence, were harming JI's popularity. Furthermore, hard-line operations that sparked heightened counterterrorism measures during this period became viewed by some JI leaders as costing them more than was gained and increasing risks of capture or death.[53] With these arguments, the political faction and the proselytizers gained influence within JI.

In contrast to the bomber faction, the political faction favors pursuing JI's objectives via overt political struggle and is generally less openly violent. This faction values cultivating contacts within their country's government with those who might sympathize with JI's cause.[54] Despite a crackdown by Indonesian police on JI, many politicians sympathize with Islamist movements and the court system often hands down lenient sentences to offenders.[55] This faction also endorses membership in the Mejelis Mujahidin Indonesia (MMI), an umbrella group of Islamists campaigning politically for the enforcement of the Shariah.[56]

Today, the proselytizer faction is the JI mainstream but includes significant elements of the other two.[57] Despite factional differences during the past few years, the organization's loose hierarchical structure downplays internal rifts and enables the group to remain strong.[58] It continues to recruit loyal followers and maintains a solid core of approximately 900 members who share a deep-rooted allegiance to the establishment of Islamic rule.[59] While the group has lost many of its battle-tested members to prison and death, others wait in the ranks to fill voids where needed. Furthermore, as members complete their often short jail sentences and return to the group, their loyalty and resolve are often strengthened.[60]

Currently, JI appears to be going through a "building and consolidation phase" as it reconstitutes and increases its capacity to take on those they perceive as the enemies of Islam.[61] Most likely, as the organization morphs in the presence of today's stricter counterterrorism environment, it will focus more on its near enemies, the national governments.[62] Despite the successes of recent counterterrorism efforts, JI's losses must not be exaggerated.[63] Elements of JI remain deadly and it poses a continuing threat to regional governments and Western interests in Southeast Asia.[64]

Origin and Historical Background

To better understand how JI's presence and power in the region developed, a brief look at its origin and history follows. Muslim influence in Southeast Asia dates back to the seventh century with the arrival of Arab merchants.[65] Since Islam came via trade instead of military conquest, its practice tended to be more moderate than that observed in the Middle East.[66] Islam was overlaid on a people who traditionally embraced animist, Hindu, or Buddhist religions, all of which were tolerant in nature.[67] Islam spread throughout most of Southeast Asia during the centuries that followed.

In the mid-1500s the Spanish and Dutch arrived and brought Catholicism which sparked conflicts between Christians and Muslims.[68] After Europeans colonized the area, Christians were placed in positions of authority over Muslims and grievances ensued. Following World War II, ethnic and religious tensions culminated in Islamic rebellions led by the Darul Islam movement.[69] Darul Islam was radical and advocated the establishment of Islamic law in Indonesia as the country emerged from colonial rule.[70] From 1948 until 1962, Darul Islam fought the Republic of Indonesia and its leader, Haji Mohammad Suharto.[71] The Suharto regime eventually defeated the rebellion in 1962, but not before it fostered a significant number of new generation Islamic radicals who continue to resist the secular government to the present day.[72]

The earliest roots of JI sprang from Darul Islam. During the 1970s, like-minded radicals gathered under the leadership of two Muslim clerics, Abdullah Sungkar and Abu Bakar Bashir. Although not members, these clerics were advocates of Darul Islam with the goal of creating an Islamic state.[73] During the 1970s and 1980s, Jemaah Islamiyah was "more an aspiration or state of mind rather than a *de facto* organization."[74]

In 1982 Sungkar and Bashir were arrested for subversion and sentenced to nine years in prison.[75] Following an early release, they fled to Malaysia and continued to promote the JI movement.[76] While in Malaysia, Sungkar was identified as the number one enemy of Indonesian President Suharto as he and Bashir continued to incubate the JI network.[77]

Gradually, through the late-1980s, Muslim scholars identifying with Jihadist-Salafi Islamic doctrine, and directly and indirectly supported by the Saudi-based Wahhabi sect of Islam, promulgated radicalism to their subjects via Islamic schools known as pesantren.[78] These teachings manipulated the region's history of violence by placing blame on the West and its allies in an effort to motivate sympathy for the movement and to persuade the students to endorse the ideal of universal jihad.[79] These efforts proved effective and resulted in most indigenous terrorist and Muslim separatist groups rejecting Western influence and endorsing the ideology of international Islamic terrorists.[80]

One of Sungkar and Bashir's initiatives involved travel to Saudi Arabia in an effort to secure funding. During this trip they established contacts with some Afghan Mujahidin.[81] This enabled Sungkar and Bashir to connect some of their members with military training and armed jihad in the Soviet-Afghan war. This quickly politicized and radicalized their thinking.[82] Additionally, Sungkar and Bashir gained financial support from Malaysian business men during this time.[83]

The JI members who fought in Afghanistan established links with Al Qaeda and bonded with their "mujahidin brothers" fighting alongside the Taliban. From this experience, these future JI leaders learned sophisticated terrorist tradecraft and connected with others dedicated to a universal jihad.[84] Upon their return to Southeast Asia, inspired by their perceived defeat of the mighty Soviets, these battle-hardened jihadists transferred their skills and connections to other members of their organization.[85] In the early 1990s as JI evolved, the group officially endorsed the use of violence to secure their ends.[86] Subsequently, following a dispute with an Indonesian-based Darul Islam leader, Sungkar and Bashir formally founded the JI organization in 1993, in Johor, Malaysia.[87]

The first JI cell held meetings weekly and consisted of eight to 10 members including Hambali, Abdul Ghani, Jamsari, Suhauime, Matsah, Adnan, and Faiz Bafana.[88] These meetings included Koranic study and jihad preparation.[89] As the organization grew, it eventually formalized its core beliefs and ideology into a book called the *Pedoman Umum Perjuangan Al-Jama'ah Al-Islamiyyah* (PUPJI).[90] Compared to its predecessor, Darul Islam, JI began with a much more defined structure and grew quickly.[91]

In 1998, the Indonesian Suharto dictatorship that had pursued Sungkar and Bashir was ousted. Subsequently, Sungkar died of natural causes in November 1999, leaving Bashir to assume the leading role within JI. No longer an enemy of the state, Bashir moved back to Indonesia.[92] By the late-1990s, heavily influenced by JI members with extensive Al Qaeda connections and Afghan battle experience, JI shifted tactics and began recruiting and training extremists for insurgent and terrorist operations.[93] Hambali, a charter member, is credited for much of this shift. He served as JI's operations chief and was Al Qaeda's Southeast Asian representative. He procured Al Qaeda funding for JI bombing operations and was key to JI's growth and training during this time.[94] Approximately 1,000 hand-picked JI members traveled to Afghan terrorist camps for specialized training while JI intensified its indigenous training capabilities at home.[95]

During this same time, philosophical divisions within JI began to emerge. Younger, more radical members including Hambali, Abdul Aziz (a.k.a. Imam Samudra), and Ali Gufron (a.k.a. Mukhlas) all felt Bashir was too weak and not aggressive enough. This group eventually became known as the bomber faction and caught the attention of the world press with its terrorist bombing offensive that extended through 2005. Today, it is seen as a factional group of JI and is led by Noordin Mohamed Top.[96] Bashir further amplified these differences when he formed the public face of JI, a politically oriented group, the Mejelis Mujahidin Indonesia (MMI, Indonesian Mujahidin Council), in August 2000.[97]

Bashir, who today is most closely identified with the political faction of JI, founded the MMI in an effort to take advantage of the new, post-Suharto Indonesian political climate that better tolerated Islamic organizations. He saw the MMI as a grassroots Islamic political umbrella organization that would pull together spurious Islamic groups into an ad-hoc coalition and thereby further JI's cause.[98] While it was not radical in appearance, the MMI exceeded 50,000 members and provided cover for more extreme-minded groups and individuals to meet and exchange ideas.[99] Al Qaeda used the MMI to network with radical elements in Southeast Asia. Since the October 12, 2002, Bali bombings, the MMI has "apparently" attempted to distance itself from extremists.[100] Whether or not this attempt is genuine or not, the MMI promoted JI's cause tremendously with the connections it facilitated and will probably continue to do so either intentionally or unintentionally.

After the 2002 Bali bombings, governments in the region intensified their pursuit of JI operatives. The strong central governments of Singapore and Malaysia outlawed the group and made numerous arrests. The Philippine government also pursued JI but with less success. These three countries cooperated in the quest to eliminate JI by sharing intelligence, assisting each other and Western allies with stings, joint investigations, and extradition of suspects. Indonesia, in contrast, basically denied the problem until the 2002 Bali bombings when it also toughened its stance on JI and passed new antiterrorism legislation and ordered arrests.[101] For political reasons the United States waited on Indonesia to acknowledge the danger JI posed before designating it as a

"Foreign Terrorist Organization" in October 2002 and declaring its suspicion that the group had ties with Al Qaeda.[102]

Despite Indonesia's policy shift following its Bali experience, it continued to maintain a relatively soft outlook on terrorism. In July 2004 its constitutional court ruled its antiterrorism laws could not be applied retroactively and most of those arrested in connection with the Bali and Marriott bombings had to be released.[103] Furthermore, Indonesian authorities were very reluctant to prosecute Bashir and when he was finally convicted for "being part of an evil conspiracy," he only received a 30 month sentence which he did not fully serve. He was released on June 14, 2006, to the outrage of much of the Western world.[104] Adding insult to injury, as soon as Bashir was released, he began touring Indonesia preaching to moderate Muslims, the majority, trying to radicalize them. Bashir's current message is anti-Western, anti-Jewish, and undermines the locally elected democratic government of Indonesia. He claims his arrest was due to U.S. pressure on the Indonesian government. He has been met with overwhelming fanfare as he attempts to energize religious zeal, idealism, and a sense of obligation to stand up for Islam.[105] In summary, Indonesia's lack of resolve to fully stamp out JI is reflected in the surge of radical Islam in a part of the world that has traditionally been moderate.[106]

Overall, the results of these counterterrorism efforts by Southeast Asian countries are having positive effects despite the weak reactions of the Indonesians. Authorities have arrested hundreds of suspected JI members across the region.[107] This includes several key operatives who have been arrested, extradited, or killed. The October 1, 2005, Bali bombing was considerably smaller in scale and less sophisticated than prior JI operations. Furthermore, the most recent attacks have been fewer and many have been thwarted by authorities. This likely reflects a combination of diminished financial means, less experienced planning expertise, counterterrorism advances, and most importantly, a change in JI's strategy[108] – a plan to expand its mass support base and selectively hold its resources in reserve for future attacks.[109]

Regardless of JI's apparent decline and philosophical changes within the group, it remains resilient and appears likely to continue to pursue its ideological cause. Thwarted plots to bomb Satya Wacana Christian University and assassinate the head of the province's attorney-general's office in March 2007 show the continuing resolve of some JI elements to inflict terror.[110] Furthermore, the seizure of 1,600 pounds of explosives, 100 pounds of TNT, approximately 200 detonators, and a large cache of weapons and ammunition during this event illustrates its lethal capability.[111] Key JI leadership, logistical, and technical expertise remain at large. The anti-Islamic conspiracy blamed on the United States, the United Kingdom, and Australia and engrained into the minds of millions of Muslims in Southeast Asia by the JI pesantren is not soon forgotten. JI remains a force to be reckoned with, and the counterterrorism pressure must continue in earnest.

Affiliations and Doctrine

The danger that JI poses as it endeavors to create an Islamic state in Southeast Asia is closely reflected in its doctrine. Abdullah Sungkar, the lead ideological force behind the organization until his death in November 1999, equated the plight of Muslims in Indonesia to that of those in Mecca under the Prophet Mohammad.[112] Sungkar was a radical committed to Islamic law and disdained non-Islamic political systems. He absolutely abhorred Christian missionary efforts in the region, and felt that JI's efforts needed to be covert to survive government opposition. He emphasized three tenets of strength for the organization: military strength, spiritual strength, and the strength of brotherhood. Keys to developing these tenets were recruitment, education, obedience, jihad, and worldwide Islamic community support.[113]

Until his death, Sungkar reportedly promoted these tenets and maintained high-level ties with Al Qaeda. In 1998, Sungkar allegedly accepted Osama bin Laden's offer to formally ally the two groups and subsequently he sent Nurjaman Riduan bin Isomuddin, a.k.a. Hambali, to Afghanistan to meet with Al Qaeda leaders, Khalid Sheikh Mohammed and Mohammed Atef, two of the 9/11 planners. This exchange led to an arrangement where JI would provide supplies and scout potential targets for Al Qaeda, which, in turn, would reciprocate with funding, expertise, and suicide bombers. Additionally, Al Qaeda would provide terrorist training to JI operatives in Afghanistan.[114]

Experts disagree on the extent of JI's links with Al Qaeda. Some equate JI's role as being Al Qaeda's Southeast Asian wing. Others argue that the two groups' objectives were not congruent since JI's were regional and Al Qaeda's were global.[115] Since 2003, no clear Al Qaeda-JI contacts can be confirmed with the JI mainstream.[116]

A letter dated July 9, 2005, from Ayman Al-Zawahiri, Al Qaeda's top deputy, to Abu Musab al-Zarqawi, Iraqi insurgent leader and commander of Al Qaeda in Iraq at the time (now deceased), further confirmed diminished ties with JI and shed light on the relationship. The letter emphasized a shift from a global focus in Al Qaeda's agenda to a narrower concentration of effort in the heart of the Islamic world, specifically Iraq. While the letter still recognized the importance of a global agenda, it did so with much less emphasis.[117] Based on the timing of the letter and the impact of U.S. led counterterrorism efforts worldwide, this refocus inevitably stemmed from Al Qaeda's weakened state and the fact that it felt compelled to concentrate its efforts on the most critical and central conflict, Iraq. While this letter did not minimize JI's importance, it did relegate it to the periphery and illustrated a deterioration in the tactical and strategic linkages between JI and Al Qaeda evident as early as 2003.[118]

JI's factional shift from its "bombing mentality" to its current mainstream (radical proselytizing) mindset during this timeframe was likely hastened by less interaction with Al Qaeda and the need to deal with increased international counterterrorism initiatives. Despite this shift, Al Qaeda and JI's loose partnership continues as JI's members draw inspiration from Al Qaeda and its leaders such as Osama bin Laden.[119] Furthermore, within the constraints mentioned in the Al-Zawahiri letter, JI and its affiliates can call upon the broad scope of capabilities that Al Qaeda's multifaceted network has to offer. As a case-in-point, the suicide bomber who drove the vehicle in the 2004 Australian embassy bombing was recruited from Al Qaeda.[120] Al Qaeda, on the other hand, gains access to JI's training camps and refuges and claims "credit" for additional terrorist events in SE Asia.

In addition to Al Qaeda, JI has other significant terrorist affiliations in Southeast Asia. Note details of these in Figure 11.2.

Figure 11.2 JI Affiliate Organizations

Abu Sayyaf Group (ASG)	Originally known as the Mujahideen Commando Freedom Fighters (MCFF) and also as Al Harakat-ul Al Islamiyya (AHAI), ASG is a militant Islamist separatist organization that fights for the establishment of an independent Islamic republic in Mindanao, the surrounding islands, and in the Sulu Archipelago of the southern Philippines.[121] Since 2005, ASG and JI have increased cooperative exchanges. These include JI operatives training in ASG camps and JI providing strategic and technical assistance including bomb-making instruction.[122] Current JI leaders, Dulmatin and Umar Patek, work closely with ASG.[123]
Arakan Rohingya (ARNO)	Burmese jihad group fighting for the independence of the Arakan region from Myanmar and self-exiled to Bangladesh.[124]
Askari Islamiyah	An alleged armed wing of JI led by Zulkarnaen that operates throughout the region.[125]
Group 272 (G272)	An informal network of Indonesian Soviet-Afghan War survivors, many of these are members of various radical groups within Indonesia.[126]
Guragan Mujahidin Islam Pattani (GMIP)	This is a small Muslim extremist group from the Pattani province of Thailand.[127]
Kumpulan Militan Malaysia (KMM)	Also known as the Malaysian Mujahidin Group, this is a satellite group of JI in Malaysia, followers of the teachings of Bashir and once led by Abu Jibril. They have been involved in multiple terrorist plots including the Jakarta Atrium bombing on August 1, 2001, and provided funding for the 2002 Bali bombing.[128] KMM has linkages with ASG and MILF. Today, KMM is led by Zulkifli bin Hir, a U.S.-trained engineer with a five million dollar bounty on his head by the U.S. Government.[129]
Laskar Mujahidin	This armed militant group is characterized by competent training and a focus on Indonesian domestic issues. It keys on Muslim/Christian issues in Ambon and Maluku and endorses a pan-Islamic ideology.[130]
Mejelis Mujahidin Indonesia (MMI)	It was founded by Bashir in August 2000 to build consensus among Islamic groups seeking the creation of an Islamic state in Indonesia. It is not a terrorist group and denies using violence to maintain favor among sympathetic Indonesian politicians. In practice, it serves as an umbrella group for many organizations, some of which use it to extend their network of terrorist contacts.[131]

Moro Islamic Liberation Front (MILF)	This is a breakaway faction from the Moro National Liberation Front and has waged a long-running separatist struggle with the Philippine government in the southern part of the country. It has 12,000 to 15,000 combatants and links with JI and Al Qaeda. Its leadership core of 500 to 700 key individuals shared Soviet-Afghan War experience with JI members. It operates numerous training bases in Mindanao frequented by JI and Al Qaeda members. It cooperated extensively with JI in the metro Manila bombings.[132] Additionally, JI and MILF Special Operations Group operatives have conducted joint urban attacks in the Philippines including bombing the Davao International Airport on March 4, 2003, and the Sasa Ferry Wharf on April 2, 2003.[133] Recently, senior MILF leadership has distanced the group from overt association with JI as it conducts peace talks with the Philippine government. Regardless of these talks, ongoing contact between members of the two groups occurs in Mindanao and between some individual MILF commanders.[134]
Rabitat ul-Mujahideen (RM)	Also known as the International Mujahideen Association, it was founded by its former spiritual leader Bashir and Hambali to coordinate militant Islamic movements throughout the region.[135] This association included JI, the MILF, Laskar Jundallah, the Republik Islam Aceh, the Thai Pattani United Liberation Organization (PULO), and the Arakanese (Myanmar) Rohingya Nationalist Organization (ARNO) together with other regional Islamic radical groups.[136]

JI's expansive network of radical Islamic organizations illustrates its reach and potential destructive capability within the region. Its network of like-minded groups enables synergy with mutually beneficial funding, training, and attack planning.[137] Currently, JI is assisting Muslim uprisings in southern Thailand and has that nation on the verge of crisis.[138] Having examined JI's doctrinal mentality and several of its network affiliates, it is now important to explore the tactics, weaponry, and methodology that JI uses to achieve its goals in the region.

Methodology, Tactics, and Weaponry

JI operates in a target-rich environment ideal for terrorist attack. Western tourists crowd the nightclubs and beaches of the region and several cities serve as critical trading nodes. Approximately 30 percent of the United States trade passes through the Strait of Malacca shared by

Indonesia, Singapore, and Malaysia along with one-quarter of the global gross national product.[139] Traditionally, JI pursues foreign interests such as these along with domestic commercial and religious targets when it executes its violence.[140] Additionally, the geographic and political landscape on which JI operates facilitates its operations. Geographically, the region's vast island network is extremely difficult for the weak central governments to patrol and offers many safe havens for terrorist activity.[141] Politically, JI draws support from the vast Muslim population of Southeast Asia that frequently sees national and international counterterrorism efforts as intrusive and a threat to their culture.[142] Furthermore, it often finds sympathy from Indonesian politicians and judges in the form of soft laws and lenient sentences.[143]

With the rise of JI's mainstream faction, the proselytizers, to prominence, the dominant JI faction remains focused on achieving an Islamic state, but now seemingly over the long-term instead of the short-term. A document found in July 2003, suggested the JI leadership has a 25 to 30 year timeline for the organization to convert more followers as it reconstitutes its strength and increases its capacity.[144] With influence from its moderate members, some in JI no longer endorse conducting attacks on Indonesian soil since such actions squander resources and potentially delay expanding JI's base of followers.[145]

While this shift in methodology from its bombing mentality in the first half of the decade may make it seem like JI is temporarily less of a threat, one should not assume that. JI's ideology is still radical to the core, and like all terrorist or revolutionary organizations, it is morphing to overcome its challenges.[146] Given JI's track record, highlighted previously in Figure 11.1, coupled with its bomber faction's propensity to operate autonomously, prudence dictates that all those concerned should expect the worst.

JI's operations manual, the PUPJI, reinforces the group's violent nature.[147] This document defines JI's indoctrination process and the loyalty expected of its members. It also prescribes rigorous military training for all JI members. The dictates of the PUPJI clearly show JI's potential for unpredictable violence and the need to exercise extreme caution when dealing with JI in all regards.[148] The PUPJI includes sections entitled, "The Progressive Methodology in Establishing the Religion" and "The General Operational Guide in Establishing the

Religion."[149] It also clearly dictates measures of secrecy such as code names and an operational security concept of "need-to-know" to ensure captured operatives cannot compromise larger elements of an operation or the organization.[150] Such militant indoctrination, training and secretive procedures certainly shapes members into a fifth column of dangerous individuals who could quickly default to violence.

In summary, JI's indoctrination, training, and procedural guidance presented in the PUPJI emphasizes the fact that JI remains potentially deadly and a definite threat to regional governments and Western interests in Southeast Asia.[151]

In its terrorist tactics, JI operatives have demonstrated the ability to develop techniques to suit varying circumstances and targets as situations dictate. Explosives are the weapons of choice, but firearms, mortars, anti-tank, and even first generation MANPADS (shoulder launched missiles) are readily available in the region, especially in Cambodia.[152] Given the JI mainstream's recent shift away from frequent violence, one must conclude that mass effect weapons, which are more likely to harm innocents and hurt their drive to become more of a mass movement, are probably low on JI's list of priorities. On the other hand, small arms caches likely remain hidden in Poso and Ambon.[153]

JI's bomb-making expertise is proven and its bombs have been well constructed and based on a combination of fertilizer and accelerants, TNT, and plastic explosives, most of which are readily available.[154] It has seemingly learned discretion from its Bali 2002 experience, so precautions not to harm innocent fellow Muslims are now taken.[155] It is certainly capable of sophisticated, coordinated, simultaneous attacks as exemplified by the complex Christmas bombings of 2000 that targeted multiple Christian places of worship across Indonesia.

While the bomber faction may still favor mass casualty effects reflecting its Al Qaeda influence, the new current mainstream leaders of JI seem content with attempting to undermine its near enemies, the state governments in the region, as well as attempting to exploit Christian and Muslim tensions while aiding Muslim insurgent groups around Southeast Asia.[156] While counterterrorism efforts have led to over 200 arrests of JI members and negated some of its finances, JI retains the capability to generate carnage with improvised explosive devices (IEDs), suicide, vehicle, and standoff bombs. When and if JI leadership decides to strike again, it has a multitude of targets to choose from and the ability to create large numbers of casualties, if desired.[157]

Organizational Structure

JI followed a clear organizational hierarchy defined in the PUPJI from 1996 to 2004.[158] As the organization morphed in response to counterterrorism setbacks and philosophical changes within the organization, a consolidation has occurred.[159] Today, specifics of these changes remain unclear, but consensus among scholars indicates that the original structure (illustrated in Figure 11.3) remains by in large the same.[160]

At the top of JI is the spiritual leader, the amir, who is the chief holder of power.[161] Currently, this vital position is vacant with the June 2007 capture of Zarkasih and Abu Dujana.[162] JI will likely pick a successor to fill the position quickly given its crucial importance to the organization. The past amirs have been revered by the JI following and have overseen a loose command structure comprised of four councils known as majelis that provide decision-making and functional expertise. These include a: (1) consultative council (majelis giyadah), (2) religious council, (3) disciplinary council, and (4) fatwa council.[163] The consultative council, also known as the governing council, controls operational mantiqis (divisions) arranged along geographical boundaries.[164] The consultative council is run by a central command (giyadah markaziyah), also referred to as a syurah, and it consists of a five member advisory panel that exerts authority over the four mantiqi leaders and theoretically controls JI operations.[165]

The four original mantiqis prescribed in the PUPJI and depicted in Figure 11.4 included the following:

- Mantiqi I (M1): Malaysia (except Sarawak and Sabah), Singapore, southern Thailand, and Cambodia;

- Mantiqi II (M2): Indonesia (except Sulawesi and Kalimantan);

- Mantiqi III (M3): Borneo (including Brunei), Sarawak and Sabah, Kalimantan and Sulawesi, southern Philippines; and

- Mantiqi IV (M4): Australia and Irian Jaya (West Papua).[166]

Figure 11.3 JI Basic Organizational Structure[167]

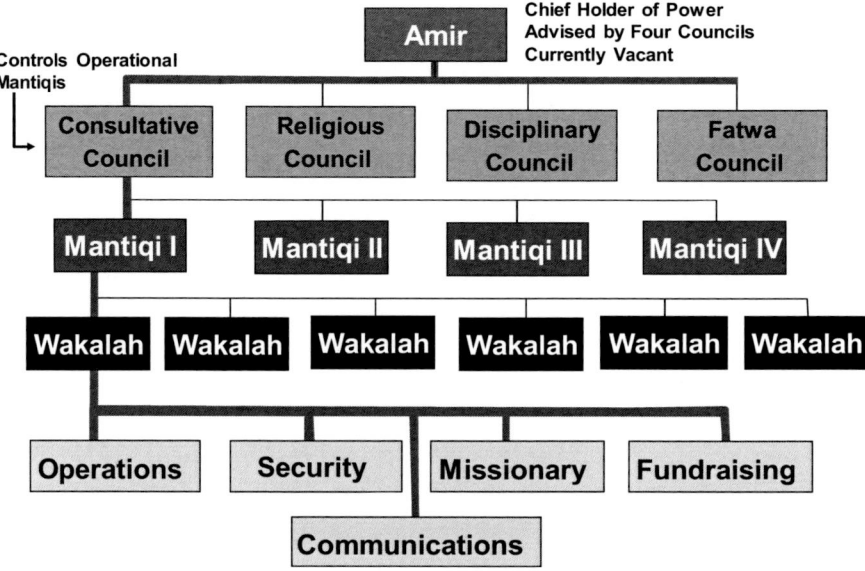

During a March 2007 capture of eight JI operatives by Indonesian counter terrorism officials in Central and East Java, a document obtained suggested that the original four Mantiqis were now consolidated administratively under the direction of Mantiqi II.[168] This does not mean that the other regions no longer have JI presence, but it does reflect the group's intention to consolidate and reconstitute.[169] Kerry B. Collison, a leading expert on JI, says that this reorganization follows the consolidation of Mantiqi III into Mantiqi II sometime after 2004.[170] Furthermore, Mantiqi I declined severely as the countries of Malaysia and Singapore executed coordinated counterterrorism efforts during the first half of the decade.[171] Additionally, Mantiqi IV, also known as "The Other Mantiqi," was always small with estimates of its strength as low as 20 members during its peak.[172] Thus, one large Mantiqi for operations is logical and probably more efficient regarding command and control.

Figure 11.4 Jemaah Islamiyah Areas of Operation[173]

Below the Mantiqi level are operational elements called wakalah (battalions). These represent an intermediate level of authority for JI operatives within a specific location. Wakalahs vary from location to location as necessary based on support and mission. By design approximately 80 members make up a wakalah with 25 +/- considered operatives. Each wakalah has five functional components: operations, security, missionary, fundraising, and communications. Each component is kept isolated from the others for security reasons.[174] Wakalahs are further divided into khatibahs (companies) which in turn are subdivided into qirdas (platoons) and then further divided into fiahs (squadrons or cells).[175] Wakalah operational components are generally comprised of four fiahs of four to five men each.[176] Again, for security reasons, a reconnaissance fiah would be isolated from an attack fiah. These compartmentalization measures prevent arrest or capture from compromising the entire wakalah. Since wakalahs vary, not all conform to the same security and operational techniques, but this is a general idea of JI's organizational set-up.[177]

This structure enables flexibility and decentralized execution of complex plans. It also empowers all levels of command to conceive objectives while the senior echelon oversees approval of such.[178] JI members display a disciplined ability to learn from their mistakes much like Al Qaeda. Its leaders analyze past operations to better adapt tactics and doctrine and prepare for future offensives. Its leadership displays sound understanding of the military tenets of momentum and the desire to seize the initiative. The small fiah units allow JI to plug in specific units of autonomous expertise while simultaneously protecting an operation's overall security. The 2004 Al Qaeda suicide bomber attack on the Australian Embassy provides a good example of this. All in all, JI's organizational set-up is efficient and facilitates its objectives and doctrine.

While the previous discussion seems to reflect exact discipline, command, and control, there are significant exceptions. At one time JI had a special operations unit, called Laskar Khos that conducted military training and other assignments. Its exact supervision was not clear.[179] Another exception involved Hambali, an Afghan mujahidin and Al Qaeda operative, who chaired the central command until just prior to his arrest in August 2003 and was involved in virtually all of the major JI operations.[180] Contrary to the PUPJI's design, Hambali often operated outside of JI's defined chain of command.[181] He pressed for the use of violence and frequently obtained funding directly from Al Qaeda.[182] This cavalier mentality often resulted in unsanctioned bloodshed and was probably much to blame for the schism that forced his bomber faction from power.[183]

Today, as the mainstream proselytizer faction reorganizes and consolidates JI into a stronger organization, it still significantly resembles its original violence-prone design, one that is battle-tested and operationally efficient. Furthermore, as of April 2007, reports from Indonesia's Anti-Terror Chief indicate JI's mainstream now has an assassination squad.[184] Its target list includes police, judges, and diplomats of its near enemy, the Indonesia government.[185]

Financing

Despite trained operatives and effective organizational structure, financial restrictions may limit JI operations. It no longer has a steady source of external funding.[186] Its primary financial means come from member contributions, business fronts, charitable contributions, and robberies.[187] In addition to these, Rohan Gunaratna, Director of the Singaporean Research Center on Terror, says JI receives funds directly on occasion from individuals in Muslim countries such as Saudi Arabia.[188] During the first part of the decade, JI received steady funding from Al Qaeda and multiple private sources in the Middle East.

Today, JI depends on charity or zakat for most of its funding. This is a religious duty expected of all Muslims by the Islamic faith to give at least 2.5 percent of their income to humanitarian causes. This may occur without the grantor knowing how their offering will ultimately be used. Quite often non-governmental organizations (NGO) provide cover for the diversion of these funds to terrorist causes. NGOs such as the International Islamic Relief Organization (IIRO) directed by Osama bin Laden's brother-in-law, Muhammad Jamal Khalifa, steer the money to various beneficiaries such as JI.[189] JI members are expected to give 2.5 to 5.0 percent of their income as an offering. Supporters in more affluent Malaysia and Singapore are expected to give a higher amount, but with stricter counterterrorism measures in place, much of these contributions no longer make their way back to JI in Indonesia.[190]

Business fronts run by JI also provide funding.[191] In Indonesia, trade, Muslim garment production, Islamic publishing, and other commercial endeavors help keep JI solvent.[192] Today, JI is can no longer depend on abundant funds and logistical support from Middle Eastern and South Asian contacts as it once did.[193] Lack of abundant funds definitely limits its capability and probably contributes to the mainstream's consolidation strategy.[194] Regardless of JI's apparent meager financial resources, its stature as the jihadist connector and shaper of radical Islamic thought in Southeast Asia enables it to attract the funds necessary to carry on.[195]

Recruitment and Training

Reliable recruitment and training is absolutely critical for JI to fulfill its objectives. Many Muslims in the region, who feel they are victims of an anti-Islamic conspiracy and are mis-ruled by their government, champion JI as it attempts to establish an Islamic Caliphate.[196] Given the vast number of Muslim subjects to pick from in Southeast Asia, JI is selective and deliberate in its recruitment process. Step one involves a recommendation for a potential recruit from a JI member.[197] Often these nominations stem from kinsman and social contacts of current members. Once nominated, recruits are sent to a pesantren for religious indoctrination where they are taught JI's radical view of current events and the plight of Muslims throughout history. During this instruction, loyalty and dedication to JI are closely assessed and those with a burning desire to promote radical Islam are identified and approached for induction. This screening period lasts for approximately 18 months and when such a candidate accepts, the individual is then placed into the JI training pipeline.[198]

Prior to the United States' Operation Enduring Freedom in Afghanistan, JI training took place in either Afghanistan or Southeast Asia. Today, JI, Al Qaeda, and their affiliates maintain numerous training sites where they send their recruits. Some of these training camps are located in Mindanao in the Philippines, Sulawesi in Indonesia, and Negri Sembilan in Malaysia. Camps have been set up throughout the region and one was even discovered near Perth, Australia.[199]

While most recruits come from families who blame the West for the plight of Islam, all trainees bound for camp receive cover stories and false documents.[200] Examples include letters from Islamic charities stating the "student" will be building mosques or participating in some other admirable undertaking.[201]

Recruits receive rigorous religious, physical, and military training. Religious curriculum includes Islamic jurisprudence, proselytization, and the theology of jihad. For physical and military training, students learn bomb-making, operation of weapons, explosives handling, demolition methodology, guerilla warfare skills, leadership, and self-defense.[202] Additionally, JI members learn computer skills and communication techniques which facilitate covert operations and minimize potential exposure to capture.[203]

While further details of JI training camps are not widely available, given many of JI's key leaders' ties and experiences with Al Qaeda, one can certainly surmise much of the curriculum. For example, *The Al-Qaeda Training Manual* provides excellent insight into a terrorist training camp's likely course of instruction. Al Qaeda training topics include: member qualifications and character traits, counterfeiting, forged documents, organizational hierarchy, hiding, communication, transportation, training, weapons transport, member safety and security, special operations, espionage, secret communication, kidnapping and assassinations, explosives, poisons, weapons, interrogation, investigations, and detention centers.[204]

An additional goal of JI's training is to cement allegiance to the group. This is reinforced with operational experience abroad in Muslim conflicts. Many of JI's most senior leaders fought in Afghanistan or Ambon/Poso and garnered critical contacts and skills from those experiences that also fostered group camaraderie.[205] Oaths administered by high-ranking religious and jihadist figures within the organization further tie new recruits to the group. Frequently, JI members marry relatives of new recruits to bind them further and make departures less likely.[206]

Member dedication and loyalty has enabled JI to weather numerous counterterrorism crackdowns. Since 2002, following the first Bali bombing, JI has lost hundreds of its members to arrest and death, but experts consistently underestimate its total strength.[207] Today, JI's core is strong. Conservative estimates project at least 900 battle-tested members.[208] This core group has undergone intense religious and military training, and shares a deep-rooted loyalty to JI's ideology and objectives.[209] Ultimately, given JI's presence in the region and a substantial number of potential jihad sympathizers to select from, it should have the capability to recruit numerous other dedicated members.

Conclusion

The United States Department of State continues to list JI as a "serious threat to Western and regional interests" in the Global War on Terrorism.[210] JI draws its strength from indigenous Muslims who feel victimized by a perceived Western-led anti-Islamic conspiracy that dates back to the colonial era, and its vision of the establishment of an Islamic caliphate and theocratic state across Southeast Asia. It maintains a regional focus and leverages the strengths of numerous like-minded radical Islamic groups across the region as it proselytizes radical militant ideology to the region's many frustrated, underemployed, and vulnerable, potential recruits and sympathizers.

While counterterrorism efforts have hindered JI especially in Malaysia and Singapore, it remains strong in Indonesia and maintains operatives throughout the entire Southeast Asian region. Awareness of JI peaked worldwide in October 2002 when one of its terrorist bombings in Bali claimed the lives of 202 innocent civilians, many of which were Westerners.

This event finally prompted the Indonesian government to acknowledge the JI threat and pursue it. Since then, counterterrorism efforts of Singapore, Malaysia, the Philippines, and Indonesia, with help from Western allies, have definitely slowed JI's pace of attacks. Authorities have arrested hundreds of JI members including three former amirs and numerous key operational leaders.

Amid this pressure, competing factions within JI emerged with the extremist bomber faction that led JI operations during the first half of the decade eventually taking a backseat to the radical proselytizing majority faction. While the proselytizers are radical to the core, they are less volatile and somewhat influenced by the minority political faction. Hopefully, as JI undergoes a leadership transition during its consolidation and reconstitution period it will give the peaceful political process a chance as it seeks to expand its base. Despite its apparent holding pattern, JI remains active and deadly, still initiating violent efforts to undermine the local governments of the region with attacks against Christian ethnic groups and Western interests.

Currently JI has at least 900 core members who have answered the call for "holy war" and maintain a deep-rooted loyalty to the group. Attrition of key leadership positions caused by ongoing counterterrorism efforts is JI's greatest challenge. Selecting leaders capable of successfully succeeding their predecessors and able to focus members on JI's ultimate objective, the establishment of an Islamic caliphate across Southeast Asia, while downplaying factional differences within the group will certainly determine JI's long-term viability. Today, JI is at a crossroads and its most immediate need is selecting a new amir. The competency and direction provided by the individual selected along with his advisors and operational leaders will dictate whether JI or counterterrorism measures gain the upper hand.

Certainly, numerous capable core JI members stand ready to fill this and other crucial positions. Inspired by radicals worldwide, JI is not likely to disappear anytime soon. Its resolve characterized by intense violence coupled with JI's regional and global Islamic terrorist connections assure this fact.

Additionally, geographical challenges, poor interagency coordination, systematic corruption, and limited government resources within Indonesia, continue to plague governmental efforts to diminish JI's presence.[211] Furthermore, sympathetic elected officials and judges who succumb to strong Muslim advocacy groups further exasperate the dilemma. Many lawmakers are hesitant to enact much needed legal reforms which would better enable law enforcement agencies to fight terror. Also, soft sentences coupled with early parole allow terrorist offenders to return to their terrorist ways wasting previous valiant efforts to capture them.[212] These failures further enable JI to radicalize the traditionally moderate population of the region. Ultimately, counterterrorism help and pressure from host countries and their Western allies must continue in substantial force to extinguish the JI threat.

Appendix—Key Figures

- **Abdullah Sungkar** was a co-founding cleric and the first spiritual leader of JI. He died of natural causes in November 1999. He favored a covert existence of JI.[213]

- **Abu Bakar Bashir** was the other co-founding cleric and the second spiritual leader of JI. As the spiritual leader, Bashir was revered as the JI amir. Some also speculate that Bashir served as an operational leader as well.[214] Additionally, he is a key leader of the Indonesian Mujahidin Council (MMI) and denies involvement in terrorism. He was released early from jail in June 2006 after serving 25 of 30 months for charges related to JI terror plots.[215] As amir, Bashir favored an overt existence of JI and appealed to the sympathies of the people.[216] He generally avoided direct involvement with violence and considered the bomber faction of JI misguided.[217]

- **Thoriqudin, a.k.a. Abu Rusydan and Hamzah**, became the next amir following Bashir's arrest in October 2002. Thoriqudin's tenure was short-lived due to arrest.[218] He was in the same group of recruits as Mukhlas and did not support the bomber faction of JI.[219]

- **Zarkasih, a.k.a. Nu'aim and Abu Irsyad**, served as JI's emergency amir following the arrest of Thoriqudin. He is credited with master-minding resurgent violence in Poso and is a first generation JI leader with Al Qaeda training and Afghan experience. Zarkasih was arrested in June 2007.[220]

- **Abu Dujana** grew up with years of Koranic tutorial in the heart of the Darul Islam underground movement. He trained in Afghanistan alongside many future JI leaders and formed personal ties with several key Al Qaeda figures. Dujana rose through the ranks of the JI Mantiqi II division and by 2000 was selected Secretary. A year later he was elected to lead the Mantiqi III division. Subsequently, in October 2002, Dujana became Thoriqudin's secretary and eventually became the operational (Syurah) leader. He was arrested in June 2007 by Indonesian counterterrorism authorities.[221] Author's note: Current information on JI is often contradictory and the source that identified Abu Dujana as the recently arrested Syurah leader had previously identified him as the new amir one year earlier.

- **Nurjaman Riduan bin Isomuddin, a.k.a. Hambali**, was the JI Logistics and Operations Chief and is now in U.S. custody.[222] He fought in the Soviet-Afghan War where he developed close links with Al Qaeda. He served as the Mantiqi I leader and was involved in every major JI operation until his arrest in August 2003 in Ayutthaya, Thailand. Also, he was suspected of being Al Qaeda's operations director for Southeast Asia and was responsible for organizing travel and accommodations for terrorists involved in the USS Cole bombing and the September 11, 2001, high-jackings.[223] Currently, he is imprisoned at the U.S. Naval Station Guantanamo Bay, Cuba detention facility.[224, 225]

- **Nasir Abas** was a former Mantiqi III leader before his arrest in August 2003. Nasir has essentially defected from the radical Islamic ranks and openly criticizes JI for targeting civilians. He has testified against JI operatives including Mukhlas and provided detailed insight into JI's ideology, structure, and activities.[226]

- **Mohammad Iqbal Abdurraham, a.k.a. Abu Jibril**, helped with the early establishment of JI and acted as a training coordinator. He was JI's primary recruiter and second-in-command until his arrest in June 2001 in Malaysia.[227] He has since been released from prison and involved in JI overt propaganda, social welfare, and outreach (dawa).[228]

- **Abdul Aziz, a.k.a. Imam Samudra**, was the field coordinator for the October 12, 2002, Bali bombings. He was arrested in Indonesia in November 2002 and later sentenced to death.[229]

- **Ali Gufron, a.k.a. Mukhlas**, was the operational commander for the October 12, 2002, Bali bombings. He took over as the JI Operations Chief for Hambali in 2002 when Hambali was under police pressure. Mukhlas was arrested December 3, 2002, in Indonesia.[230]

- **Amrozi bin Nurhasyim** is the younger brother of Mukhlas and he was an accomplice in the 2002 Bali bombings and the 2001 Philippine Ambassador's Residence bombing. He was arrested in November 2002 in East Java and later sentenced to death.[231]

- **Ali Imron** was another younger brother of Mukhlas and arrested in November 2002.[232]

- **Fathur Rahman al-Ghozi** was the senior bomb maker and field coordinator for the metro Manila bombings on December 31, 2000. He was arrested in January 2002 in Manila and later killed in a shoot-out with Philippine police in 2003.[233]

- **Dr. Azahari Husin**, a British-educated engineer, university lecturer, and an Al Qaeda trained Afghan alumnus, was JI's leading bomb maker and instructor.[234] He worked closely with Noordin Mohamed Top planning and executing both the Marriott and Australian embassy attacks before meeting his death in a shootout with Indonesian police in November 2005.[235]

- **Noordin Mohamed Top** is "one of the most wanted men in Southeast Asia."[236] He is one of the few top JI leaders without Al

Qaeda Afghan training and is nicknamed the "Moneyman." Despite his lack of Afghan experience, Top is an ultra-militant JI hardliner who followed Hambali's lead and the Al Qaeda 1998 fatwa calling for attacks against the United States and its allies.[237] He, along with Mukhlas and other hardliners, was immersed in Sungkar's boarding school, Lukmanul Hakiem. This school became the initial nerve center for JI when it was formally founded and also the base for Mantiqi I.[238] He was once considered the organization's top recruiter and strategist. He has masterminded seven suicide attacks including the Marriott and Australian Embassy attacks.[239] He is also an extremely important fundraiser for JI and currently at large.[240] Today, Top is the leader of the JI bomber faction and operates without regard to mainstream direction or approval. His group is capable of striking at will with bombs and suicide attacks.

- **Sylfullah** is an Al Qaeda bomb expert and was implicated in the Khobar Towers attack. He was in Bali the night before the October 12, 2002, attack and is believed to have supervised the final bomb-making preparations.[241]

- **Omar al-Farouq, a.k.a. Mahmoud Ahmad and Mohammed Ahmad**, was killed September 25, 2006, by British forces in Basra Iraq. Al-Farouq was a main link between Al Qaeda and JI and an expert bomb maker. He originally joined Al Qaeda in the early 1990s and trained in Afghanistan from 1992 to 1995. In 1995 he went to the Philippines for flight school but failed to gain entry. Following this, he trained in jungle warfare with JI in Mindanao. He then moved to Indonesia in 2000 and set up terrorist training camps and planned a series of attacks against Western interests and embassies throughout Southeast Asia. These attacks were scheduled to occur around the first anniversary of 9/11, but were preempted when Indonesian security officials captured al-Farouq south of Jakarta. The Indonesians turned him over to the United States and he was transferred to Bagram, Afghanistan. From there, he escaped in July 2005 and made his way to Iraq.[242]

- **Aris Sumarsono, a.k.a. Zulkernaen**, was once JI's Chief of Military Operations. He is a United States trained engineer and an

Afghanistan alumnus. He is credited with bomb-training for the Abu Sayyaf Group in the Philippines and was given sanctuary by the Moro Islamic Liberation Front when he fled Malaysia in 2003.[243]

- **Joko Pitono, a.k.a. Dulmatin**, is a suspected JI electronics and bomb-making expert and a suspect in the 2002 Bali bombing.[244] He is currently embedded with the Abu Sayyaf Group in the Philippines.[245]

- **Umar Patek** is a suspected JI recruiter and currently embedded with the Abu Sayyaf Group in the Philippines.[246]

- **Zulkifli bin Hir**, a U.S.-trained engineer with a five million dollar bounty on his head by the U.S. Government, leads Kumpulan Militan Malaysia.[247] Additionally, he conducts training in Moro Islamic Liberation Front camps in Mindanao for JI members.[248]

- **Zulkifli Marzuki** is a Malaysian national and a financial operative involved in JI front companies and charitable works with alleged links to Al Qaeda.[249]

- **Aris Munandar** is an Indonesian national and a financial operative involved in JI front companies and charitable works with alleged links to Al Qaeda.[250]

Notes

1. "Terrorism," *Anti-defamation League,* 2006, n.p., On-line, Internet, 30 August 2006, available from www.adl.org/terrorism/profiles/al_qaeda.asp and Department of State, *Country Reports: East Asia and Pacific Overview,* 30 April 2007, Chapter 2, n.p. On-line, Internet, 5 May 2007, available from http://www.state.gov/s/ct/rls/crt/2006/82731.htm.

2. Bruce Vaughn, *Islam in South and Southeast Asia*, Congressional Research Service (CRS) Report for Congress Order Code RS21903, (The Library of Congress, 8 February 2005), 1.

3. "Muslim Public Opinion on US Policy, Attacks on Civilians and al Qaeda," *WorldPublicOpinion.Org*, 24 April 2007, 4.

4. Vaughn, op. cit., 1.

5. Janes Information Group 2007, "*Indonesia*," 22 January 2007, n.p., On-line, Internet, 24 April 2007, available from Air University Library via limited access database subscription http://jtic.janes.com/subscribe/jtic/doc_view_print.jsp.

6. "Jemaah Islamiyah (JI)," *MIPT TERRORISM KNOWLEDGE BASE*, 22 August 2006, n.p., On-line, Internet, 24 August 2006, available from www.tkb.org/Group.jsp?groupID=3613.

7. Captain Wayne Turnbull, "A Tangled Web of Southeast Asian Islamic Terrorism: The Jemaah Islamiyah Terrorist Network," *Monterey Institute of International Studies*, Monterey, California, 31 July 2003, Introduction 1, On-line, Internet, 29 August 2006, available from www.terrorismcentral.com/Library/terroristgroups/JemaahIslamiyah/JITerror/JIContents.html.

8. Vaughn, op. cit., 2.

9. Kerry B. Collison, "Indonesia: Jemaah Islamiyah's Current Status," *Eye on Asia*, 4 May 2007, n.p. On-line, Internet, 15 May 2007, available from http://kerrycollison.net/index.php?/archieves/5669-Indonesia-Jemaah-Islamiyahs-current-status.html.

10. "Terrorism," *Anti-defamation League*, n.p.

11. Turnbull, Jemaah Islamiyah: Doctrine 1.

12. Department of State, *Patterns of Global Terrorism 2003*, 16.

13. Janes Information Group 2007, "*Islamist Cleric Targets Moderate Indonesia*," 7 February 2007, n.p., On-line, Internet, 24 April 2007, available from Air University Library via limited access database subscription http://jtic.janes.com/subscribe/jtic/doc_view_print.jsp.

14. U.S. Central Intelligence Agency, *World Fact Book: Indonesia*, 22 August 2006, n.p., On-line, Internet, 1 September 2006, available from www.cia.gov/cia/publications/factbook/geos/id.html.

15. U.S. Pacific Command, *Testimony before House Armed Services Committee Regarding U.S. Pacific Command Posture*, U.S. House, Statement of Admiral Thomas B. Fargo, U.S. Navy, Commander, U.S. Pacific Command, 31 March 2004, n.p., On-line, Internet, 18 January 2007, available from http://www.pacom.mil/speeches/sst2004/040331housearmedsvcscomm.shtml.

16. Ibid.

17. Ibid.

18. Department of State, *Patterns of Global Terrorism 2003*, 16.

19. Rohan Gunaratna, *Ideology in Terrorism and Counter Terrorism: Lessons from Combating Al Qaeda and Al Jemaah Al Islamiyah in Southeast Asia*, CSRC Discussion Paper 05/42, September 2005, 20-21.

20. Ibid., 20.

21. Turnbull, Introduction 1.

22. "Jemaah Islamiyah Split but Still Deadly," *BBC News,* 3 October 2005, n.p., On-line, Internet, 24 August 2006, available from http://news.bbc.co.uk/1/hi/world/asia-pacific/2983612.stm.

23. "Jemaah Islamiyah (JI)," *MIPT TERRORISM KNOWLEDGE BASE*, n.p.

24. Department of State, *Patterns of Global Terrorism 2003*, 16; also Janes Information Group 2007, *"Jemaah Islamiyya (JI),"* 30 January 2007, n.p., On-line, Internet, 24 April 2007, available from Air University Library via limited access database subscription http://jtic.janes.com/subscribe/jtic/doc_view_print.jsp.

25. "Jemaah Islamiyah," *Council on Foreign Relations*, 3 October 2005, n.p., On-line, Internet, 24 August 2006, available from www.cfr.org/publication/8948/ and "Jemaah Islamiyah," *GlobalSecurity.org*, 27 April 2005, n.p., On-line, Internet, 24 August 2006 available from www.globalsecurity.org/military/world/para/ji.htm.

26. Zachary Abuza, "Indonesia Neutralizes JI as Immediate Threat," *Terrorism Focus*, 19 June 2007, Volume IV, Issue 19, n.p., On-line, Internet, 20 June 2007, available from http://.jamestown.org/news_details.php?news_id=252.

27. Ibid., and "Indonesia: The Continuing Jemaah Islamiyah Threat," *Stratfor,* 4 April 2007, n.p., On-line, Internet, 24 April 2007, available from www.stratfor.com.

28. Indonesia: The Continuing Jemaah Islamiyah Threat," n.p.

29. Janes Information Group 2007, *"Jemaah Islamiyya (JI),"* n.p.

30. Ibid.

31. Ibid. Also, Janes Information Group 2005, "*Jemaah Islamiyya (JI),*" 16 December 2005, n.p., On-line, Internet, 14 December 2006, available from library via limited access database subscription, http://jtic.janes.com/subscribe/jtic/doc_view_print.jsp.

32. Janes Information Group 2005, n.p.

33. Ibid.

34. "Profile: Nurjaman Riduan Isamuddin," *Cooperative Research History Commons,* February-April, 1995, n.p., On-line, Internet, 1 September 2006, available from www.cooperativeresearch.org/entity.jsp?id=1521846767-2195.

35. "The Jemaah Islamiyah, Al-Qaeda Connection," *GlobalSecurity.org*, 27 April 2005, n.p., On-line, Internet, 29 August 2006, available from www.globalsecurity.org/military/world/para/ji-aq-link.htm.

36. "Top al Qaeda Terrorist Killed in Iraq," *Northeast Intelligence Network*, 25 September 2006, n.p., On-line, Internet, 28 September 2006, available from www.homelandsecurityus.com/site/modules/news/print.php?storyid=609.

37. Ibid.

38. Janes Information Group 2005, n.p.

39. "Profile: Nurjaman Riduan Isamuddin," n.p.

40. Indonesia: The Continuing Jemaah Islamiyah Threat," n.p.

41. Ibid.

42. Ibid.

43. Ibid.

44. Ibid.

45. Gunaratna, 22.

46. Janes Information Group 2007, "*Jemaah Islamiyya (JI)*," n.p.

47. Gunaratna, 21 and Janes Information Group 2007, "*Jemaah Islamiyya (JI)*," n.p.

48. David Wright-Neville, "Jemaah Islamiah Split but Still Deadly," *BBC News*, 3 October 2005, n.p. On-line, Internet, 24 August 2006, available from http://news.bbc.co.uk/1/hi/world/asia-pacific/2983612.stm.

49. Carlyle A. Thayer, "Political Terrorism and Militant Islam in Southeast Asia," *School of Humanities & Social Sciences Australian Defence Force Academy*, 24 July 2003, 17, On-line, Internet, 31 August 2006, available from www.apan-info.net/terrorism/uploaded/documents/Political%20Terrorism%20&%20Militant%20Islam.pdf.

50. Gunaratna, 21-22.

51. Janes Information Group 2007, *"Jemaah Islamiyya (JI),"* n.p.

52. "Jemaah Islamiyah Split but Still Deadly," n.p.

53. Collison, n.p.

54. Gunaratna, 22.

55. Janes Information Group 2007, *"Jemaah Islamiyya (JI),"* n.p.

56. Gunaratna, 21.

57. Ibid., 21-22.

58. Ibid., 22.

59. Collison, n.p.

60. Gunaratna, 22.

61. Collison, n.p.

62. "Indonesia: The Continuing Jemaah Islamiyah Threat," *Stratfor*, n.p.

63. Noor Huda Ismail, "JI Weakened, Yet Potential for Violence Remains," *Terrorism Focus,* 3 July 2007, Volume IV, Issue 21, n.p., On-line, Internet, 10 July 2007, available from http://www.jamestown.org/terrorism/news/article/php?articleid=2373515.

64. "Indonesia: The Continuing Jemaah Islamiyah Threat," *Stratfor*, n.p.

65. Turnbull, Historical Background 1.

66. Vaughn, 2.

67. Ibid., 2.

68. Turnbull, Historical Background 1.

69. Ibid.

70. "Jemaah Islamiyah," *GlobalSecurity.org*, n.p.

71. Gunaratna, 14.

72. Gunaratna, 14 and "Jemaah Islamiyah," *GlobalSecurity.org*, n.p.

73. "Jemaah Islamiyah (JI)," *MIPT TERRORISM KNOWLEDGE BASE*, n.p.

74. Thayer, 17.

75. Gunaratna, 15.

76. Ibid.

77. "Jemaah Islamiyah," *Council on Foreign Relations*, n.p.

78. Turnbull, Historical Background 2.

79. Ibid.

80. Department of State, *Patterns of Global Terrorism 2003*, 16.

81. Gunaratna, 15.

82. Ibid.

83. Ibid.

84. Turnbull, Historical Background 3.

85. Ibid.

86. Turnbull, Jemaah Islamiyah: Origins 1. and "Jemaah Islamiyah," *Council on Foreign Relations*, n.p.

87. Ibid.

88. Gunaratna, 15.

89. Ibid.

90. Ibid., 13.

91. Ibid., 15.

92. Turnbull, Jemaah Islamiyah: Origins 2.

93. "Jemaah Islamiyah," *Council on Foreign Relations*, n.p.

94. "The Jemaah Islamiyah, Al-Qaeda Connection," n.p.

95. Thayer, 17.

96. Janes Information Group 2007, "*Jemaah Islamiyya (JI)*," n.p.

97. Turnbull, Jemaah Islamiyah: Origins 1.

98. Janes Information Group 2005, n.p.

99. Turnbull, Historical Background 2.

100. Ibid., Jemaah Islamiyah: Origins 2.

101. "Jemaah Islamiyah," *Council on Foreign Relations*, n.p.

102. Ibid.

103. Ibid.

104. "Australia Angry as Cleric Freed," *BBC News,* 14 June 2006, n.p., On-line, Internet, 1 September 2006, available from http://newsvote.bbc.co.uk/mpapps/pagetools/print/news.bbc.co.uk/1/hi/world/asia-pacific/5078540.stm.

105. Janes Information Group 2007, "*Islamist Cleric Targets Moderate Indonesia*," n.p.

106. Ibid.

107. "Jemaah Islamiyah Split but Still Deadly," n.p.

108. Ibid., and "Jemaah Islamiyah," *Council on Foreign Relations*, n.p.

109. Janes Information Group 2007, "*Jemaah Islamiyya (JI)*," n.p.

110. "Indonesia: The Continuing Jemaah Islamiyah Threat," *Stratfor*, n.p.

111. Ibid.

112. Turnbull, Jemaah Islamiyah: Doctrine 1.

113. Ibid.

114. "Terrorism," *Anti-defamation League*, n.p.

115. "Jemaah Islamiyah," *Council on Foreign Relations*, n.p.

116. Janes Information Group 2007, *"Jemaah Islamiyya (JI),"* n.p.

117. Jonathan Ross-Harrington, "Re-Examining Jemaah Islamiyah in the Wake of the Zawahiri Letter," *Terrorism Monitor Volume III, Issue 21,* 3 November 2005, 1.

118. Ibid., 1-2.

119. "Jemaah Islamiyah Split but Still Deadly," n.p.

120. "Jemaah Islamiyah," *Council on Foreign Relations*, n.p. and "Jemaah Islamiyah Split but Still Deadly," n.p.

121. Janes Information Group 2006, *"Abu Sayyaf Group (ASG),"* 16 February 2006, n.p., On-line, Internet, 24 April 2007, available from library via limited access database subscription http://jtic.janes.com/subscribe/jtic/doc_view_print.jsp.

122. Peter Chalk and William Rosenau, "Southeast Asia, the Second Front of Global Terror?" *Nation Multimedia Group*, 21 September 2006, n.p., On-line, Internet, 22 December 2006, available from http://www.nationmultimedia.com/specials/south2years/sep2106.php and Janes Information Group 2007, *"Jemaah Islamiyya (JI),"* n.p.

123. Janes Information Group 2007, *"Jemaah Islamiyya (JI),"* n.p.

124. Turnbull, Appendix A – JI Affiliate Organizations, 1.

125. Ibid.

126. Ibid.

127. Ibid.

128. Ibid., 2.

129. "Zulkifli bin Hir: JI's U.S. Trained Engineer," *The Philippine Star*, 1 April 2007.

130. Turnbull, Appendix A – JI Affiliate Organizations, 2.

131. Ibid., 3.

132. Ibid.

133. Janes Information Group 2005, n.p.

134. Janes Information Group 2007, "*Jemaah Islamiyya (JI),*" n.p.

135. Janes Information Group 2005, n.p.

136. Ibid.

137. "Jemaah Islamiyah Split but Still Deadly," n.p.

138. Richard Halloran, "US, Asian Forces Join Hands in Battling Growing Terror Network," *Taipei Times*, 25 April 2007.

139. Regis Baldauff, Southeast Asia: The Islamist Threat of Jemaah Islamiyah," (Air War College Research Paper Maxwell AFB, AL, 9 December 2006), 2.

140. Janes Information Group 2005, n.p.

141. Ibid.

142. Ibid.

143. Ibid.

144. Janes Information Group 2007, "*Jemaah Islamiyya (JI),*" n.p.

145. Ibid.

146. Collison, n.p.

147. Gunaratna, 19.

148. Ibid.

149. Ibid.

150. Ibid.

151. "Indonesia: The Continuing Jemaah Islamiyah Threat," *Stratfor*, n.p.

152. Janes Information Group 2005, n.p.

153. Janes Information Group 2007, "*Jemaah Islamiyya (JI),*" n.p.

154. Janes Information Group 2005, n.p.

155. "Jemaah Islamiyah Split but Still Deadly," n.p.

156. "Indonesia: The Continuing Jemaah Islamiyah Threat," *Stratfor*, n.p.

157. Janes Information Group 2005, n.p.

158. Janes Information Group 2007, *"Jemaah Islamiyya (JI),"* n.p.

159. Ibid.

160. Collison, n.p.

161. Janes Information Group 2007, *"Jemaah Islamiyya (JI),"* n.p.

162. Abuza, "Indonesia Neutralizes JI as Immediate Threat," n.p.

163. Janes Information Group 2005, n.p

164. Ibid., and Turnbull, Jemaah Islamiyah: Organization and Activities 1.

165. Janes Information Group 2005, n.p., and Berry Desker, "The Jemaah Islamiyah (JI) Phenomenon in Singapore," *Institute of Defence and Strategic Studies, Nanyang Technological University, Singapore*, 1 December 2003, n.p., On-line, Internet, 20 January 2007, available from http://goliath.ecnext.com/coms2/summary_0199-615503_ITM.

166. Janes Information Group 2005, n.p, *Desker,* and Turnbull, Jemaah Islamiyah: Organization and Activities 2.

167. Janes Information Group 2007, *"Jemaah Islamiyya (JI),"* n.p.

168. Collison, n.p.

169. Ibid.

170. Ibid.

171. Janes Information Group 2007, *"Jemaah Islamiyya (JI),"* n.p.

172. Ibid.

173. Turnbull, Appendix D – Regional Maps 2.

174. Turnbull, Jemaah Islamiyah: Organization and Activities 2.

175. Janes Information Group 2005, n.p.

176. Desker, n.p.

177. Turnbull, Jemaah Islamiyah: Organization and Activities 2.

178. Ibid., The JI Terror Network: Conclusion 1.

179. Janes Information Group 2007, "*Jemaah Islamiyya (JI)*," n.p.

180. Janes Information Group 2005, n.p.

181. Janes Information Group 2007, "*Jemaah Islamiyya (JI)*," n.p.

182. Ibid.

183. Ibid.

184. Nanyang Siang Pau, "Reports Say Jemaah Islamiyah Formed Assassination Squad in Indonesia," *Malaysian, Singapore Press,* 17 April 2007.

185. Ibid., n.p.

186. Janes Information Group 2007, "*Jemaah Islamiyya (JI)*," n.p.

187. Ibid.

188. Halloran, n.p.

189. Ibid., Financing 1.

190. Janes Information Group 2007, "*Jemaah Islamiyya (JI)*," n.p.

191. Janes Information Group 2005, n.p.

192. Janes Information Group 2007, "*Jemaah Islamiyya (JI)*," n.p.

193. "Jemaah Islamiyah," *GlobalSecurity.org*, n.p.

194. Janes Information Group 2007, "*Jemaah Islamiyya (JI)*," n.p.

195. Janes Information Group 2005, n.p.

196. "Muslim Public Opinion on US Policy, Attacks on Civilians and al Qaeda," 1-5.

197. Turnbull, Recruitment and Training 1.

198. Ibid.

199. Ibid.

200. Department of State, *Patterns of Global Terrorism 2003*, 16; also Turnbull, Recruitment and Training 1.

201. Turnbull, Recruitment and Training 2.

202. Janes Information Group 2005, n.p.

203. Janes Information Group 2007, "*Jemaah Islamiyya (JI)*," n.p.

204. Jerrold M. Post, M.D., *Military Studies in the Jihad Against the Tyrants—The Al-Qaeda Training Manual*, August, 2004. USAF Counterproliferation Center, Maxwell AFB, Alabama, 11-12.

205. Turnbull, Introduction 1.

206. Janes Information Group 2007, "*Jemaah Islamiyya (JI)*," n.p.

207. Ismail, n.p.

208. Collison, n.p

209. Janes Information Group 2007, "*Jemaah Islamiyya (JI)*," n.p.

210. Department of State, *Country Reports: East Asia and Pacific Overview*, n.p.

211. Ibid.

212. Ibid., and Janes Information Group 2007, "*Jemaah Islamiyya (JI)*," n.p.

213. Gunaratna, 21.

214. "Jemaah Islamiyah," *GlobalSecurity.org*, n.p.

215. "Australia Angry as Cleric Freed," n.p.

216. Gunaratna, 21.

217. Janes Information Group 2007, "*Islamist Cleric Targets Moderate Indonesia*," n.p.

218. Zachary Abuza, "Abu Dujana: Jemaah Islamiyah's New al Qaeda Linked Leader," *Terrorism Focus*, 4 April 2006, n.p., On-line, Internet, 18 January 2007, available from http://.jamestown.org/terrorism/news/article.php?article=2369948&printthis=1.

219. Janes Information Group 2007, "*Jemaah Islamiyya (JI)*," n.p.

220. Abuza, "Indonesia Neutralizes JI as Immediate Threat," n.p.

221. Ibid., and Abuza, "Abu Dujana: Jemaah Islamiyah's New al Qaeda Linked Leader," n.p. and "Indonesia: The Continuing Jemaah Islamiyah Threat," *Stratfor*, n.p.

222. "The Jemaah Islamiyah, Al-Qaeda Connection," n.p.

223. "Jemaah Islamiyah," *Council on Foreign Relations*, n.p.

224. "Hambali – Jamaah Islamiya Operations Chief," *GlobalSecurity.org*, 11 January 2007, n.p., On-line, Internet, 18 January 2007, available from www.globalsecurity.org/military/world/para/ji-aq-link.htm.

225. Simon Elegant, "Asia's Own Osama," *TIME Asia.com*, 1 April 2002, n.p., On-line, Internet, 22 December 2006, available from http://www.time.com/time/asia/features/malay_terror/hambali.html.

226. "Al-Qaeda—Indonesia and the Informer," *BBC World Services*, September 2006, n.p., On-line, Internet, 31 January 2007, available from http://www.bbc.co.uk/worldservice/specials/1516_assignment/page12.shtml.

227. "Jemaah Islamiyah," *Council on Foreign Relations*, n.p.

228. Abuza, "Indonesia Neutralizes JI as Immediate Threat," n.p.

229. Turnbull, Appendix B – Index of Names 4.

230. Ibid.

231. Ibid.

232. "Jemaah Islamiyah: Special Report," *Western Resistance: Jemaah Islamiyah: Special Report*, 2 October 2005, n.p., On-line, Internet, 22 December 2006, available from http://www.westernresistance.com/blog/archieves/000304.html.

233. "Jemaah Islamiyah Split but Still Deadly," n.p.

234. "Azahari's Death Not the End of JI," *Australian Broadcasting Corporation*, 14 November 2005, n.p., On-line, Internet, 18 January 2007, available from http://www.abc.net.au/ra/news/infocus/s1506306.htm.

235. "Jemaah Islamiyah: Special Report," n.p.

236. Janes Information Group 2006, "*Noordin Muhammad Top*," 7 November 2006, n.p., On-line, Internet, 14 December 2006, available from library limited access database subscription http://jtic.janes.com/subscribe/jtic/doc_view_print.jsp.

237. Ibid.

238. Ibid.

239. "JI's Moneyman and Top Recruiter: A Profile of Noordin Mohammad Top," *The Jamestown Foundation*, 26 July 2006, n.p., On-line, Internet, 22 December 2006, available from http://www.jamestown.org/news_details.php?news_id=190.

240. "Jemaah Islamiyah Split but Still Deadly," n.p.

241. Turnbull, Appendix B – Index of Names 4; also "The Jemaah Islamiyah, Al-Qaeda Connection," n.p.

242. "Top al Qaeda Terrorist Killed in Iraq," n.p.

243. Abuza, "Abu Dujana: Jemaah Islamiyah's New al Qaeda Linked Leader," n.p.

244. Janes Information Group 2007, "*Southeast Asia's Tri-Border Black Spot*," 23 April 2007, n.p., On-line, Internet, 24 April 2007, available from Air University Library via limited access database subscription http://jtic.janes.com/subscribe/jtic/doc_view_print.jsp.

245. Abuza, "Indonesia Neutralizes JI as Immediate Threat," n.p.

246. Ibid.

247. "Zulkifli bin Hir: JI's U.S. Trained Engineer," *The Philippine Star*, 1 April 2007.

248. Abuza, "Indonesia Neutralizes JI as Immediate Threat," n.p.

249. Ibid.

250. Ibid.

CHAPTER 12

The Mexican Drug Cartels: At War for Control of the U.S.–Mexico Border

Dario E. Teicher

While the United States focuses on threats from overseas, a crisis is brewing on the nation's southwestern border. Mexican cartels primarily financed by the lucrative drug trade are waging war against each other, Mexican and U.S. authorities, and anyone willing to oppose their drive to control crossing-points that can access every corner of the United States for the conduct of their nefarious enterprises. Available evidence also indicates that these organizations have expanded to include domination of human smuggling and weapons trafficking at the U.S.-Mexico border. In a post 9/11 world, the person smuggled across into the United States might be an Al Qaeda or Hezbollah terrorist, and the weapons flowing into Mexico may destabilize an oil-rich economic partner and neighbor.

This chapter first places U.S.-Mexican interaction in historical and strategic context. It is a relationship that while friendly, remains far from intimate, which limits security cooperation and coordination. In essence, the Americans accuse Mexican authorities of corruption and the Mexicans accuse U.S. counterparts of being lackadaisical, specifically in preventing illegal arms from flowing south. Consequently, these animosities have contributed to the Mexican cartels ability to exploit the common border in the conduct of their illicit business, making them fabulously wealthy and lethal.

Radical Islam is well-known to be notorious; its followers are the enemy in the so-called War on Terror. By comparison, despite being a vicious threat next door, the cartels remain fairly unknown to most Americans, particularly, those living well beyond the U.S. southwestern border. While it is well-known that the border is open to illegal migrants seeking a better economic situation, less understood is that the nation's inability to deter this migration also allows other illicit dealings (drugs, kidnapping, weapons, laundered money, false documents, etc.) to be trafficked across the common border.

The Mexican cartels routinely operate on both sides of the U.S.-Mexico border, waging a war of their own, albeit with irreligious goals. The intent here is to shed light on the Mexican cartels and their border war, provide information on the efforts of U.S. and Mexican authorities to stem this enemy, and offer an explanation as to why the aims of the cartels represent an increasing and serious threat to U.S. national security.

Strategic Setting

The United States and Mexico enjoy friendly relations fostered by strong economic bonds. For example, the liberalization of the Mexican economy in the mid-1980s encouraged U.S. commercial access and the inauguration of the North American Free Trade Area on January 1, 1994, which removed all trade barriers, further strengthening ties. Additionally, the steady flow of 80 percent of Mexico's oil into the United States' economy has created a binding relationship.[1] Nevertheless, the common land boundary has always been a source of friction.

Nearly 2,000 miles of border are shared by these two countries. Historically, this border has never been well policed, allowing the criminal element on both sides of the boundary to conduct their activities with relative impunity. This border tension has forced two major U.S. military interventions in Mexico. The first was the U.S.–Mexican War of 1846 to 1848, which cost Mexico nearly two-thirds of its national territory. The second was during Mexico's Revolutionary War (1910 – 1921). In this conflict, Mexican bandits and irregular forces would cross into U.S. territory to rob, buy weapons, traffic in opium, and engage in other illicit activities. The best remembered incident occurred on March 9, 1916, when a Mexican irregular force under the outlaw turned Mexican revolutionary hero, Pancho Villa, attacked Columbus, New Mexico. The raid was a small disaster for Villa but 17 United States citizens were killed and it forced U.S. President Woodrow Wilson to authorize the second U.S.

intervention in Mexico (March 10, 1916 – February 5, 1917).[2] The result of this history has been to keep U.S.-Mexican security cooperation and coordination seriously limited.

It was during the Mexican Revolutionary War period that Mexico became a major supplier of heroin and marijuana to the U.S. market. Until the 1970s, the problem was treated as a nuisance but demand in the United States kept increasing. During the 1940s and 1950s, the United States would file a diplomatic complaint and the Mexicans would promptly have a drug-related corruption scandal leading to the removal of senior officials to pacify the Americans. In 1969, under strong pressure from U.S. President Richard Nixon, Mexico launched *Operation Condor*. The Mexican military deployed 10,000 troops to destroy the drug market along its northern border. Although the operation was scored a success, by the 1980s, the problem had taken a quantum leap for the worse. The Colombian Cali and Medellin mega-cartels were at the zenith of their power and they were pushing vast quantities of cocaine and marijuana into the United States. They controlled the entire drug distribution network from the source in the Andean Ridge of South America (particularly, Colombia, Peru, and Bolivia) to the distribution centers inside the United States.[3]

Latin American governments and the United States fought back. By the early 1990s, the power of the Cali and Medellin Cartels in Colombia was broken. Peru and Bolivia witnessed dramatic drops in cocaine production during this period. However, production moved into the southern jungles of Colombia, where smaller cartels working with leftist guerillas and right-wing illegal armed groups were still able to export drugs north. The 2002 election of President Alvaro Uribe in Colombia and his subsequent tough approach against the narcotics traffickers further eroded the power of the Colombian cartels.[4] Unfortunately, success in Colombia may have caused the focal point of drug trafficking to swing in favor of the Mexican cartels. The power they are gaining and the violence they have unleashed could threaten the stability of Mexico. One may conclude that perhaps a process of *Colombianization* is unfolding in Mexico, i.e., "…a state of all-out war between the government and the cartels… [leading to] massive bloodshed.[5]"

Origins of the Mexican Cartels

A Brief History

The Mexican revolutionary bandits of the early 20th century, who never strayed too far from the border, have been replaced by cartels able to engage in infinite brutality and operate throughout the contiguous 48 states. Colombian, Asian, Russian, Jamaican, and Dominican mafias operate in regions of the United States and Mexico, but today only the Mexicans can claim coast-to-coast drug trafficking influence in the United States.[6]

In the 1960s, small Mexican crime rings operated in the border areas pushing relatively small quantities of marijuana and opium across the frontier. By the 1970s, the appetite for drugs and particularly cocaine began to grow exponentially in the United States.[7] The Andean Ridge nations of South America (predominantly, Colombia, Peru, and Bolivia) became major cocaine production centers to meet the U.S. demand. The primary lines of communication for moving the drugs were across the Caribbean Sea, to the islands, and onward to the United States. The Mexican land route was then secondary, which kept the Mexican cartels weak and under the control of the Colombian mega-cartels.[8]

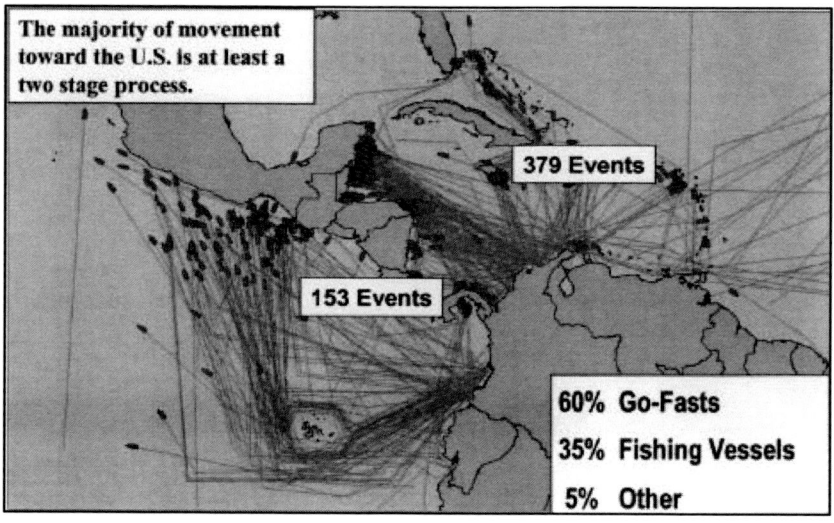

Figure 12.1 Known Maritime Drug Smuggling Tracks in 2005[9]

In the late 1980s, the balance began to shift. The U.S. Navy and Coast Guard started to aggressively interdict the Caribbean smuggling routes. While in Colombia, the government forces with U.S. support engaged in a bloody conflict to destroy the Medellin and Cali Cartels. The eventual demise of the mega cartels allowed the rise of smaller, less easy to detect, cartels in Colombia. They moved the primary routes for drug shipments out of Colombia away from a Caribbean crossing towards the islands and instead hugged the Central American coastlines or headed into the wide expanse of the Pacific Ocean before turning to Mexico for onward land movement north into the United States. (See Figure 12.1.) These cartels did not have the power to control the entire drug distribution network and instead relied on criminal partnerships with Mexican counterparts. The Mexican cartels, and particularly those that controlled key border crossing points, were now able to exploit a position of advantage and their power grew.[10]

The Evolution of Cartels

One can see that through the decades the Mexican cartels have evolved along a path observed by Professor Max Manwaring in *Street Gangs: the New Urban Insurgency*. According to Manwaring:

> An analysis of urban street gangs shows that some of these criminal entities have evolved through three generations of development. The *first generation* – or traditional street gangs – is primarily turf-oriented. They have loose and unsophisticated leadership and focus their attention on turf protection to gain petty cash and on gang loyalty within their immediate environs (designated city blocks or neighborhoods). When first generation street gangs engage in criminal enterprise, it is largely opportunistic.... *Second generation* gangs [are] ...organized for business and commercial gain. These gangs have a more centralized leadership, and members tend to focus on drug trafficking and market protection. At the same time, they operate in a broader spatial or geographic area that may include neighboring cities and other nation-states. *Third generation*

> gangs …continue first and second generation actions as they expand the geographical parameters, as well as their commercial and political objectives. As they evolve, they develop into more seasoned organizations with broader drug related markets, as well as very sophisticated transnational criminal organizations…. In this connection, they inevitably begin to control ungoverned territory within a nation-state and/or begin to acquire political power…. [The] gang and its leadership challenge the legitimate state monopoly on the exercise of control and use of violence…[11]

In Mexico, the early 20th century gangs that raided across the border had, by the 1950s, given way to second generation wealthy crime families. These organizations achieved a high degree of loyalty early on by making drug smuggling the family business. This practice continues today. The upper echelon and senior lieutenants are often family members and close personal friends, who literally grow-up in the business, making infiltration of the organization difficult. Meanwhile, the muscle (the lower echelon) is usually hired from first generation gangs, and underpaid police and military personnel to take advantage of their weapons training.

One typical example is the Arellano Family, who run the Tijuana Cartel. Their lieutenants are trusted friends, which police in Mexico refer to as the *Juniors*. The Juniors are not involved because of economic circumstances. They usually come from wealthy families and are well-educated. The Juniors join because of family ties, friendships, and to wield power. Due to their association to the Arellanos, the local police regard them as above-the-law even when they murder. In the lower ranks of the cartel, besides recruiting Mexican police officers, the Arellanos enlist their enforcers from gangs in Mexico or across the border in San Diego. Of course, the hiring of a gangster who is a U.S. citizen includes the ability to hold a genuine American passport for legal access into the United States. The cost to the Arellanos for maintaining this armed force is reasonable, when one considers the billions of dollars in drug profit. A hired gang member normally is on a weekly retainer of $1,000, with additional pay for actual operations. For example, a Junior may earn "…$15,000 for an afternoon of smuggling…."[12]

Undoubtedly, the Mexican cartels have displaced the Colombians as the mega-cartels of the early 21st century. For example, on January 8, 2007, the Dallas Morning News reported on Mexican cartel operations in Peru, which in this case involved "...nourishing the re-emergence of the Shining Path guerillas[13] [and] ...the killing of a federal judge...."[14] The article does not identify which Mexican cartel is in Peru, but the Arellanos' Tijuana Cartel is organized for international trafficking and is one of several crime organizations in Mexico, which have transitioned into Manwaring's third generation.

The Aims and Objectives of the Mexican Cartels

The Aims

According to the U.S. Department of Defense (DoD), a terrorist is "...an individual who commits an act or acts of violence or threatens violence in pursuit of political, religious, or ideological objectives."[15] The Mexican cartels are international terrorists under the DoD definition. They are certainly not pursuing religious objectives and they are not promoting an ideology. However, they do brandish political power in that they seek to undermine any political system to allow them to engage in their illicit international activities. Therefore, the aims of the Mexican drug cartels cannot be determined through analysis of their religious, ideological, or even their political goals. They are instead defined by their greed and the corruption that they propagate, the addictive and destructive nature of their products, and their absolute commitment to survival at any cost. Summarily, their aims are to maximize profits and ensure the survival of the organization in what is a Darwinian environment.[16]

In the late 1980s, the Mexican cartels attempted to organize the flow of drugs into the United States by common agreement. The head of the then most powerful Tijuana Organization (Miguel Angel Felix Gallardo), a former policeman and also regarded as the first Mexican drug boss to establish business ties to Colombian counterparts "...convoked the main Mexican drug lords in 1989 and under his leadership they split the territory reducing conflict and improving cooperation." The prime real state was the border. "In the agreement, every drug lord obtained a territory and control of the different cities along the U.S.–Mexican border."[17]

The Objectives

The secure and affordable access to Mexico's northern border can be considered a cartels overarching or strategic objective. Per Figure 12.1, the predominant illicit sea lines of communication run to Mexico, but the major market is in the United States. The transit of drugs north through Mexico involves a relatively minor degree of risk. Corruption is rampant within the government security forces; "salaries are low, [Mexico] …does not have a clear anti-narcotics strategy …and cooperation among federal and state police is minimal."[18] Hence, major risk does not occur until the crossing points are reached in the sister cities[19] along the border because here the smugglers encounter U.S. law enforcement. Therefore, the cartels invest considerable resources to control and facilitate illicit transit at these crossing points. As a result, one can consider the control of passage through the sister cities the tangible or operational objective of the Mexican cartels effort to maintain illicit access to the border and the United States.[20]

The Plazas

In the traffickers parlance, the crossing points within the two sister cities are called *the plazas* and to own one is to be considered its *gatekeeper*. It is the responsibility of the gatekeeper to ensure safe passage through the plaza of any illicit contraband (e.g., drugs, weapons, laundered cash, humans, etc.), whose owner has paid a hefty transit tax. For example, the tax on the movement of "…a kilo of cocaine is approximately $500, while the tax on $1 million in cash heading south is about $10,000."[21] Since trafficking involves tons of drugs and it is a multibillion dollar industry, a gatekeeper makes vast sums of money in collected taxes for every illicit transaction to permit the crossing through his plaza.[22]

The cartel established as gatekeeper ensures safe passage of illicit traffic by operating "…in whatever manner best suits a given circumstance: intimidation, extortion or violence. Of course, one of their main jobs is to ensure that corrupt Mexican police and military are paid off so plaza operations can proceed undisturbed."[23] The cartel may also invest in sophisticated cross-border tunneling, with lighting and in some cases wide enough to fit a vehicle. Since September 11, 2001, U.S. authorities, perhaps monitoring more closely, have increased their yearly discoveries of cartel tunnels from one to ten. Most of the tunneling has occurred from Tijuana across the border into San Diego and from Mexicali to Calexico.[24] In support of these illicit operations, the gatekeeper will obtain warehouses to stash drugs, set up safe-houses to hide their enforcers, and will recruit drivers to transport the drugs across the border and throughout the United States.[25] Furthermore, the smugglers can obtain counterfeit and even genuine documents at the crossing points.[26] Additionally, the gatekeepers also move money:

> Because some provisions of the U.S. Patriot Act have made wiring money out of the United States more complicated than before – forcing the cartels to physically transfer money between operatives along the border – the gatekeepers also must ensure that these operations run smoothly. To facilitate this, the gatekeepers operate the cartels' money laundering operations, using small businesses along the border....[27]

Finally, while in previous years cartels would avoid a shootout with U.S. authorities and even abandon their cargo if discovered, now they are prepared to fight, employing "...military style weapons and technology, utilizing counter surveillance techniques and acting aggressively against both law enforcement and competitors."[28]

The Mexican Cartels at War

Threat Warning

"In 1996, [U.S. Drug Enforcement Agency] DEA Director Thomas A. Constantine denounced the existence of a Mexican drug trafficking federation made up of four major cartels; the Tijuana Organization, the

Sonora Cartel, the Juarez Cartel, and the Gulf Group. (See Figure 12.2.)"[29] This was the coalition forged in 1989 by Felix Gallardo as head of the Tijuana Cartel. They were the most powerful of the Mexican mafias because they controlled the plazas, which are the key to the U.S.-Mexico border and access to the United States.

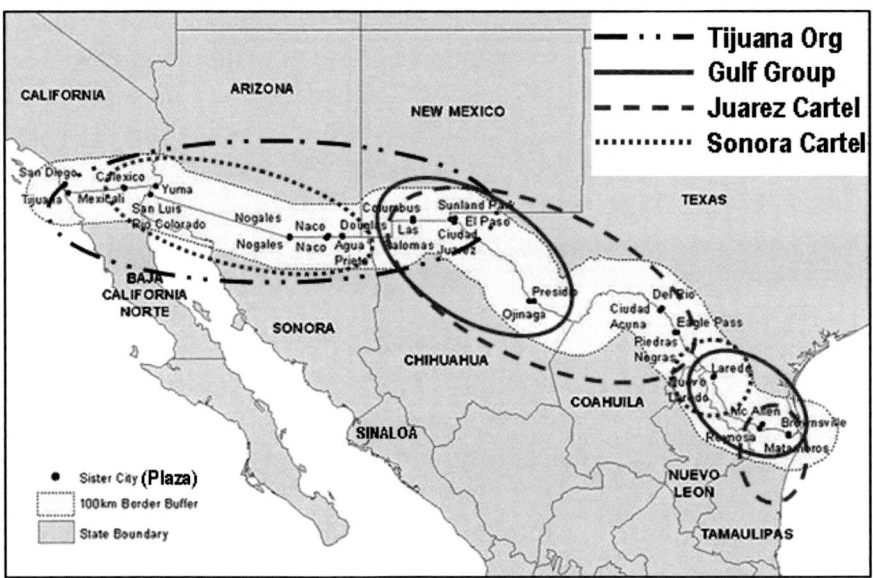

Figure 12.2 Mexican Cartels with Influence in the Border Areas, circa 2001[30]

It had been estimated in the 1990s that the drug lords of Mexico earned $6 billion to $15 billion per year.[31] However, according to United Nations' 2005 statistics, the Mexican drug cartels sit on top of "…a $142 billion a year business in cocaine, heroin, marijuana, methamphetamine, and other illicit drugs."[32] Furthermore, the major drug cartels, which control the plazas, tax or directly control profitable human smuggling rings. The cost to an illegal alien ranges from $1,500 for a Mexican peasant[33] to $60,000 for a non-Mexican desiring a secure and even comfortable transit across the border. Additionally, human smuggling carries less risk because, if the smuggler is caught by the U.S. Border Patrol, the likely outcome is release and repatriation.[34] The bottom-line is that the major Mexican cartels are well-financed to defend their enterprises and wage war for control of the U.S.-Mexico border.

The Mexican Cartel War Commences

In April 1989, the head of the Tijuana Organization, Miguel Felix Gallardo, was captured and sent to jail in Mexico for the 1985 savage kidnapping and slaying of DEA Agent Enrique Camarena. Nonetheless, due to Mexican government corruption, Felix Gallardo was able to continue to direct his cartel from prison. However, under U.S. pressure, Mexico moved him to a high security prison. His departure brought to power his nephews, the seven Arellano Brothers, with Benjamin Arellano as "Chief Executive Officer."[35] Perhaps, due to the temporary power vacuum caused by Felix Gallardo's removal or the new policies of the Arellanos, the net result was a split in the Tijuana Cartel. The new organization became known as the Sinaloa Cartel because it was centered in the Mexican State of Sinaloa.

The Arellanos' new policy was to end cooperation based on common agreement and instead moved to take absolute control of the Tijuana and Mexicali Plazas. By 1992, they had achieved their goal and during a summit of major drug lords they unilaterally raised taxes for the use of their plazas. The Sinaloa Cartel saw this as a direct affront, since they needed these two corridors to push their drugs into the U.S. market. Their response was to send gunmen to assassinate the Arellanos while they were gathered in a crowded discotheque; the attempt failed. The Arellanos retaliated by attempting to kill the head of the Sinaloa Cartel, Joaquin "Chapo" Guzman, in Guadalajara Airport. They misidentified their target and instead killed Catholic Cardinal Juan Jesus Posadas Ocampo, who coincidently arrived at the airport in a similar car as Mr. Guzman. By 1996, despite DEA Chief Constantine's belief that there was an overarching drug federation, the Mexican Cartel War for control of the plazas was underway in earnest.[36]

The Cartels Organize for War

In 1998, perhaps in an effort to shore up its war effort against the Sinaloa organization, the Tijuana Cartel entered into "...an understanding of collaboration…" with the smaller Sonora Cartel, which amounted to a merger.[37] In the following years, the various syndicates all sought alliances, hired better trained personnel, bought better technology, and acquired heavier weapons in an effort to organize and endure in a very cruel war. In fact, the surviving Mexican cartels evolved into very robust unconventional war fighting organizations able to absorb their cartel war losses, keep organizational cohesion, and maintain their profit margin. Note the Tijuana cartel's division of labor and organization in Figure 12.3.

Element	Purpose
Leadership	• Arellano Felix Family and a Council of Advisers o Makes the key decisions and provides orders to the five divisions defined below.
Intelligence & Negotiations	• Collects and provides information to the Leadership. • Infiltrates government institutions and law enforcement agencies. • Makes contact with foreign criminal organizations. • Negotiates agreements (e.g., number of shipments, quotas, prices, distribution, etc.)
Assassins	• Eliminates rivals, law enforcement agents, and traitors. • Provides Leadership protection. • Escorts drug cargoes.
Finances	• Conducts money laundering activities. • Decides where to invest drug wealth to minimize detection by the authorities.
Logistics	• Receives and distributes drug shipments and other illicit trafficking.
Special Intelligence	• Collects and provides information on the competition to the Leadership. • Manages spies whose prime responsibility is to monitor rival cartel activity.

Figure 12.3 Tijuana Cartel's Organization[38]

Figure 12.3 shows the organizational elements and their purpose in a typical cartel. Time and again, U.S. and Mexican officials have reported the demise of a Mexican cartel only to find that it had merely joined with another cartel or managed to reorganize. This was the case in the early months of 2002, when the Sinaloa Cartel made a major push to seize the Tijuana Plaza from the Arellano Felix Organization. They had assumed incorrectly that the death of Ramon Arellano Felix (head of the Tijuana Organization) in a police shootout might have weakened or disorganized the Tijuana Cartel. The miscalculation caused over 220 people to be murdered in a very short period, mostly from the Sinaloa Cartel, who failed to gain control of the plaza.[39]

The police gunned down Ramon Arellano in Matzatlan, in the Mexican State of Sinaloa. He was there leading a group of assassins in search of "El Mayo" Zambada, head of a new mid-sized cartel that operates out of Sinaloa, which was refusing to pay the Arellano Felix Organization $20 million in "taxes" owed for the use of the Tijuana Plaza. However, El Mayo survived and his Zambada Cartel joined the Sinaloa Federation.[40]

Chapo Guzman may have formed the Federation in response to a meeting in jail between Benjamin Arellano (Head of Tijuana Organization) and Osiel Cardenas (Head of the Gulf Group), which resulted in an alliance. Cardenas was imprisoned in March 2003 and Arellano the previous year. One issue that facilitated collaboration was that they controlled plazas at opposite ends of the U.S.-Mexico border as shown in Figure 12.4. Another issue was that both groups were under pressure from new organizations. For example, in Mexico's northeastern border, the Millennium Cartel, a new group with strong Colombian ties was making incursions into Gulf Cartel territory, specifically the plazas of Nuevo Laredo and Matamoros. (See Figure 12.4.) Meanwhile, the Juarez Cartel, who was fighting the Gulf Group, had key leaders arrested and its remaining members chose to join with Guzman's Sinaloa Federation.[41]

Although the Arellanos may have triggered the war by charging excessive taxes, U.S. border officials regard Chapo Guzman's ambition as the primary driver in the continuing cartel war.[42] After being checked in his attempt to seize the Tijuana and Mexicali Plazas, his cartel pushed into Sonora territory, apparently absorbing or displacing lesser drug cartels and human smuggling rings in that area. Guzman's aim was to control all illicit trafficking operations into Arizona. The U.S. Border Patrol believes that to this point he has won; a Border Patrol spokesman for the Tucson, Arizona, sector referred to the plazas as "…Chapo Guzman's territory."

Another U.S. law enforcement official was quoted as saying, "Chapo's ambition is nothing short of taking control of the Mexican border."[43]

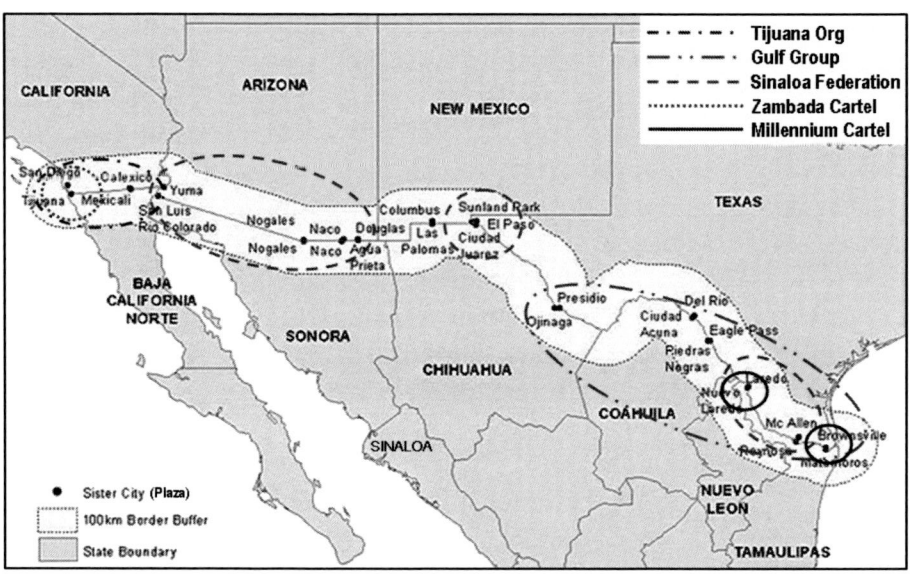

Figure 12.4 Mexican Cartels with Influence in the Border Areas, circa 2006[44]

The Violence Escalates and Spreads

In Colombia, *La Violencia* is the name given to a period (1948-1958) during which "…a state of undeclared civil war… claimed over 200,000 lives…."[45] In fact, the violence morphed from a public desire for socioeconomic change into a war against and among narco terrorists, which continues to this day.[46] Similarly, Mexico today is engulfed in a conflict where uneven socioeconomic development coupled to the drug trade has given opportunities for violent smuggling enterprises to grow powerful for waging war against each other and the state.

Effectively, by 2006, two major camps were engaged in the Mexican Drug Cartel War. One was the Sinaloa Federation, including the Zambada Cartel, and the other being the alliance of the Tijuana and Gulf organizations. While these drug coalitions battled, interlopers such as the

Millennium Cartel took the opportunity to attempt to gain a foothold on the border. Additionally, the war gave the Colombians a chance to reestablish themselves in Mexico. One such organization is the Arias Cartel and another is the FARC (Revolutionary Armed Forces of Colombia), a leftist narco-terrorist organization that has largely abandoned its ideological roots in favor of the lucrative drug market. Another reason for the return of the Colombians was to protect their drug interests, from which Mexican cartels and Central American gangs had been stealing.[47]

All these criminal organizations are fighting in the Mexican cities along the border, but often the conflict spills into the United States. For example, "In 2005, [U.S.] law enforcement linked at least three drug related killings in the Dallas area to the Zetas [former members of the Mexican Special Forces working for the Gulf Group as an elite paramilitary outfit]. Texas law enforcement authorities believe a squad of Zeta members, as many as ten, might be operating inside Texas...."[48]

One can surmise that the Zetas cross-border operations are related to the three-way conflict raging in Nuevo Laredo, Mexico. The Gulf Group is defending this plaza while the Sinaloa Federation and the Millennium Cartel aim to wrest control of the area from them. The value of the Nuevo Laredo-Laredo plaza is related to the considerable law-abiding commercial traffic; specifically:

> The Laredo Port of Entry is the busiest and most heavily traversed land port of entry on the southwest border, handling approximately 6,000 commercial vehicles a day. [Forty] percent of all Mexican exports cross into Laredo, Texas, where Interstate 35 connects directly to Dallas, and from there throughout the United States.[49]

The cartel calculations must show that when embedded in a high volume of lawful commerce unlawful smuggling has a better probability of success. Similarly, another busy commercial crossing point is Tijuana, Mexico, into San Diego, California; consequently, this is another Mexican city involved in terrible violence. In fact, every border city throughout Mexico has witnessed increases in violence as the cartels ferociously fought with challengers and the authorities in defense of their claimed territory.

"Attack with Grenades," "7 bodies found," "Three Kidnapped and Others Murdered," and "Two De-Quartered Bodies Found": These are not Iraq news headlines but, rather, they are headlines from daily newspapers across Mexico reporting on drug-related violence. Available statistics show that in 2006 between 1,800 to 2,200 people were murdered in gangland violence, and in the first three months of 2007 at least 535 suspected drug-related murders took place including those of 78 policemen. The rest of the casualties were participants in the cartel war, but too often innocent bystanders are caught in the crossfire.[50]

Cartel methods of killing and intimidation include decapitations and publicly displaying the severed heads, boiling human beings in acid, and burning a tire around the victim's neck.[51] They have put Mexico in a state of fear and the local police and the media have been intimidated. For example, in Villa Madero, Michoacán, the entire town's 32-member police force quit en masse in response to cartel threats. The media in Mexico is also afraid to report on the corruption and the violence in meaningful detail. For example, they seldom name names for fear of retribution from the cartels. President Vicente Fox proclaimed freedom of the press following his election, which ended the 71-year reign of the Institutional Revolutionary Party (PRI). However, gunmen have brazenly attacked crowded newsrooms and "...now [Mexico] ranks only second to Colombia in terms of murdered journalists...."[52]

The Mexican Authorities

The Problem of Defections

In general, Mexican security forces are underpaid, poorly equipped, and demoralized to the point that even elite units defect to the cartels. The most shocking example was when in early 2000 Mexican authorities began to take note of highly trained and well-armed assassins working for the Gulf Cartel. The unit is called the Zetas and they were previously members of Mexico's most elite special forces – the Airmobile Special Forces Group (GAFE). It is believed that since at least 1991, members of the GAFE have been encouraged to defect and operate as a private army for the Cardenas Family. There may be over 500 members, who are vicious, armed with high-tech equipment, and employ sophisticated combat tactics. "The Zetas are believed to be a serious threat to public safety on both sides of the Southwest border."[53]

The formation of this unit was an escalation in the lethality of the cartel war. The Zetas have expanded recruitment to include Mexican local and federal law enforcement personnel, as well as, gang members and ex-Kaibil soldiers (Guatemala's elite jungle fighters renowned for their toughness and brutality). Since the introduction of the Zetas, all cartels fighting for the border plazas have formed militias armed with heavy weapons. In particular, the Sinaloa Federation countered the Gulf Group with its own heavily armed private army called Los Negros (a.k.a. Los Pelones), which is recruited in the same fashion as the Zetas. In Nuevo Laredo, during an 18-month period, the two paramilitary forces clashed, killing over 230 people and wounding hundreds more.[54] Mexico's local and even federal police cannot stem the violence and too often become victims of the cartel war.

The Mexican Police

Reporting on a Tijuana police call, a *Los Angeles Times* article stated, "A convoy of 40 vehicles carrying 70 heavily armed and masked men was prowling the streets of Rosarito Beach on Tuesday evening [June 20, 2006]. The three police officers who arrived were quickly abducted. The next morning their mutilated bodies turned up in an empty lot. Their heads were found in the Tijuana River later that day."[55] In Nuevo Laredo, on June 8, 2005, a new police chief assumed office promising to be tough on crime and police corruption; he was murdered six hours later. In response, Mexican President Vicente Fox ordered the military and federal police to remove the local police and assume the responsibilities until a new vetted police force was formed. Three-hundred and five of 765 police officers were dismissed due to corruption; 41 of them shamelessly fought against the federal police and had to be arrested.[56] In another disregard for the Mexican authorities, in 2004, 40 men armed with AK-47 and R-15 rifles stormed a prison in Apatzingan in the State of Michoacán. They were wearing Mexican Army and Federal Agency of Investigation (Mexico's FBI) uniforms. According to the Mexican Office of the Attorney General, the assumption was that they were Zetas since five leading members of the Gulf Group were freed, along with another fourteen prisoners perhaps to create confusion.[57]

Despite the Zetas, Thomas Constantine's testimony of 1997 remains true; he said, "The Government of Mexico, as a result of continuing incidents of corruption in the civilian law enforcement institutions, transferred much of the narcotics enforcement efforts from the police to the Government of Mexico military."[58] The Mexican police have failed miserably to measure up to the requirements of their jobs. For example, regarding Nuevo Laredo, in 2006, U.S. Ambassador to Mexico Tony Garza was forced to take "…an unprecedented number of actions to address the escalating crisis," including a reassessment of U.S. consulate security, sending diplomatic notes to complain about the border violence, and issuing an advisory to Americans traveling to Mexico.[59] Earlier in 2005, President Fox reinforced the police in Nuevo Laredo, with 1,500 soldiers. Nevertheless, the results were dismal. By May 2006, the murder rate in the city had doubled, when compared to the same five month period of the previous year.[60]

The Mexican Military

In general, Mexican officials do not publicly impugn their police or military organizations for their inability to stop the violence. Paradoxically, they blame the increase in violence on the U.S. authorities' inability to control the border, through which a flood of illegal weapons are crossing into Mexico and the U.S. consumers of the cartels illegal products. In February 2007, the Mexican military in Matamoros, just south of Brownsville, Texas, stopped a tractor trailer being escorted by men in a pickup truck, which was fitted with armor and bulletproof glass. The trailer was carrying weapons, which included, "…18 M-16 assault rifles, one equipped with an M-203 40mm grenade launcher…, several M-4 carbines, 17 handguns…, 200 magazines for various weapons, 8,000 rounds of ammunition, assault vests and other military accessories." Although the point of origin was not immediately determined, the vehicles were headed south when intercepted.[61]

Although Mexico has a point regarding the flow of illegal weapons to Mexico from the United States, another problem is a lack of trust between the Mexican military, and federal and local police. In 2002, it was the

GAFE that captured Benjamin Arellano (Leader of the Tijuana Cartel); this action was taken by the military without prior coordination with the Office of the Attorney General (PGR) or local police.[62] The United States applauded President Fox's decision to deploy the military against the cartels. In December 2006, shortly after taking office and in response to the U.S. ambassador, Mexico's President Felipe Calderon signaled that he would be even tougher on the cartels, when he ordered an additional 3,300 troops to operate between Nuevo Laredo and Matamoros on Mexico's northeastern border.[63] Clearly, it is now on the shoulders of the Mexican military to turn the tide against the cartels and it is an effort that the United States has been willing to support for some time.

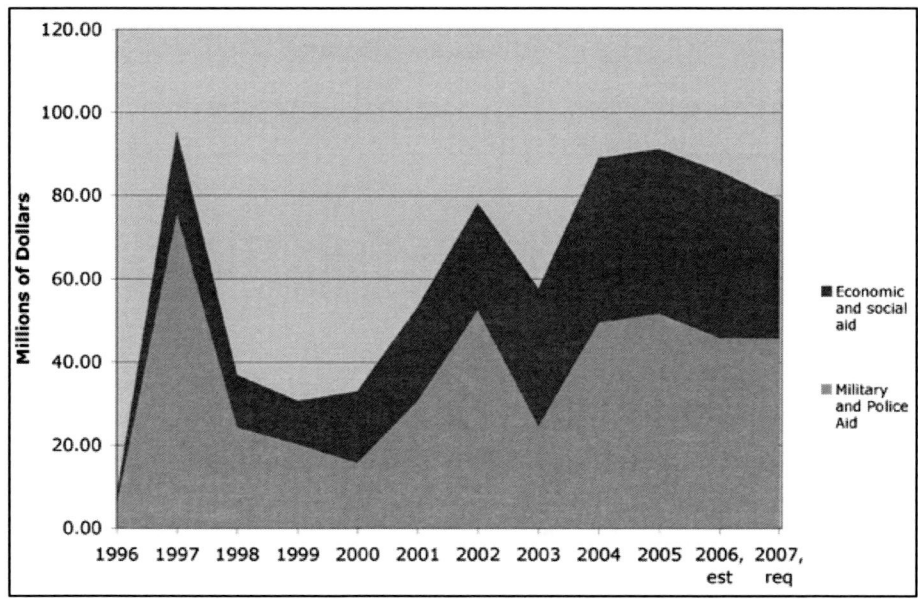

Figure 12.5 United States Aid to Mexico[64]

Unfortunately, unlike Colombia, where U.S. authorities enjoy a very close working relationship, the association in Mexico can best be described as professional but distant. One must blame history; the Mexican population still smarts from the outcome of the U.S.-Mexican War and the 1916 U.S. military "punitive" operation in Mexico that have acted as stumbling blocks to a close security cooperation. Regardless, the relationship began to improve in 1995, when for the first time a U.S. Secretary of Defense, William Perry, visited Mexico. As a result, U.S. aid to Mexico increased dramatically. (See Figure 12.5.) Regrettably, military cooperation remains uneven with Mexico's two defense ministries: the predominant Ministry of Defense (Army and Air Force) and the lesser Ministry of the Navy.[65]

The Mexican Navy, perhaps because their operations occur beyond the eyes of the Mexican media and politicians, has been willing to work closely with the U.S. Navy and Coast Guard. Whereas the Ministry of Defense, while ready to send military personnel to train in the United States at U.S. expense, seldom allows U.S. mobile training teams into their country and military-to-military border cooperation usually amounts to some information-sharing but not much actual coordination. This has had significant negative impact on efforts to address the cartel problem.[66]

The American Authorities

The U.S. Drug Enforcement Agency (DEA)

DEA is the lead government agency for U.S. counter-drug operations inside Mexico; as such, they maintain very good relations with the PGR and Mexican Navy. The relationship is not as close with the Ministry of Defense. Consequently, the bulk of U.S. aid has been targeted towards the PGR and Ministry of the Navy.[67] However, DEA, despite some headline grabbing achievements against narco-traffickers, continues to claim overall success despite facts to the contrary. In June 3, 2004, a special unit of the Federal Agency of Investigation (AFI), in coordination with U.S. authorities, captured two key members of the Tijuana Cartel (Jorge Arellano-Felix and Efrain Perez) in *Operation United Eagle*. DEA Administrator Karen P. Tandy declared, "The Arellano-Felix Organization is now in ruins…"[68] This turned out to be both premature and completely inaccurate.

If the Tijuana Cartel was finished, then who was cruising Tijuana on the night of June 20, 2006, in "…a convoy of 40 vehicles carrying 70 heavily armed and masked men…" willing to kill and decapitate three police officers? The DEA has conducted many successful operations, capturing traffickers, weapons, and vast amounts of cash and drugs, e.g., *Operation Imperial Emperor* (concluded in 2007), *United Eagle* (2004), *Impunity and Millennium* (1999), etc. Nevertheless, the strategic objective must be to regain control of the U.S. southwest border. In this undertaking, the DEA plays a supporting role to the U.S. Border Patrol.

The U.S. Border Patrol

While the DEA bathes in the accolades of the big bust and temporary success against the Mexican cartels, the U.S. Border Patrol (USBP) must struggle day-to-day in the porous trenches of the U.S. southwestern border. Only 12,300 Border Patrol agents are available to man border checkpoints covering over 5,000 miles of border with Canada, 9,500 miles of shoreline, and the nearly 2,000 miles of border with Mexico.[69] On the Canadian border, there are approximately 1,000 agents. Nearly 8,000 are deployed to the southwestern region of the United States and it is not enough. The National Border Patrol Strategy states, "CBP [Customs and Border Protection] Border Patrol has strengthened its partnerships with Canadian law enforcement and intelligence officials...." It does not make the same claim regarding Mexico. Instead, it admits, "...The southwest border is not under operational control..." and warns, "The Border Patrol arrests hundreds of aliens each year from "special interest" (sic) countries [the Department of State identifies such countries as presenting a potential terrorist threat]."[70]

The U.S. relationship with Mexican authorities that patrol the common border must be considered poor. For example, on January 24, 2006, Sara Carter, an investigative journalist for the *Inland Valley Daily Bulletin*, reported on MSNBC's *Scarborough Country* that Mexican military units were routinely crossing into the United States, providing security to drug smugglers. She claimed to have documented proof of at least 216 incidents over a 10-year period.[71] During this same MSNBC segment, T.J. Bonner, President of the National Border Patrol Council, confirmed Carter's story and assured viewers the number was much higher and that on several occasions, U.S. Border Patrol had been fired upon and taken casualties.[72]

Despite the use of military grade equipment and the professional tactics employed by Mexican cartel paramilitaries, perhaps some of these incidents did not involve Mexican personnel. Nevertheless, one issue is certain. United States law enforcement has little faith in their Mexican counterparts. Furthermore, USBP and local sheriffs and their deputies are outgunned at the border. This situation is made even worse because the cartels have also implemented more aggressive tactics:

> At one time, members or associates of Mexican drug cartels would drop the drugs or abandon their vehicles when confronted by U.S. law enforcement. Similarly, human smugglers would simply give up when approached or stopped on the highway. This is no longer the case. The drug cartels no longer tolerate compliance. Loads of both drugs and humans are vigorously protected by direct confrontation, high speed chases, and standoffs at the Rio Grande River.[73]

The growing incidents of violence originating from Mexico confirm that neither Mexico nor the United States have taken appropriate measures to deter the cartels. "From 2004 to 2005, violent incidents against Border Patrol agents on the southwest border have increased 108 [percent]." During 2006, the USBP suffered "…746 violent incidents…, [including] 46 vehicle assaults, and 43 were firearm assaults." Other violent crime blamed on the de facto open border includes 49 reported abductions of U.S. citizens between May 2004 and July 2006; a number believed to "…represent only a fraction of the actual occurrences, since many kidnappings of U.S. citizens go unreported." Primarily due to inferior weaponry, U.S. sheriffs in border cities and towns have advised their deputies to "back-off," when confronted by cartel members.[74]

The Border Crisis Finally Gets National Attention

Militarizing the U.S. Southwestern Border

President George W. Bush addressed the nation on May 15, 2006. He was primarily addressing the issue of illegal migration, when he provided strategic guidance to the government agencies involved in the form of "five clear objectives." The first objective dealt with securing the borders. Regarding the border with Mexico, the President said, "The border should be open to trade and lawful immigration, and shut to illegal immigrants, as well as criminals, drug dealers, and terrorists."[75]

The President's speech was nearly 5-years overdue. Despite the 9/11 terrorist attack, President Bush candidly admitted, "For decades the United States has not been in complete control of its borders." President Bush did remind listeners that he had already "…expanded the Border Patrol from 9,000 to 12,000 agents." Considering the very high level of border violence and the volume of illicit trafficking across the border, this number remains insignificant and fails to act as much of a deterrent to daily violations of the U.S.-Mexico border. President Bush has also promised 6,000 more agents, along with "…high-tech fences in urban corridors…, motion sensors, infrared cameras, and unmanned aerial vehicles…." However, President Bush also declared, "The United States is not going to militarize the southern border…."[76]

Arguably, President Bush's statement on militarization is simply meant to placate Mexican sentiments. Los Pelones, los Zetas, and corrupt Mexican military units are using "…rocket propelled grenades, automatic assault weapons, and "level-four" (sic) body armor and Kevlar helmets…" in the conduct of their drug and alien smuggling operations. The USBP even believes that the cartels are able to break radio communication encryptions.[77] The United States must respond to this threat and, although the Department of Defense was not tasked, President Bush did direct as many as 6,000 National Guardsmen to the southwestern border. It's called *Operation Jump Start* and it tasks the Guard with supporting the USBP for at least 2-years to allow time for the training and deployment of additional border patrol agents. The Guardsmen will engage in non-law enforcement duties, such as, surveillance, construction, and training of USBP personnel. The intent is to release USBP agents from these roles and move them to the border.[78] While President Bush may not fully militarize the border with Mexico, he has taken initial steps to better arm, train, and equip the U.S. Border Patrol. These actions are necessary if the USBP hopes to deter the Mexican cartels and one day reclaim operational control of the nation's border with Mexico.

The Threat within Human Smuggling

Despite the Al Qaeda 9/11 incident and the ongoing violence in the Mexican border cities, America's leaders' unwillingness to fully secure its southwestern border is irresponsible. Following the recent defeat of immigration reform in Congress, President Bush said that he would, "...continue to take every possible step to build upon the progress already made in strengthening our borders, enforcing our worksite laws, keeping our economy well-supplied with *vital workers*...."[79] Immigration reform failed in Congress because it was viewed as not doing enough to regain control of the nation's border with Mexico. The prevailing attitude in government circles, including the President, is that illegal migrants are "vital workers" for the U.S. economy, i.e., cheap labor for the nation to compete in a globalized market. However, one can also surmise that most American citizens considered the illegal migrants as lawbreakers; a daily reminder of the prevailing smuggling problem and the threat that among the economic refugees streaming across the border there may also be a number of Islamic terrorists bent on inflicting catastrophic harm to the nation.[80]

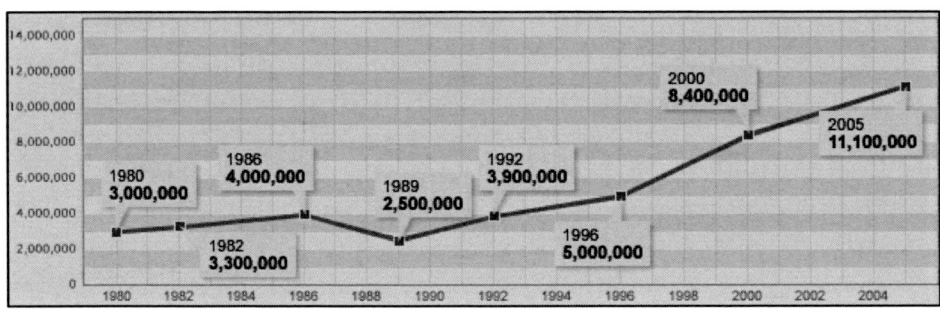

Figure 12.6 Estimated Number of Illegal Immigrants in the United States[81]

Seeing the opportunity, Mexican cartels have expanded their trafficking operations to include human smuggling. Today, Mexico's human smugglers contribute to over 80 percent of the illegal migration into the United States every year. This is approximately a half of a million undocumented aliens entering the United States annually through the southwest border. (See Figure 12.6.)[82] Regrettably, Mexico is fueled by a culture of corruption that keeps over 40 percent of the population in poverty and without financial opportunity. By way of comparison, Mexico has a per capita income of less than $10,700 to America's over $44,000.[83] As a result, the United States acts as an economic relief valve for millions of undocumented Mexicans to work in the United States, instead of placing demands for change on their own government.

Nevertheless, the United States must crack down at the U.S.-Mexico border for reasons of homeland security. The evidence is strong that the Islamic terrorist enemy is at the southwest gate and may already be inside. The number of illegal aliens from countries "Other Than Mexico" (OTM) entering the United States across the southwestern border has climbed dramatically in the last five years. OTM apprehensions in 2005 numbered 165,178, whereas in 2002 it had been 37,316 arrests. The overwhelming numbers of OTM entries are from Latin America but U.S. authorities must be cautious because 15,000 to 20,000 apprehensions per year are from special interest countries (SIC), including those classified as a state sponsor of terrorism (SST).[84] This also raises the question about how many of these SIC and SST infiltrators were not apprehended and now live among us.

Furthermore, alarms should be ringing because USBP is finding evidence of possible Islamic terrorist activity on the border. For example, during a patrol along the Rio Grande, USBP agents found… "A jacket with patches from countries where [Al Qaeda] is known to operate…. The patches on the jacket show an Arabic military badge with one depicting an airplane flying over a building and heading towards a tower…. The bottom of one patch read 'martyr,' 'way to eternal life' or 'way to immortality' (sic)."[85] Also, on September 8, 2004, U.S. Immigration and Customs Enforcement (ICE) testified on having dismantled a human smuggling ring, which specialized in moving Iraqi, Jordanian, and Syrian nationals across the border from Mexico. Most alarming was one case where, "On March 1, 2005, Mahmoud Youssef Kourani pleaded guilty to providing material support to Hezbollah. Kourani is an illegal alien who had been smuggled across the U.S.-Mexico border…. [He is also] …the brother of the Hezbollah chief of military operations in southern Lebanon."[86]

One could argue that the cartels will not risk a U.S. crackdown along the common border by knowingly transporting Islamic terrorists into the United States. Of course, the immediate flaw in this argument is that it places the security of the United States in the hands of outlaws whose primary interest is in making money. Kourani entered the United States "…after bribing a Mexican consular official in Beirut for a visa to travel to Mexico. Kourani and a Middle Eastern traveling partner then paid coyotes in Mexico to guide them into the United States…."[87] Apparently, cartel gatekeepers are not very stringent on who they allow to cross into the United States. U.S. authorities must assume that cartel plazas for accessing the United States are available to anyone willing to pay.

Measures of Ineffectiveness

In an effort to show improvement, the USBP compared two 5-month periods, October 2005 to February 2006 and October 2006 to February 2007, and reported a 30 percent decrease in arrests at the Mexico border. Therefore, they conclude that border security was improving and less people were trying to cross for fear of arrest.[88] Certainly, the availability of more agents at the border due to the deployment of the National Guard may be a factor. Additionally, President Bush and the U.S. Congress are paying closer attention to the southwestern border; hence, there is greater scrutiny on USBP actions, perhaps causing a surge on their part.

Of course, there are other possibilities. For example, less people are crossing because some coyotes cannot afford to pay the tax to the gatekeepers, who control the border plazas. Also, the increased violence caused by the ongoing Mexican Cartel War may deter some from crossing. Finally, one cannot discount the possibility that human smugglers might have become more successful at avoiding detection.[89]

One good indicator as to whether less illegal migration is a measure of greater U.S. control and security at the border is to read the drug data. According to the DEA, "Approximately 72 percent of the cocaine entering the United States moves across the Southwest Border."[90] Reported decreases in border crossings have not affected cocaine smuggling operations. The numbers of cocaine seizures have gone up dramatically over the last 20 years, increasing from 100,000 kg to over 600,000 kg per year.[91] Disappointingly, this measure is indicative of greater drug smuggling and not necessarily greater proficiency on the part of the counter-drug authorities. One simply has to look at the decreasing street value of cocaine to understand that the U.S.-Mexico border remains porous. (See Figure 12.7.) Therefore, the USBP claim of less human smuggling does not relate to better U.S. border controls because drugs are still getting through and in vast quantities.

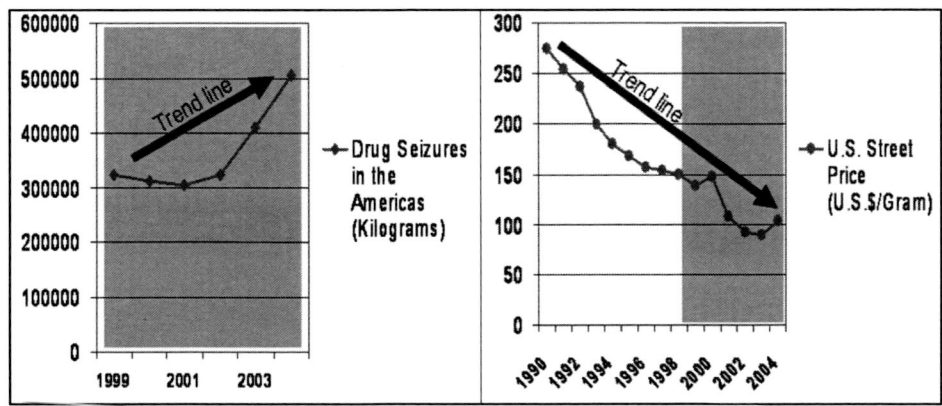

Figure 12.7 Cocaine Seizures vs. U.S. Street Value of Cocaine[92]

Conclusion

In 2007, the Mexican Cartel War raged on, with the balance of power tilting in favor of the Sinaloa Federation. The Gulf Group and Tijuana Organization alliance was shredded by Mexican military and Sinaloa Federation operations. The weakening of the Gulf Cartel may leave the Zetas without a master and under pressure from Sinaloa forces. The Zetas could seek sanctuary inside the United States, bringing their style of violence into Texas and beyond. The Tijuana Organization has also lost ground against the Sinaloa cartel along Mexico's northwestern border. The latter controls the Mexicali Plaza now, and the Arellano Brothers only control the Tijuana Plaza. The Sinaloa Federation is poised to press the war in Nuevo Laredo against the Gulf Group and in Tijuana, to perhaps finally finish the Tijuana Organization.[93]

Chapo Guzman's goal of controlling the entire U.S.-Mexico border may be within his grasp. However, the history of the Mexican drug wars is replete with inconclusive outcomes. There is always another gang or cartel waiting for an opportunity to gain control of the border action. The evidence shows that drugs are flowing almost unabated north into the United States and sophisticated weapons south into Mexico. The northern border cities of Mexico are becoming ungovernable. It will require a formidable military effort and much bloodshed for the government forces to deprive Guzman's Sinaloa Federation, or the other aspiring cartels and gangs, control of Mexico's northern frontier. One should conclude that Mexico has been "Colombinized."

Some U.S. and Mexican officials may have reasoned that an open border was a benefit to both nations. The United States would have access to cheap labor and Mexico an economic relief valve as one means of national stability. However, the Mexican cartels undermined this equation when they seized control of the border. They are polluting the United States with drugs and crime; while the money and weapons coming into Mexico are empowering cartels, which slowly undermine the rule of law in the Mexican border cities and throughout the country. Furthermore, Radical Islam has discovered the exposed soft underbelly of America, the U.S. southwestern border. They also know that the cartels have a common thread; they are all for-profit organizations. For the right price, a gatekeeper will facilitate unimpeded entry into the United States.

The U.S. Government is planning to fence long sections of the border. Fencing may deter small-time coyotes, who cannot afford a gatekeeper's taxes. However, the Mexican cartels own the plazas. They use the major highways to intermingle with the legal trade and lawful immigration, and when necessary, they tunnel their way across. Therefore, illicit trafficking, high crime, and the threat of Islamic terrorism will likely continue unabated. In addition to strengthening border security of the north side of the southwest border, and in doing a better job in educating and persuading our population not to consume illegal drugs, the United States must also increase political pressure on the Mexican authorities to allow closer security cooperation and coordination. The strong trade relations we enjoy with Mexico beyond these illegalities and U.S. reticence to use military force inside Mexico will prevent an armed intervention. In the end, the Mexican Ministry of Defense must be convinced to tolerate close ties with U.S. authorities as to develop a common winning campaign against the Mexican cartels. Otherwise, the United States will drastically militarize the border, either to defend against potential terrorism or in the aftermath of another 9/11 event originating from Mexico.

Notes

1. "External Affairs: Mexico," *Jane's Sentinel Security Assessment – Central America and The Caribbean,* 15 March 2007, Jane's Information Group, On-line, Internet, 21 April 2007, available from www8.janes.com/Search.

2. Friedrich Katz, *The Life and Times of Pancho Villa*, Stanford University Press, 1998, 560-570.

3. J. Chabat, "Mexico's War on Drugs: No Margin for Maneuver," in the *Annals of the American Academy of Political and Social Science,* Vol. 582, Cross-National Drug Policy, Sage Publications, Inc., July 2002, 135-136.

4. D.E. Teicher, "The Decisive Phase of Colombia's War on Narco-Terrorism," Counterproliferation Papers, Future Warfare Series No. 28, Maxwell AFB, AL: USAF Counterproliferation Center, January 2005, 21.

5. D.E. Schulz, *Between a Rock and a Hard Place: The United States, Mexico, and the Agony of National Security*, Strategic Studies Institute Special Report, U.S. Army War College, 24 June 1997, 2.

6. Ibid.

7. Chabat, op. cit., 135.

8. M. Goodman, "Muerto, Inc.," *Frontline*, 1997, On-line, Internet, 16 August 2007, available from www.pbs.org/wgbb/pages/frontline/shows/mexico/readings.

9. "Suspect Maritime Activity: 1 January 2005 – 20 December 2005," U.S. Southern Command, DoD, unclassified, PPT Slide showing Joint Interagency Task Force South maritime tracks of known smugglers embarked on go-fast boats (a 30-40 ft. vessel, with four or more outboard engines, designed for high speed), fishing boats, and other vessels, which refers to larger ocean-going ships. A movement of drugs is considered a two stage process because *stage 1* is the maritime crossing to Mexico, and often to Guatemala or Belize, then *stage 2* is the land crossing of Mexico north into the United States.

10. O. Becerra, "Tijuana Cartel Fights for its Future," 15 November 2002, in *Jane's Intelligence Review, Systematic Transnational Crime,* 1 December 2002, On-line, Internet, 22 April 2007, available from www8.janes.com/Search.

11. M. G. Manwaring, *Street Gangs: The New Urban Insurgency*, Strategic Studies Institute, March 2005, 9-10.

12. Goodman, op. cit.

13. A. Corchado, "Mexican Drug Cartels Move into Peru," 8 January 2007, in *The Dallas Morning News*, On-line, Internet, 15 August 2007, available from www.dallasnews.com/sharedcontent/dws/news/world/mexico/stories. The Shinning Path was once a violent and powerful Maoist guerilla movement, which may be regaining strength thanks largely to drug traffickers.

14. Ibid.

15. "Department of Defense Dictionary of Military and Associated Terms (as Amended through 13 June 2007,)" *Joint Publication 1-02*, Joint Staff, 12 April 2001, 540.

16. W.L. Burnham, Maj., U.S. Army, "Drug Epidemic not War," CSC, 1992, *GlobalSecurity.Org*, On-line, Internet, 15 August 2007, available from www.globalsecurity.org/military/library/report/1992/BWI.htm.

17. Becerra, "Tijuana Cartel Fights for its Future," op. cit.

18. Ibid.

19. Sister City – Along the U.S.-Mexico Border, a Mexican city usually stands next to an American city, e.g., Tijuana and San Diego (See Figure 12.2).

20. "Mexico: The Vital Role of 'Gatekeepers' in the Smuggling Business," 22 December 2006, *Strategic Forecasting, Inc.*, 2007, On-line, Internet, 24 April 2007, available from www.stratfor.com/products/premium.

21. Ibid.

22. "A Line in the Sand: Confronting the Threat at the Southwest Border," prepared by the Majority Staff of the House Committee on Homeland Security, Subcommittee on Investigations, a 2006 interim report, 11.

23. "Mexico: The Vital Role of 'Gatekeepers' in the Smuggling Business," op. cit.

24. C. Kahn, "Tunnels under the U.S.-Mexico Border," 18 August 2007, *NPR*, 2007, On-line, Internet, 19 August 2007, available from www.npr.org/templates/story.

25. "A Line in the Sand: Confronting the Threat at the Southwest Border," op. cit., 9-10.

26. W. Tucker, "Broken Borders: Document Forgers Thrive," *Lou Dobbs Tonight*, 4 July 2007, On-line, Internet, 19 August 2007, available from youtube.com/watch?v=TI7H0rmPkIY.

27. "Mexico: The Vital Role of 'Gatekeepers' in the Smuggling Business," op. cit.

28. "A Line in the Sand: Confronting the Threat at the Southwest Border," op. cit., 6.

29. Chabat, op. cit., 136.

30. R.J. Miro and G.E. Curtis, *Organized Crime and Terrorist Activity in Mexico, 1999-2002*, Federal Research Division, Library of Congress, February 2003, 46.

31. Ibid., 137.

32. "Mexico: Drug Cartels a Growing Threat," 2 November 2006, *Viewpoints*, 2007, On-line, Internet, 23 April 2007, available from www.worldpress.org.

33. "A Line in the Sand: Confronting the Threat at the Southwest Border," 17. Alien smuggling organizations show complete disregard for peasants. The women can expect to be raped; the peasants have been left to die by the coyotes for various reasons (e.g., a deal gone-bad or avoiding capture); and often, work in America is as slave labor because the peasant may not have the means to pay for the transit across.

34. Ibid., 14-15.

35. P. Lupsha, "Transnational Narco-Corruption and Narco-Investment: A Focus on Mexico," *Transnational Organized Crime Journal*, 1995, in Frontline Readings, On-line, Internet, 25 April 2007, available from www.pbs.org/wgbh/pages/frontline/shows/mexico/readings.

36. T. Padgett and E. Shannon, "The Border Monsters: Mexico's Top Drug Lords, the Bloodthirsty Arellano Felix Brothers, Horrify even Tijuana," *The New Frontier*, 2001, Time.Com, On-line, Internet, 25 April 2007, available from www.time.com/time/covers.

37. "Mexican Drug Trafficking in a Globalizing World," *Drug Wars*, 2006, On-line, Internet, 25 April 2007, available from www.accd.edu/sac/earthsci/lambert/projects/drugs-us-mex.

38. Becerra, "Tijuana Cartel Fights for its Future," op. cit.

39. Ibid.

40. Ibid.

41. O. Becerra, "New Traffickers Struggle for Control of Mexican Drug Trade," 17 August 2004, in *Jane's Intelligence Review, Systematic Transnational Crime*, 1 September 2004, On-line, Internet, 22 April 2007, available from www8.janes.com/Search.

42. D. Solis, "Drug Cartels want Migrants' Routes: Fight to Control Corridors on Arizona Border turns Violent," *The Dallas Morning News*, 19 February 2007, DallasNews.com, On-line, Internet, 23 April 2007, available from www.dallasnews.com/sharedcontent/dws/world/mexico/stories.

43. Ibid.

44. "Mexico: The Vital Role of 'Gatekeepers' in the Smuggling Business," op. cit.

45. D.M. Hanratty and S.W. Meditz, editors, *Colombia: A Country Study*, Washington: GPO for the Library of Congress, 1988, On-line, Internet, 24 August 2007, available from http://countrystudies.us/colombia.

46. D.E. Teicher, op. cit., 1-3.

47. D. Solis, op. cit.

48. "A Line in the Sand: Confronting the Threat at the Southwest Border," op. cit., 17.

49. Ibid., 10.

50. "Security & Law Enforcement," *Frontera NorteSur*, April – June 2007, On-line, Internet, 26 April 2007, available from www.nmsu.edu/~frontera/secr.html.

51. "A Line in the Sand: Confronting the Threat at the Southwest Border," op. cit., 12.

52. "Mexico: Drug Cartels a Growing Threat," op. cit.

53. "A Line in the Sand: Confronting the Threat at the Southwest Border," op. cit., 11.

54. Ibid., 11-14.

55. R. Marosi, "Mexico's Cartels Escalate Drug War," 23 June 2006, in *Los Angeles Times*, 2006, On-line, Internet, 23 April 2007, available from www.latimes.com/news/printededition.

56. T.G. Carpenter, "Mexico is Becoming the Next Colombia," Foreign Policy Briefing, No. 87, 13 November 2005, CATO Institute.

57. Becerra, "New Traffickers Struggle for Control of Mexican Drug Trade," op. cit.

58. "Mexico: 1999 Narrative," 2 September 2003, in *Just the Facts: A Civilians Guide to U.S. Defense and Security Assistance to Latin America and the Caribbean*, Latin American Working Group Education Fund and Center for International Policy, On-line, Internet, 28 April 2007, available from www.ciponline.org/facts.

59. "A Line in the Sand: Confronting the Threat at the Southwest Border," op. cit., 21-22.

60. "Mexico: The Vital Role of 'Gatekeepers' in the Smuggling Business," op. cit.

61. J. Seper, "Officers Outgunned on U.S. Border," 9 March 2007, in *The Washington Times*, News World Communications, Inc., 2007, On-line, Internet, available from www.washigntontimes.com/national.

62. Becerra, "Tijuana Cartel Fights for its Future," op. cit.

63. Seper, op. cit.

64. "Mexico," 25 September 2006, in *Just the Facts: A Civilians Guide to U.S. Defense and Security Assistance to Latin America and the Caribbean*, Latin American Working Group Education Fund and Center for International Policy, On-line, Internet, 28 April 2007, available from www.ciponline.org/facts. In Figure 12.5, the 1999 decrease in military aid was caused by Mexico returning 73 Vietnam-era UH-H1 helicopters, which had too many mechanical problems.

65. "Mexico: 1999 Narrative," op. cit.

66. "Mexico: 1999 Narrative," 2 September 2003, in *Just the Facts: A Civilians Guide to U.S. Defense and Security Assistance to Latin America and the Caribbean*, Latin American Working Group Education Fund and Center for International Policy, On-line, Internet, 28 April 2007, available from www.ciponline.org/facts.

67. "Mexico: 1999 Narrative," op cit.

68. "Major Cartel Lieutenants Arrested in Mexico," 7 June 2004, Operation United Eagle, Drug Enforcement Agency, U.S. Department of Justice, On-line, Internet, 27 April 2007, available from www.usdoj.gov/dea.

69. "On a Typical Day…," *Fact Sheet*, 2006, U.S. Customs and Border Protection.

70. *National Border Patrol Strategy*, Office of Border Patrol and The Office of Policy and Planning, U.S. Customs and Border Protection, (Washington, D.C.: September 2004), 4-6.

71. S. Carter and T.J. Bonner, interviewed by J. Scarborough, MSNBC, "Border Wars," 24 January 2006, *Scarborough Country*. The National Border Patrol Council is the labor organization, which represents U.S. Border Patrol employees. The *Inland Valley Daily Bulletin* is an Ontario, California newspaper.

72. Ibid.

73. "A Line in the Sand: Confronting the Threat at the Southwest Border," op. cit., 19.

74. Ibid., 18, 20, 22.

75. "President Bush Addresses the Nation on Immigration Reform," 15 May 2006, *Office of the Press Secretary, The White House*, transcript, On-line, Internet, 28 April 2007, available from www.whitehouse.gov/news/releases/2007.

76. Ibid.

77. "A Line in the Sand: Confronting the Threat at the Southwest Border," op. cit., 23-24.

78. "Operation Jump Start," *Fact Sheet*, 2006, U.S. Customs and Border Protection.

79. "President Bush Addresses Border Security and Immigration Challenges," 10 August 2007, *Office of the Press Secretary, The White House,* transcript, On-line, Internet, 28 April 2007, available from www.whitehouse.gov/news/releases/2007.

80. M. Allen, "Bush Orders New Crackdown on U.S. Border," 10 August 2007, *The Politico*, On-line, Internet, 10 August 2007, available from http://dyn.politico.com/prinstory.cfm?uuid=4D4320A1-3048-5C12-0002D819781B61BE.

81. "U.S. Immigration Statistics," Pew Hispanic Center, *cnn.com*, 14 May 2007, On-line, Internet, available from www.cnn.com/interactive/us/0603/charts.immigration. The graph (Figure 12.6) shows a decrease in 1989. This is not an actual decrease but the

effects of the 1986 immigration reform act, which included an amnesty clause for illegal aliens already in the United States.

82. "A Line in the Sand: Confronting the Threat at the Southwest Border," op. cit., 8-9.

83. "The World Factbook," *CIA*, 13 July 2007, On-line, Internet, 25 August 2007, available from www.cia.gov/library/publications/the-world-factbook/docs.

84. "Detention and Removal of Illegal Aliens," OIG-06-33, U.S. Immigration and Customs Enforcement, U.S. Department of Homeland Security, April 2006, 10.

85. "A Line in the Sand: Confronting the Threat at the Southwest Border," op. cit., 28.

86. Ibid., 29-30.

87. Ibid., 30.

88. T. Hendricks, "On the Border," *San Francisco Chronicle*, 12 March 2007, LexisNexis Academic, On-line, Internet, 21 April 2007, available from web.lexis-nexis.com/universe/primdoc.

89. D. Solis, "Drug Cartels want Migrants' Routes: Fight to Control Corridors on Arizona Border turns Violent." The *coyotes* is the name given to those who smuggle humans for profit across the U.S.–Mexican Border. Along the Mexico–Arizona Border, independent coyotes have had their vehicles burned and they have even been killed by the Sinaloa Cartel, who is in control of the crossing points.

90. "Statement of Karen P. Tandy, Administrator, Drug Enforcement Agency, Before the Committee on Appropriations Subcommittee for the Departments of Commerce, Justice, State, the Judiciary and Related Agencies, United States House of Representatives," 24 March 2004, in *DEA Congressional Testimony*, Drug Enforcement Administration, 24 March 2004, On-line, Internet, 2 May 2007, available from www.dea.gov/pubs/cngrtest/2004.html.

91. Ibid., 302-303, 368.

92. *2006 World Drug Report*, vol. 2: Statistics, United Nations Office of Drugs and Crime, United Nations Publication, 302-303, 368.

93. Fred Burton, "Mexico: The Price of Peace in the Cartel Wars," *Stratfor Terrorism Intelligence Report*, 2 May 2007, Strategic Forecasting, Inc., 2007, On-line, Internet, 1 October 2007, available from www.stratford.com/products/premium/read_article.php?id=288017&selected=Stratfor+Weekly.

CHAPTER 13

Revolutionary Armed Forces of Colombia (FARC)

Jerrold M. Post

FARC does not engage in war for the sake of war, but ...engages in war in search of peace.

—Commander Raúl Reyes[1]

War isn't just about shooting a gun. War is a fight against hunger and a struggle so that you don't die. War is a fight so that you have clothes. War is a fight to have a roof and to not get rained on. War is a fight to be able to read and not be illiterate. What I mean is that war is a fight so that you don't die.

—Fabian Ramirez[2]

Introduction

The Revolutionary Armed Forces of Colombia (FARC) was founded in 1964 as a social revolutionary organization with Marxist-Leninist ideological foundations with the declared intent to overthrow the democratic Colombian government. FARC is Latin America's oldest, largest, most capable, and best-equipped insurgency with perhaps 12,000 fighters and are located mostly in rural areas of Colombia, South America's oldest democracy.[3] While FARC no longer retains the strictest adherence to this original ideology, the group's senior members still consider themselves Marxist-Leninist, and much of the documentary material obtained in recent years still employs strong Marxist-Leninist rhetoric.[4] In addition to its attacks on Colombian military, political, and economic targets, FARC has been heavily involved in narcotics trafficking, kidnapping for ransom, extortion, murder, and other criminal acts, to the point where the group is better known for its major role in the illicit narcotics industry than for its insurgent activities. Yet its leadership is still committed to its social revolutionary goals and employs terrorist tactics to intimidate its political adversaries.

History: Origins of Major Players and Major Issues

The history of Colombia is bathed in blood. The current internal crises there are but the latest phase of a civil war that started over a century ago. The culmination of the civil war between the Liberals and the Conservatives was the "national bloodletting," referred to as the La Violencia, from about 1948 to 1958, which resulted in an estimated 200,000 deaths. The basic catalyst for violence was the refusal of government officials to comply with the people's demands for socioeconomic reform. At the beginning of La Violencia, Manuel Marulanda described the fear, desperation, and sense of marginalization that led to the formation of FARC, "I started to look for a solution. Already you heard people saying, 'Who do we get? Who will join us? Guns? Where are the guns, and how do we get them? If we stay quiet, they're going to kill us all. We couldn't take any more punishment.'"[5]

Such statements reflect the initial general attitudes, considerations, and motivating forces of Latin American social revolutionary groups seeking to overthrow the capitalist economic and social order that, in the case of Colombia, led to corrupt and violent practices inflicted by the landed elite on the peasant settlers. Besides FARC, a number of other social revolutionary terrorist groups were formed and became active during the same period, including Moviemiento de Abril 19 (M-19) and Ejército de Liberacion Nacional ELN (The National Liberation Army) of Colombia and Sendero Luminoso (the Shining Path) and Túpac Amaru in Peru.

A military coup ended La Violencia and a power-sharing arrangement led to the liberals and conservatives forming the National Front (Frente Nacional, 1958-1974). However, during this violent period, landless locals banded together in self-defense communities, forming *autodefensas* under the leadership of Marulanda, who was on the left wing of the

Liberal party. The families, who described themselves as a movement of rural workers, had cleared land for farming, with the support of the Colombian Communist party, and had asked the government to build roads and schools and grant them access to loans to expand their agricultural efforts. In the absence of government support, the peasant communities declared themselves Marxist-Leninist agrarian "independent republics."[6] The largest cooperative, Marquetalia, which had 1,000 members, was located in the remote mountainous regions in the Andean plains. In the late 1950s, after the civil war, the Colombian government, with the assistance of a U.S. assessment team, put together a pacification strategy, Plan Lazo, and struggled to reassert its control over the state and reduce the number of subversive groups, including the communist republics in southern and central Colombia.[7]

In the early 1960s the government attempted unsuccessfully to occupy Marquetalia, which increasingly was perceived as "the epicentre of the revolution."[8] On May 18, 1964, approximately 2,000 soldiers surrounded the peasant enclave and blocked the entrance of food and medicine. This Operation Marquetalia lasted three months and formed part of Plan Lazo, which was supported by the U.S. military. The survivors of this siege, who were able to escape along secret paths on the night of June 14, 1964, declared war against the government of Colombia and founded the Southern Bloc.

The Founding of FARC

Two years later, in 1966, at an annual conference of guerrilla leaders, the Southern Bloc expanded its military efforts into a nationwide group, the Fuerzas Armadas Revolucionarias de Colombia (FARC, Revolutionary Armed Forces of Colombia). Since its inception, FARC has been led by former peasant farmer Pedro Antonio Marín, who is generally referred to as Manuel Marulanda-Vélez and whose enemies refer to as "Tirofijo," Spanish for "Sureshot." Referring to the siege, Marulanda stated, "The self-organized and self-led resistance of the potential victims, the peasants, emerged [due to] reactionary violence."[9]

The Founding Generation

Pedro Antonio Marín, or Marulanda, was born between 1928 and 1930 into a peasant family in a coffee-growing region of west-central Colombia. He had only four years of formal education. His family supported the Liberal party, and when a civil war began in 1948 following the assassination of a Liberal president, Marulanda and a few cousins moved to the mountains and became guerrillas.[10] Marulanda is considered to be a professional survivor and a determined commander.

Only five feet tall, he is a charismatic chieftain who has been personally involved in combat and inspired unrivaled confidence in his followers. Marulanda's peasant origins and his sense of military strategy have earned him nationwide recognition as a leader in leftist political and guerrilla circles. According to one of his top commanders, Raúl Reyes:

> Commander Manuel Marulanda, who lives in the mountains with the rest of the guerillas, occupies himself with teaching…forms of battle to the masses of the villages. [Marulanda] is the teacher and guide who is most clear and experimental in the political, military, and organizational [aspects] of the formation of the new combatant staff. [Marulanda spends] a good part of time in designing and controlling the practice of the political-military plans of all FARC groups.[11]

Jacobo Arenas, Marulanda's close friend, second-in-command, and FARC's political founder, aspired to establish an agrarian communist state, with small-size industries. Arenas integrated a political agenda with FARC's military strategy of overthrowing a government it perceived to be plagued by elitism and corruption.

As conceptualized by the founding generation, there are two primary goals for FARC: to overthrow the state and to establish a communist-agrarian state in its place.[12] Such aims will be accomplished to the extent that solidarity is achieved among the entire Latin American Communist revolutionary movement.

For decades following the La Violencia, the insurgent groups, including FARC, remained largely outside the focus of the government, patiently creating an alternative society.[13] During the 1970s and 1980s, like Hamas in its formative stage in Gaza, FARC established its own schools, judicial system, health care, and agrarian economy, thereby creating its own de facto state in remote regions of southern Colombia and building significant social capital. Eventually, there were in effect two Colombias: the remote area east of the mountains, which is the domain of key insurgent groups, characterized by harsh mountain and forest regions with undeveloped, dirt roads, and scattered villages, and the more developed regions west of the mountains, where the landed elite live. The internecine conflicts in Colombia have always been about power, and in this country, power stems from control of the land. As long as the guerrilla groups confined their activities to their section of Colombia, the government would leave them alone, acting only when the insurgents' actions demanded a response. However, FARC became more ambitious.

Creating a Revolutionary Army Funded by Narcotics

In a pivotal meeting at a party conference held in May 1982, FARC decided that the priority task was to create a revolutionary army that would be able to take on the security forces. In order to fund this effort, FARC decided to exploit the narcotics trade. By taxing all aspects of the drug trade, it could reap profits; by protecting and controlling production areas, it would not only secure its income but would also be able to recruit from the marginalized peoples living in these regions.

As the crops became more lucrative, FARC began levying a 10 percent tax on fields of coca and opium poppies, the raw material for cocaine and heroin, and collecting fees for every narcotics flight leaving controlled regions. Indeed, the ability to employ tactics that may have at once seemed counter to FARC's original Marxist-Leninist ideology signifies what Commander Reyes rationalizes as FARC's ability and obligation to adapt to changing times:

> FARC is characterized as a political force that is nurtured by the Marxist-Leninist principles…under the assumption that Marxist-Leninism is not a dogma but has to be a guide for revolutionary action. For this reason, we consider that on today's stage, it is necessary that each time we are able

to innovate more and learn from various experiences in the revolutionary battle, so as not to fall into using obsolete schemes that would distance us from reality.[14]

In examining motivations for Colombians' involvement in FARC and FARC's involvement in drugs, it is clear that the concepts of narco-terrorism and political terrorism are not mutually exclusive. Indeed, FARC is involved in the narcotics trade as a way of "funding the revolution." While the group did consider the negative aspects of links to the drug trade, the benefits with regard to financial resources and popular support were too great. The money and the manpower led to FARC's remarkable resurgence. In 1982 FARC was a small organization of 15 fronts with approximately 2,000 guerrilla fighters, worried about attracting followers. By 1990, as a consequence of the large infusion of drug-related funds, it had expanded its forces to 43 fronts with about 5,000 fighters. The practical benefits of such a size increase include the ability to move to mobile warfare and to use large units capable of directly confronting military units of equal size and of overrunning military instillations and smaller units.[15] FARC's views on the legitimacy of drug trafficking are interesting: "We tax everything under our control. Everybody else lives on this money. Why shouldn't we? We regulate drug areas, defending the rights of campesinos who have little other opportunities."[16]

A number of commentators have asserted that FARC camouflages its illegal activities under the cover of political ideology, that hiding behind a political screen has allowed it to maintain the appearance of a semi-legitimate political force in Colombia while continuing to engage in criminal activities and fill its coffers with illegal profits. As FARC defector Carlos Ploter notes, drug money is creating "false needs" among guerrilla fighters and distracting them from their initial objective of fighting for social justice. FARC members have succumbed to consumerism and long for luxuries, such as expensive cars and watches. Moreover, as *Washington Post*'s Marcela Sanchez notes, those FARC members caught in the middle of a conflict that began 40 years ago and that is now part of both the war on drugs and war on terrorism have "achieved little else other than a twisted sense of upward mobility."[17]

One FARC defector, "José," describes the link between FARC and the drug trade: "To end the war you have to end the guerrillas. As long as there are guerrillas there are drugs. They exist together."[18]

However, there is a consensus among those who have followed FARC since its inception that the Marxist-Leninist ideology of the founding fathers remains a powerful, indeed the core, motivating force. Thomas Marks, Professor of Insurgency, Terrorism and Counterterrorism at the National Defense University and a noted expert on revolutionary warfare and FARC, observes that "in all of its basics – from vocabulary to analytical categories to societal analysis to combat doctrine, FARC remains Marxist-Leninist."[19] The members' mind-set is communist; the communist watchword "God is party" still pertains. FARC's ideological rigidity is almost akin to evangelical belief. Its national strategy is of a prolonged people's war and occupation of territory. FARC plans a gradual encirclement of Colombia's principal cities and a final assault on Bogotá.[20]

Group Profile and Membership

An analysis of the group makeup provides further insights into motivations for joining FARC and involvement in its activities. Sociologist James Peters states that 80 percent of FARC's members are peasants. Most are young, poorly educated people from rural areas, some of whom indicate that they are more attracted to FARC for its "relatively good salary and revolutionary adventurism than for its ideology."[21] In contrast to most other Latin American guerrilla and terrorist groups, FARC leaders also generally are poorly educated peasants. For example, Manuel Marulanda, FARC's chief leader, had only four years of grammar school education. His predecessor, Jacobo Arenas, had only two years of school.

Many new recruits do not seem to have a choice about whether to join FARC. Although FARC has stipulated that 15 was the minimum age for recruitment, this standard has not been respected.[22] According to Colombian authorities, a 10-year-old used by FARC to deliver a bomb was killed on April 17, 2002, after the bicycle he rode up to a military checkpoint exploded. Members also reportedly pressure indigenous people to become involved in the conflict, and media reports indicate that FARC had recruited adolescents from native Amazonian tribes in Brazil. FARC has been accused of forcibly conscripting Colombian youth in areas where it has difficulties recruiting or in instances in which landowners are unable to meet FARC demands for "war taxes."[23] A 19-year-old pleading for refugee status before a U.S. court of appeals stated that he was working on his family's farm when he was approached by a group of men who identified themselves as members of FARC. The youth testified that the guerrillas asked him to join the group and stated that "*life could be rough*" if he refused. He refused and later received two phone calls demanding that he join. After he again refused, the guerrillas told him that "[he] should be careful because the offence [he] had made against them was unforgivable."[24]

While for some, there does still seem to be ideological motivation for joining FARC, poor farmers and teenagers join out of boredom or simply because it pays them about $350 a month, which is $100 more than a Colombian army conscript. Considering the financial benefits, forced conscription, and lack of alternatives, FARC would seem to have a weaker ideological base than it professes to have, but some new recruits do subscribe to FARC's original Marxist-Leninist social revolutionary ideological platform. Ramón, a 17-year-old guerrilla, told a *Washington Post* reporter, "I don't know the word 'Marxism,' but I joined FARC for the cause of the country...for the cause of the poor."[25]

For the leadership echelon, Marxist-Leninist doctrine continues to reign supreme. While there are a few members of the younger generation in the secretariat, they are careful not to overstep their bounds, must be careful about being "pure," and do not have much influence. This is not likely to change in the near term unless Marulanda dies, which emphasizes the importance of the health status of this aging leader.[26]

Aging Leader

Marulanda has been pronounced dead several times in army communiqués, but reports of his demise were premature, as he has always reappeared in guerrilla actions. He is approximately 80-years-old and his health is a point of concern for the group. His age is significantly affecting his leadership and vitality, probably accounting for the paralysis in FARC leadership and decision-making in recent years. While he is still at the helm, few changes can occur, and new ventures or policy shifts are not anticipated.

However, the power of Marulanda, the leader of the moderate faction, who favors a political solution, is limited to some extent by FARC's main decision-making body, the seven member secretariat.[27] As there is no clear successor, when Marulanda dies, there will probably be a power struggle. Jorge Briceño ("Mono Jojoy") represents FARC hard-liners, who favor military solutions and oppose the peace process. Marulanda's death will likely lead to domination of FARC by Jojoy and his fellow hard-liners. Mono Jojoy reportedly has been the primary cause for a division and contention between FARC's political and military branches.

Regardless of generational differences FARC, as noted by Commander Reyes, old members and new, strongly assert that their violent actions are simply a response to the government's military actions: "there is no force directed to make policy through arms. However, if the enemy…insists on war, FARC has a responsibility of responding to that challenge each time [with greater force] and for that reason FARC requires the support and the solidarity of everyone."[28]

FARC recognizes the harm that its actions impose on the Colombian citizenry but states that despite such harm (and the resulting harm to FARC's public image), the violence will continue:

> Never are we going to renounce peaceful means, but if we are obliged to take part in armed battle, then we will also continue with such battle, with the pain that is implied for many people; in the field of combat there are many dead and destruction and pain for many people, and we hope to avoid all that.[29]

Such statements create the impression that FARC members are the victims of violence. In calling for solidarity among the masses, FARC perpetuates the impression that the masses should consider themselves victims of the government and should bear arms against "the enemy," alongside FARC.

Self-Defense Forces of Colombia

In Colombia, there are several paramilitary self-defense organizations, the majority of which are grouped under the umbrella organization called the AUC (Autodefensas Unidas de Colombia, or the Self-Defense Forces of Colombia). Its founding leader, Carlos Castaño, who was assassinated several years ago, trained a generation of paramilitary militia. The atrocities committed during La Violencia by the semi-official armed groups referred to as "chulavitas" are carried out today by paramilitary groups. These are not government-sponsored "death squads" but rather appear to be more akin to vigilante groups.[30] Today's paramilitary militias were formed in the 1980s, with assistance from the landed elites, the Colombian army, and the drug traffickers who owned large plots of the country's best land. The peace talks begun in 2003 with the AUC involved a hasty de facto pardoning of murders and drug trafficking charges.[31]

Transformation of Colombia under President Uribe

When President Alvaro Uribe came to power in 2002, Colombia was mired in armed conflict and its economy was struggling out of its first recession in seven decades. Many Colombians assert that Uribe has helped transform the country since he came to office.[32] The economy has grown at an annual rate of 4.4 percent, rising to 5 percent in 2005, helped by high prices for oil and metal exports. Under his "democratic security" strategy (which has received strong support from the White House), life in the main cities is more secure, and it is becoming increasingly possible to drive between these cities with little likelihood of being kidnapped by FARC and other insurgent groups. Murders and kidnappings are at their lowest rates in two decades, according to government figures. Uribe, who came to office promising to bring a new, heightened level of security to Colombia, has made remarkable progress in achieving this goal. The number of murders has been cut in half, from 32,000 per year at its peak. Polls demonstrate that support for Uribe's program, which earlier was mainly confined to the urban middle and upper classes, now extends throughout the country.[33]

With some 12,000 members, FARC has continued to be active throughout Colombia and governs a region the size of Switzerland. It has, however, never really had mass support, and functions more like a *foco*,[34] with the combatants being the movement. This fact, in turn, has permitted the government to focus its security efforts on the FARC paramilitary adversary without being concerned with a broader population supporting

FARC, in contrast to Hamas, where there is broad county support for the Hamas militants. FARC has waged its revolutionary struggle for more than 40 years, and its doctrine has emphasized patience and persistence in what inevitably will be a long struggle.

FARC members claim that they do not want to be thought of simply as terrorists who work outside the law:

> [I]t is so very important that we can also count on the support of many friends on the level of the distinguished members of parliament, on the level of distinguished social, intellectual, democratic, communist, and revolutionary organizations and of friends of peace for Colombia, in order to achieve the recognition of force for FARC that would permit FARC to compete for the favor of the popular masses in the public place, without the stigma of being an organization that is not recognized by international laws. This is an urgent necessity that exists.[35]

There is evidence linking FARC and other terrorist organizations, such as the IRA in Northern Ireland and ETA in the Basque region of Spain, to provide weapons, training, and safe havens. Links between the IRA and FARC reportedly go back several years and were established through the current relationship between FARC and ETA. These relationships demonstrate the extent of FARC business networking and operations, including extensive arms trading and technology exchanges.

Speaking to other communist groups in the Latin American region, Commander Reyes notes the solidarity FARC members are hoping to bridge with such marginalized sectors:

> [These groups] know that in FARC they have friends... confronted with the politicians of the imperialism of the United States of America and the Colombian oligarchy, who are determined to perpetuate their power at the costs of the pain, the exploitation, the misery, and the state repression of the dispossessed and marginalized individuals of our homeland.[36]

Although now in a period of strategic retreat, FARC does not believe it is losing. Rather, it has had to drop back to a different phase of Maoist struggle, planning to return to a more active struggle once Uribe is out of office.[37]

Joaquin Villalobo, former commander of the Farabundo Marti Liberation Front (FMLN) of El Salvador, has observed that FARC has been on the decline during the Uribe years, having had difficulty responding to the Colombian army's reorganization. While FARC has existed for 40 years, it was more than 10 years ago that the group seriously challenged the state and less than five years ago that the state decided to confront the group. Colombia, in Villalobo's opinion, has "achieved the most national and international legitimacy in its struggle against the insurgency, and FARC is the most illegitimate guerilla organization the region has known."[38]

FARC is increasingly isolated internationally and will have difficulties overcoming its political incapacity and military weakness "unless it received direct support from a neighboring government, which would mean covert logistics operations on a grand scale and a nearby rearguard."[39] And that is exactly what the populist socialist leadership of Hugo Chavez in neighboring Venezuela has been providing.

Since Chavez came to power in Venezuela, he has provided financial support as well as weapons to his fellow social revolutionaries in FARC. The purchase of 100,000 AK-103s from Russia and the revised Venezuelan military doctrine, which emphasizes the "war of the fleas," i.e., a campaign of terrorism and insurgency, suggests this trend will increase.[40]

Notes

1. Interview with Commander Raúl Reyes, "Nivel de lucha cada vez más definitorio," Farcep.org, 4 May 2002, On-line, Internet, 6 November 2007, available from www.farcep.org/?node=2,765,1.

2. Steven Dudley, "On the Road with FARC," *The Progressive*, (November 2003).

3. "House International Relations Committee, Summary of Committee Investigation of 'IRA Links to FARC Narco-Terrorists in Colombia,'" Center for International Policy's Colombia Program, Committee on International Relations, U.S. House of

Representatives, 24 April 2002, On-line, Internet, 6 November 2007, available from www.ciponline.org/colombia/02042401.htm.

4. Dudley, "On the Road with FARC."

5. Ibid.

6. "Colombia's Civil Revolutionary Armed Forces of Colombia (FARC)," *Online NewsHour*, 2003, On-line, Internet, 6 November 2007, available from http://cocaine.org/colombia/farc.html.

7. Thomas Marks, personal communication, 15 March 2007.

8. Constanza Vieria, *Colombia: Five Decades of a Struggle for Land that Became a War*, (New York: Global Information Network, 2004).

9. Ibid.

10. Rex A. Hudson, *The Sociology and Psychology of Terrorism: Who Becomes a Terrorist and Why?*, Report prepared under an interagency agreement by the Federal Research Division, (Washington, D.C.: Library of Congress, 1999), 107.

11. "Entrevista con el Comandante Raúl Reyes," Farcep.org, 6 February 2006, On-line, Internet, 6 November 2007, available from www.farcep.org/?node=2,1880,1.

12. "FARC: We Don't Own Any Coca Fields," New Colombia News Agency (ANNCOL), www.anncol.org/uk/site/doc.php?id=253, site no longer available.

13. Thomas Marks, *Colombian Army Adaptation to FARC Insurgency* (Carlisle, PA: The Strategic Studies Institute, 2002), 4.

14. Interview with Commander Raúl Reyes, "Nivel de lucha cada vez más definitorio," Farcep.org, 4 May 2002.

15. Marks, *Colombian Army Adaptation to FARC Insurgency*, 7.

16. Ibid.

17. Marcela Sanchez. "Concern for Colombia's Little Guy," *Washington Post*, 24 June 2004.

18. Shannon McCaffrey, "Program to Battle Colombian Drug Trafficking Gets Fresh Scrutiny," Knight Ridder, 15 September 2005.

19. Marks, personal communication.

20. Commentary of Malcolm Deas, St. Anthony's College, Oxford, at Colombian Security Forum, "What Are FARC's Current Political and Military Strategies," 12 November 2003, summarized by Jay Cope, personal communication, 15 March 2007. Cope concurs with Thomas Marks that Marxist-Leninist ideology remains at the core of FARC's strategic goals.

21. Hudson, *Sociology and Psychology of Terrorism*, 106.

22. "Child Soldier Use 2003: A Briefing for the 4th UN Security Council Open Debate on Children and Armed Conflict," *Human Rights Watch* (January 2003), On-line, Internet, 6 November 2007, available from http://hrw.org/reports/2004/childsoldiers0104/5.htm.

23. Hudson, *Sociology and Psychology of Terrorism*.

24. *Carlos A. Betancur López, Petitioner, v. Alberto González, Attorney General, Respondent Petition for Review of an Order of the Board of Immigration Appeals*, United States Court of Appeals for the First Circuit, On-line, Internet, 6 November 2007, available from www.ca1.uscourts.gov/cgi-bin/getopn.pl?OPINION=05-2092.01A.

25. Hudson, *Sociology and Psychology of Terrorism*.

26. Marks, personal communication.

27. Hudson, *Sociology and Psychology of Terrorism*, 107.

28. Interview with Commander Raúl Reyes.

29. Ibid.

30. Marks, personal communication.

31. "Disarming, Bit by Bit," *The Economist*, 31 January 2004.

32. "An Encore for Uribe," *The Economist*, 24 May 2006.

33. Marks, personal communication.

34. Inspired by Ernest "Che" Gueverra in the 1959 Cuban Revolution, and formalized as revolutionary doctrine by Regis Debray, the *foco* theory of urban guerrilla warfare is that a small cadre of mobile guerrillas can serve as a focus (*foco* in Spanish) and mobilize popular discontent against the regime and lead to a general insurrection.

35. Ibid.

36. "Entrevista con el Comandante Raúl Reyes."

37. Jay Cope, personal communication, 15 March 2007.

38. Joaquin Villalobos, "Colombia: Expert Analyzes How FARC Is Losing Domestic Conflict," *Bogotá Semana*, 7 July 2003.

39. Ibid.

40. Jerrold Post, "'El Fenomeno Chavez': Hugo Chavez of Venezuela, Modern Day Bolivar," Monograph #39, Future Warfare Series, (Maxwell Air Force Base, AL: USAF Counterproliferation Center, 2007).

CHAPTER 14

Mara Salvatrucha: A Threat to U.S. and Central American Security

Tina S. Strickland

Introduction

Transnational street gangs are growing at an alarming rate in the United States and in Central America. They are becoming more violent and committing more crimes; they are dispersing throughout the country and infiltrating communities that have been immune to this violence in the past; and their organization appears to be increasingly more structured. These gangs are a new type of enemy to be reckoned with as non-state actors.

Consequently, American communities are scared and law enforcement agencies have stepped up to the plate and are taking action to combat these enemies on American soil. The Federal Bureau of Investigation (FBI) and the Department of Homeland Security (DHS) are taking serious measures in prevention and deterrence of these gangs, but current efforts are not enough to rollback their growing strength and potential to become a serious threat to our nation's security. Unless action is taken to address the underlying social causes of these criminal elements, they will continue to grow and threaten the United States. The possibility definitely exists for transnational gang networks to be employed by terrorist groups to smuggle agents and/or weapons, even weapons of mass destruction (WMD), into our country. They do not necessarily care about who they do business with; they are only interested in the payment to finance their own criminal activities and organizations. These individuals are terrorists in their own right operating under an ideology of violence without regard to America's homeland.

The U.S. military is also playing a role – engaging in security cooperation with Central American countries to establish regional partnerships for confronting the security challenges posed by these gangs and developing regional solutions to combat them. There is also a potential threat to the military services in terms of gang members infiltrating the ranks to gain experience in weapons training and combat techniques.

The United States needs to take a more serious look at this threat and realize transnational gangs are becoming a significant risk to our nation's domestic and national security interests. They are a danger to society at all levels – local, state, national, and perhaps most importantly, internationally. Solutions to the gang problems will not be easily implemented since they are multi-agency and multinational, and require resources, time, and a balanced approach with prevention programs, law enforcement, and rehabilitation opportunities.

Background

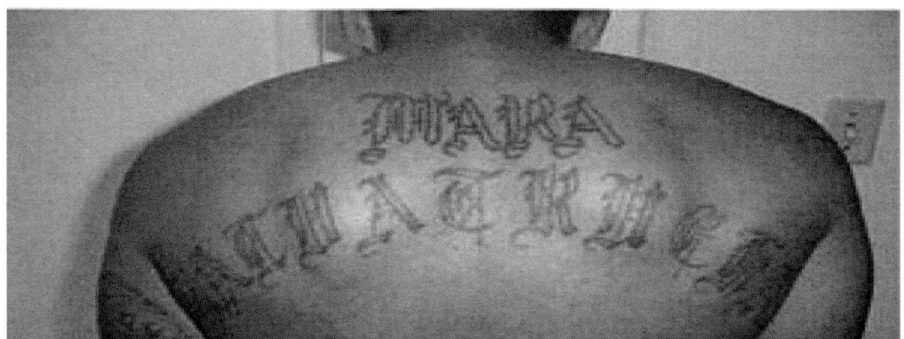

Figure 14.1 MS-13 member marked with tattoos

Street gangs have been part of American culture for years. Most are relatively innocuous but some are becoming more violent and territorial. In 2005, the FBI reported that there are around 30,000 gangs with 800,000 members affecting communities all over the United States.[1] The most violent and rapidly spreading gang in the United States is the Mara Salvatrucha-13, generally known as MS-13.[2] "It's considered the fastest growing, most violent and least understood of the nation's street gangs…" which is now operating in 33 states.[3] The largest concentration is in

California, Northern Virginia, and New York but they are also appearing in other large cities in Texas, Illinois, North Carolina, Nebraska, and Oregon.[4] MS-13 is dispersing across the country beyond major cities and into suburban areas like Fairfax County in Northern Virginia and the suburbs of Maryland in close proximity to Washington, D.C. They have become more mobile to acquire new market territory for drug sales and distribution, and to maintain family and social ties as their families migrate throughout the United States.[5] Their movement and dispersal in the country appears to be socially important as well as a business imperative.

The origin of the MS-13 and other violent gangs such as the M-18 (a rival to MS-13) can be traced to Los Angeles in the 1980s.[6] They initially came from Salvadoran families who fled to the United States from the civil war that was taking place in their own country. They were coming from an environment of war and violence and arrived in the United States already skilled in use of weapons, machetes, and combat tactics. As a minority group in the United States, they were marginalized and discriminated against within their new society. They subsequently banded together for support and protection from other gangs. They also learned new skills and techniques for violent crimes from gangs already present in Los Angeles such as the Crips and the Bloods.[7] Robert Mueller, FBI Director, states that "Los Angeles is ground zero for modern gang activity."[8] Los Angeles is where gang members originally migrated and where today gang violence continues to grow and evolve into more dangerous organizations.

Gang culture and customs are essential elements of membership. These individuals are often recruited at very young ages and normally come from poor families with very little education. Because opportunities are limited, children in these situations are often driven to seeking out activity and acceptance on the streets with others from similar circumstances. More often than not, they end up as members in various street gangs who engage in theft, drug distribution, and other violent crimes.

Initiation rituals and procedures are well established within the MS-13 culture. To become a member, the individual has to submit to a 13-second beating (or longer) from other gang members.[9] Then as a new member, they must commit a robbery or some other petty crime to prove they can do it.[10] MS-13 members have unique forms of identification including special tattoos, which normally have MS and 13 in gothic lettering on the chest.[11] Many members are donned with tattoos from head to toe, even on their eye lids. Each one is supposed to include a message. For example, some display on their bodies a trinity of three dots indicates hospital, prison, and graveyard – the three possible outcomes in the life of an MS-13 member.[12] They use hand signs to communicate and wear certain articles of clothing for identification, and prefer Nike shoes.[13] It is this inclusive culture that makes it very difficult, mostly impossible, for these individuals to escape.

Once they become full fledged members, the violence starts and never ceases. Their crimes are all over the map – from petty theft to drug distribution to murder. They also smuggle individuals across borders along with drugs and weapons. Even kidnapping is within their repertoire.[14] In Virginia, MS-13 members have used machetes to commit violence.[15] One MS-13 member was convicted of an attack with a machete that severed three fingers of a rival gang member.[16] Machetes are common weapons of choice since they are also used by Central American peasants.[17] Stabbings at local Virginia malls were becoming common occurrences.[18] MS-13 members are also reported to be responsible for the December 2004 bus bombing in Honduras in which 28 people were killed.[19] The list of crimes they commit is exhaustive – they have no mercy on their victims or conscience regarding their deeds. They do it for the money and because it is core to their culture and way of life.

Another important aspect of the gang culture is what goes on in the prisons in Central America. The gang members are very successful at continuing to maintain their control and organization while serving jail terms.[20] The structure of the gang appears to stay intact while they are inside prison. Some prisons experience more gang violence than others and some must keep rival gang members separated in order to maintain control. In August 2005, a long-standing truce between MS-13 and M-18 was broken when MS-13 members killed 35 M-18 members in a coordinated effort across a number of Guatemalan jails.[21] One official stated that "the jails are nothing more than schools of crime."[22]

In the early 1990s in an effort to deal with the growing problem posed by MS-13, the U.S. Government began deportation of these gang members back to El Salvador after they spent time in U.S. jails. Unfortunately, these deportations and extraditions were not coordinated with their home country and the respective law enforcement agencies were unprepared to manage the level of organized violence perpetrated by these deportees. Because these gang members were not guilty of crimes in their home country, once they arrived from the United States they established gangs in Salvadoran towns and gained additional territory and strength at home while still keeping their ties to members in the United States. Not only were they able to quickly expand networks throughout their home country with links to their U.S. counterparts, they also spread across the region into other Central American countries. This began development of their international networks and marked the beginning of serious problems for both the United States and Central American governments in controlling and managing the movement and growth of these gangs.[23] It is this transnational reach and ability to easily move between countries – the United States, Mexico, and Central America, with associated communication and transportation channels that makes MS-13 a unique threat to the United States and the region.

Despite growing awareness of the problem, it is not completely clear how many MS-13 or M-18 members exist in any country. Given the informal and secretive nature of these gangs, it may be impossible to determine the actual strength of these organizations. There are many disparate accounts because reliable and accurate data is lacking. The number of members reported in each country varies from source to source but those cited below from *Security and Foreign Forces* in March 2006 appear to be the most comprehensive and representative from one source.[24]

- Honduras – 36,000
- United States – 25,000
- El Salvador – 11,000
- Nicaragua – 5,000
- Canada – 4,000
- Costa Rica – 2,500
- Belize – 100

Also, Guatemala is reported to have 14,000 members.[25] In January 2006, the *Economist* reported 25,000 in El Salvador and comparable numbers in the United States, Honduras, and Guatemala, concluding that MS-13 and M-18 is the "...largest criminal network in the Americas..."[26] As a reference point, there are estimated to be approximately 50,000 Al Qaeda members, several thousand members of Hezbollah, more than 10,000 Al Fatah members, and more than 1,000 members of Hamas.[27,28,29,30] Based on size alone, MS-13 warrants attention. Since it appears to be approaching a membership of 100,000, it is certainly of formidable size in comparison and is creating an increased threat to these governments in terms of security, political and economic stability, and potential corruption of security and law enforcement officials.[31]

These gangs finance their operations through many different criminal activities to include robbery, muggings, extortion, drug trafficking and distribution, weapons smuggling, prostitution rings, car theft, and even murder.[32] However, drug sales and distribution account for an estimated 80 percent of their finances.[33] In large cities, they extort money from local businesses, similar to a tax. The businesses pay for fear of the destruction and potential loss these gang members may cause to their property, and fear of other threats the gang members might impose upon them.[34] They are likely to extort payoffs from other operators on their territory such as taxi drivers and possibly even homeowners. These gang members are thugs and aim to inflict fear and violence upon anyone or anything that might hinder their activities or provide an opportunity for them to make a profit. Such financial gains allow them to buy weapons, engage in recruiting activities, develop their organization and infrastructure, acquire technology for communications, and procure means to travel and migrate from location to location within the United States and other countries.

Technology offers these gangs communication options that they have not had in the past, which in turn provides increased opportunity for their interclique collaboration. They use disposable cell phones and the Internet, both of which are readily available at low cost. There is speculation that they may be using the Internet in the same fashion as terrorist groups.[35] It could provide them enhanced opportunities and ways to control and organize, recruit, train, raise funds, and distribute propaganda. It may also help them maintain awareness of law enforcement activities and plans, and provide them access to technical information such as how to make bombs. This knowledge could increase their level of violence and render them more effective.

Technology helps to remove the traditional geographic barriers for gangs both within and outside the United States. Today, they do not have to be mobile to operate. This could foster their opportunities for growth and unity which could mean an organization that becomes more controlled and centralized. Although there is no data available, one caution to note regarding their use of the Internet for information is the illiteracy rate may be relatively high among these individuals. A high illiteracy rate among these gang members could curtail use and effectiveness of the Internet as a network-enhancing tool. Also, these gang members may not have the technical skills necessary to develop and maintain websites. However, such services could be easily purchased.

These gangs are now a transnational entity and technology has assisted them in many ways to include facilitating their organizational structure. They organize themselves into regional groups called cliques which are an integral part of their operation and provide the basis on which they coordinate their activities.[36] These cliques normally have a leader who coordinates the local activities and decides on issues such as reprimands and sanctions for those who do not obey the rules of the gang. This person is referred to as the "shot caller" for obvious reasons. Although they primarily operate within their own clique, they are also known to commit crimes with members outside of their clique.

Although it appears that these gangs are well organized at the clique level, intelligence data indicates they lack an overarching and centralized structure and leadership.[37] However, there have been reports indicating that clique leaders have begun to conduct meetings with other cliques in which they coordinate and collaborate on activities, discuss differences in their operations, and share information about known law enforcement activities.[38] This indicates an increase in their interclique organization and cooperation, which could potentially evolve into something more structured resembling an organized crime syndicate.[39] However, there is still no solid evidence of a central leader overseeing the activities of the gang at large. This lack of central leadership may reduce the risk of coordinated or large scale attacks in the near future. However, much remains unknown and U.S. Government agencies and our regional partners need improved intelligence data and information to better parse out the organization and structure of MS-13.

Threats to Domestic and National Security

Social and Economic Impacts

Although social and economic impacts of these transnational gangs in the United States might be small in comparison to the threats imposed by other terrorists groups and criminal organizations such as Al Qaeda, they are still very significant. First and foremost, law enforcement communities at the local, state, and federal level are expending considerable resources to combat this growing problem. This is a significant issue for the law enforcement community as a whole and one that requires political attention, social attention, and funds for complementary programs for deterrence and prevention.

The crimes these gang members commit are often quite violent and this instills fear and intimidation in the public around them. Citizens become afraid to spend time in their communities and provide less patronage to local businesses and community organizations. In addition, the extortion of a "gang tax" from some local businesses can also have a significant impact on their ability to make a profit and continue to operate within the community.[40] Eventually, some of these smaller businesses may decide the sacrifices and hardships to keep their businesses within the territory of an MS-13 clique are just not worth the price to them emotionally and economically. This in turn provides fewer services to community citizens and forces them to find alternative sources of goods and services. Their neighborhoods will continue to decline as the gangs take full control. This results in sections of cities becoming more violent which leads to greater stress on the law enforcement organizations and the city governments. This pattern can be seen in countries throughout the region including the United States.

In these communities, gang members are impacting the school systems within their territorial boundaries. They prey on students, commit crimes at school locations, and use these schools as prime recruiting locations. Consequently, schools must spend additional resources on security to control these members. Academic and other school-related programs suffer accordingly as their funding and resources are decreased to accommodate for the increase in school security programs. Parents become unhappy and complain, and schools must spend considerable energy and resources to alleviate their concerns. This is a growing problem for public school systems in the United States, especially in the major metropolitan areas in which the gang problem continues to grow.

The cost to the governments and citizens of Central American countries is even more devastating. For example, the cost of violence to El Salvador in 2003 was $1.7 billion which was 11.5 percent of its GDP for that year.[41] It is purported that the region's per capita GDP would be 25 percent higher if violence could be reduced to the world average.[42] This is a significant economic loss and provides an indication of how these gangs can have serious impacts on entire nations. Murder rates in these countries are also alarming. The *Inter Press Service News Agency* reports that 6 people a day are murdered in Honduras with a population of 6 million; 8 per day in El Salvador with 6.2 million; and 14 per day in Guatemala with a population of 12 million.[43] The violence continues at a tremendous cost to citizens, law enforcement, and political/government security. Although the economic impact of MS-13 on the United States is clearly not this powerful, it is likely that its impact on local communities in which it is active are comparable.

Transnational Smuggling and Possible Terrorist Ties

In addition to the social and economic impacts at a local and national level, these gang members pose a significant threat transnationally through illegal smuggling of goods and transportation of people across borders, particularly U.S. borders. Perhaps the greatest threat MS-13 gang members may pose to the United States would be through cooperation with terrorist groups. This cooperation would occur where the capabilities of MS-13 meet the needs of terrorist groups. It is this intersection that presents a special risk and requires more exploration. The necessary ingredients are all in place. MS-13 has demonstrated the capability to smuggle people and weapons; terrorist groups want to enter the United States; and there is ample evidence that cooperation between these groups is likely if money and profit is involved for MS-13 members.

The Department of State differentiates between the actions of human smuggling and human trafficking.[44] Trafficking of people is based on exploitation of people through criminal acts which take away their rights and freedoms. The Department of State defines human smuggling as

"...the facilitation, transportation, attempted transportation or illegal entry of a person(s) across an international border, in violation of one or more countries laws, either clandestinely or through deception, such as the use of fraudulent documents."[45] It further states that smuggling normally involves financial gain for the smuggler and that most people that are being smuggled do so with knowledge and are generally cooperating with and paying the smuggler in hopes of gaining access to another country. Once individuals are smuggled into a country, they are on their own and the smuggler moves on to locate more customers. MS-13 members are mostly smugglers, not human traffickers. It is these activities and capabilities that create an additional potential threat to U.S. security.

The MS-13 and M-18 members have been crossing the border between the United States and Mexico since the 1980s. Border security with Mexico is problematic and illegal immigration, smuggling, and drug trafficking occur every day. MS-13 is already known for their illegal smuggling activities of both people and weapons from Central American countries into the United States.[46] The ability of MS-13 to subvert U.S. security in transporting goods and services across our borders is well established. What remains unclear is the extent to which this capability may purposefully or unknowingly aid terrorist groups. Thus, a significant potential threat which transnational gangs pose to the national security interests of the United States is in the form of human smuggling of terrorists and smuggling of WMD into our country.[47]

At the present time, some gang members are purported to be linked to terrorists. In January 2006, the Department of Justice reported that 10 foreign nationals from Colombia were indicted by a federal grand jury in Miami, Florida on charges of providing material support to a foreign terrorist organization and alien smuggling.[48] Assisted were members of the Revolutionary Armed Forces of Colombia, also known as the FARC, a foreign terrorist organization. The defendants supposedly provided these FARC members with false documentation and helped them procure weapons and drugs. Although the defendants were not MS-13 members, in June of 2004, the Colombian police indicated that the FARC and other drug cartels had ties to MS-13 cliques in El Salvador.[49] The Colombian police believed the MS-13 members were being hired by the FARC to engage in illegal drug activities in exchange for weapons. The important point to note is the link of the FARC to MS-13. While the transactions between FARC and MS-13 operatives is more natural due to common language and culture, it is not inconceivable that MS-13 might also conduct business with other terrorist organizations (not even knowing they are terrorists) such as Al Qaeda or Hezbollah.

At least one connection between MS-13 and Al Qaeda has already been reported. In September 2004, the *Washington Times* reported an Al Qaeda/MS-13 connection in Honduras in which a key Al Qaeda cell leader, Adnan G. El Shukrijumah, was supposed to have met with MS-13 leaders.[50] Subsequent sources stated that this meeting was never verified by authorities in Honduras. Two other sources allege that MS-13 has a major smuggling center in Matamoras, Mexico.[51] If this is, in fact, a reality, it poses a potential major security risk to the United States. These possibilities are cause for concern and alarm.

In the testimony of Diego Rodriguez of the FBI to the Committee on House Government Reform in July 2006, he stated that "MS-13 has gained notoriety for its flexibility and willingness to participate in any type of criminal activity at any time."[52] Rodriguez believes that the gang's potential to grow and spread both nationally and internationally has enabled it to participate in more criminal activities and become more violent, and that it is this growth and potential size and organization growth where its greatest threat lies.[53]

On the other hand, there are arguments against MS-13 cooperation with terrorist groups. The *Terrorism Monitor* cites four reasons that cooperation between the Mara gangs and Al Qaeda is unlikely.[54] First is the lack of structure and organization within the gang network. The lack of a central decision-making authority makes any lasting or complex relationship improbable. The second factor is the Maras' lack of an anti-American agenda. The third reason is that the Maras are public and visible, and a secretive organization like Al Qaeda would not connect with them due to the risk of detection by law enforcement agencies. Further, Al Qaeda might not trust that MS-13 operatives will not betray them, especially if it might prove more profitable to the gang. Finally, because the Mexican border is well known and under constant surveillance, it may not be the first choice of entry for Al Qaeda; entry through Canada or by sea into a port or beach along the Atlantic or Pacific coastlines may be a more likely choice. Other sources also point out reasons that MS-13 gang members and terrorists would be unlikely Al Qaeda associates. Virtually none of them are Muslims. Also, language and cultural barriers would divide them and lack of trust of individuals outside of particular Al Qaeda networks could be factors retarding the development of potential partnerships.[55] Terrorist organizations and gangs are both close and tight-knit; they trust no one outside of their respective organizations. It would be unlikely for either of them to trust the other, especially in a major operation.

While some argue that ideology would preclude MS-13 and Al Qaeda from developing a meaningful relationship, others argue that Al Qaeda could buy the gang's services and use their smuggling operations to get terrorists and weapons into the United States.[56] They might also hire them as assassins to eliminate specific U.S. leaders. MS-13 does not have to know that they are dealing with a terrorist organization; they would just provide the illegal services. There is no evidence to suggest that MS-13 would reject smuggling terrorists into the United States or operating as contract killers if they are paid to do so. They conduct criminal acts strictly for the money and profit. They also have no particular alliance to an ideology that would make them unwilling to aid anyone willing to pay for their services. Even the *Terrorism Monitor* accepts that cliques in Mexico may provide smuggling services for payment.[57]

The opportunity exists for collaboration between MS-13 and terrorist groups and the risk it creates should not be overlooked. Because Al Qaeda and MS-13 lack a common type of organization, ideology, agenda, or common goals, meaningful cooperation or relationships between them are not probable but are possible.

It should also be noted that not only is the U.S.-Mexican border very open to penetration, so too is the U.S.-Canadian border.[58] Indeed, Canada has its own criminal gangs. The Jamestown Crew is one in Toronto (similar to MS-13), but it is also estimated that 4,000 Maras are working in Canada.[59] This, too, increases the opportunity for transnational operations to develop as the Canadian border is not under the same degree of surveillance as is the Mexican border.

Law Enforcement Efforts

United States

Due to the increased risk to U.S. national security interests and public safety, the U.S. Government has been increasing its law enforcement efforts against gang activity since the 1990s. Although there have been efforts in the past decade, the 9/11 terrorist attacks had a significant negative impact on resources dedicated to the gang problem. Now that some years have passed since these attacks, priorities are again shifting and law enforcement agencies are beginning to increase efforts and resources directed toward combating these criminals.[60] The FBI appears to have the lead and is embarking on a number of programs and strategies to attack this issue. These initiatives primarily involve coordinating investigations with other agencies, improving anti-gang operations, and enhancing communications efforts and collection of information and intelligence.

The FBI established the MS-13 National Gang Task Force (NGTF) in early 2004.[61] This task force is designed to be a coordinated effort among law enforcement agencies at the federal, state, and local levels, as well as with international partners in Central America. Coordination and communication are essential to the success of this task force. In September 2005, over 650 arrests were made in 12 states and 5 countries – 73 in the United States, about 237 in El Salvador, 162 in Honduras, 98 in Guatemala, and 90 in Mexico with assistance from numerous agencies and governments.[62] Although the arrests were conducted as separate operations in each country and state, this demonstrates the effects of coordination, cooperation, and collaboration at all levels of involvement. The FBI believes the NGTF to be crucial to information sharing at the national and international levels.[63] Before development of this task force, few partnership efforts existed between countries or agencies which resulted in little cooperation and a lack of successful law enforcement operations. Although arrests have been made in the past by various groups and organizations, none have produced results comparable to that of the NGTF.

In an effort to further enhance law enforcement efforts, the FBI also created the National Gang Intelligence Center (NGIC) in 2005. The NGIC is also a multi-agency effort that attempts to integrate intelligence across all law enforcement levels on the various gang activities that pose a threat to the United States.[64] Similar to the NGTF, the goal is to centralize and coordinate the collection of gang-related information at a national level, analyze it, and then distribute it to affected law enforcement agencies in the United States.[65] In recent FBI testimony to Congress, Robert Loosle, FBI Special Agent in Los Angeles, stated his belief that the NGIC will enable analysts to determine links between gangs and ongoing investigations, learn more about gang members, identify trends in their behavior and activities, and enable law enforcement authorities to better gauge the threat they pose.[66] These are all great steps in helping to identify, deter, and dismantle their structure and leadership.

The Department of Homeland Security is also conducting anti-gang law enforcement efforts. In February 2005, the Immigration and Customs Enforcement (ICE) stood up *Operation Community Shield* which focuses on law enforcement efforts against criminal street gangs in the United States.[67] The focus started on MS-13 but has now expanded to all street gangs that are considered to be a security threat.[68] As with the other efforts discussed above, ICE's *Operation Community Shield* also focuses on developing partnerships and integrating with other law enforcement agencies, and promoting the sharing of information and intelligence to combat gang activities.

ICE also wants to promote public awareness about law enforcement efforts against gang violence. *Operation Community Shield* has proved to be very effective. Since its February 2005 start, 533 criminal arrests and 1,855 administrative immigration arrests have been made. Of these, 51 were gang leaders and 1,075 had violent criminal histories. About 153 have been sentenced from prosecution under this program.[69]

As DHS Secretary Michael Chertoff stated, "Gang members are some of the people who are shooting at our border patrol agents and committing acts of violence on both sides of the border, and that is, in and of itself, a very, very serious national security issue."[70]

The Department of Justice has taken the lead to coordinate the national anti-gang activities by creating a new task force called the National Gang Targeting, Enforcement, and Coordination Center (GangTECC) which has members from multiple agencies – FBI; the Bureau of Alcohol, Tobacco, and Firearms; the Bureau of Prisons; the

Drug Enforcement Agency; the Marshals Service; and the U.S. Immigration and Customs Enforcement.[71] The GangTECC serves as the point of coordination among these agencies for investigations and intelligence sharing, and works closely with the NGIC. Because this program falls under the Department of Justice and includes the FBI, it has become the central coordination mechanism and authority for U.S. federal law enforcement agencies.

Although the United States is increasing its efforts and placing more focus and resources on the gang problem, this is just a start with the multiple law enforcement communities. Arrests and prosecutions are critical to deterrence and communicating the message of zero tolerance to both the gang members and the public, but it is only a partial solution to the gang problem. U.S. law enforcement agencies must continue to strengthen their efforts by better coordination, collaboration, and sharing of data and information. It is reported that information sharing is still lacking among agencies such as sharing of databases or development of a comprehensive database with all known gangs and criminals.[72] Improvement in this area is critical to becoming more effective in understanding and analyzing the issues, and developing strategies to combat these gangs' criminal activities. Because data is lacking, relatively little is known about these gangs. More accurate and reliable information and intelligence will assistance the law enforcement community in developing better methods to manage and address this problem at all levels of government and between country partners. The U.S. Government must improve its vigilance in maintaining the critical coordination and collaboration across these programs since different department and agencies are involved with no clear indication of which one is actually in the lead.

Central America

Gang violence also poses a serious threat to the national and regional security of many Central American countries by weakening their economic and political stability. In addition to efforts by U.S. law enforcement agencies, a number of countries in Central America are also taking action against these gangs with law enforcement legislation.

The short-term law enforcement approach has helped these countries gain some control, but each of them needs to address the social, economic, and environmental issues that are the basic causes of gang development and continuance. These include lack of education, poverty, domestic abuse, lack of employment opportunity, corruption, drugs, etc. Law enforcement initiatives are necessary but they only address the symptoms and do not get at solutions to the root causes. These approaches also do not address prevention or rehabilitation, and they often create new problems that only exacerbate present problems such as prison overcrowding.

Many of the Central American countries have taken some aggressive actions against the gang violence taking place in their countries. The governments of Honduras, Guatemala, and El Salvador have instituted law enforcement efforts designed to curb and take control of the ongoing violence. In August 2003, Honduras launched *Operation Liberty*, a nationwide law enforcement operation to curb gang activities.[73] The Honduran government enacted legislation that can punish gang leaders with 9 – 12 years in prison and fines up to $12,000. Within about a year, over 15,000 members were arrested. However, according to the U.S. Agency for International Development (USAID), very little funding is allocated to support programs for prevention and rehabilitation in Honduras.[74]

Guatemala has also taken a law enforcement approach but has not yet passed specific legislation to curb their gang violence.[75] The focus in Guatemala has been in particular communities where crime levels are very high. This has resulted in high arrests but has contributed relatively little to solving the underlying problems.

In July of 2003, El Salvador launched *Operation Firm Hand*, which allows gang members over 12 years of age to be tried as adults and receive up to 20 years in prison.[76] However, this legislation has been controversial in El Salvador as judges do not believe it is fair to these young gang members and therefore do not enforce it. According to the USAID, it has also resulted in serious prison overcrowding and debate over the constitutionality of the law.[77] USAID reports that Mexico has not enacted specific anti-gang legislation but did start a program called *Operation Blade* under which hundreds of members were arrested.[78] Mexico is of particular importance in these efforts as it is the gateway these gangs use to gain access to the United States. Unless efforts to curb gang activity in Mexico are pursued and taken seriously, the United States will continue to experience the migration of these gang members and others they might bring into our country. Then the duty comes back to the United States and its ability to control the Southwest border with Mexico.

All of these operations are effective law enforcement actions that result in more arrests but they do not necessarily reduce the crime threat and are limited in dealing with the root causes of the problem. Programs to prevent gang membership early on and/or to rehabilitate later for a second chance are basically ignored in law enforcement which leads governments and communities into a false sense of security. If law enforcement is proactive and working to make lots of arrests, then the problem is seen as being solved. Law enforcement efforts also result in overcrowding of Central American prisons which in turn creates a whole new set of issues to contend with that revolve around lack of human rights and repression. These members can be incarcerated at a very early age with virtually no chance to rehabilitate, while also suffering the horrible conditions of overcrowded prisons. Additionally, incarceration of young people in such an environment provides the opportunity to learn even more tricks of the gang trade.

The United States and these Central American countries need to continue to work together on the transnational issues of gang violence and address cross-border links with Mexico as a critical point. Figure 14.2, taken directly from the April 2006 USAID report, provides an overview of the Central American gang problem with legislation and government focus.[79] The emphasis on law enforcement solutions does not necessarily consider the transnational issues and could possibly worsen the situation in some countries as did the U.S. deportation of MS-13 members back to El Salvador.

Unintended Consequences

Although law enforcement efforts in both the United States and Central America are laudable, they are narrowly focused and have produced unintended consequences. Because the focus and placement of resources has been primarily on law enforcement, systemic issues that foster gang membership (e.g., poverty, lack of education, lack of employment opportunities) and rehabilitation options (e.g., counseling, employment, development of technical job skills) after arrest or incarceration have received virtually no attention or funding priority in any of the impacted countries.

Figure 14.2 Central American Gang Issues

State	Problem	Legislation	Programs
El Salvador	Gang problem is international and severe. Despite heavy-handed anti-gang laws, homicides are still on the rise.	Anti-gang law	Law enforcement is emphasis, with active government and NGO prevention and some intervention efforts.
Honduras	Gang problem is severe with international aspects that warrant concern. Homicides are increasing notwithstanding anti-gang legislation.	Anti-gang law	Law enforcement is emphasis with limited resource support; There is limited prevention and intervention.
Nicaragua	Gang problem is relatively minor and localized. Gang activity continues due to drug trafficking, poverty, and lack of opportunities.	An Anti-gang law was debated but not accepted by Congress.	Approach weighted more towards prevention and intervention, with law enforcement involvement.
Guatemala	Gang problem is severe but localized. There are increasing reports of social cleansing of gangs appearing in international news.	Anti-gang law is under consideration.	Law enforcement is the emphasis, with some prevention and intervention.
Mexico (Southern and Northern Borders)	Gang problem along the borders is considered both local and international, but is not widely recognized. Southern border offers drugs/arms/human trafficking opportunities for gangs. The Northern border gangs are cooperating with drug cartels.	There is no anti-gang law.	Law enforcement is the emphasis, with some NGO and government prevention and intervention effort.

From the 1990s to the present, one of the most notable consequences that has resulted from deportation of members from the United States back to Central America has been the facilitation of the transnational development of these gangs. Gang members sent back to Central America spread violence in those communities and provide links for new recruits to move to the United States. This exacerbates the problem in both the United

States and the country of origin.[80] Deported members returning to their former countries in Central America often continue their violence at home and plan their later return to the United States. Salvadoran police estimate that 90 percent of these deportees return to the United States as soon as possible.[81] It is ironic that the U.S. deportation of these gang members has caused the problem to swell in both Central America and the United States.[82] The map at Figure 14.3 indicates the transnational flow of gang members from Central America to the United States through Mexico. These gang members continue to travel back and forth across the borders of all of these countries. U.S. deportation laws are essentially supporting the mobility of gang members which makes this a major transnational issue.

Figure 14.3 Map of Transnational Gang Movement

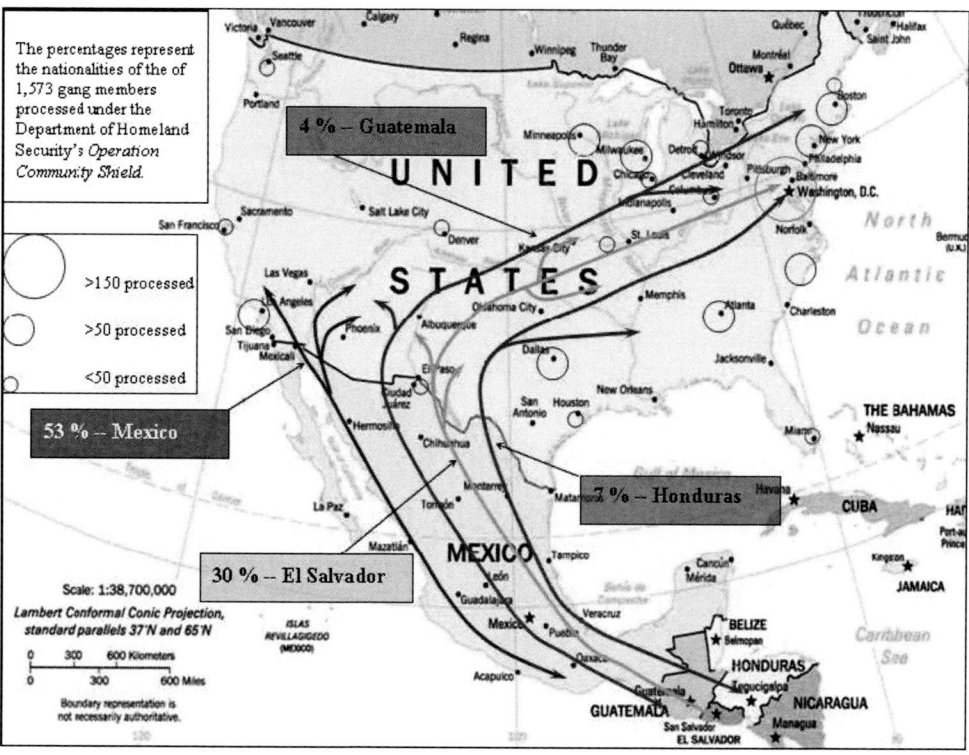

The U.S. Agency for International Aid (USAID) described this transnational issue as the "revolving door" phenomenon.[83] Since it is so easy for these criminals to cross borders, they continue to flow from north to south and south to north. They sometimes use this to their advantage and manipulate the law enforcement systems while doing so. For example, some may intentionally get arrested in order to get a trip back home to Central America at the expense of the U.S. taxpayers. Others flee Central America if they feel law enforcement pressure is heightened or if other adversarial encounters seem likely. The shuttle of gang members between countries continues at a high rate.

The *LA Times* reported on the case of Melvin "Joker" Cruz-Mendoza who was deported four times back to San Salvador over an 8-year period.[84] This illustrates how deportations continue to reinforce transnational activities. A member gets convicted of a crime in the United States, serves time, gets out of jail, gets deported back to San Salvador, commits crimes there as well, and then returns to the United States to repeat the process. "Deportations have helped create an 'unending chain' of gang members moving between the U.S. and Central America…It's a merry-go-round" stated Rodrigo Avila, El Salvador's vice minister of security.[85] U.S. Immigration and Customs Enforcement officials report that while at least 70 percent of arrested gang members are deported – only 30 percent are actually arrested and charged with crimes.[86] Again, the evidence is overwhelming – this is a serious problem needing attention, as their continual movement between countries allows these gang members to strengthen their networks in both countries for smuggling drugs, weapons, and people. U.S. deportation processes are enhancing opportunities for gangs to potentially smuggle terrorists and WMD into our country.

The second serious issue that both the U.S. Government and Central American governments have to face, also compounded by U.S. deportation, is the prison overcrowding that results from major law enforcement efforts. There is not enough prison capacity in any of these countries (the United States included) to accommodate the arrests that are made. It appears to be a no-win situation. In addition, their time in prison also allows them the opportunity to hone their skills in conducting violence – they learn from others already in prison. This is a vicious circle – law enforcement efforts get gang members off the streets, they go to jail, then are deported by the United States back to Central America where they are imprisoned in prisons that are far above their intended capacity and, thus tend to be unmanageable. So, once jailed, the MS-13 members are soon released. Then, they cause more crime there. Eventually, many (if not most) make their way back to the United States to continue the cycle of crime. It has been stated that the Maras "...have become the most serious challenge to peace in the region since the end of the civil wars of the 1980s" and that the deportation policies of the United States has been a major contributor.[87]

Potential Solutions

There are a myriad of actions and solutions that need to be taken to address the problem of gang violence in both the United States and Central America. Law enforcement actions have considerable merit but do not provide a comprehensive approach to all the issues or address the root causes of the problem. In addition, law enforcement actions create other problems that must also be tackled. A more comprehensive solution is needed to eliminate most gang violence in the United States. It will require considerable resources and funding for programs in the United States, and the continuation and strengthening of relationships with our Central American partners to combat this problem. Thus far, programs have focused mainly on law enforcement, whereas little support has been given to a more balanced approach that includes prevention programs and intervention. However, efforts in this direction are beginning to unfold.

In February 2005, a variety of individuals from both the United States and Central America that work in social services, academia, government, and law enforcement came together to discuss initiatives and research on youth gang violence in Central America.[88] Six themes emerged from the conference addressing solutions to the problems of gang violence.[89] Although these solutions were primarily focused on Central America, they apply equally to the problems and issues in the United States. These are:[90]

1. There is a need for integrated multi-agency effort that promotes cooperation between all involved organizations.

2. Required is a better understanding of the social factors which enhance risk of membership such as marginalization and discrimination.

3. Governments need to scale back on heavy-handed law enforcement approaches.

4. Efforts are needed to reduce the availability of drugs and weapons, with more focus put upon investigating organized criminal networks.

5. It will be helpful to curtail media attention which tends to instill public fear and stigmatizes members.

6. There is a need for more gang data and gang research to get a clearer picture of their activities.

These themes are certainly valid and represent the need for a more comprehensive approach to dealing with gang activity and violence. Even U.S. law enforcement agencies recognize the need for a more comprehensive and integrated solution to the problem. In testimony to Congress, Robert Loosle, FBI Special Agent in Los Angeles, suggested a three-pronged approach of prevention, intervention, and rehabilitation.[91] Prevention efforts need to focus on taking action to change the culture and conditions that encourage young individuals to join gangs. Most of these individuals grow up in poverty, suffer domestic abuse, receive little formal education, and essentially have no skills to market to an employer. They wind up in the streets and turn to violence to make ends meet and satisfy social needs.

Intervention is more law enforcement oriented and serves as a proactive approach to break up gang activities and behavior, making it more difficult for them to operate and commit crimes. Rehabilitation requires educational programs, multi-agency cooperation, and other social and psychological initiatives that will be instrumental to achieving the long-term goal of dismantling these violent gangs.[92] Opportunities must be available for the post-gang membership/post-incarceration phase for those who want to change their behavior and start a new life. The tattoos and other markings made during gang membership make it difficult to leave the gang as employers may be hesitant to hire former members and current members can seek to punish those who have left the group. Loosle also stated that Los Angeles and five other sites are each receiving $2.5 million in state and local grants for these types of programs.[93] These offer merely a start for the work that must be done in this area. These programs must also be closely studied and benchmarked throughout the United States and Central America to achieve positive benefit.

USAID also offers a number of very important conclusions and recommendations from their recent evaluation and analysis.[94] Although these are focused on Central American gangs, there is ample applicability to the United States. In addition, there should be few differences between the solutions for all impacted countries due to the transnational nature of gang activity. It will be important to pursue the following guidelines.

1. Solutions to gang problems will require U.S. Government involvement with cooperation from all agencies and the Central American countries. Independent action alone will not be fully effective.

2. There must be a balanced approach with law enforcement and prevention programs which is the only way to achieve a long-term solution.

3. It is necessary to expand community-based policing that brings together the community, police, and legal counterparts to combat the problem in an integrated fashion.

4. The players must promote information exchange between affected countries to assess costs, share lessons learned, and to discuss anti-gang efforts, plans, and programs.

5. Authorities must continue to collect gang data and promote the need for reliable research so that policies are reliably based on facts.

These recommendations highlight common themes that need to be addressed in order to tackle this difficult problem. The most important step is understanding the gang problem and taking a long-term approach to its solution with development and implementation of social programs that address the underlying cultural and environmental factors that foster gang formation. Some of these include poverty, marginalization, discrimination, community support and services, lack of employment opportunities, and poor access to education. Law enforcement action is not addressing these core problems. Thus, solution to gang problems will take time, resources, funds, and the will to follow through with a long-term approach. U.S. leadership in the region will be paramount.

There have been some successes with a balanced approach that addresses these multiple causes of gang membership. One study was done on members who were both victims and perpetrators of violence and were able to remove themselves from that lifestyle.[95] Over time, the study showed that availability of support structures and psychological help facilitated changes and improvements to their well-being and new capabilities to function without violence. Northern Virginia has also taken positive action to implement a more rounded approach through a regional anti-gang task force which coordinates between law enforcement, prevention, and intervention actions with police and community members.[96] These approaches are more difficult and require long-term sustainability to be effective, but there is some data to show that they can be effective.

Guatemala, with the assistance of USAID, has had some success with programs that have helped former gang members go straight. An effort was initiated with Guatemala's government and private businesses in the country to give at-risk individuals some alternative life-style choices.[97] These include job training and other community programs to learn life and technical skills without the need to resort to a life of violence. According to USAID, since this program was initiated in 2004, 1,200 youths received life and job skills training, some primary education, and approximately 100 youths have been placed in jobs.[98]

Another recent initiative in Guatemala was a 2006 reality TV show in which former gang members acted out the parts of small business owners.[99] This program, funded by USAID and small business owners in Guatemala, demonstrated to these youths that there are alternatives to gang membership and violence. The participants were said to be very grateful for the opportunity and that people would give them a chance. These programs in Guatemala are just an indication of the potential pay-off that intervention and rehabilitation programs can have. USAID continues its work in Guatemala in developing prevention and rehabilitation programs for vulnerable youths and former gang members.

Role of Military Services

Not only can law enforcement, social agencies, and non-governmental agencies contribute to resolution of the gang security problem, but the military services of the affected countries are also working together to enhance cooperation and collaboration to confront common issues and difficulties. For example, the U.S. military services are involved in combating illegal immigration across the U.S.-Mexico border.[100] The National Guard is participating with the U.S. Customs and Border Protection (CBP) in *Operation Jump Start* in which National Guardsmen deploy for 2 years to the U.S.-Mexico border areas to provide total support to the CBP.[101] The Guard will be helping to develop technology for detection systems, provide communications, support analysis of intelligence, and help develop border security systems.

Although the U.S. military is pitching in to help combat the flow of gang members into the United States, it may also be unintentionally serving as a training ground for some gang members in use of weapons and military tactics. No data was located to indicate whether Mara gang members are doing this, but a number of cases are cited in which neo-Nazi members in the United States are using the military for this purpose.[102] Military members receive training in the armed services that is unparalleled anywhere else. They are trained in the use of weapons and combat methods. Specialized training in explosives and military tactics would also be of interest to gang members. This could present a future potential threat to the United States.

Although the number of gang members in the military is unknown, it is believed that gang members are not likely to be able to enlist in the U.S. military services because of the standard screening process that checks the background, criminal records, and outward appearance of individuals before they are admitted. Criminal records preclude enlistment in the military without a waiver and physical attributes such as extensive tattoos could be warning flags that would thwart enlistment.

However, gang membership cannot always be determined during the screening process as some individuals are able to conceal their arrest histories or other criminal activities.[103] Recruiting pressures might also be a factor for recruiters who need to meet quotas. It is difficult for recruiters to have a full and complete picture of an enlistee's entire background, and furthermore, they are not likely to spend a lot of time looking for facts they do not already know that would disqualify a recruit from enlisting. If a recruiter is aware of the fact that a potential enlistee is a current or previous gang member, they just might ignore it if the conditions are right and recruiting pressure is high. Since the population of young adults in the United States is the potential recruit population for both the military and gangs, the military services will need to continue to improve their screening processes to preclude gang members from enlisting and to ensure that recruiters remain honest in the process.

The U.S. military realizes the importance of regional security with our Central American neighbors. Consequently, the Department of Defense has been engaging in establishing cooperation and regional partnerships to confront the security challenges in the region. U.S. Southern Command has the lead for these actions.[104] The goal is to develop strong partnerships so that the impacted countries can work together on mutual security interests such as gangs, drug trafficking, narco-terrorism, or any other threat to their regional security. Through these security cooperation programs, good military relations are encouraged in the region through efforts to build partner capabilities and economic programs. This is accomplished through a variety of operations, exercises, and program initiatives with our partners.[105]

Joint Interagency Task Force (JIATF) South is an interagency and international effort to help protect borders through surveillance and interdiction operations.[106] Per the JIATF South website, the task force "conducts counter illicit trafficking operations, intelligence fusion and multi-censor correlation to detect, monitor, and handoff suspected illicit trafficking targets; promotes security cooperation and coordinates country team and partner nation initiatives in order to defeat the flow of illicit traffic."[107] Cooperation, collaboration, and sharing data and intelligence are working to ensure the success of the task force. In the last 6 years, JIATF South has supported activities that have led to an increase in cocaine seizures with a record high recorded in 2005.[108]

The Conference of Central American Armed Forces (CFAC) is another effort in which multiple military organizations are partnering in regional security cooperation. These countries are El Salvador, Guatemala, Honduras, Nicaragua, and the United States.[109] The purpose is to engage these regional military forces in cooperation and mutual support in combating common security threats against stable governments. The Global Peace Operation Initiative is also a component of this effort which is working to develop a multinational peacekeeping battalion in the region to support peacekeeping efforts.[110] Each of these efforts can contribute to increasing security and military presence, and aim to facilitate control of the rampant gang activity in the region.

Conclusions and Recommendations

The gang problem in both the United States and Central America is one that should be of grave concern to their respective governments. Although gang activities and associated crimes may seem to pale in comparison to other salient issues such as terrorism, these criminal gangs are non-state actors that do pose a threat to the security of the nations in the region including the United States. They are some of the largest offenders of illegal immigration/smuggling of people and illicit drug activity across the U.S.-Mexico border. Drug related activities alone cause more than 21,000 U.S. deaths each year, seven times the casualties caused by Al Qaeda once in 2001 in the 9/11 attacks. Thus, from 2001 through 2007, there have been an estimated 147,000 drug-related deaths in the United States.[111] Gang help might provide Al Qaeda with a prime opportunity to smuggle terrorists and/or weapons, perhaps even WMD into the United States. Ideological and cultural differences would prevent any lasting alliances between gangs and Islamic terrorists, but they could still do business together to transit people or WMD across the U.S.-Mexico or U.S.-Canadian borders. These are threats the U.S. Government must address now to avoid a potential catastrophe in the future.

Funding and resources are scarce to combat the gang problem, Nevertheless, U.S. law enforcement agencies must continue their efforts, while others simultaneously execute prevention and rehabilitation programs for there to be success in the long-term. Law enforcement efforts are necessary, if not sufficient, and their success is essential in combating this problem. Information sharing and coordination at all government levels are also crucial in attacking and solving this problem. DOJ and DHS are implementing efforts such as the FBI's MS-13 National Gang Task Force and National Gang Intelligence Center, the Department of Justice's National Gang Targeting, Enforcement, and Coordination Center, and Immigration and Customs Enforcement's Operation Community Shield. These are an excellent start, but those executing the anti-gang programs need to be diligent and continue to find more ways to share information and data and work together in understanding and solving the problem.

However, law enforcement is only one part of the solution. It mostly attacks the symptoms of a much larger problem and fails to address the underlying conditions that foster gang membership in the first place. If those could be addressed, the root causes might be substantially eliminated. It is not realistic to think that gangs can be eradicated totally, but if actions can be taken to curtail them so that they are mostly ineffective and unable to threaten our security, then much of the goal will be achieved.

It is evident from the literature that data about gang activity is relatively sparse. There are a multitude of unknowns and many speculations. Because there is a dearth of data, government agencies really do not thoroughly understand the problem of gang activities, their membership, and why they do what they do. Government agencies need to make gang data collection, intelligence gathering, and research a top priority. Without data and intelligence, analysis will be weak. Without adequate and accurate analysis of the problem and issues, solutions will be off the mark and unsuccessful. Accurate data and solid analysis are also needed for research and development of programs for prevention and intervention along with methods for rehabilitation once incarcerated.

Interagency cooperation within the United States and international cooperation between the United States and its neighboring states are both essential if the gang problem is to be reduced. Given the ability of gang members to cross the U.S. borders almost at will, the efforts of the United States will never be successful unless we can work with our partner nations in this endeavor. Therefore, partnership and collaboration with the Central American countries through will be essential to our success in combating these non-state actors. Transnational problems need transnational solutions.

U.S. Government agencies at all levels need to evaluate the counter-gang programs that already exist at the federal, state, and local levels. Rather than starting from scratch, building upon programs that already exist could provide a quick start-up and might require fewer resources than creating and implementing new anti-gang programs. Agencies need to make the constant evaluation and assessment of current efforts a priority. Metrics to measure shortfalls and progress of counter-gang programs are essential. Proof of counter-gang program effectiveness should assist in gaining further financial support for such programs that can then provide a model for other such parallel programs and identifying which programs should serve as models.

Based on these conclusions, the United States should make the following recommendations a priority in combating gang violence:

- First, data, intelligence, and research must be improved. Current information is lacking to make sound decisions and develop the right programs. Collecting more data and intelligence, in collaboration with other affected countries, will help in designing the proper counter-gang strategies. Improved intelligence sharing across nations will improve the chances of detecting any cooperation and interaction between MS-13 gangs and terrorists. Military intelligence and the FBI can combine forces in assisting governments to develop integrated systems to collect information and foster collaboration. The U.S. military must continue its security agreements with Central American governments, and expand these to examine gangs as a security threat to ensure we have transnational cooperation and assistance. If gangs and terrorists are working together to enter the United States, we must know about it sooner rather that later. Improved intelligence and sharing of that intelligence provides us the advantage.

- Second, it is imperative to treat the MS-13 gang threat as a transnational problem and ensure that our actions and solutions are also transnational. The United States cannot go it alone. Deportation reform, curbing illegal drug trade and human smuggling, and focusing on reducing the demand for drugs in the United States are essential for aggressive action and reform. These are major issues and will take time, resources, and multi-agency and Congressional support. We must provide leadership and resources to assist our Southern neighbors to fully address this problem.

- Finally, the United States must focus on a more balanced approach. Law enforcement means alone cannot fix the problem – it only provides short-term fixes that, in many cases, make the situation worse. The government needs to use current social programs already in place to take gang members off the streets and into jobs with a future. We must continue to prevent gang membership, interfere with their organization and operations, suppress the conditions that foster gang development, and rehabilitate those that are ready and capable.

All of this will require sustained and focused attention in an environment where many other threats are present. Although we may never totally eliminate gang violence, through a combination of improved understanding, international cooperation, and a balanced approach, we may be successful in minimizing the threat of gangs to both the United States and the region.

Notes

1. Federal Bureau of Investigation, "Gangs in America…and Beyond: FBI Exec Outlines Anti-Gang Strategy to Congress," *Headline Archives*, 20 April 2005, On-line, Internet, 20 November 2007, available from http://www.fbi.gov/page2/april05/swecker042005.htm.

2. ICE Fact Sheet, *Operation Community Shield*, 10 March 2006.

3. Arian Flores, "The Most Dangerous Gang in America," *Newsweek*, 145, no.13 (28 March 2005), 22-25.

4. Federal Bureau of Investigation, "Cracking Down on Violent Gangs: International Effort Nets 650 Arrests," *Headline Archives*, 9 September 2005, On-line, Internet, 20 November 2007, available from http://www.fbi.gov/page2/sept05/ngtf090905.htm.

5. Maj Jodi M. Vittori, "The Gang's All Here: The Globalization of Gang Activity," Research Report no. CI04-1748, Wright Patterson AFB, OH; AFIT, 2006, 8.

6. No specific reference provided since this information is practically in all sources and becomes common knowledge after doing lots of reading on the subject.

7. "*Jane's Sentinel Security Assessment – Central America and the Caribbean,*" Security and Foreign Forces, 9 March 2006.

8. Robert S. Mueller III, Director, Federal Bureau of Investigation, (remarks to Los Angeles Chamber of Commerce, Los Angeles, CA, 18 January 2007).

9. Andrew Romano, "Machetes on the Mean Streets," *Newsweek* 145, no.13, (28 March 2005), 24-25.

10. Ana Arana, "How the Street Gangs Took Central America," *Foreign Affairs*, 84, no. 3, (May-June 2005), 98-110.

11. Romano, op. cit.

12. Special Report: Criminal Gangs in the Americas, "Out of the Underworld," *Economist* 378, no. 8459, (7 January 2006): 23-26.

13. Romano, op. cit.

14. "Gonzales seeks death penalty against MS-13 members," *Spero News*, 9 May 2007, On-line, Internet, 14 August 2007, available from www.speroforum.com/site/article.asp?id=9300.

15. Michelle Malkin, "Alien Gangstas Menace D.C. Suburbs," *Human Events*, 61, no. 30, (5 September 2005), 2-3.

16. Ibid.

17. Arana, op. cit.

18. Malkin, op. cit.

19. Arian Campo-Flores, "The most Dangerous Gang in America," *Newsweek*, 145, no. 13, (28 March 2005), 22-25.

20. Special Report: Criminal Gangs in the Americas, op. cit.

21. Ibid.

22. Ibid.

23. *Jane's Sentinel Security Assessment – Central America and the Caribbean*, op. cit.

24. Ibid.

25. Joseph Farah's G2 Bulletin, "Criminals, jihadists threaten U.S. border-Unholy alliance of terrorists, gangs, revolutionaries pose new security risk," *WorldNetDaily.com*, 17 January 2005.

26. Special Report; Criminal Gangs in the Americas, op. cit.

27. MIPT Terrorism Knowledge Base, "Al-Qaeda group profile," On-line, Internet, 21 February 2007, available from http://www.tkb.org/Group.jsp?groupID=6.

28. CFR.org Staff, "Backgrounder Hezbollah," On-line, Internet, 21 February 2007, available from http://www.cfr.org/publication/9155/.

29. MIPT Terrorism Knowledge Base, "Al-Fatah group profile," On-line, Internet, 21 February 2007, available from http://www.tkb.org/Group.jsp?groupID=128.

30. MIPT Terrorism Knowledge Base, "Hamas group profile," On-line, Internet, 21 February 2007, available from http://www.tkb.org/Group.jsp?groupID=49.

31. Jeremy McDermott, "Criminal 'Mara' gangs pose threat to Central America," *Jane's Intelligence Review*, 1 June 2004.

32. Marian Leerburger, "Mara Salvatrucha: A Significant Homeland Security Threat," *Journal of Counterterrorism and Homeland Security International* 11, no. 3, (Fall 2005), 34-36.

33. *Jane's Sentinel Security Assessment – Central America and the Caribbean*, op. cit.

34. *World's Most Dangerous Gang*, DVD, National Geographic, 2006.

35. Vittori, op. cit.

36. House, Testimony of Diego G. Rodriguez, Special Agent in Charge, Criminal Division, Washington Field Office FBI before the Committee on House Government Reform, Washington, D.C., 14 July 2006.

37. Ibid.

38. Fred Burton, "Mara Salvatrucha: The New Face of Organized Crime?" *Stratfor*, 29 March 2006, On-line, Internet, 14 August 2007, available from http://stratfor.com/products/premium/print.php?storyId=264131.

39. Ibid.

40. *World's Most Dangerous Gang*, op. cit.

41. Special Report, "Out of the Underworld," op. cit.

42. Ibid.

43. Manuel Bermudez, "Central America: Gang Violence and Anti-Gang Death Squads," 6 September 2005, On-line, Internet 30 January 2007, available from http://ipsnews.net/print.asp?idnews=30163.

44. U.S. Department of State Human Smuggling and Trafficking Center Fact Sheet, *Distinctions between Human Smuggling and Human Trafficking*, January 2005.

45. Ibid.

46. Leerburger, op. cit.

47. Ibid.

48. U.S. Department of Justice, "Foreign Nationals Charged with Attempting to Provide Material Support to Terrorists and Alien Smuggling," Release #06-042, 27 January 2006.

49. Leerburger, op. cit.

50. Jerry Seper, "Al Qaeda seeks tie to local gangs," *The Washington Times*, 28 September 2004.

51. Ibid.

52. House, Testimony of Diego G. Rodriguez.

53. Ibid.

54. Carlos Mauricio Pineda Cruz, "Al Qaeda's Unlikely Allies in Central America," *Terrorism Monitor*, 3, no. 1, 13 January 2005, On-line, Internet, 14 August 2007, available from http://www.jamestown.org/terrorism/news/article.php?articleid=2369091.

55. "El Salvador gang member: I'm no terrorist," *Miami Herald*, 2 February 2005.

56. Burton, op. cit.

57. Ibid.

58. John Hill, "Gunning for trouble? Canadian street gangs and illegal firearms?" *Jane's Intelligence Review*, August 2006.

59. Ibid.

60. Chitra Ragavan, Monika Guttman, and Jon Elliston, "Terror on the Streets," *U.S. News and World Report*, 13 December 2004.

61. Federal Bureau of Investigation, "Violent Gangs," On-line, Internet, 20 November 2007, available from http://www.fbi.gov/hq/cid/ngic/violent_gangs.htm.

62. Federal Bureau of Investigation, "Cracking Down on Violent Gangs: International Effort Nets 650 Arrests."

63. Federal Bureau of Investigation, "Gangs in America…and Beyond: FBI Exec Outlines Anti-Gang Strategy to Congress."

64. Federal Bureau of Investigation, "Violent Gangs," op. cit.

65. House, Testimony of Robert B. Loosle, Special Agent in Charge, Criminal Division, Los Angeles Field Office FBI before the House Committee on Government, Subcommittee on Criminal Justice, Drug Policy and Human Resources, Los Angeles, California, 3 October 2006.

66. Ibid.

67. ICE Fact Sheet, *Operation Community Shield*, 10 March 2006.

68. Ibid.

69. Ibid.

70. Moonisha Bansal, "Chertoff: Street Gangs a Threat to National Security," CNSNEWS.com, 13 March 2006, On-line, Internet, 14 August 2007 available from http://www.cnsnews.com/ViewNation.asp?Page=%5CNation%5Carchive%5C200603%5CNAT20060313b.html.

71. Ibid.

72. Special Report, "Out of the Underworld," op. cit.

73. McDermott.

74. Bureau for Latin American and Caribbean Affairs, Office of Regional Sustainable Development, United States Agency for International Development (USAID), Central America and Mexico Gang Assessment, staff study, April 2006.

75. Ibid.

76. McDermott, op. cit.

77. USAID staff study, op. cit.

78. Ibid., and McDermott, op. cit.

79. USAID staff study, op. cit.

80. Arana, "How the Street Gangs Took Central America," op. cit.

81. "Maras," *Jane's Sentinel Security Assessment-North America*, 15 September 2006, On-line, Internet, http://janes.com/janesdata/sent/namsu/_nam9999.htm#top.

82. Arana, "How the Street Gangs Took Central America," op. cit.

83. USAID staff study, op. cit.

84. Robert Lopez, Rich Connell, and Chris Kraul, "Gang Uses Deportation to Its Advantage to Flourish in U.S.," *LA Times*, 30 October 2005.

85. Ibid.

86. Special Report, "Out of the Underworld," op. cit.

87. Ana Arana, "Crime without Borders," On-line, Internet, available from http://www.enjeux-internationaux.org/aritcles/num11/en/crime.htm.

88. A Conference Report, "Voices from the Field: Local Initiative and new Research on Central American Youth Gang Violence," August 2005.

89. Ibid.

90. Ibid.

91. House, Testimony of Robert B. Loosle.

92. Ibid.

93. Ibid.

94. USAID staff study, op. cit.

95. A Conference Report, "Voices from the Field," op. cit.

96. Ibid.

97. USAID, "Ex-Gang Member Gets Second Chance," Press release, 10 October 2006, On-line, Internet, 14 August 2007, available from http://www.usaid.gov/stories/guatemala/fp_guatemala_gangs.html.

98. Ibid.

99. USAID, "From Firearms to Open Arms," USAID Frontlines, March 2006, On-line, Internet, 14 August 2007, available from http://www.usaid.gov/press/frontlines/fl_mar06/feature.htm.

100. U.S. House Committee on Homeland Security, *A Line in the Sand: Confronting the Threat at the Southwest Border*, Subcommittee on Investigations.

101. Ibid.

102. David Holthouse, "A Few Bad Men," *Southern Poverty Law Center Intelligence Report*, Summer 2006, On-line, Internet, 20 November 2007, available from http://www.splcenter.org/intel/news/item.jsp?aid=66.

103. Kathryn E. Tierney, *Study of Navy and Marine Corps Prison Inmates Affiliated with Gangs and Extremist Groups: Trends and Issues for Enlistment Screening*, Naval Postgraduate School (Monterey CA, March 1998): 6, 60.

104. Senate, Posture Statement of General Bantz J. Craddock, U.S. Army, Commander, U.S, Southern Command before the 109th Congress, Senate Armed Services Committee, 14 March 2006.

105. Ibid.

106. Ibid.

107. Joint Interagency Task Force South main page, information section, mission, On-line, Internet, 3 February 2007, available from http://www.jiatfs.southcom.mil/cg/mission.htm.

108. Senate, Posture Statement of General Bantz J. Craddock, op. cit.

109. Ibid.

110. Ibid.

111. Statement of Gen James T. Hill to 108th Senate Committee on Foreign Relations, 26 October 2003, On-line, Internet, 14 August 2007, available from http://bogota.usembassy.gov/wwwsjh02.shtml.

Contributors

Ms. Farhana Ali joined the RAND Corporation in August 2005 as a Policy Analyst. Her research is focused on the ideological roots of global terrorism, Al Qaeda in Pakistan, and female suicide bombers. For nearly a decade, she has examined the emerging trend of women's role in Al Qaeda and local jihadi groups, paying particular attention to women's roles in emerging conflicts such as Iraq. Ms. Ali has published several articles on this topic. She is the author of "Muslim Female Terrorists on the Rise," *Oxford Analytica*, "Women in Black: A Look at Pakistan's Radical Women," *Terrorism Monitor*, "Rocking the Cradle to Rocking the World: The Role of Muslim Female Fighters," *Journal of International Women's Studies*, "Women Central to the Al-Qaeda Family," *Terrorism Focus*, "The Bomber Behind the Veil," *The Baltimore Sun,* and "The Mujahidaat: Tracing the Early Female Warrior of Islam to Modern Day Suicide Bombers," a chapter to be published in a forthcoming book by the Institute for National Strategic Studies. She is a sought-after lecturer on violent women and has presented her work to diverse audiences, including Oxford University, Tufts University, the International Institute of Strategic Affairs in London, and has appeared on BBC World News, CNN International and Headlines news, National Public Radio, Voice of America, ABC News, Canadian national television, and Al-Jazeera. Prior to RAND, she worked in the U.S. Government for five years as an analyst and received Meritorious Awards for her outstanding service and expertise on Islamic doctrinal issues. Ms. Ali is proficient in French, Urdu, Punjabi, and modern standard Arabic. She has a Master's Degree in Security Policy Studies from George Washington University.

Dr. Stephen F. Burgess is Associate Professor, Department of International Security, U.S. Air War College and an Associate Director (Regional Affairs) of the U.S. Air Force Counterproliferation Center. His three books are *South Africa's Weapons of Mass Destruction* (with Helen Purkitt, Indiana University Press, 2005), *Smallholders and Political Voice in Zimbabwe,* and *The United Nations under Boutros Boutros-Ghali,*

1992-97. Dr. Burgess co-authored a monograph, *The Rollback of the South African Chemical and Biological Warfare Program*, featured on *60 Minutes* and in *The New York Times* and *The Washington Post.* He researches and publishes on African, South Asian, United Nations, and counterproliferation security issues. Since 1999, he has taught courses on U.S. national security decision-making, global security, international organizations and peace and stability operations, and African politics and security. Before 1999, Dr. Burgess was a faculty member at Vanderbilt University, the University of Zambia, and Hofstra University. He completed his Ph.D. at Michigan State University and was a Fulbright-Hays fellow at the University of Zimbabwe.

Dr. James J.F. Forest is Director of Terrorism Studies and Associate Professor in the Combating Terrorism Center at West Point. He has published over 10 books on terrorism and counterterrorism, including *Teaching Terror* (Rowman & Littlefield, 2006), *Weapons of Mass Destruction and Terrorism* (McGraw-Hill, 2007), and *Countering Terrorism and Insurgency in the 21st Century* (Praeger, 2007). His research has also appeared in academic journals including the *Cambridge Review of International Affairs,* the *Journal of Political Science Education,* and the international journal *Democracy and Security.* Dr. Forest was selected in 2006 and 2007 by the Center for American Progress and *Foreign Policy* magazine as one of "100 of America's most esteemed terrorism and national security experts," and is regularly invited to give lectures and participate in research projects in the United States and abroad. Dr. Forest received his graduate degrees from Stanford University and Boston College, and undergraduate degrees from Georgetown University and De Anza College.

Mr. Gregory F. Giles is a Senior Director with Hicks and Associates, a wholly owned subsidiary of Science Applications International Corporation (SAIC). He is a recognized senior expert on Iran, weapons of mass destruction (WMD), and terrorism, with over 18 years experience supporting various U.S. Government clients. Currently, Mr. Giles is providing analytical and planning support to U.S. Strategic Command on Iran's leadership and how best to deter it. He has briefed the results of this analysis to U.S. Central Command and the Principal Assistant Secretary of Defense/SOLIC. He is also advising senior officials at the National Nuclear Security Administration on Iran's nuclear negotiating goals, strategies, and tactics. In this regard, he has assessed Iran's motives to pursue nuclear weapons, anticipated actual Iranian nuclear moves, and postulated likely Iranian reactions to various U.S. courses of action. Mr. Giles produced two in-depth studies on Iranian WMD threats for the Advanced Systems and Concepts Office of the Defense Threat Reduction Agency. This work included a detailed profile of Iranian President Ahmadinejad and identified 75 possible U.S. initiatives to deter Iranian WMD activity. Mr. Giles briefed results from this work at the National Security Council, State Department, OSD, and National Defense University. In September 2005, Mr. Giles testified before the House Homeland Security Committee on the threat of Iranian WMD terrorism against the U.S. homeland. Mr. Giles is a regular guest speaker at the USAF Counterproliferation Center, the Air War College, and the U.S. Army War College. Mr. Giles also taught the WMD strategies and command and control arrangements of rogue states and terrorist groups at the Defense Nuclear Weapons School. Among his publications are: "Command and Control Challenges of an Iranian Nuclear Force," in *Deterring the Ayatollahs,* Policy Focus No. 72, July 2007, Washington Institute for Near East Policy, Patrick Clawson and Michael Eisenstadt, editors; "The Crucible of Radical Islam: Iran's Leaders and Strategic Culture," in *Know Thy Enemy*, Dr. Barry Schneider and Dr. Jerrold Post, editors, USAF Counterproliferation Center, November 2002; "The Islamic Republic of Iran and Nuclear, Biological, and Chemical Weapons," in *Planning the Unthinkable*, Scott Sagan, et al., editors, Cornell University Press, August 2000. Mr. Giles is a graduate of Dickinson College and received his Master's Degree in International Security Policy from Columbia University.

Lieutenant Colonel (Dr.) Michael T. Kindt is currently the Director of Counterterrorism Studies at the USAF Counterproliferation Center. Prior to this assignment he was a student at the Air War College where he earned a Masters of Strategic Studies with academic distinction. Lt Col Kindt has a M.A. and Ph.D. in clinical psychology from Bowling Green State University and is licensed to practice clinical psychology in the state of Alabama. His previous assignments include directing provision of mental health services at Moody Air Force Base, Georgia, and RAF Molesworth, UK. He also has extensive experience in education and training, having worked as an instructor, flight commander, and squadron commander of the 382d Medical Training Squadron at Sheppard Air Force Base, Texas. In this role he directed 40 resident and distance learning courses in a wide-range of medical specialties training over 5,500 students annually. He has published a monograph entitled "Building Population Resilience to Terror Attacks: Unlearned Lessons from Military and Civilian Experience," (CPC, 2006)

Dr. Jerrold M. Post is Professor of Psychiatry, Political Psychology and International Affairs and Director of the Political Psychology Program at The George Washington University. Dr. Post has devoted his entire career to the field of political psychology. Dr. Post came to George Washington after a 21-year career with the Central Intelligence Agency where he was the founding director of the Center for the Analysis of Personality and Political Behavior. He played the lead role in developing the "Camp David profiles" of Menachem Begin and Anwar Sadat for President Jimmy Carter and initiated the U.S. Government program in understanding the psychology of terrorism. In recognition of his leadership at the Center, Dr. Post was awarded the Intelligence Medal of Merit in 1979. He served as expert witness in the trial in the spring of 2001 for the Al Qaeda terrorists responsible for the bombing of the U.S. embassies in Kenya and Tanzania, and, since 9/11, has testified on terrorist psychology before the Senate, the House of Representatives, and the United Nations. He is a widely published author, whose most recent books include *Leaders and their Followers in a Dangerous World* (Cornell Univ. Press, 2004) and *The Mind of the Terrorist: The Psychology of Terrorism from the IRA to al-Qaeda* (Palgrave-Macmillan, 2007). Dr. Post chaired the Committee on the Psychological Roots of Terrorism for the International Summit on Democracy, Terrorism and Security in 2005. Dr. Post is a frequent commentator on national and international media on such topics as leadership, leader illness, treason, the psychology of terrorism, suicide terrorism, weapons of mass destruction, Saddam Hussein, Osama bin Laden, Hugo Chavez, Mahmoud Ahmadinejad, and Kim Jong Il.

Dr. Barry R. Schneider is the Director of the USAF Counterproliferation Center (CPC) at Maxwell Air Force Base, Alabama, and is also a Professor of International Relations at the Air War College. Dr. Schneider specializes in WMD counterproliferation and nonproliferation issues as well as the profiles of adversary leaders and their strategic cultures. He is the author of *Future War and Counterproliferation: U.S. Military Responses to NBC Proliferation Threats* (Praeger, 1999); Editor, *Middle East Security Issues, In the Shadow of Weapons of Mass Destruction Proliferation* (CPC, 1999); and contributor to and co-editor of *Avoiding the Abyss: Progress, Shortfalls and the Way Ahead in Combating WMD* (CPC, 2005; Praeger, 2006); *Know Thy Enemy: Profiles of Adversary Leaders and Their Strategic Cultures* (CPC, 2003); *The Gathering Biological Warfare Storm* (CPC, 2002); *Pulling back from the Nuclear Brink: Reducing and Countering Nuclear Threats* (Frank Cass Ltd., 1998); *Battlefield of the Future: 21st Century Warfare Issues* (Air University Press, 1998); *Missiles for the Nineties: ICBMs and Strategic Policy* (Westview, 1984); and *Current Issues in U.S. Defense Policy* (Praeger, 1976). He has served as a Foreign Affairs Officer (GS-14) and Public Affairs Officer (GS-15) at the U.S. Arms Control and Disarmament Agency, as a Congressional staffer on arms control and defense issues, and was a Senior Defense Analyst at The Harris Group and the National Institute for Public Policy. He has taught at the Air War College since 1993. As a faculty member he has taught Air War College core courses of instruction and elective courses such as International Rivals, Homeland Security Issues, International Flashpoints, Counterproliferation Issues, 21st Century Warfare Issues, and CBW Issues for the USAF. He has taught at five other colleges and universities, and has a Ph.D. in Political Science from Columbia University.

Ms. Tina S. Strickland is assigned to the Joint Staff, J8, Joint Forces Structure, Resources, and Assessment, at the Pentagon as a Force Management and Personnel Programs Senior Analyst. In this capacity, Ms. Strickland oversees manpower and personnel issues, and assesses their impacts on force structure. Her previous assignment was at the Air War College at Maxwell Air Force Base, Alabama. It was during this assignment as a student that she developed a keen interest in the threat of transnational gangs to U.S. security. Prior to being a student at the Air

War College, she was Chief of the Special Programs Branch, Force Management Division, Headquarters Air Force A1P. A civilian government employee for over 20 years, Ms. Strickland's earlier assignments include management positions at the Air Force Personnel Center and the U.S. Office of Personnel Management, and personnel research psychologist positions at the U.S. Office of Personnel Management, the Air Education and Training Command, and the Air Force Materiel Command. Ms. Strickland's career has been varied; however, her primary focus has been on issues surrounding the selection, training, and promotion of military personnel and U.S. civil service employees. At the same time, her interests include the larger questions of the labor supply in the United States and the effects of demographic changes on the federal government's ability to maintain a qualified and diverse staff. Ms. Strickland has master's degrees in strategic studies from the Air War College and psychology from St. Mary's University.

Mr. Dario E. Teicher is a Senior Defense Analyst, specializing in Combating Weapons of Mass Destruction, at U.S. Central Command. He is also a Professor of Joint Military Operations in the Naval War College Distance Education Program. He holds a B.S. in Computer Science from the State University of New York, Maritime College, a Master of Science in Telecommunications from the Naval Postgraduate School, and is a graduate from the U.S. Army Command and General Staff College, the Joint Forces Staff College, and the U.S. Air Force Air War College where he received a Master of Strategic Studies degree. Prior to his retirement from the U.S. Navy, Mr. Teicher was a resident professor at the U.S. Naval War College in the Joint Military Operations Department. He was also a Surface Warfare Officer, a Joint Specialty Officer, and a Foreign Area Officer (specializing in the Western Hemisphere) having served as the Naval Section Chief for the U.S. Military Group, El Salvador, and as the Chief of Security Cooperation Plans for U.S. Southern Command during which time he was actively involved in Colombia's military offensive against narco-terrorism and Haiti's effort to reestablish a security force immediately following Operation UPHOLD DEMOCRACY. Mr. Teicher is the author of *The Decisive Phase of Colombia's War on Narco-Terrorism* and contributed to *The Homeland*

Security Papers, authoring "The Colombian War and the Narco-Terrorist Threat."

Major James C. "Chris" Whitmire, USAFR, is an Individual Mobilization Augmentee (IMA) assigned to the USAF Counterproliferation Center (CPC). He received his commission from the U.S. Air Force Academy in 1990 where he graduated in the top one percent of his class with military and academic honors. He is a senior pilot with over 3,800 hours in military and commercial aircraft and 21 combat sorties. He holds an FAA Airline Transport Pilot certificate with type ratings in the Boeing 707/720 and multiple Learjet models. He served on full-time active duty from 1990 to 2000 with three operational flying assignments including two as a KC-135 tanker pilot and one as a C-21 VIP airlift pilot. During this time he received numerous airmanship awards and served in many leadership capacities including training chief, evaluator, functional check pilot, flying general instructor, and interim operations officer. Since transitioning to the reserve component, he has served as the USAF CPC Homeland Security Officer where his primary duties include developing, administering, and instructing the Air War College's Homeland Security Course, the school's highest rated elective. In addition to his homeland security duties, he is an elected official serving on the Transylvania County, NC Board of Education, realtor, and furloughed American Airlines pilot and experiences the security challenges facing the nation firsthand. This observation of America's vulnerabilities and open society provides a unique perspective in fulfilling his duties. His education includes a Bachelor of Science Degree in Civil Engineering from the U.S. Air Force Academy where he graduated as the department's top graduate. He also has a Master of Science Degree from the Institute of Aerodynamic Flight Structures, Columbia University, which he completed as a Guggenheim Scholar. He was the Air War College IMA of the Year for 2003 and an Air Education and Training Command finalist. He has contributed to numerous USAF CPC publications. Most notably, he was the lead editor and contributing author to *The Homeland Security Papers: Stemming the Tide of Terror*, which was reviewed and acted on by the United States House Select Committee for Intelligence. It was also selectively republished by McGraw-Hill in its best-selling undergraduate and graduate text, *Homeland Security:*

Controlling the New Security Environment. His latest publication is *Shoulder Launched Missiles (A.K.A. MANPADS)—The Ominous Threat to Commercial Aviation.* This highly acclaimed monograph has garnered national attention for its exploration of the lucrative appeal of the airline industry to terrorist attack, associated repercussions, and solution strategy.

Dr. James E. Winkates, Research Professor of International Affairs, teaches in the Department of International Security Studies, Air War College, Maxwell Air Force Base, Alabama. He earned his B.A. in History from Beloit College (Wisconsin), and his M.A. and Ph.D. in international affairs from the University of Virginia. He has taught the terrorism elective course at the Air War College since 1986. His expertise draws upon field visits to DoD, USAF, and Army defense installations as well as to the nation's premier civilian specialized institutions such as the Center for Disease Control in Atlanta. Current research projects include comparative assessments of hard and soft power counterterrorism policy instruments, analysis of suicide terrorism, and the utility of political, military, and economic responses to deter and defend against non-state threats. He has taught a wide-range of courses, including international security, U.S. foreign and defense policy, Sub-Saharan Africa, and terrorism. His major publications include "Suicide Terrorism: Martyrdom for Organizational Objectives," (2006); "The Transformation of the South African National Defence Force: A Good Beginning," *Armed Forces & Society* (Spring 2000); and "U.S. Policy Toward East Africa: Crisis Response Amid Limited Interests," in Karl Magyar, Ed., *United States Interests and Policies in Africa: Transition to a New Era* (Macmillan, 2000). Among his other related publications are *U.S. Foreign Policy in Transition* (Nelson Hall, 1994); "Toward an International Counterterrorist Policy," in *Global Policy Studies* (Macmillan, 1990); "Terrorism: War by Another Name?" *Quarterly Journal of Ideology* (1988); *Low Intensity Warfare* (1986); and "Hostage Rescue in a Hostile Environment," in *Political Terrorism and Business* (Praeger, 1979). In previous years he twice earned the AWC Faculty Research Award. He is a past President, International Studies Association/South, a 400-member professional body.

INDEX

9

9/11 attacks, *See also* September 11, 2001, 1, 2, 5, 6, 16, 19, 20-27, 45, 47-52, 58, 146, 149, 171, 198, 199, 201, 210, 211, 239, 289, 290, 292, 300, 310, 317, 334, 349, 371, 372, 377, 413, 427

A

A.Q. Khan Laboratories, 50
Abas, Nasir, 332
Abdurraham, Mohammad Aqbal (a.k.a. Abu Jibril), 333
Abu Sayyaf Group, *See also* ASG, 210, 298, 319, 335
Ahmadinejad, Mahmoud, 168, 171, 173, 174, 179
al Dawa, 169
Al Qaeda, vii, viii, ix, 4, 6, 8, 13, 19, 20, 21, 23, 26, 37-47, 49-55, 57, 58, 65, 70, 77, 85, 86, 88, 90, 93, 94, 98, 99, 102, 103, 113, 116-118, 121, 125, 131, 137, 138, 140, 142, 146, 148-151, 167, 170, 171, 177, 178, 184, 185, 197, 198, 200, 201, 209-213, 215-218, 223, 224, 226, 256, 289-300, 302, 303, 307-311, 314-318, 320, 322, 326-328, 332-335, 349, 372, 373, 406, 408, 411, 412, 427
Al Qaeda 1.0, 37-39, 41, 43, 44-47, 54, 58, 292
Al Qaeda 2.0, ix, 37, 41, 43-46, 58, 289
Al-Aqsa Martyrs Brigade, 4, 8, 9, 121, 184
al-Banna, Hassan, 213, 263
al-Fahd, Nassir bin Hamad, 53, 216, 217
al-Farouq, Omar (a.k.a. Mahmoud Ahmad), 310, 334
al-Ghozi, Fathur Rahman, 310, 333
al-Manar, 244, 250
al-Masri, Abdul Aziz, 185
Al-Masri, Abu Obaidah, 297
al-Muhajir, Abu Hamza, 215
al-Qassam Brigades, 267, 273, 280
al-Wahhab, Ibn Abd, 213

Al-Yazid, Mustafa Abu, 297
Al-Zawahiri, Ayman, 39, 45, 46, 48, 51-53, 58, 148, 210, 212, 217, 289, 290, 291, 294-297, 302, 318
AMAL, 236, 237, 239, 242, 247, 248, 257
anthrax letter attacks, 52, 68
Arafat, Yasser, 9, 72, 171, 266, 267
Arakan Rohingya (ARNO), 319
Arenas, Jacobo, 388, 391
ASG, *See also* Abu Sayyaf Group, 298, 299, 319
Atef, Muhammed, 290
Aum Shinrikyo, 55, 68, 199, 201, 202, 204, 206, 208, 217, 219

B

Bali, 8, 197, 292, 298, 308-310, 315, 316, 319, 322, 329, 330, 333-335
Barkun, Michael, 207
Barot, Dhiren, 211, 215
Bashir, Abu Bakar, 310, 313- 316, 319, 320, 331
Bayazid, Muhammed, 51
Berri, Nabih, 236
bin Hir, Zulkifli, 319, 335
bin Laden, Osama, 20, 23, 37, 38, 39, 41, 43, 45-51, 54, 55, 58, 70, 78, 86, 92, 93, 140, 144, 210, 212, 216, 217, 276, 289-294, 296-299, 302, 317, 318, 327
bin Nurhasyim, Amrozi, 310, 333
Bojinka plot, 299
bomber faction, 309, 311, 315, 321, 322, 326, 330-332, 334
Bourgass, Kamel, 200, 211
Briceño, Jorge, 393
Buenos Aires, Argentina, 5, 170, 179, 249
Bush, President George W., 22, 48, 49, 102, 291, 370-372, 374

C

Calderon, Felipe, 367
caliphate, 38, 205, 214, 307, 329, 330
Cardenas, Osiel, 361, 364

445

catastrophic terrorism, 198, 205, 209, 217, 222, 225, 226
CBRN (chemical, biological, radiological, nuclear) threats, 49, 53, 55, 198, 201-203, 221
Chechens, 209
Coercion Hypothesis, 38
Colombia, ix, 67, 76, 184, 208, 351-353, 362, 364, 367, 385-391, 393-396, 410
Combating Terrorism Center at West Point, 202, 214, 224

D

Darul Islam, 298, 313, 314, 332
Department 9000, 178
deportation, 266, 404, 417, 418, 420
diasporas, 300-302
Dujana, Abu, 309, 323, 332

E

Earth Liberation Front, *See also* ELF, 65, 69
Ejército de Liberacion Nacional, *See also* ELN, 386
ELF, *See also* Earth Liberation Front, 69
ELN, *See also* Ejército de Liberacion Nacional, 386

F

Fadlallah, Ayatollah Muhammed Hussein, 237, 241, 243, 246, 247
FARC, *See also* Revolutionary Armed Forces of Colombia, ix, 68, 76, 184, 208, 363, 385-395, 396, 410
FATAH, 9, 10, 68, 72, 73, 79, 87, 184, 257, 266, 267, 277, 279, 281, 283, 406
Federal Agency of Investigation, 365, 368
Female suicide bombers, viii, 12, 13, 113-119, 121-126, 133, 135, 138-150
Fox, President Vicente, 364, 365
Franchise hypothesis, 44
Franz, Dave, 202

G

G272, *See also* Group 272, 319
Gallardo, Felix, 355, 358, 359

gang activities, 403, 413, 414, 416, 422, 423, 427, 428
gang membership, 417, 422, 424, 425, 428, 430
gang threat, 429
gang violence, 403, 404, 414-417, 421, 429, 430
gangs, 403, 413-415, 418, 419, 427
Ghaith, Abu, 51
Global War on Terrorism, *See also* GWOT, 8, 18, 38, 41, 98, 329
GMIP, *See also* Guragan Mujahidin Islam Pattani, 319
Group 272, *See also* G272, 319
Gufron, Ali (a.k.a. Mukhlas), 333
Gulf Group, 358, 361, 363, 365, 366, 375
Guragan Mujahidin Islam Pattani, *See also* GMIP, 319
Guzman, Joaquin, 76, 289, 359, 361, 376
GWOT, *See also* Global War on Terrorism, 1, 18, 19, 21, 41, 98

H

Hamas, viii, ix, 4, 8-10, 12, 15, 17, 24, 78, 79, 87, 106, 136, 147, 170, 178, 182-184, 186, 263-283, 296, 389, 395, 406
Hambali, 310, 311, 314, 315, 320, 326, 333, 334
Haniya, Ismail, 270, 275
Hezbollah, viii, ix, 4-6, 9, 86, 167, 169-171, 178, 181, 182, 184, 186, 233-258, 263, 266, 279, 296, 349, 373, 406, 411
Hoffman, Bruce, 199, 210, 264
human smuggling, 349, 358, 361, 370, 372-375, 409, 410, 429
Husin, Dr. Azahari, 333
Hussein, Saddam, 67, 169-171, 248, 267

I

ideology, 19, 49, 88, 103, 120, 184, 205, 208, 209, 212-215, 217, 218, 220, 223, 224, 226, 246, 264, 271, 278, 279, 296, 313, 314, 319, 321, 329, 333, 355, 385, 389, 390, 391, 401, 412
IIRO, *See also* International Islamic Relief Organization, 327

ILM, *See also* Office of Islamic Liberation Movements, 177, 181
Imron, Ali, 333
Indonesia, 2, 210, 298, 307, 310, 311, 313-317, 319-323, 326-328, 330, 331, 333, 334
International Islamic Relief Organization, *See also* IIRO, 327
intifada, 1, 2, 6, 8, 9, 12, 23, 80, 129, 137, 171, 250, 263- 269, 271, 273, 275, 276, 278
IRA, *See also* Irish Republican Army, 68, 75, 395
Iran, vii, viii, 5, 6, 15, 67, 89, 128, 129, 167-172, 174- 189, 236-239, 241, 242, 244, 248, 251, 255, 256-258
Irish Republican Army, *See also* IRA, 68, 75, 208
Islam, viii, 3, 4, 11, 14, 18, 19, 26, 38, 42, 79, 85, 87-89, 91-97, 99-107, 120, 123-136, 138-140, 146, 148, 169, 172-174, 207, 211, 213-218, 223-226, 257, 263, 264, 271, 274, 278, 279, 290, 292-294, 296, 307, 312, 313, 316, 320, 328, 349, 376
Islamic law, 4, 88, 144, 147, 213, 225, 250, 313, 317
Islamic Revolutionary Guard Corps, 167, 177, 238, 245
Islamiyah, Askari, 319
Isomuddin, Nurjaman Riduan (a.k.a. Hambali), 317, 332
Israel, 4, 5, 10, 11, 17, 22, 23, 26, 47, 71, 121, 139, 147, 167, 171, 173-175, 186, 215, 233, 235, 237, 238, 240, 242, 243, 245, 248-257, 263-266, 269-271, 274, 276, 277, 279, 281-283

J

Jafari, Major General Mohammad Ali Aziz, 180
Jemaah Islamiyah, *See also* JI, viii, ix, 4, 8, 42, 210, 298, 307, 309, 313, 325
Jenkins, Brian, 5, 220
JI mainstream, 312, 318, 322
JI, *See also* Jemaah Islamiyah, 8, 42, 298, 299, 307-335

jihad/jihadis, viii, 4, 16, 39, 41, 42, 44, 51, 52, 58, 78, 80, 92, 98, 113, 115, 116, 118-120, 122, 125, 126, 129-136, 138-140, 142, 144-153, 169, 174, 184, 210, 213-217, 223-226, 239, 245, 263, 266, 267, 271, 274, 277, 279, 280, 289, 293-296, 299-303, 307, 313, 314, 317, 319, 328, 329
Juarez Cartel, 358, 361

K

Karbala, 128, 183, 188
Khalid Sheikh Mohammed, 46, 48, 290, 310, 317
Khan, A.Q., 50
Khobar Towers, 5, 16, 19, 171, 334
Khomeini, Ayatollah Ruhollah, 129, 167, 169, 172, 173, 177, 183, 236, 237
kidnapping, 252, 266, 329, 350, 359, 386, 404
KMM, *See also* Kumpulan Militan Malaysia, 319
Koran, 3, 14, 18, 79, 80, 81, 123, 126, 127, 130, 131, 132, 133, 134, 137, 207, 213, 217, 224, 247, 274
Kumpulan Militan Malaysia, *See also* KMM, 319, 335
Kurdistan Workers Party, *See also* PKK, 184

L

La Violencia, 362, 386, 388, 394
Laskar Khos, 326
Laskar Mujahidin, 319
Lebanon, 4-6, 10, 11, 129, 167, 169-171, 174, 175, 178, 183, 184, 233-244, 246-257, 266, 271, 275, 279, 373
lessons learned, 23, 292, 423
Liberation Tigers of Tamil Eelam, *See also* LTTE, 4, 6, 199
Los Negros, 365
Los Pelones, 365, 371
LTTE, *See also* Liberation Tigers of Tamil Eelam, 4, 6, 7, 9, 12, 15, 75, 116, 199, 204
Luminoso, Sendero, 76, 208, 289, 290, 386

M

Mahmood, Sultan Bashirrodan, 50
Mahmoud Zahhar, 275
Majeed, Chadri Andul, 50
Mara Salvatrucha, *See also* MS-13, ix, 401, 402
Marquetalia, 387
martyrdom, 3, 6, 13-15, 18, 74, 80, 81, 114, 118-121, 124-127, 130-136, 138-140, 145, 147, 238, 240, 247, 268, 272-274, 276, 277, 279, 280
Marulanda, Manuel, 76, 386-388, 391
Marzuki, Zulkifli, 335
Marzuq, Abu, 269
McCants, Will, 214
Mejelis Mujahidin Indonesia, *See also* MMI, 312, 315, 319
MFA, *See also* Ministry of Foreign Affairs, 167, 178-181
MILF, *See also* Moro Islamic Liberation Front, 319, 320
Millennium Cartel, 361, 363
Ministry of Foreign Affairs, *See also* MFA, 12, 177, 178
Ministry of Intelligence and Security, *See also* MOIS, 177
mirror imaging, 25, 26
MMI, *See also* Mejelis Mujahidin Indonesia, 312, 315, 319, 331
MOIS, *See also* Ministry of Intelligence and Security, 167, 177, 179-181
Moro Islamic Liberation Front, *See also* MILF, 210, 320, 335
MS-13, *See also* Mara Salvatrucha, 402-414, 417, 421, 427, 429
Mugniyeh, Imad, 241
mujahidaat, 113-116, 118, 122, 124-126, 149, 152
Munandar, Aris, 335
Muslim Brotherhood, 85, 87, 213, 263, 264, 267, 268, 275

N

Najaf, Iraq, 237, 246, 248
Nasrallah, Hassan, 5, 241, 243, 245-248, 254, 257
National Intelligence Estimate, *See also* NIE, 37, 49, 209
new breed terrorist, 19, 20
Nidal, Abu, 10, 71, 72, 136
NIE, *See also* National Intelligence Estimate, 37, 44

O

Ocalan, Abdullah, 9, 12, 75, 289
Office of Islamic Liberation Movements, *See also* ILM, 177
Oslo, 9, 17, 266

P

Palestinian Islamic Jihad, *See also* PIJ, 4, 8, 10, 170, 182, 184, 272
Parachini, John, 201, 204
Patek, Umar, 319, 335
Pedro Antonio Marín, 387, 388
PFLP, *See also* Popular Front for the Liberation of Palestine, 4, 9, 68, 182, 184
PFLP-GC, *See also* Popular Front for Liberation of Palestine – General Command, 182, 184
PIJ, *See also* Palestinian Islamic Jihad, 4, 8-10, 170, 182-184
Pitono, Joko (a.k.a. Dulmatin), 335
PKK, *See also* Kurdistan Workers Party, 4, 9, 12, 75, 76, 184, 289, 290
Plan Lazo, 387
Plazas, 356, 358, 359, 361, 365, 374, 376
PLO, *See also* Palestinian Liberation Organization, 17, 237, 266, 267
political faction, 168, 175, 311, 315, 330
political terrorism, 67, 390
Popular Front for Liberation of Palestine – General Command, *See also* PFLP-GC, 182, 184
Popular Front for the Liberation of Palestine, *See also* PFLP, 4, 8
propaganda, 123, 133, 138, 139, 333, 406
proselytizers, 312, 326
PUPJI, 314, 321-323, 326

Q

Qods (Jerusalem) Force, 177, 178, 179, 180, 181, 183, 188
Qutb, Sayyid, 214, 215, 224

R

Rabitat ul-Mujahideen, *See also* RM, 320
radioactive material, 201, 211
Red Army Faction, 68, 70, 76
Red Brigades, 68, 76
Regional security, 415, 426
Ressam, Ahmed, 211
Revolutionary Armed Forces of Colombia, *See also* FARC, 68, 184, 363, 385, 387, 410
Rezaq, Mohammad, 71
ricin, 51, 52, 200, 201, 211

S

Sadr, Imam Musa, 142, 236, 237, 247, 248
salafi/salafis, 41, 117, 213-217, 223-226, 289, 299-301, 303, 307, 313
Salafi-Jihadi ideology, 215, 217, 223, 225, 226
Salafi-Jihadi movement, 213, 214
sarin gas, 68, 199, 204
schism, 311, 326
September 11, 2001, *See also* 9/11 attacks, 1, 19, 26, 39, 44, 46, 85, 91, 93, 101, 105, 171, 197, 217, 226, 291, 292, 332, 357
Shebaa farms, 250, 251
Shining Path, 76, 289, 355, 386
Sinai, Joshua, 221
Sinaloa Cartel, 359, 361
smuggle terrorists, 420, 427
Sonora Cartel, 358, 360
Southern Bloc, 387
Soviet-Afghan war, 314
Sri Lanka, 4, 6, 9, 75, 116, 199
Strait of Malacca, 320
street gangs, 353, 401, 402, 403, 414
Subway cyanide attacks, 53
Suharto, Haji Mohammad, 298, 313, 314, 315
suicide bombing, 1- 3, 5, 8, 9, 11, 12, 14-18, 26, 40, 80-82, 114, 115, 117-119, 121, 122, 129, 133, 138, 141-144, 146, 149, 171, 174, 183, 211, 238, 239, 266, 272, 273, 277, 309, 310, 317, 318, 326
Sumarsono, Aris (a.k.a. Zulkernaen), 334
Sungkar, Abdullah, 298, 313, 314, 317, 331, 334
Supreme Council for the Islamic Revolution in Iraq, 169
Supreme National Security Council, 179, 180
Sylfullah, 334
Syria, 67, 184, 235, 236, 242, 243, 248, 250, 251, 253

T

Taliban, 26, 41, 50, 88-90, 92-94, 98, 99, 102, 103, 106, 144, 171, 182, 184, 289, 297, 314
Tamil Tigers, 4, 16, 75, 116
Tamiyya, Ibn, 213
Tenet, George, 26, 49, 51, 186
The Call for a Global Islamic Resistance, 44
Thoriqudin (a.k.a. Abu Rusydan and Hamzah), 331
TICs, *See also* Toxic Industrial Chemicals, 52, 53, 200
Tijuana Cartel, 354, 355, 358, 359, 360, 361, 367, 368
TIMs, *See also* Toxic Industrial Materials, 52, 53
Top, Noordin Mohamed, 309, 315, 333
Toxic Industrial Chemicals, *See also* TICs, 53
Toxic Industrial Materials, *See also* TIMs, 53
transnational gang networks, 401
Tucker, Jonathan, 201, 203, 206
Turkish Government, 9
TWA 847, 241

U

U.S. Critical Infrastructure and Key Assets, 55
U.S. vulnerabilities, 1
United States, vii, viii, ix, 2, 5, 18, 20, 23-26, 37, 38, 44, 47-55, 57, 58, 68, 85-87, 89, 94, 97, 100, 101, 103, 104, 116, 125,

140, 143, 167-169, 176, 180, 182-184, 186-188, 197, 198, 200, 206, 211, 212, 215-219, 224, 225, 233, 239, 240, 241, 244, 249, 251, 256-258, 282, 283, 294, 307, 308, 311, 315, 317, 320, 328, 329, 334, 349-358, 363, 366-376, 395, 401-403, 405-418, 420, 421, 423, 425-429, 430
Uribe, President Alvaro, 351, 394, 396

W

Wahhabi, 86, 307, 313
WMD, 1, 23, 49, 51, 53-55, 58, 168, 176, 182, 185-189, 197-204, 207-209, 215-222-226, 401, 410, 420, 427
WMD attack, 23, 49, 51, 54, 186, 201, 207, 208, 215, 219, 224-226
WMD terrorism, *See also* CBRN threats, 185, 187, 188, 198-202, 220, 225

Y

Yassin, Sheikh Ahmad, 263, 264, 266, 267, 270
Yazdi, Ayatollah Taghi Mesbah, 173
Yousef, Mona, 274, 275
Yousef, Ramzi, 20, 299, 310

Z

zakat, 327
Zambada Cartel, 361, 362
Zarkasih (a.k.a. Nu'aim and Abu Irsyad), 309, 323, 332
Zarqawi, Abu Musab, 117, 293- 296, 318
Zetas, 363-366, 371, 375
Zubaydah, Abu, 290